The Thugs Or Phansigars Of India: Comprising A History Of The Rise And Progress Of That Extraordinary Fraternity Of Assassins, And A Description Of The System Which It Pursues And Of The Measures Which Have Been Adopted By The Supreme Government Of India

Sir William Henry Sleeman

81 Thuggee began near Agra

THE

THUGS

OR

PHANSIGARS OF INDIA:

COMPRISING A

HISTORY OF THE RISE AND PROGRESS

OF THAT

EXTRAORDINARY FRATERNITY OF ASSASSINS;

AND A

DESCRIPTION OF THE SYSTEM WHICH IT PURSUES, AND OF THE

MEASURES WHICH HAVE BEEN ADOPTED BY THE SUPREME

GOVERNMENT OF INDIA FOR ITS SUPPRESSION.

———————

Compiled from Original and Authentic Documents published

By CAPTAIN W. H. SLEEMAN,

SUPERINTENDENT OF THUG POLICE.

———————

PHILADELPHIA :

CAREY & HART.

1839.

PREFACE.

THE history of the Thugs, comprised in the following pages, has been chiefly compiled from a volume published in Calcutta in 1836, entitled, " Ramaseana, or a Vocabulary of the peculiar " Language used by the Thugs, with an Introduc- " tion and Appendix, descriptive of the System " pursued by that Fraternity, and of the Measures " adopted by the Supreme Government of India " for it suppression."

The author, Captain W. H. Sleeman of the Indian military service, who has recently occupied the station of Superintendent of the Thug Police, has devoted but a few pages of his voluminous work to the vocabulary referred to in the title. The remainder of the work is composed of an Introduction, comprising notices of the system of the Thugs, and of the operations pursued by the government for extirpating them; a series of con- versations with Thug informers, containing full and most extraordinary disclosures respecting their superstitions and crimes; and an immense mass of official papers relating to the apprehension of various gangs of Thugs, their trials and executions.

From this repository of undigested materials, the compiler of the volume now offered to the public, has endeavoured to form a clear and succinct account of the Thugs, their peculiar superstitions, their methods of proceeding in robbing and murdering travellers, and the operations of the British government in India for the extirpation of this singular and unparalled system of assassination and plunder. To this he has added an Appendix, containing the vocabulary of their language, the disclosures made to Captain Sleeman by Thug informers, and a specimen of the trials of some of the criminals; which serves to exhibit the careful and impartial system pursued by the British authorities in bringing these atrocious criminals to justice.

The information contained in the following pages, will be found to exhibit a most extraordinary and interesting chapter in the history of human character. It brings to light the astounding fact, that for a period of two hundred years, there has existed in India a secret association of assassins, bound together by a peculiar system of superstition, and successfully pursuing robbery and murder as a regular means of subsistence; that this association was, or rather *is*, composed of many thousand persons; that by a process of early education and gradual training its members are brought to consider murder and robbery as no crimes, but rather as religious acts, well pleasing to their tutelary deity; and finally, that their measures have been so cunningly concerted, and carefully pursued, that until within a very recent period, not one in a hundred of them has ever been brought to answer to any human tribunal for his atrocious crimes. The reader will have the satisfaction, however, of learning, that the energetic measures now in operation for suppressing this abominable fraternity, afford a fair presumption that its existence will speedily terminate.

Aware that the principal value of the work depends upon the amount of authentic information which it comprises, the compiler has presented the several portions of it as nearly in the state in which each is furnished by the original writer, as was consistent with the clearness and brevity necessary to commend it to the notice of the general reader. The arrangement which he has adopted, is believed to be such as will afford the reader a satisfactory general view of the subject in the main body of the work; with the means of gratifying curiosity, as to its minuter details and ramifications, in the Appendix. To the inquirer into human character and the motives and springs of action which influence the conduct of men under extraordinary circumstances, the whole will form a most curious and interesting study.

CONTENTS.

HISTORY

THUGS OR PHANSIGARS.

————————

[THE first satisfactory general notice which we find of the Thugs, is contained in the following account from the pen of Doctor Richard C. Sherwood, Surgeon on the Establishment of Fort St. George. It was written in 1816; and refers to the Thugs as they were found at that time in the southern part of Hindoostan, under the name of Phansigars. The notes which illustrate it were written by Captain Sleeman, with all the advantages of his subsequent investigations, personal and historical, in 1816.]

WHILE Europeans have journeyed through the extensive territories subject to the Government of Fort St. George, with a degree of security no where surpassed, the path of the native traveller has been beset with perils little known or suspected, into which numbers annually falling, have mysteriously disappeared, the victims of villains as subtle, rapacious, and cruel, as any who are to be met with in the records of human depravity.

The Phansigars, or stranglers, are thus designated from the Hindustani word *phansi*, a noose. In the more northern parts of India, these mur-

2

derers are called *Thugs*, signifying deceivers : in the Tamul language, they are called *Ari Tulucar*, or Mussulman noosers : in Canarese, *Tanti Calleru*, implying thieves, who use a wire or cat-gut noose : and in Telagu, *Warlu Wahndlu*, or *Warlu Vayshay Wahndloo*, meaning people who use the noose.

There is no reason to believe that Europeans were aware of the existence of such criminals as Phansigars, until shortly after the conquest of Seringapatan in 1799 ; when about a hundred were apprehended in the vicinity of Bangalore. They did not engage general attention ; nor would it appear that they were suspected to belong to a distinct class of hereditary murderers and plunderers, settled in various parts of India, and alike remarkable for the singularity of their practice, and the extent of their depredations. In the year 1807, between Chittoor and Arcot, several Phansigars were apprehended, belonging to a gang which had just returned, laden with booty, from an expedition to Travancore, and information was then obtained, which ultimately led to the developement of the habits, artifices, and combinations of these atrocious delinquents.

The Phansigars that infested the South of India a few years ago, were settled in Mysore, on the borders of that kingdom and the Carnatic, in the Balaghat districts, ceded to the Company by the Nizam in 1800, and they were particularly numerous in the Poliums of Chittoor. The sequestered part of the country, which comprehended these Poliums, maintaining little intercourse with the neighbouring districts, abounding in hills and fastnesses, and being immediately subject to several Polygars, afforded the Phansigars a convenient

and secure retreat; and the protection of the Polygars was extended to them, in common with other
classes of robbers, in consideration of a settled
contribution, or, which was more frequent, of
sharing in the fruits of their rapacity.

It was impossible that such criminals as Phansigars, living by systematic plans of depredation,
could long remain in the same place in safety, unless
their practices were encouraged or connived at by
persons in authority. .Hence, after the establishment of the Company's Government over the Carnatic, and the Districts ceded by the Nizam, and
the consequent extinction of the power and influence of the Polygars, some of whom had succeeded
in rendering themselves virtually independent of
the former government, these murderers very
generally changed their abodes, and frequently
assumed other names.

While they lived under the protection of Polygars and other petty local authorities, and among
people whose habits were in some respects analogous to their own, it was unnecessary to dissemble
that they subsisted by depredation. They and
their families lived peaceably with their neighbours,
whom they never attempted to molest, and between
whom there subsisted a reciprocation of interest in
the purchase and disposal of the plunder which
the Phansigars brought with them on returning
from their expeditions. Afterwards, on the extension of the English government, it was usual for
the Phansigars, while they continued their former
practices, ostensibly to engage in the cultivation of
land or some other occupation, to screen themselves
from suspicion to which they must otherwise have
been obnoxious.*

* They at all times engaged in the tillage of land even under

Phansigars never commit robbery unaccompanied by murder, their practice being first to strangle and then to rifle their victims. It is also a principle with them to allow no one to escape of a party however numerous, which they assail, that there may be no witnesses of their atrocities. The only admitted exception to this rule is in the instance of boys of very tender age, who are spared, adopted by the Phansigars, and, on attaining the requisite age, initiated into their horrible mysteries.*

A gang of Phansigars consists of from ten to fifty, or even a greater number of persons, a large majority of whom are Mussulmans; but Hindus, and particularly those of the Rajput tribe, are often associated with them.† Bramins, too, though rarely, are found in the gangs.‡ Emerging from their haunts, they sometimes perform long journeys, being absent from home many months, and prowl along the eastern and western coasts to Hyderabad and Cape Comorin. In general, however, they do

the Native Chiefs when they had settled habitations. They either sowed the lands or prepared them for the seed during the season they remained at home, and left the care of them to their old men, women and children while on their expeditions.   W. H. S.

* Girls of very tender age and high cast are also often spared, and when they grow up married to the sons of Thugs. Women too are often separated from the parties of travellers on some pretence or other and saved by most classes of Thugs.   W. H. S.

† The gangs have often consisted of two and three hundred, though on such occasions they commonly follow each other in small parties of ten or twenty, or operate on roads parallel to each other, and prepared to concentrate on any point when necessary.   W. H. S.

‡ Bramins, it is probable, do not assist in the actual perpetration of murder, but are employed to procure intelligence, in obtaining which their peculiar privileges afford them great facilities.

Bramins strangle just as often as others; and are strangled by them without distinction.   W. H. S.

not roam to such a distance, but make one or two
excursions every year.* Their victims are almost
exclusively travellers whom they fall in with on
the road. Each gang has its sirdar or leader, who,
directs its movements. Of a numerous gang, some
usually remain at home, while the rest are engaged
in the work of pillage and murder. Those that
are abroad are often divided into separate parties
of ten or fifteen persons, who either follow each
other at some distance, or, the parties taking different routes, they rendezvous at an appointed
place in advance, measures being at the same time
taken to secure a speedy junction of the gang,
should this be requisite for the purpose of attacking
several travellers at once. Different gangs sometimes act in concert, occasionally apprising one
another of the approach of travellers whose destruction promises a rich booty.

Phansigars have the appearance of ordinary
inoffensive travellers, and seldom assume any particular disguise. They indeed not unfrequently
pretend to be traders, and there is reason to believe
that they sometimes come from the Dukhun clothed
in the garb of Bairagis. Formerly, when Phan-
sigary was practised to a greater extent, and in a
more daring manner than at present, the leader,
especially if enriched by former spoliations, often
travelled on horseback, with a tent, and passed for
a person of consequence or a wealthy merchant,

* In the districts between the Ganges and Jumna, there were
some associations of Thugs that seldom went far from home, and
who made short and frequent expeditions. So the Jumaldehee
Thugs of Oude and the neighbouring districts, so some of the
Thug families in Bundelcund. Generally, however, the Thugs
north of the Nurbudda, have been in the habit of making long
expeditions, and remaining absent from six to eight months on
each. W. H. S.

otherwise he appeared at first in a more humble character, and assumed in the course of his rapacious progress one of more importance, as he became possessed of horses and bullocks, which while they afforded him carriage for the plundered property, subserved the purpose of giving countenance and support to his feigned character.*

Phansigars are accustomed to wait at Choultries on the high roads, or near to towns where travellers are wont to rest. They arrive at such places and enter towns and villages in straggling parties of three or four persons, appearing to meet by accident and to have had no previous acquaintance. On such occasions, some of the gang are employed as emissaries to collect information, and especially to learn if any persons with property in their possession are about to undertake a journey. They are often accompanied by children of ten years of age and upwards, who, while they perform menial offices, are initiated into the horrid practices of the Phansigars, and contribute to prevent suspicion of their real character. Skilled in the arts of deception, they enter into conversation and insinuate themselves, by obsequious attentions, into the confidence of travellers of all descriptions, to learn from them whence they come, whither and for what purpose they are journeying, and of what property they are possessed ;—thus—

> " ——— under fair pretence of friendly ends,
> And well placed words of glozing courtesy,
> Baited with reasons not unplausible,
> Wind them into the easy-hearted man;
> And hug them into snares."

* They still continue to assume all kinds of disguises, and in every considerable gang there are some who feign to be men of high rank, as merchants or the public servants of some Native Government.

When the Phansigars determine, after obtaining such information as they deem requisite, to attack a traveller, they usually propose to him, under the specious plea of mutual safety, or for the sake of society, to travel together, or else they follow him at a little distance, and on arriving at a convenient place, and a fit opportunity presenting for effectuating their purpose, one of the gang suddenly puts a rope or sash round the neck of the unfortunate person, while others assist in depriving him of life.*

Two Phansigars are considered to be indispensable to effect the murder of one man, and commonly three are engaged. There is some variation in the manner in which the act is perpetrated, but the following is perhaps the most general. While travelling along, one of the Phansigars suddenly puts the cloth round the neck of the person they mean to kill, and retains hold of one end, while the other end is seized by an accomplice; the instrument crossed behind the neck is drawn tight, the two Phansigars pressing the head forwards; at the same time the third villain, in readiness behind the traveller, seizes his legs, and he is thrown forward upon the ground. In this situation he can make little resistance. The man holding the legs of the miserable sufferer, now kicks him in those parts of

---

They become acquainted with some officers of rank about Court whom they conciliate by handsome presents, who can serve them in time of need, and about whom they can always talk familiarly to travellers of rank whom they intend to kill. W. H. S.

* If the traveller suspects one small party, he soon falls in with another, who seem to enter into his feelings of distrust. The first party is shaken off and the second destroys him. If there is only one party, or the travellers suspect and avoid the whole, two men are placed to watch their motions: and one follows them up, while the other informs the gang of their movements. W. H. S.

the body endowed with most sensibility, and he is quickly despatched.*

Antecedently to the perpetration of the murder, some of the gang are sent in advance, and some left in rear of the place, to keep watch and prevent intrusion by giving notice, on occasion, to those engaged in the act. Should any persons unexpectedly appear on the road, before the murdered body is buried, some artifice is practised to prevent discovery, such as covering the body with a cloth, while lamentations are made professedly on account of the sickness or death of one of their comrades; or one of the watchers falls down, apparently writhing with pain, in order to excite the pity of the intruding travellers and to detain them from the scene of murder.

Such are the perseverance and caution of the Phansigars, that a convenient opportunity not offering, they will sometimes travel in company with, or pursue persons whom they have devoted to destruction several days before they execute their intention. If circumstances favour them, they generally commit murder in a jungle or in an unfrequently part of the country, and near to a sandy place or dry water-course.† A hole three or four

---

* Some Thugs pride themselves upon being able to strangle a man single-handed; and, in speaking of an absent or deceased Thug, mention this as the highest compliment they could pay him. A man who has been able unassisted to pull a man from his horse and strangle him will confer a distinction upon his family for several generations. Such a man was Bukshee, whose head was preserved by Doctor Spry, and I have heard of a few others.
W. H. S.

† Particular tracts were chosen in every part of India where they could murder their victims with the greatest convenience and security. Much frequented roads passing through extensive jungles, where the ground was soft for the grave, or the jungle thick to cover them, and the local authorities took no notice of the bodies.

feet in depth, in such a spot, is dug with facility, in which the body being placed, with the face downwards, it is shockingly mangled. Deep and continued gashes are often made in it in both sides, from the shoulders to the hands and to the feet, which lay open the abdomen and divide the tendon at the heel. Wounds are also made between the ribs into the chest, and sometimes if the hole be short, the knees are disjointed, and the legs turned back upon the body. The hole is then filled with earth. The body is thus cut and disfigured to expedite its dissolution, as well as to prevent its inflation, which, by raising or causing fissures in the superincumbent sand might attract jackals, and lead to the exposure of the corpse. When the amount of the property is less than they expected to find; the villains sometimes give vent to their disappointment in wanton indignities on the dead body.

If, when a murder is perpetrated, a convenient place for interring the body be not near, or if the Phansigars be apprehensive of discovery, it is either tied in a sack and carried to some spot, where it is not likely to be found, or it is put into a well;* or which is frequently practised, a shallow hole is dug, in which the corpse is buried, till a fit place for interring it can be discovered, when it is

The Thugs speak of such places with affection and enthusiasm, as other men would of the most delightful scenes of their early life. The most noted were among the Thugs of Hindostan.   W. H. S.

* In Oude where the fields are almost all irrigated from wells, the bodies are generally thrown into them, and when the Cultivators discovered them, they hardly ever thought it worth while to ask how they got there, so accustomed were they to find them. In Bengal and Behar where the most frequented roads pass along, or frequently across rivers, the bodies are commonly thrown into them.   W. H. S.

removed and cut in the manner already mentioned.
If the traveller had a dog, it is also killed, lest the
faithful animal should cause the discovery of the
body of his murdered master.   The office of
mangling the dead body is usually assigned to a
particular person of the gang.   The Phansigars
are always provided with knives and pick axes,
which they conceal from observation.

From the foregoing account it will be obvious,
that the system of the Phansigars is but too well
adapted for concealment.   The precautions they
take, the artifices they practise, the mode of destroying their victims, calculated at once to preclude
almost the possibility of rescue or escape—of witnesses of the deed—of noise or cries for help—of
effusion of blood—and, in general, of all traces of
murder :—these circumstances conspire to throw
a veil of darkness over their atrocities.*

I now proceed to notice various particulars,
more fully illustrating the practices, habits, and
character of these criminals.

It is not improbable that formerly a long string,
with a running noose, might have been used by
Phansigars for seizing travellers, and that they
robbed on horseback.   But be this as it may, a
noose is now, I believe, never thrown by them from
a distance, in this part of India.   They sometimes
use a short rope, with a loop at one end, but a turban or a dothi (a long narrow cloth, or sash worn
about the waist,) are more commonly employed ;
these serve the purpose as effectually as a regularly
prepared noose, with this advantage that they do
not tend to excite suspicion.   When such a cloth

---

* If a Thug has been wounded in strangling a traveller, they
pretend to have been attacked by robbers, and take him to the
nearest station without any fear of discovery.   W. H. S.

is used, it is, previously to applying it, doubled to the length of two or two and a half feet, and a knot is formed at the double extremity, and about eighteen inches from it a slip knot is tied. In regulating the distance of the two knots, so that the intervening space when tightly twisted, may be adapted to embrace the neck, the Phansigar who prepares the instrument ties it upon his own knee. The two knots give the Phansigars a firm hold of the cloth, and prevent its slipping through their hands in the act of applying it. After the person they attack has been brought to the ground, in the manner already described, the slip knot is loosed by the Phansigar who has hold of that part of the cloth, and he makes another fold of it round the neck, upon which, placing his foot, he draws the cloth tight, in a manner similar to that (to use the expression of my Phansigar informer) " of packing a bundle of straw."

Sometimes the Phansigars have not time to observe all the precautions I have mentioned in cutting and interring a body; apprehensions for their own safety inducing them to leave it slightly buried. Sometimes, also, when a murder is perpetrated in a part of the country which exposes them to the risk of observation, they put up a screen, or the wall for a tent, and bury the body within the inclosure, pretending if inquiries are made, that their women are within the screen. On such occasions, these obdurate wretches do not hesitate to dress and eat their food on the very spot where their victim is inhumed.

If, which scarcely ever happens, a traveller escape from the persons attempting to strangle him, he incurs the hazard of being dispatched by one of the parties on watch.* Should he finally escape, or should any other circumstance occur to excite alarm or apprehensions of being seised, the gang immediately disperses, having previously agreed to re-assemble at an appointed time, at some distant place.

Travellers resting in the same Choultry with Phansigars are sometimes destroyed in the night, and their bodies conveyed to a distance and buried. On these occasions, a person is not always murdered when asleep; as, while he is in a recumbent posture, the Phansigars find a difficulty in applying the cloth. The usual practice is first to awaken him suddenly with an alarm of a snake or a scorpion, and then to strangle him.†

In attacking a traveller on horseback, the Phansigars range themselves in the following manner. One of the gang goes in front of the horse, and another has his station in the rear : a third, walking by the side of the traveller, keeps him engaged in conversation till, finding that he is off his guard, he suddenly seizes the traveller by the arm and drags him to the ground, the horse at the same time being seized by the foremost villain. The miserable sufferer is then strangled in the usual manner.

Against Phansigars it must be obvious, that arms and the ordinary precautions taken against robbers, are unavailing. When a person is armed with a dagger, it is usual for one of the villains to secure his hands. It sometimes happens, that a party of travellers, consisting of several persons, and pos-

---

* These men have swords, and will endeavour to cut down any man who escapes from the stranglers.   W. H. S.

† Travellers have been very often buried in the rooms in which they have been strangled in Suraes, and large towns. If the house be occupied, the occupants are in league with the Thugs, of course.   W. H. S.

sessed of valuable effects, are, while journeying in imaginary security, suddenly cut off; and the lifeless and despoiled bodies being removed and interred, not a vestige of them appears.* Instances are said to have occurred, of twelve and fourteen persons being simultaneously destroyed. But such occurrences must be rare; and, in general, the property taken is not considerable. Such, indeed, are the cruelty and cupidity of these detestable wretches, that, on the presumption of every traveller possessing concealed treasure, or some property, however trifling, even indigence affords not its wonted security.

Formerly, if good horses, shawls, or other valuable articles, were among the booty, they were commonly reserved for the Polygar, in payment of protection. A portion of the plunder was usually appropriated to defraying the expenses of religious ceremonies; and sometimes, a part was also allotted for the benefit of widows and families of deceased members of the gang. The residue of the booty, being divided into several parts, was usually shared as follows:—to the leader two shares; to the men actually concerned in perpetrating the murder, and to the person who cut the dead body, each one share and a half, and to the remainder of the gang

* Near Sadras, about ten years ago, three *golah* peons were killed, having on them money in different coins, to the amount of 16,000 rupees. In 1805, five persons were killed in Coimbatoor, and cash to the amount of 2,500 pagodas, the property of the Collector of the district, was taken. In the same year, two respectable natives, proceeding on horseback from Madras to the Malabar coast, with five attendants, were all killed. In 1807, five persons, besides two others who had joined them on the road, were killed near Bangalore, and robbed of property to the amount of 1,000 pagodas, belonging to an officer of engineers. And in 1815, three persons were killed in the district of Masulipatam, and 2,500 rupees taken.

each one share. The plunder was almost always carried home by the Phansigars and sold greatly below its value. It was never disposed of near to the place where the person to whom it belonged was murdered, nor where it was likely to be recognized, of which the Phansigars were enabled to judge by the information imparted to them by the credulous sufferers.*

The frequent association of the most abject superstition, with the deepest guilt, has been often noticed. The justness of the observation is exemplified in the conduct of most, perhaps of all classes of Indian delinquents, and remarkably so in that of the Phansigars. Their system, indeed, seems to be founded on the basis of superstition. They pay the most servile regard to omens; and they never leave their abodes to go on an expedition, without a previous persuasion, derived from modes of divination in use among them, that it will be attended with success. Though the Phansigars are almost all Mussulmans, they have nevertheless universally adopted, on certain occasions, the idolatrous worship of Hindu deities. *Cali* or *Marriatta* (the goddess of small pox of the Carnatic) is regarded as their tutelary deity, and is the object of their adoration. She is usually invoked by them under the name of *Javi* or *Ayi* and of *Tuljapuri*.† Before

---

* The property was generally disposed of near the place where the murders were perpetrated when the travellers were from distant parts; but at villages off the main road or in advance of the place, and not at places where the travellers had rested or been seen.   W. H. S.

† Colonel Colin Mackenzie, so well known for his successful researches into Indian history and antiquities, observes in a letter to me, " that it was the custom of many of the ancient heads of families, that have raised themselves by depredation to rank and power, to conciliate *Cali*; hence the sacrifices of human kind, of offerings of horses and ultimately of sheep by the Rajahs of Mysore,

an expedition is determined on, an entertainment is given, when the ceremony of sacrificing a sheep to *Jyu* is performed; and though perhaps not always, yet it would seem generally in the following manner. A silver or brazen image of the goddess, with certain paraphernalia pertaining to her; and sometimes also, one of *Ganesa;* and the images of a lizard and a snake, reptiles from which presages are drawn; together with the implements of Phansigari, as a noose, knife, and pick-axe, being placed together, flowers are scattered over them, and offerings of fruit, cakes, spirits, &c. are made; oderiferous powders are burned, and prayers are offered for success. The head of the sheep being cut off, it is placed, with a burning lamp upon it and the right forefoot in the mouth, before the image of *Jayi,* and the goddess is entreated to reveal to them, whether she approves of the expedition they are meditating. Her consent is supposed to be declared, should certain tremulous or convulsive movements be observed, during the invocation, in the mouth and nostrils, while some fluid is poured upon those parts. But the absence of those agitations is considered as indicating the disapprobation of the goddess, and the expedition is postponed.

and now the commutation of cocoanuts at the hill of Mysore, which derives its name from *Mahes Asura Mardana,* another name for *Cali.*

"At Chitteldroog also, the ancient Polygars worshipped and sacrificed to *Cali,* and even still at *Taljupur* on the western ghauts, 300 miles west of Hydrabed, on the road to Poonah. I was there in March 1797. It is a celebrated temple of *Cali,* where the poojah is performed by a low tribe, and not by bramins, who abhor these rites. It is even so much suspected that infamous rites and human victims were offered there, that my head bramin (the late valued *Boriar,*) horror-struck by the accounts he received, urged my departure from *Taljepur,* and was not easy till we got away.

About ten or twenty days afterwards, the ceremony is repeated; and if auspicious inferences be
drawn from it, the Phansigars prepare to depart.
But before they determine towards what quarter to
proceed, some persons of the gang are sent on the
high road, in the direction they wish to take, to
observe the flight of crows and other birds, and to
listen to the chirping of lizards. Should success
be betokened, the same path is taken. If the signs
be adverse, the sirdar sends some of the gang to
make observations on another road, or at a place
where two roads meet, and these votaries of superstition proceed in that direction, which promises,
as they infer, the best success.

In the course of their progress, they observe the
same scrupulous regard to omens. Emboldened
by favourable ones, they are greatly discouraged
by those of an opposite tendency. If they have
not proceeded far from home, when unlucky signs
are descried, they regard them as premonitions to
return: under other circumstances they either perform certain ceremonies, or they halt for a few
days, till the malignant influence, denoted by them,
is supposed to be past, or else they bend their
course in a different direction. To the intervention
of bad omens, a traveller, over whom destruction
was impending, is sometimes indebted for his
safety.*

---

* It would be tedious to enumerate all the omens by which they
allow themselves to be influenced in their proceedings. I shall
briefly mention a few of both kinds, prosperous and adverse.

The following are favourable signs: A lizard chirping, and a crow
making a noise on a living tree on the left side. A tiger appearing
is deemed rather a good sign. The noise of a partridge on the
right side, denotes that they will meet with good booty on the very
spot, and they, therefore, are accustomed to make a halt.

These betoken misfortune. A hare or a snake crossing the

On returning also from a successful expedition, ceremonies are performed to *Jayi*.

The Phansigars keep the Hindu festivals of the *Dipivali* and the *Desserah*, which they celebrate in a manner similar to that observed among Hindus.

A tradition is current among Phansigars, that about the period of the commencement of the *Cali Yug*, *Mariatta* co-operated with them so far, as to relieve them of the trouble of interring the dead bodies, by devouring them herself. On one occasion, after destroying a traveller, the body was, as usual, left unburied; and a novice unguardedly looking behind him, saw the goddess in the act of feasting upon it, half of it hanging out of her mouth. She, upon this, declared that she would no longer devour those whom the Phansigars slaughtered; but she condescended to present them with one of her teeth for a pickaxe, a rib for a knife, and the hem of her lower garment for a noose, and ordered them, for the future, to cut and bury the bodies of those whom they destroyed.

White and yellow being considered the favourite colours of their patroness, and those in which she is arrayed; the cloths for strangling are of one or other of these, to the exclusion, I believe, of all other colours.

Ridiculous as their superstitions must appear, they are not devoid of effect. They serve the important purposes of cementing the union of the gang; of kindling courage and confidence; and, by an appeal to religious texts deemed infallible, of

road before them. A crow sitting and making a noise on a rock or a dead tree. An ass braying while sitting. An owl screeching. The noise of a single jackal. If a dog should carry off the head of a sheep which they have sacrificed, they consider it to betoken that they will get no booty for many years.

imparting to their atrocities the semblance of divine sanction.

To the ascendancy of the same superstitious feeling is also to be ascribed the curious circumstance that Phansigars are accustomed to refrain from murdering females, and persons of the Camala cast; which includes gold, iron, and brass-smiths, carpenters and stone-cutters, washermen, pot-makers, pariahs, chucklers, lepers; the blind and mutilated, a man driving a cow or a female goat, are also spared. These persons appear to be regarded either as the descendants or servants of *Jayi*, as her constant worshippers; or as having claims to the especial protection of the goddess, and are for these reasons exempted from slaughter.

When this rule is respected, any one of these persons, travelling with others of different castes, proves a safeguard to the whole party; the same principle which prompts the Phansigars to destroy every individual of a party, forbidding them to kill any unless the whole.

Many Phansigars, who have become informers, have declared that they never knew any of the above-mentioned persons to have been destroyed, and conceived that no pecuniary temptation could be sufficiently powerful to occasion a violation of the rule. Others have stated that they had heard of a gang of Phansigars who, having murdered a woman, never afterwards prospered, and were at length destroyed. Notwithstanding the reasons for acquiescing generally in the truth of the statement, that women, and men of particular castes, are spared, the following occurrences, in the latter of which not fewer than nine persons disappeared, and who were almost beyond doubt murdered by Phansigars, shew that their religious scruples on this point are, when the temptation is great, at least sometimes overcome.

In the latter end of 1800, Mohamed Rous, the Subadar who commanded the escort of the Resident of Mysore, being ordered to join the force then forming against the Southern Polygars, sent some of his family, among whom were two, if not three, women, to Madras. They were never heard of until June 1801, when a man was seized at Bangalore, having in his possession a bullock which was recognized to have belonged to Mahomed Rous. This man was a Phansigar, and gave a clear account of the murder, by a gang to which he belonged, of the Subadar's family.

The wife of Kistna Row, in company with his nephew, and attended by a bramin cook, two female servants, two private peons, and two coolies, set out from Poonah with four horses to join Kistna Row, then at Nagpur. They had nearly completed their journey, having arrived at a village about fifteen miles from the place of their destination, and sent to apprize Kistna Row of their approach. Two persons were sent by him to conduct the party to Nagpur; but subsequently to the departure of the travellers from the village above-mentioned no intelligence could be obtained—no traces whatever could be discovered of them; and though about four years have since elapsed, all inquiries have been fruitless.*

---

* I have stated that nine persons were cut off on this occasion, though there is some reason to believe that the party consisted of even a greater number.

Kistna Row had been formerly employed in the confidential situation of Shirishtedar under Colonel Read, when this gentleman held the Collectorship of the Territories ceded by Tippoo, on the conclusion of the war of 1793. He afterwards served under Colonel Close, at the Residency at Poonah, where he is still employed by the British Government.

The utility to such criminals as Phansigars of signs, and of words and phrases not understood by others, as channels of communication, must be obvious. It is accordingly found that several such are employed by them. Some of those in more frequent use I shall mention; and the catalogue might have been easily extended.

Drawing the back of the hand along the chin, from the throat outwards, implies that caution is requisite—that some stranger is approaching. Putting the open hand over the mouth and drawing it gently down implies that there is no longer cause for alarm. If an advanced party of Phansigars overtake any traveller whom they design to destroy, but have need of more assistance, they make certain marks on the roads, by which those of the gang who follow understand that they are required to hasten forwards. A party in advance also leaves certain marks where a road branches off, as intimations to those who follow of the route their comrades have taken.

The following list comprehends several slang terms and phrases in use among them. This language they denominate *Pheraseri-ci-bat;* or as the term may be rendered, the language of dispatch or emergency:

Yetu,	one.	Sitcale,	pagoda.
Bitri,	two.	Burce,	rupee.
Sancod,	three.	Chilta,	fanam.
Wodli,	four.	Sitac,	gold.
Panchuru,	five.	Cawridga,	silver.
Serlu and Cheru,	six.	Curp,	a horse.
Sathuni,	seven.	Curpani,	a mare.
Desur,	ten.	Newala,	sheep.
Mahi,	one hundred.	Samcani,	a hare.
Hacade,	one thousand.	Moz (per)	bullock.
Doacade,	two thousand.	Agasi,	turban.
Desacade,	ten thousand.	Raclan (per)	jackal.

Comuda (h) ....cock.
Comudi (h)..............hen.
Sendri, ...coral.
Pandur-phali,...........pearl.
Shaick-ji, or Ma- } Mussulman
  homed Khan, } stranger.
Bhitu,.............Hindu do.
Cantger (per).......watcher.
Chaicari, ...intelligencer.
Worawal,.. { Persons appoint-
            ed to seize horse-
            men.
Mahi,..............pickaxe.
Cathmi, ... { knife for cutting
            the dead body.

Rumal, { handker-
         chief worn
         as a turban.
Cancha (h).. } sash
Dhoti (tel) .. }
Newar (h).....tape
Nar Muctem,.......
Sir-ghant..........chief knot.
Der-ghant.....1½ or slip knot.
Man, . { a convenient place for
          murdering.
Cont, . { name of an enter-
          tainment given by
          Phansigars to their
          friends.

Various articles used for strangling.

	Literally.	Phansigar Acceptation.
Nyamet,..........	A delicacy,........	A rich man.
Lacra, ...	A stick, ...	A man of no property.
Phankana, ...	....	Ditto.
Dhol, ...	A barber's drum,...	An old man.
Man Jharcerdo,....	Sweep the place,...	See that no person is near.
Kantna pantelao,...	Bring firewood,....	Take your allotted posts.
Pan ka rumal nicalo,............	Take out the hand-kerchief with the beetle,..........	Get out the doti, &c.
Pan Khao,........	Eat beetle, ...	Despatch him.

Ronacero, ... Implies a slight burial, with the face downwards, the body whole and covered only with sufficient earth to conceal it.

Kedbi Gidbi, Dekho, Look after the straw, ... Look after the corpse, that is, the Phansigars proceed to a village after the slight burial, and send out the appointed persons to bury the body properly, keeping watch that no person is looking.

Kedba bahir pariya. The straw is come out,....... Jackals have taken out the corpse, you must not go that way.

Bhavani Puter, Descendants of Bhowani, ... Bhavani Putur, Town of Bhowani Puter, ...	Phansigars?

Used interrogatively to ascertain without the risk of exposing themselves, whether persons whom they meet on their journeys, and whom they suspect to be of the same fraternity, are so or not. When caution is particularly requisite, the question is put in the latter and less suspicious shape. The first syllable *put*, ascertains the point of their connexion with *Bhavani*, whilst from the termination *ur*, which signifies a town or village, they would appear to a stranger to be inquiring only about some particnlar place.

Phansigars bring up all their male children to the profession, unless bodily defects prevent them from following it. The method observed in initiating a boy is very gradual. At the age of ten or twelve years, he is first permitted to accompany a party of Phansigars. One of the gang, generally a near relation, becomes his *ustad* or tutor, whom the child is taught to regard with great respect, and whom he usually serves in a menial capacity, carrying a bundle, and dressing food for him. Frequently the father acts as the preceptor to his son. In the event of being questioned by travellers whom he may meet, the boy is enjoined to give no information further than that they are proceeding from some one place to another. He is instructed to consider his interest as opposed to that of society in general, and to deprive a human being of life is represented as an act merely analogous and equivalent to that of killing a fowl or a sheep. At first, while a murder is committing, the boy is sent to some distance from the scene, along with one of the watchers: then allowed to see only the dead body : afterwards more and more of the secret is imparted to him—and at length, the whole is disclosed. In the mean time a share of the booty is usually assigned to him. He is allowed afterwards to assist in matters of minor importance, while the murder is perpetrating : but it is not until he has attained the age of 18, 20, or 22 years, according to the bodily strength he may have acquired, and the prudence and resolution he may have evinced, that he is deemed capable of applying the *Dhouti*, nor is he allowed to do so, until he has been formally presented with one by his *ustad.* For this purpose a fortunate day being fixed upon, and the time of the *Desserah* is deemed particularly auspicious, the preceptor takes his pupil apart and presents him with a *Dhouti*, which he tells him to use in the name of *Jayi;* he observes to him that on it he is to rely for the means of subsistence, and he exhorts him to be discreet and courageous. On the conclusion of this ceremony his education is considered to be complete, he is deemed qualified to act as a Phansigar, and he applies the noose on the next occasion that offers.

After his initiation, a Phansigar continues to treat his preceptor with great respect. He occasionally makes him presents, and assists him in his old age; and, on meeting him after a long absence, he touches his feet in token of reverence.

Such is the effect of the course of education I have described, strengthened by habit, that Phansigars become strongly attached to their detestable occupation. They rarely, if ever abandon it.*

* Three are known to have engaged in the service of the company as Sepoys. When closely pursued, Thugs often enter the regiments of Native Chiefs, or engage in some other service till the

Some, narrowly escaping the merited vengeance of the law, and released from prison under security, could not refrain from resuming their old employment; and those who, bending under the weight of years and infirmities, are no longer able to bear an active or principal part, continue to aid the cause by keeping watch, procuring intelligence, or dressing the food of their younger confederates.

The bonds of social union among Phansigars are drawn still closer by intermarriages. Though not of frequent occurrence, instances are not wanting in which they have married into families deemed honest and respectable. The women are not ignorant of the proceedings of their husbands. Persons of mature age are very rarely admitted into the fraternity, and when this has been done, it was only after long and intimate intercourse had enabled the Phansigars fully to appreciate the character of their confederates.*

To the influence of personal character are Phansigars usually indebted for becoming the heads of gangs. Like others, who follow lawless and abandoned courses, the Phansigars are profligate and improvident, and addicted to the use of *bang*, so that the wealth they may acquire, even though considerable, is soon wasted.

Whether any Phansigar were ever capitally

danger is over. A great many of the most noted Thugs now in India, are in Scindheea's Regiments, at Gwalior, and in those of Oudepore, Joudpore, Jypore, &c., and it is almost impossible to get them, as they always make friends of the Commandants by their presents and their manners. Some are in the Baroda Rajah's service, others were in the King of Oude's service, but that is not now a safe one for them.   W. H. S.

* North of the Nurbudda, the Thugs had for many years been in the habit of admitting into their gangs men of all ages and all casts.   W. H. S.

punished by the Nabobs of the Carnatic, I know not. One gang, settled in the Polium of Chargal, near the Paidnaigdrug Pass, between the upper and lower Carnatic, was apprehended about 17 years ago, and fined to the amount of 5,000 rupees by the Subahdar of the province; a mode of punishment so far from being justifiable, that it could hardly have been imposed except from sordid motives: nor could it fail to give new impulse to the activity of the Phansigars, and to render them more than ever rapacious and secret in their barbarous practices.*

Hyder Alli proceeded against these criminals in a very summary manner. and destroyed several of them. In the reign of Tippoo, some were sentenced to hard labour, and others suffered mutilation of the limbs. While Purniah was Dewan of Mysore, during the minority of the present Rajah, highway robbery being frequent, was made capital, and several Phansigars were executed.

It must be obvious that no estimate, except what is extremely vague and unsatisfactory, can be formed of the number of persons that have annually fallen victims to Phansigars in the south of India. The number has varied greatly at different periods. There is reason to believe, that from the time of the conquest of Mysore in 1799 to 1807 and 1808 the practice of Phansigari, in this part of India, had reached its acme, and that hundreds of persons, were annually destroyed.† The great political

---

* Native Hindoo Princes, hardly ever punished these people, unless they had by some accident murdered some priest or public officer of the Court, in whom they feel particularly interested. While their grief or resentment lasted, they were seized and punished, but no longer. W. H. S.

† In one of his reports, the magistrate of Chittur observes—" I believe that some of the Phansigars have been concerned in above

changes, which marked the commencement of that period, and the introduction of a new system of government in Mysore, the ceded districts and the Carnatic, though infinitely preferable to the former, yet was it in many respects less zealous and vigilant, and afforded facilities of communication before unknown, between distant countries, of which the Phansigars and other criminals availed themselves to overspread the country: and it may be conjectured that many persons deprived by the declension of the Mohammedan power of their wonted resources, were tempted to resort to criminal courses to obtain a subsistence.

The foregoing description of the Phansigars is meant to be more particularly applicable to those gangs that were settled in the northern parts of the Carnatic and in the ceded districts, antecedently to the year 1808. Since that time, they have become well known to the English Courts of Justice, and their habits have undergone some changes. Many have left the Company's territories, and fled to those of the Nizam and of the Mahrattas. But though the number of them is greatly diminished, Phansigars still infest the dominions of the Company. The gangs indeed, consist of fewer persons than formerly; their plans are less systematic;

two hundred murders; nor will this estimate appear extravagant, if it be remembered, that murder was their profession, frequently their only means of gaining a subsistence: every man of fifty years of age, has probably been actively engaged during twenty-five years of his life in murder, and on the most moderate computation, it may be reckoned, that he has made one excursion a year, and met each time with ten victims."

Yet Francis Bartolomeo says, in a note page 69—" During a residence of 13 or 14 years in India, I never heard of any traveller being robbed or murdered on the highway."—*Travels in India, translated by Forster.*

their range is less ample; they roam the country more secretly; more frequently changing their names and places of abode; and adopting other precautionary measures to screen themselves from justice. Unfortunately few of the numerous Phansigars that have at different times been apprehended could be convicted in accordance with the evidence required by the Mohammedan criminal law; which admitting not the testimony of accomplices, and rarely the sufficiency of strong circumstantial evidence, unless confirmed by the confession of the culprits, their adherence to protestations of innocence has alone, but too frequently, exempted them from punishment. Those that have been tried and released becoming greater adepts in deceit, have, together with their old propensities, carried with them a knowledge of the form of trial, and of the nature of the evidence requisite to their conviction.

The habits and proceedings of the Phansigars, it is reasonable to conclude, have been modified and varied by different circumstances and events of a local or political nature in the several states infested by them, in some places approximating more than in others to the foregoing description. There is every reason to believe that in the Deccan, and more particularly in the territories of the Nizam, Phansigars are very numerous. They will be naturally encouraged to settle in greater numbers, and to carry on their practises with less caution and secresy, in a country a prey to anarchy or invasion, where the administration is feeble or corrupt, or where crimes are constantly committed with impunity. It is also not unreasonable to suppose, that they may occasionally act in concert with other classes of delinquents, and that their proceedings may sometimes be of a mixed nature,

partaking of the peculiarities of those with whom
they may be in league. In those countries, too,
where Phansigari has been long practised, it may
be presumed, that the ordinary artifices will at
length become known, and as the success of those
murderers must chiefly depend on the ignorance of
travellers of their devices, they will perhaps find it
necessary to resort to novel and unsuspected strat-
gems.*

I have heard of no instance in which a European
was murdered by Phansigars. The manner in
which they are accustomed to travel in India, is
perhaps sufficient to exempt them from danger;
added to which, apprehension of the consequences
of strict inquiry and search, should an European
be missing, may be supposed to intimidate the
Phansigars, at least in the dominions of the company. Similar reasons influence them in sparing
coolies and parties charged with the property of
English gentlemen, combined with the consideration that while such articles would generally be
useless to the Phansigars, they would find difficulty
in disposing of them, and might incur imminent
danger of detection in the attempt.

That the disappearance of such numbers of
natives should have excited so little interest and
inquiry as not to have led to a general knowledge
of those combinations of criminals will naturally
appear extraordinary. Such ignorance, certainly,
could not have prevailed in England, where the

* There are a class of Byragee and Gosaen Thugs, who travel
about the country as religious mendicants, and rob and murder
occasionally. They pretend to alchemy, and getting the silver of
the credulous under a promise of converting it into gold, they make
off with it. They are well known to the Thugs, and often join
them in their murders, when they meet on the roads.

W. H. S.

absence, if unaccounted for, of even a single person, seldom fails to produce suspicion, with consec-
utive investigation and discovery. In India the
case is far otherwise: and such on event, unless
occurring to a person of some consequence, would
scarcely be known beyond the precincts of the
place of residence or the village of the unfortunate sufferer. Many that fall victims to the Phansigars are the subjects of other and distant states,
many have no settled abodes. It must also be
remembered that Phansigars refrain from murdering the inhabitants of towns and villages near to
which they are halting; neither are they accustomed to murder near to their own habitations,
circumstances which not only prevent suspicion
attaching to them as the murderers, and to the
local authority as protecting and sharing the booty
with them, but tend to throw it upon others, who
reside near to the spot whither a traveller may
have been traced, and where he was last seen.
Besides a person setting out on a journey is often
unable to fix any period for his return; and though
he should not revisit his home, at the expected
time, his delay will, for a while, excite little alarm,
in the minds of his friends. He is supposed to be
unexpectedly detained—to be ill—to have met
with some ordinary accident—to have deserted his
family—to have died. Should suspicion arise that
he has been murdered, the act is attributed to
ordinary highway robbers, and it is but seldom
that minute inquiries can be instituted by his
bereaved relatives. But supposing that this is
done, and the progress of the missing traveller
traced to a particular place and not beyond it, still
suspicion would be apt to attach to any, rather
than to a few apparently inoffensive travellers,

journeying either for the purpose of traffic, as is imagined; or, as is often pretended, to see their relations, or to be present at some marriage, and who, if ever noticed, have perhaps been long since forgotten. If notwithstanding all these improbabilities, suspicion should fall upon the actual perpetrators, where could they be found?*

Thus with respect to Sepoys, who having obtained leave of absence, never rejoined their corps, the conclusion generally formed has been, that they had deserted,—when, in various instances, they had fallen sacrifices to the wiles of the Phansigars. The same observation is particularly applicable to golah peons, charged with the conveyance of money and valuables; many of whom having disappeared, no doubt was entertained that they had absconded, and appropriated the property to their own use. Even the apprehension, which an indistinct idea of danger tends to create in the minds of these and other travellers would render them only more liable to fall into the snare. Less persuasion would be requisite to induce them to join a party of Phansigars, prompted by the belief that they were thus providing, in the most effectual manner, for their own safety.

What constitutes the most odious feature in the character of these murderers is, that prodigal as they are of human life, they can rarely claim the benefit of even the palliating circumstance of strong pecuniary temptation. They are equally strangers to compassion and remorse—they are never re-

---

* To whom were the friends of the murdered to complain? it was equally unavailing to complain to the authorities of the district in which they were supposed to be murdered—that in which the suspected murderers resided, and that in which they themselves resided; and they had no others to complain to.

strained from the commission of crimes by commiseration for the unfortunate traveller—and they are exempted from the compunctive visitings of conscience, which usually follow, sooner or later, the steps of guilt. "Phansigari," they observe with cold indifference, blended with a degree of surprise, when questioned on this subject, "is their business," which, with reference to the tenets of fatalism, they conceive themselves to have been pre-ordained to follow. By an application of the same doctrine, they have compared themselves, not inaptly, to tigers, maintaining that as these ferocious beasts are impelled by irresistible necessity, and fulfil the designs of nature in preying on other animals, so the appropriate victims of the Phansigars are men, and that the destiny of those whom they kill "was written on their foreheads."*

This state of moral insensibility and debasement is calculated to give birth to pity, while it aggravates the horror with which we contemplate their atrocities. It ought not to be forgotten that, unlike many who adopt criminal courses, the Phansigars had not previously to divest themselves of upright principles, to oppose their practice to their feelings; but, that, on the contrary, having been trained up from their childhood to the profession, they acquired habits unfitting them for honest and industrious exertion: that a detestable superstition lent its sanctions to their enormities: and that they did but obey the instructions, and imitate the examples of their fathers.

* A Thug will never kill a tiger, and believes that no man who has violated this rule ever survived long. They believe that no tiger will ever kill a Thug, unless he has secreted some booty, or cheated some of the gang out of their just share. A mere tyro or understrapper, they think a tiger may kill, provided he be not of good Thug descent. W. H. S.

The Thugs* in the more northern parts of India
may be divided into three classes. The first consists chiefly of Mahomedans who originally resided
under the protection of Zemindars of large estates,
as Hura Sing, Dia Ram, &c., and in the district of
Etawab, including also a few stranglers at other
villages.† The second class is composed of Hindus,
who are for the most part of the Lodeh caste, and
is much more numerous than the former.‡ They
resided in great numbers in their eastern part of
Etawah, and the adjoining district of Cawnpore,
until alarmed by the active exertions of the magistrates by whom many were apprehended.§ These
Thugs had long escaped suspicion by engaging in
tillage, and by always carrying on their depredations at a distance from home. The third class is
more considerable in respect to number, and extends
over a larger tract of country than either of the
foregoing classes. It consists of a desperate association of all castes, which grew up in the Pergunnahs
of Sindouse and Purhara, and the neighbouring
villages in the Mahratta territories.‖ ·They travel
in large bodies, and are more bold and adventurous

* The term Thug is not unknown in the South of India, but is
not applied to the Phansigars, but to a class of delinquents to whom
it seems more appropriate, viz. to cheats and swindlers, who often
appearing as pearl and coral sellers, practise various fraudulent
arts, particularly in substituting bad coins for good, which they
receive under pretence of giving or taking change.

† These are the Sindouse men, and those of the adjoining Purguna of Sursae.   W. H. S.

‡ These were the Behareepore, Tirwa and Oureya men, of the
districts of Cawnpore, and Furruckabad, and Belha. W. H. S.

§ Messrs. Stockwell, Halhed, Perry, Wright, and others.
                                                      W. H. S.

‖ These were the Sindouse and Sursae men, the same as first
named. The Sindouse villages were held by the Kuchwaha Rajpoots, and for that reason called Kuchwahadhar. The Sursae
villages were held by Purheear Rajpoots, and therefore called

than the Thugs in the Company's provinces. Their predatory excursions are chiefly confined to the country that lies to the eastward and southward of Gwalior, and to the province of Bundelcund.

Thevenot, in the following passage, evidently alludes to the Phansigars or Thugs.

" Though the road I have been speaking of from " Delhi to Agra be tolerable, yet hath it many " inconveniences. One may meet with tigers, " panthers, and lions upon it, and one had best also " have a care of robbers, and above all things not " to suffer any body to come near one upon the " road. The cunningest robbers in the world are " in that country. They use a certain slip with a " running noose, which they can cast with so much " sleight about a man's neck, when they are within " reach of him, that they never fail, so that they " strangle him in a trice. They have another " cunning trick also to catch travellers with. They " send out a handsome woman upon the road, who " with her hair dishevelled seems to be all in tears, " sighing and complaining of some misfortunes " which she pretends has befallen her. Now, as " she takes the same way that the traveller goes, " he easily falls into conversation with her, and " finding her beautiful, offers her his assistance, " which she accepts ; but he hath no sooner taken " her up behind him on horseback, but she throws " the snare about his neck and strangles him, or at " least stuns him, until the robbers (who lie hid)

Purbeeara. All Bundelcund and the Saugor and Nurbudda territories were supplied with the seed from which all their gangs arose from this great store-room. Some were Brahmans, some were Mussulmans, but all men whose ancestors had been Thugs for many generations, and being themselves fully initiated and noted men, they formed new gangs with great facility wherever they went.   W. H. S.

" come running into her assistance and complete
" what she hath begun.* But besides that, there
" are men in those quarters so skilful in casting the
" snare, that they succeed as well at a distance as
" near at hand; and if an ox or any other beast
" belonging to a caravan run away, as sometimes
" it happens, they fail not to catch it by the neck."†

Travellers in the south of India also are sometimes decoyed through the allurements of women
into situations where they are murdered and plundered by persons lying in wait for them; but
whether by that class of criminals who are properly called Phansigars, I am uncertain.‡ This
method, as well as that of administering intoxicat-
ing and poisonous mixtures to travellers, though
inconsonant with the habits of the large gangs
who are not accompanted in their excursions by
women, may perhaps be resorted to by smaller and
more needy parties, who rob near to their own
abodes, or who having no fixed habitation, con-
tinually roam with their families from place to
place.§

How long the country south of the Kistna has

* This may have been the case in the sixteenth century, but is
so no where now I believe. The Thugs who reside in fixed habitations and intermarry with other people, never allow their women
to accompany them or take any part in their murders. The only
exception to this rule that I am aware of is the wife of Bukhtawur
Jemadar of Jypore, after whom we have been long searching in
vain.   W. H. S.

† Thevenot's Travels, part III. page 41.

‡ The wandering bands of Thugs, who seem to retain the usages
of their ancestors, are assisted by their women in all their operations, I believe.   W. H. S.

§ I have mentioned that bands of thieves in the disguise of
Gosaens and Byragies are to be found in all parts of India; and
these men often commit murder, and generally after stupifying
their victims with Dutera and other drugs. Other bands wander
about as Benjaras, Khunjurs, Nats, &c. &c. &c.   W. H. S.

been infested by Phansigars I know not, though it is certain that they have been settled in the Poliums of Chittoor for at least a century. On this point the Phansigars themselves are quite ignorant, knowing in general little more than that their fathers and grandfathers followed the same horrid employment, and taught it to their children. There is however no reason to suppose that the practice in this part of India is of great antiquity. It may also be a question whether to the Hindus or to the Musselmans ought to be considered as attaching the reproach of inventing this detestable system of pillage and murder. The respect paid by Musselman Phansigars to the omens and modes of divination, and to the religious and idolatrous rites of the Hindus—a respect apparently not accidental, but which pervades and seems interwoven with their whole system—affords grounds for the belief, that to them, rather than to the Musselmans, is to be ascribed the invention.*

On the other hand it may be argued, that had these bands of murderers consisted primarily of Hindus, it would probably have appeared that the practice was of considerable antiquity; in which case there could hardly have been that prevailing ignorance among the Hindus with regard to it, which is found to exist. It is a practice more in unison with the habits and customs of the Musselmans than with those of the Hindus. The gangs at least in the southern parts of India, consist chiefly of Musselmans, and similar practices it appeared,

* It seems to me quite clear, that the system had its origin in some bands of robbers who had become Musselmans, and who infested the roads about Delhi above two centuries ago—that they came from the north-west, but from what country I cannot venture to guess. W. H. S.

prevailed in Hindustan in the time of Shah Jehan and Aurung Zeb, and probably much anterior to the reigns of these monarchs, and have continued to the present day ; and if, as I have been informed, Arabia and Persia be infested by Phansigars, little room is left to doubt that these murderers came along with the Mohammedan conquerors into India, and that they have followed the progress southward of the Mohammedan arms. In support of this opinion it may be observed, further, that in the more southern provinces which were never, or which fell latest, a prey to Mohammedan conquerors, Phansigars do not appear even yet to have established themselves. I have not heard of any gangs being found to the south of Salem in Bara-mahal; and even these there is reason to believe, but recently migrated thither from the Poliums of Chittoor and the Zillah of Cuddapah. With respect to the Hindu usages, adverting to the disposition observable among the lower orders of both nations to adopt the rites and customs of each other, they may have been introduced and eagerly received among ignorant and superstitious offenders, ever prone to embrace a scheme which serves the purpose of tranquillizing the mind without requiring the abandonment of criminal habits either by Hindu converts to Islamism, or by such Hindu criminals as retaining their religion, attached themselves to bands of Phansigars.

Such is Dr. Sherwood's account of Thuggee, so far as it was known in 1816. We now proceed to bring under the notice of the reader the circumstances in the condition and the customs of India, which favoured the practices of these murderers, and afforded them the means of concealment. Among these circumstances the usual mode of travelling in that country is the most remarkable and important in its relation to this matter.

Such conveniences as stage coaches,* public wagons, and boats, (excepting the Ganges steamers just established by government,) do not exist. There are not even any conveyances which a person may hire from stage to stage, unless in a very few parts of the country, where a traveller might, for a short distance, be supplied at each stage with a pony which would go at the rate of about three miles an hour; and he could hire a few porters to carry his baggage. The only attempt at any thing like travelling posts is by going in a palkee (*Anglicè,* palanquin) carried by bearers.

Travelling *dâk,* or in a palanquin, is a mode of conveyance only available to the rich. A palkee holds but one, and the charge is never less than one, sometimes two, shillings a mile, as dear as posting in England. The traveller is obliged to give from two to five days' notice to the post-master, according to the distance; and the average rate of proceeding is about four miles an hour.

In ordinary journeying in India, the traveller is obliged to carry every thing with him. If a rich man is accompanied by his family, his goings forth are like those of the patriarchs of old, with his "flocks and herds, his camels, and his beasts of burden, his men-servants and his maid-servants;" he travels on his own horses, or on an elephant, while his tents, beds, cooking vessels, &c. &c., are

* See Foreign Quarterly Review No. XLI.

carried on camels or in carts. Some of his attendants accompany him on horseback, or on ponies;
and the rest walk, at the rate of ten or twelve
miles a day. Should he travel by water, he hires
a comfortable boat for himself and his family, with
as many more as he requires for his kitchen and
baggage, and embarks with all his retinue. Individuals of less wealth convey their property in a
few carts, and are content to sleep and eat under
the shelter of trees, or of one of those magnificent
groves, mango and others, which are found at a
few miles interval in many parts of India. According to the rank or wealth of the individual, his
mode of travelling and number of attendants varies;
some have only a pony to carry their baggage,
while they walk on foot; and the poorest not only
walk, but carry their own stores, consisting of a
blanket or quilt for a bed, a pot of brass or copper
tinned* to boil pulse in or make a curry, a smaller
one to drink out of, and a round plate of sheet-iron,
on which, supported by two stones or lumps of
earth, and with a few sticks or a little cow-dung
underneath for fuel, he bakes his cakes of unleaven-
ed bread, which is merely flour and water, kneaded
for a few minutes. Merchants who have goods to
despatch hire either boats, carts, camels, pack-
horses, or bullocks, to convey their wares to their
destination; and the same conveyances, and the
same drivers or conductors, proceed the whole
distance, although it may be five hundred or even
a thousand miles. Large sums of treasure or
jewellery, amounting sometimes to several thousand
pounds at a time, are constantly dispatched by the

---

* It is a curious distinction between the Hindoos and Musselmans, that the former all use brass vessels, the latter those made
of copper tinned.

bankers of one town to their correspondents at several hundred miles distance, by the hands of common porters. These men, instead of going in large parties well armed, usually travel in small numbers, without any arms whatever; trusting for protection to the appearance of utmost poverty which they assume. They, however, often fall victims to the ruthless vigilance of the Thugs.

There are but few inns or serais in India; the best of them consist but of a quadrangle of arches or arcades. Some of these, raised under the Mohammedan princes, are beautiful specimens of Oriental architecture, with lofty gateways and battlements; but the greater part are more like what are built on the foundation of a new street in London, to be afterwards converted into cellars. Under the native rulers, these buildings were rather numerous and kept in tolerable order; a regular establishment of guards and servants was maintained at them; and there were private doors and apartments for women. Our readers, who are familiar with Oriental tales and the Arabian Nights, will remember them, under the name of caravanserais or khans, as the scene of so many of the adventures therein described. Under the extortion of the earlier English government in India, however, and the consequent impoverishment of the country, all have suffered, more or less, and many of the most splendid are gone entirely to ruin. There are generally a few shops within the square; and, in places of considerable thoroughfare, a few people of a class called Buttearas, who cook dinners for travellers. Where there are no serais, travellers sleep in the verandahs of houses or in any open sheds they can find; but the climate of India is such as not to render shelter necessary for nine months in the year; and none but single travellers or very small parties care for serais or houses. All who are rich enough to carry tents, or those who travel in tolerable numbers, usually prefer encamping under the shade of trees, at some distance from the dirty serais or villages; and when one party is so encamped under a shady grove, a single traveller, or even several together, will easily be induced to join them, and often ask permission to do so, for the sake of protection.

It is the existence of such customs which renders the operations of the Thugs so practicable.

Our readers will almost deem it impossible that such organised gangs of murderers, amounting to several thousands, could carry on their villainy almost undiscovered so long; for two or three centuries at least. The difficulty, however, nearly vanishes when we reflect on the mode of travelling in India, just described, and on the peculiar system of the Thugs. In the first place they seldom murder near their own homes; but even this would be a point of little importance when we consider, secondly, that travellers, and generally from a distant part of the country, are their victims: thirdly, that they invariably murder before they rob.

Lastly, they avoid exciting suspicion by being careful to leave behind them no marks even of a crime having been committed. The travellers who became their victims were men seeking for service; or returning home with the savings of years; merchants going on business to a distant town; or others journeying either for business or pleasure. They might be murdered in the morning twilight within half a mile of the serai or village in which they had passed the night; while the Thugs who watched and had marked them for their prey were encamped at a short distance. No one missed them: the people of the serai or village which they had left took it for granted that they had proceeded on their way; and those of the next halting-place in advance were ignorant of their approach. It is not till days, weeks, months, or even years had passed away that their relations, hearing nothing of their arrival at their intended destinations, make inquiries, and it is seldom that they can ascertain even the place about which the travellers were probably murdered. Unless the inquiry be made within a short time, and there may have been something in the appearance or equipage of the travellers to attract attention, the villagers and others who reside along the road would not recollect whether those inquired for had passed or not. But even supposing (as has occasionally occurred) that the relations succeed in tracing the travellers to a certain spot, beyond which all clue is lost; this gives a moral certainty that they have been murdered at no great distance, that is, within a few miles adjacent.—But how, within such a space, are they to pitch upon the spot where the bodies are interred?—and more,—where are the murderers? probably hundreds of miles away; and even should they by chance be again encamped on the very spot, what means are there of detection? In ordinary thefts, and by local thieves, the tracing and discovery of stolen property affords a very powerful means of bringing the matter home to the perpetrators; but this has but little effect against Thugs. They contrive to obtain full knowledge of the persons, residence, and destination of those they murder, and are careful not to dispose of any recognisable articles where they might by chance be perceived. Such as have any peculiar marks are destroyed.

Considering all these circumstances, it is not astonishing that so little has been done towards suppressing this association of miscreants. The fact is, that until these five or six years, no one had any correct notion of its extent: all that was known up to that period was, that travellers were occasionally enticed and murdered by people called Thugs, who assumed the garb of inoffensive wayfarers. By some extraordinary chance, such as one of the victims having made his escape, or some of the stolen property being unexpectedly recognised, or one of the gang having turned informer in consequence of a quarrel for the division of the spoil, a few of these miscreants were occasionally discovered and punished. Even had the various governments into which India is divided, been aware of the extent of the evil and anxious to destroy it, they would have been unable to do so: insulated efforts would have produced little or no benefit; the jealousies which existed would have prevented their combining for the purpose; and for a century and a half or more, there has not existed any paramount power which could devise a general plan of operations, and compel the rest to submit to it.

Other causes are not wanting which tended to prevent any attempts being made, even in detail, to arrest the proceedings of the different gangs of Thugs. Some of the native chiefs knowingly harboured and protected them as a source of revenue from which they derived considerable sums annually out of the profits of their plunder. The

Thugs lived in villages like other people, and generally cultivated small portions of ground to maintain appearances: so that the native chiefs, if questioned, pretended of course to know nothing of their real character; asserting that these people lived, cultivated, and paid their rent like others, and accounting for the absence of most of the male population during several months, by saying that they went for service and returned periodically with the amount of their earnings. In other cases, native chiefs who would have readily punished a gang of thieves when apprehended, were deterred from doing so by superstitious dread. The Thugs always endeavoured to impress the belief that they were acting according to the injunctions of their deity Bhowanee, and that all who opposed them would feel the vengeance of their goddess. The few instances in which Thugs were put to death by native chiefs were generally cases of personal vengeance, because these villains had murdered some relation or dependent of the chief, and were by good fortune apprehended immediately, "in the red-hand." It has unfortunately in several instances occurred that after punishing Thugs, the chief himself, his son, or some relation has died within a short time : whether some of the Thug fraternity took secret means to insure such an occurrence, cannot be ascertained; but they seized all such opportunities to substantiate the belief which they endeavoured to inculcate. In general, a native chief would merely extort a sum of money from the Thugs, or keep them in confinement for a short time, after which they were released; and not unfrequently they were discharged at once. Their own superstition however, as has just been explained, is now beginning to operate against them.

The following will show what extraordinary proceedings occur sometimes in India. A dispatch of dollars to the value of four thousand pounds sterling, made on account of a rich merchant of Indoor, Dhun Raj, was carried off by Thugs, who murdered the attendant guards, near a place called Burwaha Ghaut, on the Nerbudda. He contrived to ascertain who the Thugs were, and, being a man of considerable influence, to occasion their arrest and detention in gaol by the native chiefs in whose jurisdiction they lived: after some time an agreement was made with the Thugs to release them, if they would refund the money or its amount.

Some paid out of the fruits of former expeditions, others borrowed in anticipation of future success; and those who had neither money nor credit, pledged themselves to pay part of their future earnings.

The Thugs durst not break their engagements for fear of Dhun Raj, and after some time he realized the full sum of which he had been plundered. Finding, however, that he could turn his power and influence to so good an account, he began to assume the character of a patron of Thugs: he had always some of the principal leaders about his person, and yearly exacted large sums of money from the principal gangs in return for his protection, threatened those who refused with arrest and punishment: and such was his influence, that he could procure the release of a gang from almost any gaol in central India.

Though the British Indian government was free from the superstitions or the corruptions which prevented the native chiefs from punishing Thugs, it was not the less hampered by prejudices of its own, and by real difficulties which lay in the way of the object desired. Regarding the prejudices alluded to, it is necessary to explain a little of the secret springs that actuated the government. The members at the head of the administration have always had a tolerably correct idea of the oppressive nature of the British rule in India, and of the light in which it is held by the natives; but it has always been a primary object to prevent this knowledge from reaching the English public. To effect this, the reports forwarded to the Court of Directors, have always descanted on the admirable system of internal government which has been established in their territories; the blessings which the native subjects enjoy; and their consequent gratitude. The feeling descends through the various ranks of government servants, who generally take their cue accordingly. It may be observed too, that the majority of the officers of government, civil or military, are extremely ignorant of the natives of India, and of their real sentiments; and are therefore easily misled by a few designing favourites, who alone possess their ear, and have their own ends to serve.

To acknowledge, even had they been fully aware of it, the existence of such an evil as Thuggee over the whole of the British provinces, was by no means agreeable to the government, it would have contradicted their repeated assertions and representations. If an evil could be suppressed quietly and without incurring any additional expense, it would have been a source of deep satisfaction; but the proceedings of government have almost warranted a belief that they would prefer the existence of an evil, provided it were not generally known, even to the discovery of a remedy, if this should tend to produce a considerable sensation and excite inquiry. We could at least instance several public officers who have brought considerable annoyance upon themselves by too broadly bringing to notice the existence of evils, or the enormous extent to which crimes of the deepest dye, such as murders, gang robbery, and others, are perpetrated. Appearances are, however, kept up. The zeal and ability of the officer are praised, and his praiseworthy motives duly appreciated ;—but then come certain remarks indicating an " apprehension of his being misinformed ;" doubts that " the evil is not so bad as he has represented ;" with a concluding observation that copies of the correspondence will be sent to the superintendent of police, judge of circuit, or some superior officer, who will be desired to report on the subject. This individual, if he have any tact, or any thing to hope or fear from the favour of government, frames his report according to what he sees is wished or expected from him ; states the district to be not in worse order than others (which perhaps is true enough, owing to the vigorous measures of the magistrate in question, by which crime has been abated) ; and, by a careful adjustment of words and phrases, contrives to do away entirely with the impression which, in accordance with truth, ought to have been received. Occasionally, where the magistrate has persisted in his representations, the affair has actually ended by his removal, while his successor has reaped the full benefit of his exertions, and gained the entire credit of them.

A strong instance of the way in which the ends of justice may be defeated by a mistaken anxiety in public officers to gain a good name with the government by making it appear that crime does not exist, occurred in the district of Chupra in 1827. Two men were murdered by a gang of Thugs, who, almost immediately after, got drunk and quarrelled. Four of them in consequence gave information against the others, who were arrested with the property of the murdered men in their possession; these were committed for trial, and the four first allowed to turn King's evidence. The state of the case is as follows:—There was, first, the evidence of the approvers; second, the deposition of the wives of the men, who swore to the property found; and thirdly, the men accused of being Thugs could give no satisfactory account of themselves. The defence was merely a denial, and an assertion that the property claimed by the widows was their (the prisoners') own. The judgment given will scarce be credited by our readers. The prisoners were released; the approvers and the police were severely punished for perjury and for oppression; government was led to believe that no such crime as Thuggee existed in that part of the country; and the magistrate, Mr. Pringle, who had been active in apprehending many Thugs, and had reported the same, received a severe reprimand.

One fact yet remains to be mentioned, which will show the difficulties of the case. The judge, Mr. Elliot, ordered the property which was claimed by the widows to be retained in court, while all the rest of the property found on the prisoners was returned to them. Now, for whom was the above to be retained? It could not belong to any third person, but either to the prisoners or to the murdered men. If the judge disbelieved the whole story for the prosecution, and deemed the prisoners innocent, he should have restored to them this property along with the rest that was found upon them, and which they claimed as their own. If he believed the statement of the widows, that those things belonged to their husbands, then must the prisoners have been punished as the murderers, and the property would have been given to the widows. This little fact is one of those which either show a strange perversion of judgment, or denote a vacillation of mind indicating that the judge himself felt that all was not right in the orders he gave.* The truth of all that was stated on the part of the prosecution has since been fully proved by depositions of other Thug approvers; and not only so, but that Thuggee existed to a great extent in those districts, at the very time that Mr. Elliot was assuring government that no such crime occurred.

Many of the English magistrates were actuated by the same feelings. Some would not allow that Thuggee could exist in their districts, and even were excessively indignant at such statements being made by the officers employed in the suppression of this crime: they were perfectly astounded, when men dispatched by those officers proceeded to dig up the bodies of persons recently murdered in various places, sometimes within a short distance of the police functionary's residence. Others admitted that such a thing might occur occasionally; while a few boldly and openly stated what they had discovered, and gave much valuable information. Our limits do not permit us to add here, extracts from the official papers: we must,

---

* No mention of this order to retain that portion of the property is to be found in Capt. Sleeman's book. We derive it from a statement publicly made by Mr. Pringle.

therefore, refer our readers to various letters from Mr. Wright, a Madras magistrate.

But even if all the English magistrates in India had been aware of and cordially co-operated with each other, they would have effected little towards the suppression of Thuggee. The ordinary tribunals and modes of proceeding, which answered in some degree for the detection and punishment of ordinary offenders, were of little avail against Thugs. Except in the rare instance of a gang being apprehended with stolen property in possession, which the relations of the murdered persons were there to identify, the only witnesses who could ever be brought against them were some of their own fraternity; and the evidence of men whose preliminary step must be to confess themselves the most ruthless villains in existence, is naturally received with distrust, of which the case commemorated by Mr. Pringle is a memorable example, and doubtless may plead for the judge.

Such being the English mode of proceeding, it is no wonder that approvers and informers were slow to come forward; for no sooner did they lose the protection of the functionaries, than they were murdered by their accomplices. The dilatoriness and inefficiency of the courts; the great power which the subordinate police and court officers possess to disguise the real merits of a case; the influence which the Thugs contrived to obtain over these by means of bribes; the few instances in which stolen property or bodies were discovered; all conspired to increase the difficulty under which the ordinary magistrates laboured in detecting the perpetrators of this crime. But even where the bodies were found in wells, which was a common way of disposing of them when in a hurry or likely to be disturbed, in the Doab, Oude, and other parts, the owner of the ground and his neighbuors generally buried them as quickly as possible that the police officers might know nothing of the matter; and if these did become acquainted with the circumstance, a bribe would usually prevent their reporting it to the magistrate. The farmers and others had just grounds for what they did, owing to the ;strange mode in which the English government conducts its police affairs. In such cases as those now mentioned the common practice is to summon to court the owners of the neighbouring lands, and many of the neighbours;—at a distance, perhaps, from ten to eighty miles, and to fine them severely as a matter of course, if they could not produce the perpetrators of the murders.

But even when an insulated gang was actually brought to justice, it was but a drop in the ocean towards the suppression of Thuggee :—nor would, nor will any thing effect this, but a general system, which shall be in operation all over India. Different magistrates might receive information which, if it were combined and compared together, might prove of the greatest value, but which becomes useless when frittered away among separate officers, who have no communication with each other. The whole business too was so little understood, that few could bring themselves to credit the extent of such an organized system of murder. Although sufficient was known, so far back as 1810, to induce the commander-in-chief to issue a general order to the native soldiery who went on leave, urging them to take bills on the different treasuries for the amount of their savings, instead of carrying cash for fear of being robbed on the road, yet year after year passed, and men did not join their corps: but it was always supposed they had deserted, and little suspicion apparently was entertained of their being murdered, which however, was since discovered to have been the case in almost every instance. The scattered residences of the Thugs was another obstacle, and rendered them much more difficult to deal with than ordinary criminals, who inhabit the same locality. The members of a single gang often came from different parts of the country, some of which were hundreds of miles asunder. Numbers of them, perhaps the greater part, were residents of foreign states over which the magistrates had no control; and, although the British government might have requested the co-operation of the different princes, little or no good would have been effected. Even a system of Thug police, such as has now been established, if confined to the British provinces, could have been of no permanent use. The Thugs would have emigrated for the time to the native states, and although the crime might for a while cease in the British territories, as soon as the special Thug police was abolished, those miscreants would all have returned and prosecuted their trade as vigorously as ever.

Occasionally when a gang, residents of a foreign territory, were arrested, and moral proof against them was strong, but legal proof, according to the English system, failing; if the government made them over to their native chief in the hope that he would punish them, this usually ended in their being released by paying a sum of money—sometimes without. On the other hand, when British subjects were apprehended on a Thug expedition in a native state, they sometimes contrived, by flattering English prejudices, to obtain the protection of the functionaries. The established creed of the govern-

ment is the superior excellence of their own administration, and the blessings enjoyed by their native
subjects; and they descant largely on the tyranny
and oppression in all native states.   This is well
known to the native dependents and officials, who
play their part accordingly.   With many of them
the Thugs maintained a good understanding, and
when any of those wretches, residents of British territories, were arrested by a native chief, a pitiable
story was presented to some English functionary of
"poor innocent British subjects on a trading expedition," or something of the sort, having been confined by a tyrannical chief, in order to extort
money from them.   Of course, a due proportion of
compliments and flattery of the English was mixed
up with the representation, and this would produce,
often without the slightest inquiry, a strong letter
from the English functionary to the native chief on
the injustice of his proceedings, and generally in-
sured the release of the Thugs.

MEASURES OF THE BRITISH GOVERNMENT IN INDIA FOR THE SUPPRESSION OF THUGGEE.

We now proceed to notice the measures taken
by the British authorities in India for the suppression of Thuggee.   The writer in the Foreign
Quarterly Review, upon whose authority as well
as that of Captain Sleeman, the following statements
are made, seems to have had access to the most
authentic original sources of information.

The state of society in India being such as we
have just described, it is not surprising that so well
organized a system of murder and robbery as that

of the Thugs should have remained so long in full vigour.

* Things had gone on in this way for years, chequered occasionally by the vigorous attempt of some individual functionary to eradicate the evil, but without any solid benefit. The most notorious of these efforts was an attack made by Messrs. Halhed and Stockwell, in the year 1812, on the stronghold of a large body of Thugs, in the province of Sindouse, in the Gualior territory. They had formed a large village there, whence they issued annually on their excursions, and paid a regular tribute to that state for their protection. Many were killed; but the greater part, being driven away, scattered themselves all over India, joining other gangs or forming new ones wherever they went: so that the enterprize, from not being followed up on a system of information derived from some of those who were captured, actually in its results produced more evil than good.

The next event which occurred, and which ultimately laid the foundation of the successful measures that have been since pursued, was the arrest of a gang of a hundred and fifteen, near Jubulpoor, in 1823; it was accomplished by the following means. A noted leader of Thugs, named Kulian, was in the Jubulpoor gaol. Seeing the proof strong against him, he offered to turn informer to save himself; and was promised his life in the event of his doing good service. He accordingly desired his brother, Motee, to accompany the first large gang he should meet, travelling in that direction; to note well the murders and places where the bodies should be buried: and, as the gang

* For. Quart. Rev. No. xli.
6*

approached Jubulpoor, to give information to Mr. Molony, agent to the governor-general. The gang which Motee joined was that of Dhunnee Khan: he strictly fulfilled his instructions, and 'caused the apprehension of the whole; this has been already related; and also how Dhunnee Khan contrived to persuade Mr. Molony to order their release. In despair at this, Motee followed the gang, and, by dint of frightening some of them with assurances of speedy re-apprehension, persuaded a few to return with him to Mr. Molony, and declare what they really were. On this additional evidence, a large police force was sent after the gang, and succeeded in capturing a hundred and three, who were safely lodged in gaol. Mr. Molony unfortu-nately died soon after this: his successor apparently did not know how to proceed in the case, until Mr. F. C. Smith took it up in 1830, shortly after his appointment as governor-general's agent at Jubul-poor; seventy-five were convicted; the others having died in gaol, excepting some who were made informers.

Another considerable gang was apprehended in the same territories in 1826 by Captain Wardlow, employed there as a civil officer; a third by Cap-tain Sleeman, in Bhopal, in the beginning of 1830; and a fourth by Major Borthwick, political agent of Mahidpoor.

Of all these gangs, some of the members, fright-ened at what had already occurred, turned appro-vers, in order to save themselves; but the evidence of these men, in particular of a Brahmin approver, named Ferringhea, was perfectly astounding, and laid open a scene of barefaced villainy which could scarcely be credited: nevertheless, every statement hitherto made by them, and by others, have been corroborated. *ib.*

The disclosures made by these different approvers, and the information given, threw open so fine a field for a general plan of operations, that the matter was warmly taken up by Mr. Smith, agent to the governor-general, and Captain Sleeman, district officer of Nursingpoor, each zealously co-operating with the other. On the 21st September, 1830, Mr. Smith wrote to government, and intimated the necessity of some such plan : but the eyes of the latter had been opened, and before the receipt of Mr. Smith's dispatch, a letter from government, dated 8th October, was addressed to him, requesting his opinion on the subject. In reply, he submitted a plan, of which the following is an outline.

1st. That an officer, to be termed superintendent of operations against Thuggee, should be appointed, with power to send out parties to apprehend those against whom he might have information in any part of the country.

2d. The superintendent to commit all whom he deems guilty for trial, before the governor-general's agent in the Saugor and Nerbudda territories.

3d. Lists to be made out against all upon whom suspicion rests, and sent to the different English functionaries.

4th. The residents at native courts also to give their assistance.

The draught likewise contains several minor provisions regarding the search for dead bodies ; rewards to those who deserve such a mark of approbation ; penalties for harbouring Thugs ; prevention of abuses by approvers ; and other clauses not worth enumerating here, although highly useful in practice.

The suggestions were, however, but partially adopted by government, for unfortunately Lord William Bentinck, at that time at the head of affairs, was not in the habit of indulging in a general or comprehensive view of any question ; and his mind, while in India, was chiefly occupied in the minor details of government and the consideration of petty economical retrenchments. Captain Sleeman was, in January, 1831, removed to Saugor district, authorized to act as superintendent, to send out parties for the arrest of Thugs, and proceed as above proposed ; but he was still expected to perform all his duties as civil officer of the Saugor district, without any additional pay, such being Lord William Bentinck's system. Still under so able and indefatigable an officer as Captain Sleeman much benefit occurred, and numerous arrests were made ; but it soon became evident, from the extensive nature of the Thug operations, that more aid must be granted. Accordingly, in January, 1832, another officer was appointed to take charge of the revenue and civil duties of the Saugor district, over which Captain Sleeman then presided, leaving to the latter only the magistracy department ; thus allowing him more leisure to devote to Thug affairs. Three junior officers were appointed his assistants, and detached to apprehend such Thugs as they could obtain information of.

Still, the more that was done the more seemed requisite to do. Every arrest brought to light new combinations and associations of these professed assassins, and discovered new scenes in which their dreadful trade was at work. It was obvious that nothing but a general system, undertaken by a paramount power, strong enough to bear down all opposition by interested native chiefs, could ever eradicate such well-organized villainy; and the other members of government at length succeeded in persuaded Lord William Bentinck that it was incumbent upon a government calling itself enlightened to take the lead in so good a work; and that a moderate expense would be well bestowed in suppressing an association which was causing the annual murder of some thousands of his fellow creatures. In prosecution of the extended system of operations, Captain Sleeman was in January, 1835, relieved altogether from ordinary civil duties, and appointed superintendent; and several additional officers were nominated to act under him in various parts of the country.

Jubulpoor, the residence of the agent to the governor-general in the Saugor and Nerbudda territories, was appointed Captain Sleeman's head-quarters. All Thugs apprehended within those territories Jeypoor, Hyderabad, Nagpoor, and other contiguous native states, are tried by the agent at Jubulpoor. Those of Oude and Indore by the residents of those courts; and such as have committed crimes in what are called the regulation provinces, are tried by the officers who are there stationed. Operations have lately extended into Bombay, Madras, the eastern parts of Bengal, and the north westernmost parts of the Indian continent; and there is no doubt that, to ensure complete success it will be necessary to nominate additional superintendents as well as subordinate officers for each of these divisions: to which should be added functionaries specially appointed for the trial of those committed.

The success of the combined operations has been

beyond hope; and if properly followed up, it will be almost impossible for a Thug to remain at large. The mode of proceeding is, to take the deposition of those who turn approvers, wherever this may happen to be. These men are then required to give, to the best of their recollection, a full account of every expedition on which they have been, mentioning the dates of every one, and the detail of every murder; together with the names of those who had formed the gangs, their residence, caste, &c., &c. All this is registered in the office of the general-superintendent, and lists of those to be apprehended are sent to the different subordinate officers, who are all provided with approvers and guards. These officers also take the depositions in full of all whom they may apprehend, copies of which are sent to the general-superintendent. It is obvious that when depositions, thus taken almost simultaneously from different people hundreds of miles apart, who have had no means of collusion, and none of them expecting to be apprehended, agree in describing the same scenes and the same actors, it is obviously next to impossible to refuse belief. But another test is applied. When a Thug is arrested, he is brought direct to the officers' residence, and placed in a row between unconcerned people. The approvers, who have been detained at the stations, are then sent for singly, and required to point out any individual of the party whom they may know. If they all fix on the same individual, and their statements also agree with those previously made by others, it is impossible that better evidence can be had.

We mention this, because we are aware that a prejudice has gone forth against the mode of conducting both the previous investigations and the

sessions part of the business in Thug trials.   That
a man who has only seen or heard the latter should
have some suspicions is not surprising; for the
whole evidence of events long past is given so
glibly, that it appears to bear strong marks of
fabrication.   But in fact the sessions part of the
business is the least to be relied on: if that were
all a man had before him to enable him to form his
judgment, few Thugs would have been punished:
before the trials come on, the approvers have all
been brought together; have had opportunities
of seeing the prisoners, and of fabricating what
tales they please.   But this they dare not do; they
know well that what passes in the sessions, though
the actual trial, yet serves chiefly to inspect the
papers and operations of the subordinate officers,
in order to ascertain that all has been correctly
conducted; and that in reality, the previous proceedings form the evidence mainly relied upon.
The whole association of Thugs is, in fact, different
from that of any other known villains in existence.
Their system is such, that they are beyond the
reach of the ordinary tribunals of the country, and
a special system must be put in force against them.
That some petty abuses have been committed, we
allow.   Money has occasionally been extorted
from people, under threat of accusing them of being
Thugs; and others, though innocent, have suffered
a temporary imprisonment.   But there is no system,
however well organized, that may not be open to
imperfections; and what are such evils as the
above, which are the sum total of all that has
occurred, to ridding the world of some hundreds
of professed assassins.

We are fully convinced, after taking everthing
into consideration, that there are no trials in which

a man may with so safe a conscience pronounce
sentence, as those of the Thugs; in proof of which
we have only to refer to the table in p. 38 of Captain Sleeman's work. No less than eleven different
functionaries, judicial and political, are there mentioned as having held Thug trials; yet the general
result is the same in all, as to the proportion found
guilty and acquitted. We could mention many
individual instances in proof of the correctness of
the information obtained and evidence brought forward, but will content ourselves with one very
striking case from Hyderabad. About eighty
Thugs had been arrested in various parts of that
kingdom by different parties of approvers; they
were collected into a gang and sent off to Jubulpoor
under a guard. As they were passing the residence of the local governor of one of the Hyderabad provinces, he gave in charge to the guard
eleven men whom he had apprehended on suspicion. The whole were safely brought to Jubulpoor;
but it so happened that the papers and documents
relating to their arrest had not been received by
the time of their arrival; and the officer commanding the guard made no report as to whence
the different men who composed the gang under
his charge had been received; they were, therefore, as a matter of course, supposed to be all
Thugs who had been arrested by the approvers.
Nevertheless the usual form was proceeded in, *i. e.*
the approvers who remained at Jubulpoor were
sent for singly to inspect the gang; all were
recognized to be Thugs excepting eleven men, of
whom the approvers said they knew nothing. On
the receipt of the documents a few days afterwards,
these eleven proved to be the party given in charge

to the guard by the local governor, with whose arrest the approvers had no concern.

The success which has attended the exertions of the officers employed to suppress this crime, has hitherto equalled the most sanguine expectations. In most parts of central India, Bundlecund, Bogle-cund, and from Allahabad to the Himalayah, Thuggee now scarcely exists: the great proof of which is, that the servants of English gentlemen, and Sepahees, who go on leave into those parts of the country, have, during the last three years, all returned in safety; whereas previously, not a year passed without many of them being missed. We mention these two classes, for their movements only can we correctly ascertain; but it is a fair inference that other natives have travelled in equal safety. There can be no doubt that if the British government will pursue vigorous measures for a few years, the system will, with proper supervision on the part of the ordinary police, be completely eradicated, never again to rise; but if exertions are slackened, and any fully initiated Thugs left at large, they would infallibly raise new gangs, and Thuggee would again flourish all over India. It is certainly incumbent on a government which assumes to itself the character of enlightened, and which is now paramount in India, to exert itself for the suppression of such an atrocious system. It is impossible to ascertain with accuracy the extent to which it has been carried annually, and, could it be done, the statement would scarcely be credited. Reckoning the number of Thugs in all India to be ten thousand, and that, on the average, each Thug murders three victims a year, this will give an amount of thirty thousand murders annually committed for many years past, of which, till lately,

scarcely any thing was known. Frightfully enormous as this may appear, it is probable that both
estimates are under the mark, which is warranted
by what appears on the trials, where, of course,
but a small portion of the crimes actually committed are proved.

In the sessions of 1836, lately held by the
Honourable F. I. Shore at Jubulpoor, two hundred
and forty-one prisoners were convicted of the murder of four hundred and seventy-four individuals, of
whose corpses three hundred and fourteen were
disinterred, and inquests held upon them.

The results have been hitherto highly satisfactory. Within these few years more than two
thousand Thugs have been arrested by the officers
attached to the Jubulpoor and Central India establishment alone. Of these about three hundred
have been made approvers; eighteen hundred and
three were committed for trial.* Of these four
hundred and nineteen were sentenced to death;
one thousand and eighty to transportation for life ;†
ninety-five to imprisonment for life; leaving two
hundred and nine, who were either sentenced to
limited imprisonment, allowed to turn approvers,
died in gaol, or were otherwise disposed of. Only
twenty-one of the whole have been acquitted; and
this proves the extraordinary care with which the
cases are prepared by the officers to whom this
duty has been intrusted, and the strong nature of
the evidence adduced. We cannot but wish them
every success in exterminating a system which

---

* This result reaches to the year 1836, and is consequently
greater than that given in a paper of Captain Sleeman's, in a subsequent part of the work.

† These sentences are at once carried into execution, and not
commuted, as is so common in England.

spares neither sex nor age; whose members never abandon their profession as long as they possess the power to engage in an expedition; who watch for their prey like wild beasts or vultures; and talk of the principal scenes of their crimes as a sportsman would of his favourite preserves. We trust also that no miserable fit of economy on the part of government may arise to thwart the measures in progress, but that every co-operation will be given to those praiseworthy exertions.

CAPTAIN SLEEMAN'S NOTICE OF THE THUGS, THEIR LANGUAGE, SUPERSTITIONS AND CUSTOMS.

WE now present the reader with the account of the Thugs, by Captain Sleeman, the Superintendent of the Thug Police. This account is prefixed by the author to his Ramaseana or Vocabulary of the Thug dialect. It brings down the history to the year 1836. The vocabulary itself will be found in the Appendix to this work.

I have, I believe, entered in this Vocabulary every thing to which Thugs in any part of India have thought it necessary to assign a peculiar term; and every term peculiar to their associations with which I have yet become acquainted. I am satisfied that there is no term, no rite, no ceremony, no opinion, no omen or usage that they have intentionally concealed from me; and if any have been accidently omitted after the numerous narratives that I have had to record, and cases to investigate, they can be but comparatively very few and unimportant.

Their peculiar dialect the Thugs call Ramasee;

and every word entered in this Vocabulary is Ramasee in the sense assigned to it; while but few of them are to be found at all in any language with which I am acquainted. Their verbs have all Hindostanee terminations, and auxiliaries, such as Kurna to make, Lena to take, Dena to give, Jana to go, Lana to bring, Dalna to throw.

Different terms have often been invented for the same thing by different gangs, situated at a great distance from each other. Many of the members of the seven original clans who emigrated into remote parts of India, after their flight from Delhi, had, perhaps, forgotten many of the terms in use among them before they had the means of forming new gangs out of the rude materials around them in their new abodes, or before their own children became old enough to obviate the necessity of raising new recruits from among their neighbours, and been obliged to adopt new ones. As the new gangs became too large to be satisfied with occasional murders upon the roads in their neighbourhood, they extended their expeditions into remote parts, and had frequent occasions of meeting and acting in conjunction with each other; when it became necessary that all should become so familiarly acquainted with the different terms used by different gangs to denote the same thing, as to be able to use them indifferently and at the moment when occasion required.

It is not perhaps above fifty or sixty years that the gangs of Hindoostan have been in the habit of frequently extending their depredations into the districts south of the Nurbudda; and to these depredations they were invited chiefly by the Pindaree system, which rendered the roads leading from these districts across the Nurbudda to the

Gangetic provinces, and to Hindoostan generally, very insecure; and caused the wealth to flow by those of Surgooja and Sumbulpore; and by the remittances made in jewels and specie from Bombay and Surat, to Indore and Ragpootana after the suppression of that system under the Marquis of Hastings, and the introduction of the opium monopoly into Malwa; which created an extraordinary demand for money to be advanced to the cultivators of that article.

There are in almost all parts of India money-carriers by profession, who, though in the very lowest classes of society in point of circumstances, are entrusted by merchants with the conveyance to distant parts of enormous sums in gold and jewels; and sent without a guard, and often without arms to defend themselves. Their fidelity, sagacity, and beggarly appearance are relied upon as a sufficient security; and though I have had to investigate the cases of, I may say hundreds, who have been murdered in the discharge of their duty, I have never yet heard of one who betrayed his trust. It was generally by these men, that the merchants of Bombay and Surat sent their remittances in gold and jewels through Kandeish and Malwa to Indore and Rajpootana; and from the year 1824, to the commencement of our operations in 1830, the sums taken from them by gangs of Thugs from Hindoostan, or countries north of the Nurbudda were immense. Of the following sums, we have authentic records.

	Rs.
1826, at Choupara on the Taptee—murder of 14 persons at one time, and plunder of - - - -	25,000

1827, Malagow in Kandeish—murder of
7 persons at one time, and plunder of - 22,000
1828, Dhorecote in Kandeish—murder of
3 persons at one time, and plunder of - 12,000
1828, Burwahagat on the Nurbudda—
murder of 9 persons at one time, and
plunder of   -   -   -   - 40,000
1829, Dhoree in Kandeish—murder of 6
persons at one time, and plunder of   - 82,000
1830, Baroda—murder of 25 persons, and
plunder of   -   -   -   - 10,000

In the Choupara affair, 150 Thugs were engaged, and of these there are only 33 at large. In the Burwahaghat affair, 125 were engaged, and of these only 12 are now at large. In the Dhoree affair, 150 were engaged, and of these only 30 are now at large. In the Dhorecote affair, 125 were engaged, and of these 25 only are at large. In the Dholeea and Malagow affair, 350 were either present or within a stage or two of the place and shared in the booty, and of these only 36 are now at large.*

There are Thugs at Jubulpore from all quarters of India; from Lodheeana to the Carnatic, and from the Indus to the Ganges. Some of them have been in the habit of holding, what I may fairly call unreserved communication with European gentlemen for more than twelve years; and yet there is not among them one who doubts *the divine origin of the system of Thuggee*—not one who doubts, that

---

* Total 136, but in reality there are only 69 of the Thugs engaged in these affairs now at large, as many were engaged in more than one of them. The total number engaged would appear to be 900, but in reality there were only between 500 and 600 for the same reason.

he and all who have followed the trade of murder
with the prescribed rites and observances, were
acting under the immediate orders and auspices of
the Goddess Devee, Durga, Kalee or Bhawanee,
as she is indifferently called, and consequently there
is not one who feels the slightest remorse for the
murders which he may, in the course of his vocation, have perpetrated or assisted in perpetrating.
A Thug considers the persons murdered precisely
in the light of victims offering up to the Goddess;
and he remembers them, as a Priest of Jupiter
remembered the oxen, and a Priest of Saturn the
children sacrificed upon their altars.   He meditates
his murders without any misgivings, he perpetrates
them without any emotions of pity, and he remembers them without any feelings of remorse.   They
trouble not his dreams, nor does their recollection
ever cause him inquietude in darkness, in solitude,
or in the hour of death.

I must at the same time state that I have very
rarely discovered any instance of what may, perhaps, be termed *wanton cruelty*; that is pain inflicted beyond what was necessary to deprive the
person of life—pain either to the mind or body.
The murder of women is a violation of their rules
to which they attribute much of the success against
the system, because it is considered to have given
offence to their patroness; but no Thug was ever
known to offer insult either in act or in speech to
the women they were to murder.   No gang would
ever dare to murder a woman with whom one of
its members should be suspected of having had
criminal intercourse.   In Bengal, Behar, and Or-
rissa, and in the countries east of the Jumna and
Ganges, they have not I believe yet ventured to
violate this rule against the murder of females;

and in the countries south of the Nurbudda river they have rarely violated it, I am told, except in the case of old women whom they could not conveniently separate from parties of travellers, or whom they supposed to be very wealthy. The gangs who inhabited the countries between the rivers Indus, Jumna, and Nurbudda, are the only ones that have yet ventured to murder women indiscriminately; and the belief that they owe their downfall in great measure to their having done so, will effectually prevent the practice from extending to other countries. The Thugs who resided between the Ganges and Jumna, did not, however, much scruple to participate in the murder of females while associated with the gangs of Bundelcund and Gwalior in their expeditions to the west of the Jumna, and south of the Nurbudda.

I have never found a Thug by birth, or one who had been fully initiated in its mysteries, who doubted the *inspiration of the pick-axe*,[*] when consecrated in due form,—not one who doubted that the omens described in this work were all-sufficient to guide them to their prey, or to warn them from their danger; or that they were the signs ordained by the Goddess expressly for these purposes,—not one who doubted, that if these omens had been attended to, and the prescribed rules observed, the system of Thuggee must have flourished under the auspices of its divine patroness, in spite of all the efforts for its suppression.

There is every reason to believe that the system of Thuggee or Phansegeeree, originated with some parties of vagrant Mahommuduns, who infested the roads about the ancient capital of India. Hero-

[*] See vocabulary in the Appendix, article *Kussee*.

dotus, in his Polymnia, mentions, as a part of the army with which Xerxes invaded Greece, a body of horse from among the Sagartii, a pastoral people of Persian descent, and who spoke the Persian language. Their only offensive weapons were a dagger, and a cord made of twisted leather with a noose at one end. With this cord they entangled their enemies or their horses, and when they got them down they easily put them to death. Thievenot, in the passage quoted by Doctor Sherwood from his Travels, part 3d, page 41, states,— " Though the road I have been speaking of from " Delhi to Agra be tolerable, yet hath it many " inconveniences. One may meet with tygers. " panthers, and lyons upon it; and one had best " also have a care of robbers, and above all things " not to suffer any body to come near one upon " the road. The cunningest robbers in the world " are in that country. They use a certain rope " with a running noose, which they can cast " with so much sleight about a man's neck " when they are within reach of him, that they " never fail, so that they strangle him in a trice, " &c. &c. But, besides that there are men in " those quarters so skilful in casting the snare that " they succeed as well at a distance as near at " hand, and if an ox or any other beast belonging " to a caravan run away, as sometimes it happens, " they fail not to catch it by the neck."*

Now, though there is a vast interval of time between the Persian invasion of Greece and the travels of Thievenot, and of space between the seat of Sagartii and that of the ancient capital of

---

* Thievenot was born 1621—he died 1692, and his travels were published 1687.

India, I am still inclined to think that the vagrant bands, who, in the sixteenth century infested the roads, as above described, between Delhi and Agra, came from some wild tribe and country of the kind: and I feel myself no doubt, that from these vagrant bands are descended the seven clans of Mahommudun Thugs, Bhys, Bursote, Kachunee, Huttar, Ganoo, and Tundel,* who, by the common consent of all Thugs throughout India, whether Hindoos or Mahommuduns, are admitted to be the most ancient, and the great original trunk upon which all others have at different times and in different places been grafted. Bands of these vagrants, under various denominations, are to be found in all parts of India, but are most numerous, I believe, to the north and west. They all retain in some degree their pristine habits and usages; and taking their families with them, they allow their women to assist in the murders which they perpetrate in their encampments; but they have always some other ostensible employment, and as the other Thugs, who live among and cannot be distinguished from other men, say, " they live in " the desert and work in the desert, and their deeds " are not known!"

But whatever may have been the origin of the system, it is sufficiently manifest that their faith in its divine origin is of Indian growth, and has been gradually produced by the habit of systematically confounding coincidences of circumstances and events with cause and effect. This is a weakness in some degree inherent in human nature, and

---

* Some include also the Kathur clan who are also called Ghuga-roe, but by most they are considered to be merely a sect from one of the original clans.

common, therefore, in some degree, to all states and classes of society. The man who seriously believes that he is habitually blessed with good or cursed with bad luck at cards or dice, the mother who believes that her child sickens because her friends venture to praise its freshness or its appetite, have it in common with the poor Bhoomka of the wild tracts of India, who believes that he can charm the tiger from his village, the Garpuguree who believes that he can divert the hail storm from the corn fields of its cultivators, and the Thug, who believes that he can inspire his pick-axe.* But India is emphatically the land of super-stition, and in this land the system of Thuggee, the most extraordinary that has ever been recorded in the history of the human race, had found a con-genial soil and flourished with rank luxuriance for more than two centuries, till its roots had pene-trated and spread over almost every district within the limits of our dominions, when the present plan of operations for its suppression was adopted in 1830 by the then Governor General Lord William Bentick.

For many years up to 1829 these assassins traversed every great and much frequented road from the Himalah Mountains to the Nerbudda

---

* In many parts of Berar and Malwa, every village has its Bhoomka, whose office it is to charm the tigers; and its Garpu-guree, whose duty it is to keep off the hail storms. They are part of the village servants, and paid by the village community. After a severe storm that took place in the district of Nursingpore, of which I had the civil charge in 1823, the office of Garpuguree was restored to several villages in which it had ceased for several generations. They are all Brahmans, and take advantage of such calamities to impress the people with an opinion of their usefulness. The Bhoomkas are all Gonds, or people of the woods, who worship their own Lares and Penates.

river, and from the Ganges to the Indus, without
the fear of punishment from divine or human laws.
There is not now, I believe, within that space a
single road except in the western parts of Rajpootana and Guzerat, that is not free from their depredations; and whatever may be ultimately the
opinion of thinking men regarding the general
character and results of Lord William Bentinck's
administration, I hope all will unite in applauding
the boldness which could adopt, and the firmness
which could so steadily pursue this great measure
for relieving the native society of India from an
evil which pressed on them so heavily, and on
them alone; for these assassins had rarely if ever
attacked Europeans. It was not against their
tenets to do so, but they knew that Europeans
seldom travelled with much money or other valuable property about their persons, and that their disappearance would cause much more inquiry, and
consequently more danger to their associations
than that of native travellers.

So early as April 1810 the commander-in-chief
of the army thought it necessary to issue an order,
cautioning the native troops against this dreadful
evil to which so many brave soldiers of every
regiment in the service were annually falling victims; but all attacks upon the evil itself continued
to be, as heretofore, insulated and accidental.
They were planned and executed by individual
magistrates, who becoming by accident acquainted
with the existence of the evil within their jurisdictions applied their abilities and their energies for a
time to its suppression; but their different efforts
being unconnected either in time or in place, and
often discouraged and repressed by the incredulity

of controling powers, were found ultimately almost every where alike unavailing.*

* GENERAL ORDERS BY MAJOR GENERAL ST. LEGER, COMMANDING THE FORCES.

Head Quarters, Cawnpore, the 28th April, 1810.

" It having come to the knowledge of Government that several " Sepoys proceeding to visit their families on leave of absence from " their corps have been robbed and murdered by a description of " persons denominated *Thugs,* who infested the districts of the " Dooab and other parts of the Upper Provinces, and the insidious " means by which they prosecute their plans of robbery and assas- " sination having been ascertained, the Commander of the Forces " thinks it proper to give them publicity in General Orders to the " end that Commanding Officers of Native Corps may put their " men on their guard accordingly.

" It has been stated, that these murderers, when they obtain " information of a traveller who is supposed to have money about " his person, contrive to fall in with him on the road or in the " Serais ; and under pretence of proceeding to the same place, keep " him company, and by indirect questions get an insight into his " affairs, after which they watch for an opportunity to destroy him. " This they sometimes create by persuading the traveller to quit " the Sarais a little after midnight, pretending it is near day-break, " or by detaching him from his companions lead him under various " pretences to some solitary spot.

" It appears that in the destruction of their victim they first use " some deleterious substance, commonly the seeds of a plant called " Duttora, which they contrive to administer in tobacco, pawn, the " hookah, food or drink of the traveller. As soon as the poison " begins to take effect, by inducing a stupor or languor, they strangle " him to prevent his crying out, when, after stripping and plun- " dering him, the deed is completed by a stab in the belly on the " brink of a well into which they plunge the body so instantaneously " that no blood can stain the ground or clothes of the assassin.

" As the Company's Sepoys who proceed on leave of absence " generally carry about them the savings from their pay in specie, " and travel unarmed, they are eagerly sought out by these robbers " as the particular objects of their depredation. With a view there- " fore to guard against such atrocious deeds, the Commanding " Officers of Native Corps will caution their men when proceeding " on leave of absence.

1st. " To be strictly on their guard against all persons (particu- " larly those unarmed) whom they fall in with on the road who

That truly great and good man the Marquis of Hastings, to whom India is perhaps more indebted than to any other individual whose character and station have had any influence upon its destinies, has the following passage in his short summary of his own administration of the government of India; and yet, strange to say, of the operations of that force the Gwalior Contingent, which this Nobleman supposed to have been so effectually employed in the suppression of this system, there is now to be found neither recollection nor record either among the officers who commanded it, or the people against whom it was employed. " Scindiah had " evaded producing this contingent until after the " destruction of the Pindaries. To compensate for " such a delay, which I affected to consider as

" evince a solicitude to keep them company on pretence that they "are going the same way and are inquisitive about their affairs.

2d. " Not to quit the Sarais at a very early hour in the morning " before the rest of the travellers.

3d. " Not to receive pawn, tobacco, sweetmeat, &c. &c. from " such persons, or smoke their hookahs, particularly if offered to " them in solitary spots on the road ; and lastly to avail themselves " of the protection of sowars (horsemen) when opportunity offers, " or travel as much as possible with large bodies of people. This " last object might be attained in a great degree if the men were " persuaded, on occasions of periodical leave of absence, to keep " together on the road, as long as the several destinations of such " Native Commissioned or Non-Commissioned Officers as may be " proceeding the same way will admit.

" It has also been intimated to the Major General Commanding " the Forces, that the Residents at Delhi and Lucknow, and the " Collectors of Revenue will be authorized, on the application of " Commanding Officers of Pay Masters, to grant bills payable at " sight and at the usual exchange, on any other treasury for sums " which may be paid into their own Treasuries on account of " Sepoys wishing to remit money from one point of the country to , " another; a mode which in conformity to the views of government " is particularly to be encouraged and attended to by Officers " Commanding Corps and Detachments."

" accidental, I pressed that the corps should be
" employed in extinguishing certain mischievous
" associations in Scindiah's territories.   The de-
" scription applied not only to some bands of
" avowed robbers, but to a particular class denomi-
" nated Thugs.   This nefarious fraternity, amount-
" ing, by the first information, to above a thousand
" individuals, was scattered through different vil-
" lages often remote from each other; yet they
" pursued with a species of concert, their avocation.
" This was the making excursions to distant districts,
" where, under the appearance of journeying along
" the high roads, they endeavoured to associate
" themselves with travellers, by either obtaining
" leave to accompany them as if for protection, or,
" when that permission was refused, keeping near
" them on the same pretext.   Their business was
" to seek an opportunity of murdering the travellers
" when asleep or off their guard.   In this, three or
" four could combine without having given suspicion
" of their connection.   Though personally unac-
" quainted, they had signs and tokens by which
" each recognized the other as of the brotherhood ;
" and their object being understood, without the
" necessity of verbal communication, they shunned
" all speech with each other till the utterance of a
" mystical term or two announced the favourable
" moment, and claimed common effort.   Scindiah's
" tolerance of an evil so perfectly ascertained,
" merely because the assassinations were seldom
" committed within his own dominions, may afford
" a tolerable notion of the vitiation of society in
" Central India before this late convulsion.   There
" is reason to believe that by this time the pest in
" question has been rooted out; which, with the
" suppression of some bodies of horsemen under

"military adventurers (a service completely
"achieved by the contingent), will be no less a
"benefit to Scindiah's own government, than to
"adjacent countries."

This system has now, August, 1835, I hope, been
happily suppressed in the Saugor and Nurbudda
territories, Bhopaul, Bundelcund, Boghelcund,
Eastern Malwa, the greater part of Gwalior, the
districts between the Ganges and the Jumna. It
has also I hope been suppressed in Candeish, Go-
zerat, Berar, Rajpootana, Western Malwa, and
the Delhi territories, in as far as it arose from the
depredations of gangs that resided in the territories
above-named, within which little more I hope
remains to be done than to collect the fragments of
the general wreck of the system—the *Burkas*, or
fully initiated Thugs, who have as yet escaped us,
and are capable of creating new gangs in any part
of India that they may be permitted to inhabit;
and that they will so create them if left for any
time undisturbed in any place, no man who is well
acquainted with the system will for a moment doubt.

But that the system has been suppressed in every
part of India where it once prevailed (and I believe
that it prevailed more or less in every part) is,
however, a proposition that neither ought nor can
be affirmed *absolutely*, for, as justly observed by
the able magistrate of Chittoor in 1812, Mr. W. E.
Wright—"with respect to the crime of murder by
"Thugs or Fanseegeers, it is not possible for any
"magistrate to say how much it prevails in his
"district, in consequence of the precautions taken
"by these people in burying the bodies of the
"murdered."* To affirm absolutely that it has

* See his letter to the Secretary to the Madras Government
dated 1st July, 1812.

been suppressed while any seeds of the system remain to germinate and spread again over the land might soon render all that has been done unavailing, for there is in it a "principle of vitality" which can be found hardly in any other; and unhappily there exists every where too great a disposition to believe that we have completed what we have only successfully begun. However honourable to the individuals engaged in it and useful to the people the duty of suppressing this evil may be considered, it certainly is one of great labour and of most painful responsibility; and as almost all those who have yet devoted their abilities to the task have done so at a personal sacrifice of some kind or another to themselves, they have naturally felt anxious to see their part of the work completed as soon as possible. " Fere libenter id, quod volunt homines, credunt," was an observation of Cæsar's, the truth of which is illustrated in almost every human undertaking; and though I do not think any public officer will declare this evil suppressed within his jurisdiction before he believes it to be so, I fear many will, as heretofore, believe it to be so, long before it really is.* There were, and I believe, still are in Bundelcund, and the districts between the Ganges and the Jumna, some small gangs of these assassins who confined their operations to the roads in the neighbourhood of their residence, and the secrets of their crimes to

* It has been every where found dangerous for a magistrate to make it appear to his native police officers, that he believes or wishes to believe that the crime of Thuggee has entirely ceased within his jurisdiction, for they will always be found ready to avail themselves of such an impression to misrepresent cases that might otherwise lead to discoveries of great importance. Bodies of travellers that have been strangled by Thugs have, in numerous instances, been either concealed or represented by the police as those of men

their own families, or to a very small circle of friends and associates. They were either in their infancy, or formed by very shrewd old men who saw the danger of continuing with the large gangs and extending their expeditions into very distant parts. Bukshee Jemadar, one of the most noted Thug leaders of his day, who died in the Saugor jail in 1832, had for some fifteen years ceased to accompany the large gangs, and was supposed to have left off the trade entirely. He was settled at Chutterpore on the great road from Saugor to Culpee, with his three sons, all stout young men, who were supposed by all the old associates of their

who had died of disease, or been killed by tigers, and have been burned without further inquiry, when a careful inquest by impartial persons would have shown the marks of strangulation upon their necks. Landholders of all descriptions, whether ostensibly entrusted with the police duties of their estates or not, will in the same manner always endeavour to conceal the discovery of murders perpetrated within them by these people under a magistrate anxious to believe that the crime does not exist within his division. In some parts of India heavy penalties are injudiciously imposed upon landholders and police officers within whose estates or jurisdictions bodies of murdered men may be found unless they can produce the perpetrators, which is, in effect, to encourage the crime by discouraging the report of those discoveries that might lead to the arrest and conviction of the murderers.

Mr. Wilson writes to me on the 3d December, 1834,—" It is " painful to observe that wherever the Thugs go they are invariably " protected by the Zumeendars, and the premises of the Thakurs or " principal landholders are the certain spots to find them in." This observation so just with regard to the districts east of the Jumna, has been, unhappily, found equally applicable to every other part of India to which our operations have extended. The Zumeendars or landholders of every description have every where been found ready to receive these people under their protection from the desire to share in the fruits of their expeditions, and without the slightest feeling of religious or moral responsibility for the murders which they know must be perpetrated to secure these fruits. All that they require from them is a promise that they will not commit murders within their estates, and thereby involve them in trouble.

father never to have been initiated in the mysteries of Thuggee. They were all however arrested with their father and brought to Saugor. A trooper of the 10th cavalry came to me some time after this from the Mow Cantonments with a piteous tale of the loss and supposed murder of his younger brother, a trooper in the same regiment, whom he had a year or two before, while on their way to their homes on furlough, left in company with a small party of *extremely civil men* in the neighbourhood of Chutterpore. The young trooper's pony *had become lame* on the road, and his brother and party went on to prepare their dinner, telling him to spare his pony and come up slowly, as they would have every thing ready for him by the time he arrived. "The strangers had, he said, been very kind to "him, and very solicitous about the accident to "his pony; and promised to see him safe to the "encampment, as they were obliged to wait for a "relation who was following: but his brother could "never after be found." I took the trooper at his request to the jail, and almost as soon as he entered he put his hand upon the shoulder of Bukshee's youngest son, who was remarkable for his large eyes, saying, "What did you do with my poor brother—where did you murder and bury him?" and turning round while he yet had hold of the man, he said, "this is one of the men to whom I confided my brother." Jawahir and his brothers, who had hitherto persisted in denying that they had ever been on Thuggee, and whose father's old associates, now admitted King's evidences, used to declare that this son, Jawahir, so far from having been on Thuggee, was such a chicken-hearted lad that the very name of murder used to frighten him, now thought the charm had been

broken, and confessed that their father had initiated them from their boyhood; but having limited their expeditions to that road, and admitted only a small party of associates their proceedings had remained undiscovered. Some of the old members of these small gangs have been secured and convicted of old crimes perpetrated while they were associated with the large gangs, and they have in consequence suspended their operations; but they will resume them again when our pursuit ceases unless all their principal members be brought to punishment.

It has now become quite clear to every unprejudiced magistrate, that, as a general principle, he can never rely upon the landholder of a village either to assist him in the arrest of these people, or to prevent their following their trade of murder when they are made over to him upon his pledge to do so. His own particular interest in encouraging the system and sharing in the spoil, will always be dearer to him than any that he can hope to enjoy in common with the society at large by the suppression of it. When driven from one part of the country they never doubt of being soon able to secure the good will of such landholders in any other, for they find little or no difficulty in establishing themselves in new village communities, and in connecting their dreadful trade with the pursuits of agriculture. Left unmolested for a few years they gain recruits from among the youth of their neighbourhood; and by a lavish expenditure of the booty they acquire, and by that mild and conciliatory deportment which they find it necessary to learn and observe on all occasions for the successful prosecution of their trade, they very soon gain the good will of their new circle of society, and contrive to make every member feel interested in their security and success. No men observe more strictly in domestic life all that is enjoined by their priests, or demanded by their respective casts; nor do any men cultivate with more care the esteem of their neighbours, or court with more assiduity the good will of all constituted local authorities. In short, to men who do not know them, the principal members of these associations will always appear to be among the most amiable, most respectable, and most intelligent members of the lower, and sometimes the middle and higher classes of native society; and it is by no means to be inferred that every man who attempts to screen them from justice knows them to be murderers.*

* I will here quote a passage from a private letter of Mr. McLeod to me, written at Dholepore or the banks of the Chumbul, May, 23d, 1833. "I am about to send off Purusram, Laek's brother, without irons is search of his father's gang, accompanied only by a sowar, a sipahee or two, and a chuprassee of my own, all of whom will be directed to conceal their livery. They will be instructed on falling in with the gang to give intelligence at the nearest residence of a native functionary, and be furnished with a document requesting such functionary to have them seized as 'Companee ka chor,' and delivered over to his superior to whom application will afterwards be made for their transfer. Purusram states that he can, if necessary, dig up at every stage the bodies of men they have lately murdered to satisfy the scruples of such as doubt his information. That he will find out the gang I have not the slightest doubt, and if he prove as faithful and intelligent as I hope, we may safely calculate upon their seizure. To ensure his earnestness as far as possible, I have assured him that I will do my utmost to have his father pardoned, and that your assurance before leaving Saugor made me confident that he would be so. In your last you say he ought not to be spared as he has neglected your invitations, but I really doubt whether they can ever have reached him in an authentic form; for both Laek and his brother assert that such assurance is all he wants, and his old wife has just toddled away home fully confident that, if he returns unassisted, she will speedily conduct him into my presence or that of some European officer. When we consider the indistinct account they receive of the horrors of Saugor much allowance must be made for them in this

When Feringeea,* a Thug leader of some note, for whose arrest government paid five hundred

respect. Bhimmee Jemadar tells me that when Durgean the runaway approver joined them, he said—"Oh! my friends you had "better cut and run as fast as you can—hundreds of us Thugs are "being strung about Saugor—still more are sent to the Blackwater, "which is worse; and those that escape are cut muttee* for life "—as to the poor approvers, Sleeman Sahib is getting a large mill "made up at the Mint to grind them all to powder." They of course all took to their heels after this. Bhimmee is a mild, respectable kind of man who would certainly not appear born for a gallows, and I hope you will let him remain with me. I feel interested, too, for the whole of Laek's family, among whom I do not think there is naturally any vice, and shocking as their proceedings would appear at home, very many palliating circumstances evidently exist here, and we must be guided by what is expedient. To Laek the sentence of any of his brothers would be most disheartening. When he heard of their arrest, he repeated with great feeling a Hindostanee verse to this effect. "I was a "pearl once residing in comfort in the ocean. I surrendered myself, "believing I should repose in peace in the bosom of some fair "damsel—but alas! they have pierced me, and passed a sting "through my body, and have left me to dangle in constant pain as "as an ornament to her nose." I will have his narrative taken and sent to you.   D. F. M'LEOD.

Lieutenant Thomas, a very talented officer, writes to me from Gualior 2d September, 1835—"Munohur, the brother of Leak, (cousin not brother) has voluntarily surrendered himself, at the persuasion of his mother, who lately sent to me for Laek. Upon sending him to her, I told Laek that I would certainly intercede with you for his brother if he would place himself in my custody. He is many years younger than Laek, and has one of the most benevolent countenances that I have ever seen. He looks as though he would rather commit suicide than common, and cold blooded murder. He tells me that he can point out the homes in the Jypore and Jodhpore villages of many noted Sooseea Thugs; that Raejoo is now at his home, and that he left those gangs only a month since actually on Thuggee in Jodhpore."
      G. P. THOMAS.

    * Earth. (Ed.)

---

* This Feringeea was for several years in the service of Sir David Ochterlony, as a *Jemadar*,—a sort of sergeant, in command of the armed attendants of a great man.

rupees, was brought in to me at Saugor in December, 1830, he told me, that if his life were spared he could secure the arrest of several large gangs who were in February to rendezvous at Jypore, and proceed into Guzerat and Candeish. Seeing me disposed to doubt his authority upon a point of so much importance, he requested me to put him to the proof—to take him through the village of Selohda, which lay two stages from Saugor on the road to Seronge, and through which I was about to pass in my tour of the district, of which I had received the civil charge, and he would show me his ability and inclination to give me correct information. I did so, and my tents were pitched, where tents usually are, in the small mango grove. I reached them in the evening, and when I got up in the morning, he pointed out three places, in which he and his gang had deposited at different intervals the bodies of three parties of travellers. A Pundit and six attendants murdered in 1818, lay among the ropes of my sleeping tent, a Havildar and four Sipahaes murdered in 1824, lay under my horses, and four Brahman carriers of Ganges water, and a woman murdered soon after the

Purusram came up with his fathers' gang at Alneeabas in the Joodpore territory, where they had been arrested by the Thakur who refused to give them to our guard—beat the old man to death and released the rest.

Mr. Wilson, Sept. 1835, observes of Makeen Lodhee, one of the approvers, that " he is one of the best men I have ever known !" and I believe that Makeen may be trusted in any relation of life, save that between a Thug who has taken the *auspices* and a traveller who has something worth taking upon him. They all look upon travellers as a sportsman looks upon hares and pheasants ; and they recollect their favourite *Beles*, or places of murder, as sportsmen recollect their best sporting grounds, and talk of them, when they can, with the same kind of glee !

Pundit, lay within my sleeping tent.* The sward
had grown over the whole, and not the slightest
sign of its ever having been broken was to be seen.
The thing seemed to me incredible; but after
examining attentively a small brick terrace close
by, and the different trees around, he declared himself prepared to stake his life upon the accuracy of
his information. My wife was still sleeping over
the grave of the water-carriers unconscious of what
was doing or to be done.† I assembled the people
of the surrounding villages, and the Thanadar and
his police, who resided in the village 'of Korae
close by, and put the people to work over the
grave of the Havildar. They dug down five feet
without perceiving the slightest signs of the bodies
or of a grave. All the people assembled seemed
delighted to think that I was become weary like
themselves, and satisfied that the man was derang-
ed; but there was a calm and quiet confidence
about him that made me insist upon their going on,
and at last we came upon the bodies of the whole
five laid out precisely as he had described. My
wife, still unconscious of our object in digging, had
repaired to the breakfast tent which was pitched
at some distance from the grove; and I now had
the ropes of the tent removed, and the bodies of
the Pundit and his six companions in a much
greater state of decay, exhumed from about the
same depth, and from the exact spot pointed out.
The Cawrutties were afterwards disinterred, and

* The principal leaders of the gangs, by whom these Brahmins
were murdered, were Brahmuns, Aman, the cousin of Feringeea,
and Dirgpaal, both Subardars of Thugs.

† She has often since declared that she never had a night of such
horrid dreams, and that while asleep her soul must consequently
have become conscious of the dreadful crimes that had been there
perpetrated.

he offered to point out others in the neighbouring groves, but I was sick of the horrid work, and satisfied with what he had already done.* The gangs which were concentrating upon Jypore were pursued, and the greater part of them taken; and Feringeea's life was spared for his services.

While I was in the civil charge of the district of Nursingpore, in the valley of the Nurbuddah, in the years 1822, 23, and 24, no ordinary robbery or theft could be committed without my becoming acquainted with it; nor was there a robber or a thief of the ordinary kind in the district, with whose character I had not become acquainted in the discharge of my duty as magistrate; and if any man had then told me, that a gang of assassins by profession, resided in the village of *Kundelee*, not four hundred yards from my court, and that the extensive groves of the village of Mundesur, only one stage from me, on the road to Saugor and Bhopaul, was one of the greatest *Beles*, or places of murder in all India; and that large gangs from Hindustan and the Duckun used to rendezvous in these groves, remain in them for many days together every year, and carry on their dreadful trade along all the lines of road that pass by and branch off from them, with the knowledge and connivance of the two landholders by whose ancestors these groves had been planted, I should have thought him a fool or a madman; and yet nothing could have been more

* The proprietor of the village of Selobda connived at all this, and received the horse of the Pundit in a present. Several of the gang resided in this village, and the rest used to encamp in his grove every year in passing, and remain there for many days at a time, feasting, carousing and murdering. The people of the village and of the surrounding country knew nothing of these transactions, nor did the police of the thana of Korae.

true. The bodies of a hundred travellers lie buried in and around the *groves of Mundesur;* and a gang of assassins lived in and about the village of Kundelee, while I was magistrate of the district, and extended their depredations to the cities of Poona and Hydrabad.

The first party of men I sent into the Duckun to aid Captain Reynolds, who had been selected by Colonel Stewart to superintend the employment of our means for the suppression of the system in the Nizam's dominions, recognized in the person of one of the most respectable *linen drapers* of the cantonments of Hingolee, Huree Sing, the adopted son of Jowahir Sookul, Subahdar of Thugs, who had twenty years before been executed with twenty-one of his followers at Aggur for the murder of a party of two women and eight men close to the cantonments. On hearing that the Huree Sing of the list sent to him of noted Thugs at large in the Duckun was the Huree Sing of the Sudder Bazar, Captain Reynolds was quite astounded, for so correct had he been in his deportment and all his dealings, that he had won the esteem of all the gentlemen of the station, who used to assist him in procuring passports for his goods on their way from Bombay; and yet he had, as he has since himself shown, been carrying on his trade of murder up to the very day of his arrest with gangs of Hindustan and the Duckun on all the roads around, and close to the cantonments of Hingolee; and leading out his gang of assassins while he pretended to be on his way to Bombay for a supply of fresh linens and broad cloth. Captain Reynolds had for several years up to this time had the civil charge of the district of Hingolee, without having had the slightest suspicion of the numerous murders that he has now discovered to have been every year perpetrated within his jurisdiction.*

* The following is an extract from the narrative of this Hurree Sing alias Hureea, taken at Hingolee.

"A year and a half before I was arrested at Hingolee, in June, "1832, I set up a shop in the bazar of the Golundauz in the Hingo- "lee cantonments. I used before to bring cloths from Berar to the "cantonments for sale; and became intimately acquainted with "Maha Sing, Subahdar of the Golundauzes. I told him that I "should like to set up a shop in his bazar; and he advised me to "do so, and got the Cotwal to assign me a place. I set up a linen "draper's shop, and I went several times with other shop-keepers "to Bombay to purchase a stock of broad cloths and other articles. "The people of the cantonments knew that I used to deal to the "extent of several hundred rupees.

"When I resided at Omrowtee about seven years ago, I used to "come to Hingolee and lodge in the house of Ram Sing, Thug, "who has since been seized and sent to Jubulpore. Sometimes I "came with the gangs on Thuggee and sometimes as a merchant "with cloths for sale. When I came with cloths I used to stay for "fifteen or twenty days at a time in the Moghul Sowar lines, and "other places. After the release of Hurnagur and his gang from "Hingolee after the Girgow murders, I, with Maunkhan, the two "Nasirs, Chotee approver and others, killed three Marwaries; and "after this Imam and Chotee got seized at Saugor, and this was "reported to me by Kureem Khan and others who came to Om- "rowtee from the Nurbudda valley; and I thought that I might be "pointed out and arrested. This was my reason for leaving Om- "rowtee for Hingolee. When I was arrested I had determined to "leave off Thuggee, and intended to go and reside at Bombay. I "used to go out occasionally on Thuggee after I settled at Hingo- "lee, and when the gangs of Thugs encamped on the tank or "lodged in the Dhuramsalah, I used to converse with them; but I "never let them know where I resided. Ismael Thug, who is now "an approver, used to reside in the bazar of the fifth regiment, and "be served Captain Scott as a Gareewan. Mohna, alias Ruhman, "used also to reside here sometimes. Bahleen also used to live and "work in the bazar, but they used all three to go on the roads, as "many travellers used to pass and no one sought after Thugs. "Any skilful party might have had three or four affairs every "night without any one being the wiser for it. People knew not "what Thuggee was, nor what kind of people Thugs were. Travel- "lers were frequently reported to have been murdered by robbers, "but people thought the robbers must be in the jungles; and never "dreamed that they were murdered by the men they saw every

In Oude and other parts of India where the fields are irrigated from wells, the bodies of travellers murdered by these people are frequently found by the cultivators and landholders who take them out and bury them without any report to the police, knowing that they are the bodies of travellers so murdered, whose distant friends are not likely to trouble them with any inquiries. In some instances we have found that they save themselves this trouble by throwing in some dead carcase in order to account for the offensive smell of the putrid bodies, should any one have the curiosity to inquire the cause. Such, in short, are the precautions taken by these people to conceal their murders both before and after they take place, that they may be every year perpetrated in the district of the most vigilant magistrate without his having any knowledge or suspicion of them; and their subsequent discovery must not be considered to detract from his character as a public officer unless it can be shown that he has discouraged the free report of those circumstances that might have led to the discovery earlier.

The extent of good above described has been effected by the arrest of above two thousand Thugs, who have been tried at Indore, Hydrabad, Saugor and Jubulpore. One hundred and fifty have been tried and convicted at Indore, eighty-four at Hydrabad; and at Saugor and Jubulpore above twelve hundred have been convicted, in one hundred and sixty-seven trials, of the murder of nine hundred and forty-seven persons; while about two

---

" day about them. I never invited a Thug to my house, nor did I
" ever expose any of the articles obtained in Thuggee for sale. I
" was much respected by the people of the town and cantonments
" and never suspected till arrested."

hundred and fifty have, in all these trials at Indore, Hydrabad, Saugor and Jubulpore, been admitted as King's evidences on the conditions of exemption from the punishment of death and transportation beyond seas for all past offences, provided they placed all those offences on record when required to do so, and assisted in the arrest of their associates in crime.

These men are commonly tried for one particular case of murder, perpetrated on one expedition, in which case all the gang may have participated, and in which the evidence is the most complete. On an average more than ten of these cases have been found to occur on every expedition; and every man has, on an average, been on more than ten of these expeditions. The murders for which they are tried are not, therefore, commonly more than a hundredth part of the murders they have perpetrated in the course of their career of crime. In the last sessions held at Jubulpore by Mr. Smith for 1834-35, thirty-six cases from Hydrabad, committed by Captain Reynolds, and forty-two cases from other parts committed by myself, were tried, and two hundred and six prisoners convicted of the murder of four hundred and forty persons. Of these persons the bodies of three hundred and ninety had been disinterred and inquests held upon them, leaving only fifty-five unaccounted for.*

In the dominions of the King of Oude much has already been done by Colonel Low and Captain Paton; and I have no doubt of a successful result to our efforts in that quarter provided the pursuit

---

* These trials included several supplementary cases, or cases which had been tried before, but were brought on as other prisoners, who were not forthcoming when they were first tried, have been arrested and brought in for trial.

be actively kept up in such of our districts as border upon them, and the local magistrates continue to give the Oude authorities their cordial support and co-operation; nor have I much doubt of ultimate success in Western Malwa,* Guzerat, Rajpootana, and the Delhi territories. Great progress has been made in the extensive territories of the Nizam, south of the Nerbudda, by Captain Reynolds, under the auspices of the Resident, Colonel Stewart; and as the Bombay Government and local authorities in the conterminous districts of that Presidency have manifested the most anxious wish to co-operate, those of Madras will probably do the same, and we shall then have a fair prospect of ultimate success throughout the countries south of the Nerbudda.

Something has been done in Behar by Mr. Peploe Smith, a very active and intelligent magistrate, and by Mr. C. W. Smith and others, and what has been done may lead to more; but the provinces of Behar, Bengal, and Orissa, are those in which my hopes of final success are perhaps least sanguine. The river Thugs of Bengal, who reside chiefly in the district of Burdwan, on the banks of the Hooghly, will defy all our efforts unless some special measure be adopted by the government for the suppression of their system, and we have, to promote its success, a combination of circumstances almost too favourable to be hoped for. They are supposed to be between two and three hundred, and to employ about twenty boats, which pass up and down the Ganges during the months of November, Decem-

---

* Indeed Major Borthwick's great success in Western Malwa has left but little to accomplish in that quarter.

ber, January, and February. Each boat is provided with a crew of about fourteen persons, all
Thugs, but employed in different capacities. Some
are employed in pulling the boat along by a rope,
and appear like the dandies or rowers and pullers
of ordinary boats; some as *Sothas*, or inveiglers,
follow the boats along the roads that run, parallel
with the river, and by various arts prevail upon
travellers to embark as passengers on board their
boats, where they find many Thugs well dressed
and of the most respectable appearance, pretending
to be going on or returning from a pilgrimage to
the holy places of Guya, Benares, Allahabad, &c.
These are the stranglers and their assistants, who
on a signal given by the man at the helm on deck
(*Bykureea*), strangle the travellers, break their
back bones and push them out of a window in the
side into the river. Each boat has one of these
windows on each side, and they are thrust out of
that facing the river.

Several boats belonging to the same association
follow each other at the distance of from four to
six miles, and when the travellers show any signs
of disliking or distrusting the inveigler of one, or
any disinclination to embark at the ghat where his
boat is to be found, the inveigler of the one in
advance learns it by signs from the other, as he
and the travellers overtake him. The new inveigler gets into conversation with the travellers, and
pretends to dislike the appearance of the first, who
in his turn, pretends to be afraid of the new one,
and lags behind, while the new man and the travellers congratulate each other on having shaken
off so suspicious a character. These men never
shed blood, and if any drop touch them they must
return and offer sacrifices of some kind or other.

They never keep any article that can lead to suspicion, as their boats are constantly liable to be
searched by the custom-house officers.   Nothing I
believe could tempt them to murder a woman. This
class contains Mahommuduns and Hindoos of all
casts, and they go up the river Ganges as far as
Benares, and sometimes even as far as Cawnpore,
it is said ; and they carry on their depredations as
well going down as coming up the river.   The
Lodahas, Moteeas, and Jumaldehee Thugs, who
reside in Behar and Bengal, are all acquainted with
them, as the principal scene of their operations is.
along the banks of the Ganges and other large
rivers into which they throw the bodies of their
victims. Their resting places or Thapas, are almost
always upon the banks of these rivers, where the
large and most frequented roads approach nearest
to them ; and there they remain for a long time
together, destroying such travellers as they can
persuade to spend the night with them. When they
fall in with the boats, and see a chance of a good
prize, some of the members of their gang go on
board and assist in the murder ; and the whole
gang share equally with that of the boatmen in the
spoil.

Our present plan of operations for the suppression
of this system commenced with the arrest of a
large gang from Hindoostan on its return from an
expedition into the Duckun by Captain, now
Major Borthwick, Political Agent at Mahidpore ;*

* Major Borthwick, on the 7th of November, 1831, accompanied
by Captain McMahon and a party of two hundred of the Jowra
Cavalry Contingent, made a night march of thirty miles, and
arrested an entire gang of forty-six of these murderers, with
property to the value of about twelve thousand rupees, which they
had brought home from a recent expedition in which they had

and that of another by me in Bhopaul in the beginning of 1830.* These arrests were attended by a combination of circumstances so fortunate, that a man might consider them as providential without exposing himself to the charge of superstition. The feelings of every one whose feelings were of any importance to the cause, from the Governor General Lord Wm. Bentinck and Vice President in Council, Sir Charles Metcalfe, to the humblest individual, seemed to be deeply and simultaneously interested in promoting its success. Colonel Stewart, who was at the time the representative of the government at the Court of Indore, tried the gang arrested by Captain Borthwick, under instructions from the supreme government; and he long afterwards declared " that he considered the share " he had in bringing these men to punishment as " by far the most useful part of his public life," though few men in India have, I believe, had a more useful career. Mr. Smith, who was the Governor General's representative in the Saugor

murdered a great many persons. His exertions in the cause have been unwearied, and eminently successful, and the gangs of Western Malwa have been almost entirely extirpated by his means.

* A gang of one hundred and five was arrested by Mr. Molony as they were crossing the valley of the Nerbudda from the Duckun after the Lucknadown murders in 1823. The bodies of the murdered people were pointed out and taken up at the time, but the death of Mr. Molony and other circumstances deferred the trial till 1830. Another large gang was arrested on its return from the Duckun over the same road by Captain Wardlow in 1826, and sent to Mr. C. Fraser at Jubulpore. He had the bodies of a great number of people whom they had murdered along the road disinterred ; and having committed the case for trial to Mr. Wilder, then Agent of the Governor General at Jubulpore, they were all convicted, and punished. Another was seized by Major Henley at Bhopaul ; and these several seizures may be considered as having laid the foundation of the subsequent proceedings in having furnished such numerous sources of information.

and Nerbudda Territories, has felt the same with regard to his share in bringing the other gangs to punishment.

The government observed upon the trial of the Mahidpore gang—

"These murders having been perpetrated in "territories belonging to various native chiefs, and "the perpetrators being inhabitants of various dis- "tricts belonging to different authorities, there is "no chief in particular, to whom we could deliver "them for punishment, as their sovereign, or as the "prince of the territory in which the crime had "been committed."

"The hand of these inhuman monsters being "against every one, and there being no country "within the range of their annual excursions from "Bundelcund to Guzerat in which they have not "committed murder, it appears to His Lordship in "Council, that they may be considered like pirates, "to be placed without the pale of social law, and "be subjected to condign punishment by whatever "authority they may be seized and convicted."*

It is a principle of the law of nations, recognized I believe by every civilized people, that assassins by profession shall find in no country a sanctuary, but shall every where be delivered up to the Sovereign who reclaims them, and in whose dominions they have perpetrated their crimes; and as the crimes of these assassins are never confined to the country in which they reside, and as every country in India must now be considered as under

* See Mr. Secretary Swinton's letter to Colonel Stewart of the 23d October, 1829. To few men is the success which has attended these operations more attributable than to Mr. George Swinton, who was then Chief Secretary to Government and is now in Europe.

the protection of the supreme government in some
relation or other, that government very properly
undertook the duty which seemed to be imposed
upon it by the laws of humanity and of nations,
and determined to reclaim them from every state.
in which they might seek shelter.*

Unhappily there are in India few native chiefs
who have any great feelings of sympathy even with
the inhabitants of their own territories beyond their
own family or clan, or any particular desire to
protect them from the robber or the assassin; and
no instance can I believe be found of one extending
his sympathies or his charities to the people of any
other territory. They have, however, all a feeling
of strong pride in claiming for their own territory
the privilege of a sanctuary for the robbers and
assassins of all other territories; while their public
officers of every description and landholders of
every degree convert this privilege, when conceded
to their chiefs, into a source of revenue for themselves.

* " Although the justice of each nation ought in general to be
" confined to the punishment of crimes committed in its own terri-
" tories, we ought to except from this rule those villains, who by
" the nature and habitual frequency of their crimes violate all
" public security, and declare themselves the enemies of the human
" race. Poisoners, assassins, and incendiaries by profession,
" may be exterminated wherever they are seized : for they attack
" and injure all nations, by trampling under foot the foundations
" of their common safety. Thus pirates are sent to the gibbet by
" the first into whose hands they fall. If the sovereign of the
" country where crimes of that nature have been committed,
" reclaims the perpetrators of them in order to bring them to
" punishment, they ought to be surrendered to him, as being the
" person who is principally interested in punishing them in an
" exemplary manner. And as it is proper to have criminals regu-
" larly convicted by a trial in due form of law, this is a second
" reason for delivering up malefactors of that class to the States
" where their crimes have been committed.—*Vattel's Law of*
Nature and Nations, Book L Chap. 19.

From the time that our government assumed,
under the Marquis of Hastings, its true and digni-
fied position as the protector of the society of India
generally against the savage inroads of the Pin-
dary hordes, the native chiefs considered themselves
as standing, with regard to us, in a relation entirely new; and bound to obey our call for aid and
support in the suppression of any system prejudicial
to the general interest and welfare of the community. They all knew that this system of merciless
and indiscriminate assassination was still more
general than that of the Pindaries, that it was the
growth of ages, extending all over India, and
being founded in the faith of religious *ordinance*
and *dispensation*, had become so deeply rooted in
the soil, that nothing but the interposition, under
Providence, of the supreme government, and the
acquiescence, support and co-operation of all its
dependent chiefs, could possibly extirpate it. But,
as in the case of the Pindaries, many of these native
chiefs or their officers and landholders, nevertheless sacrificed with reluctance, the revenues they
were in the habit of deriving from these people,
and with still more the pride of being thought able
to afford to them that asylum which others were
obliged to deny, and consequently, the *reputation*
of being able to refuse with impunity an acquiescence which others were obliged to concede to
the supreme government; and such men availed
themselves with avidity of the indolence, or indifference of the European functionaries by whom
our government happened to be represented. Happily they have been very rare, and the obstacles
which they have caused very few; while the
instances of the cordial, zealous, and active co-

operation of such functionaries have been very
numerous.*

But it must be admitted that this evil has prevailed in our own provinces as much as in native
states; and if I were called upon to state any single
cause which has operated more than any other to
promote its extension, I should say it was the
illogical application in practice of the maxim,
" that it is better ten guilty men should *escape*, than
" that one innocent man should *suffer.*" It is no
doubt better that ten guilty men should *escape* the
punishment of death, and all the eternal consequences which may result from it, than that one
innocent man should suffer *that punishment;* but
it is not better that ten assassins by profession should
escape, and be left freely and impudently to follow
every where their murderous trade, than that one
innocent man should *suffer the inconvenience of
temporary restraint;* and wherever the maxim has
been so understood and acted upon, the innocent
have been necessarily punished for the guilty. In
a country like India, abounding in associations of
this kind, and with every facility they could desire
to promote their success, and with little communication of thought or feeling between the governing

* In addition to the political functionaries already named, I
should name as having given us their cordial support and valuable
aid—The Honourable R. Cavindish as Resident at the Court of
Gwalior; Major Alves as Political Agent in Bhopaul, and Agent
in Rajpootana; Colonel Spiers as Acting Agent in Rajpootana
and Political Agent at Neemuch; Mr. Wilkinson, Political Agent
in Bhopaul; Captain Wade, Political Agent at Lodheeana; Mr.
Græme and Colonel Briggs, Residents at the Court of Nagpore;
Captains Robinson and Johnstone as Assistants and Officiating
Residents at the Court of Holcar; Mr. Williams and Colonel Bal-
four at Baroda; Major Ross, Political Agent at Kota; and, though
last not least, Mr. Ainslie and Mr. Begbie, as Agents to the Governor General at Bundelcund.

and the governed, the necessity of prosecuting
gang robbers and murderers with such a maxim
so understood and acted upon, is often found to
be a greater surce of evil to the families and village
communities who have suffered, than the robbers
and murderers themselves; for the probability is
always in favour of the criminals being released,
however notorious their character and guilt, to
wreak their vengeance upon them at their leisure,
after the innocent and the sufferers have been
ruined by the loss of time and labour wasted in
attendance upon the Courts to give unavailing
evidence.

It is a maxim with these assassins, that " dead
men tell no tales," and upon this maxim they invariably act. They permit no living witness to their
crimes to escape, and therefore never attempt the
murder of any party until they can feel secure of
being able to murder the whole. They will travel
with a party of unsuspecting travellers for days,
and even weeks together, eat with them, sleep with
them, attend divine worship with them at the holy
shrines on the road, and live with them in the
closest terms of intimacy till they find time and
place suitable for the murder of the whole. Having
in the course of ages matured a system by which
the attainment of any other direct evidence to their
guilt is rendered almost impossible, they bind each
other to secresy by the most sacred oaths that thei
superstition can afford ; and such associations
never desire from any government a clearer *license*
to their merciless depredations than a copy of the
rule, " that the testimony of any number of confessing
" prisoners shall not be sufficient ground to autho-
" rize the detention of their associates ;" for if the
confessing prisoners escape the laws of the country,

they are put to death by the laws of the association.
To suppress associations of this kind in such a
country and such a society as those of India, a
departure from rules like these, however suitable
to ordinary times and circumstances, and to a
more advanced and a more rational system of
society, becomes indispensably necessary; and as
they have matured their system to deprive all
governments of every other kind of direct evidence
to their guilt but the testimony of their associates,
it behoves all governments, in order to relieve
society from so intolerable an evil, to mature another by which their testimonies shall be rendered
effectual for their conviction, without endangering
the safety of the innocent. This I hope has now
been done, but it can never be rendered so perfect
as not to depend in some measure upon the personal character of the officers entrusted with its
superintendence. There is no duty which requires
higher qualifications for its proper discharge; and
if these qualifications be not considered a point of
paramount importance in the nomination of officers
to the department, government will certainly not
do its duty to the society.

The trial of these people for murders perpetrated
in the Hydrabad and Indore dominions, was with
the consent of the Nizam and Holcar governments,
made over to the British Residents at their respective Courts, but subject to the revision and final
orders of the supreme government. That of those
charged with murders perpetrated in the Oude
territory, has, with the consent of the King, been
made over to the Resident at that Court. The
trial of those charged with murders perpetrated in
any other territory, and beyond the limits of districts in which our regulations are in force, was

made over to the Governor General's Agent in the Saugor and Nurbudda territories, who has since for the time been entrusted, for special reasons assigned by the Resident and approved by government, with the trial of those charged with the murders in the Hydrabad territories also.

Thugs charged with murders perpetrated in the districts where our regulations are in force, were to be made over for trial to the regular tribunals; but, with the sanction of government previously obtained in any particular case, the venue might be changed from the Court of any one district to that of another, or to that of the special Commissioner for the whole, Mr. Stockwell, then Commissioner of the Allahabad division, who consented to undertake that in addition to his other duties, and who conducted, in that capacity, the trial of one of our most interesting and important cases committed to him by Mr. Wilson.

When I first undertook the duty of superintending the operation for the arrest of these gangs, and of collecting the evidence for the cases in which they were to be committed for trial, the most laborious and painful that I have ever performed, I had the civil charge of the district of Jubulpore on the Nurbudda river. As that of Saugor was more central, and consequently more eligible, I was in January, 1831, transferred to the civil charge of that district during the absence of Mr. C. Fraser on sick leave to the hills. On his return in January 1832, he resumed charge of the revenue and civil duties, and left me the criminal, which I continued to discharge till January 1835, while Captain Low continued to officiate for me in the civil charge of the Jubulpore district. By the resolution of government of the 10th January, 1835, my head-quarters were transferred back to Jubulpore; and having the general superintendence of all proceedings preliminary to trial over the whole field of our operations, which had now extended from Lahore to the Carnatic, I was relieved from every other charge.

. In May 1832, Captain Reynolds was appointed to superintend our operations south of the Nurbudda. In September 1832, Mr. Wilson was appointed to superintend those between the Ganges and the Jumna; and in February 1833, Mr. McLeod was appointed to superintend those in Rajpootana, Malwa, and the Delhi territories; and three officers with higher qualifications, for the very delicate and responsible duty in their respective spheres of action could not, I believe, have been any where found.

On the 10th of January 1835, Lieutenant Briggs, a very active and intelligent officer, was appointed to succeed Mr. McLeod in Malwa and Rajpootana, and Lieutenant Elwall, an officer equally well qualified, was appointed to assist Captain Reynolds south of the Nurbudda; and Captain Paton, Assistant to the Resident at the Court of Lucknow, was withdrawn from the general duties of the Residency, that he might afford his valuable aid exclusively to this department in Oude.

In March 1831, a tuman or company of Nujeebs was added to the Jubulpore local police corps, exclusively for employment under me in this duty; and in April another company was added to the same corps for employment under Captain Reynolds, south of the Nurbudda. The officer commanding the Saugor Division, Brigadier General O'Halloran, anxious to afford his aid in promoting the success of an undertaking of so much importance to the society of India generally, and to the native army in particular, had given me the services of a detachment, under the command of an excellent native officer Rustum Khan, in Bundlecund; and Brigadier General Smith, since he succeeded to the command, has been equally anxious to afford his aid on all proper occasions. In July 1833, when our means had become inadequate for the vast field over which our operations extended, Messieurs Wilson and McLeod were, under instructions from government,* allowed by the officers commanding the divisions in which they were employed each a detachment of forty regular sipahees under a native commissioned officer, and twenty troopers from the corps of local horse under a Dufadar.

Knowing how many of their comrades used annually to be murdered by these assassins on their way home to their families on furlough, the pursuit after them is a duty which these regular sipahees very cheerfully perform, and are indeed extremely proud of; and as the knowledge which they acquire in the course of its discharge of their mode of inveigling and destroying travellers is communicated to all the men of their regiments when they rejoin, their employment on this has been unquestionably and will continue to be of great advantage to the whole native army.

Thus far our highest political functionaries have afforded their aid in the arrest and the trial of these criminals cheerfully and gratuitously. Colonel Stewart, Mr. Wellesley, Mr. Martin and Mr. Bax successively at Indore, Colonel Stewart again at

---

* 40 Sipahees under a native commissioned Officer; 20 Sowars under a Dufadar for each of those two gentlemen. See proceedings of the Governor General in Council, 28th June, 1833.

Hydrabad, and Mr. F. C. Smith in the more laborious office of the Saugor and Norbudda Agency; and proud indeed, might any man feel, however exalted his station, to be able to contribute his aid to the great work of relieving a society of one hundred millions of his fellow creatures from an evil so great, and so calculated from its character, and that of the deluded people among whom it has fallen, to penetrate and poison every source of confidence and security between man and man.

Among the people of India almost every man is married as soon as he has attained the proper age, and his parents can afford the expenses of the marriage ceremonies. The younger sons of poor but respectable families seek employment in distant public establishments, civil or military, while their wives and children remain united with the family under the care of their father or their elder brother, and the ties of duty and affection between them and their parents are never broken or impaired by any length of absence, or any new interests or connexions. During their absence these sons subject themselves to all kinds of privations in order that they may be able to send home the largest possible share of their incomes; and derive their greatest happiness from the hope of returning occasionally and enjoying for short and distant intervals, the society of their families thus united and bound together by ties so amiable. If any die their widows and children still remain with the family, and are maintained by the survivors; and all "delight to honour" the widow who honours the memory of her deceased husband. It is upon such families, who are to be found in almost every town in India, that the evil of this system of assassination presses most heavily. If the absent members do not return at the time they are expected, others proceed in search of them; and since I undertook this duty, numbers have flocked to me to inquire after the fate of those whom they had long lost. Often in my court I have seen them listening with unobtrusive grief to a circumstantial detail of the murder of their parents, brothers or children from the mouths of these cold-blooded and merciless assassins, while the tears stole down their cheeks; and taking from my stores of recovered property some sad token in arms, dress, or ornaments, of the melancholy truth to take home to the widows and children of the murdered, who might otherwise doubt their tale of sorrow, and entertain some lingering but unavailing hope of their return.*

* In January, 1831, a small gang was arrested and brought in to me at Saugor. One of the approvers, in deposing to the identity of one, mentioned that he had then on him, unaltered, the vest which they had taken some time before from Purtapa, a man whom they had murdered with his friend at Gola pass, on their way from Indore to Bhopaul. I had it taken off and sent immediately by the letter dawk to the resident at Indore, Mr. Wellesley. He was absent, but Captain Johnstone, the assistant resident, made the requisite inquiries and sent me the result. The reader may find it interesting. In the early stage of our proceedings such occurrences were very common.

Indore, 2d *February,* 1831.

Humeerchund, merchant of Indore, being called into court, gives the following statement:

"On Sunday, the 10th of the month of Poos, Sumbut, 1886,
"(20th December, 1829,) my brother Purtapa and my wife's
"brother Sooklall, proceeded towards Sehore with a tattoo, on
"which was loaded about 400 rupees worth of English Chintz,
"Mushroo, &c. They also carried with them 105 Halee rupees
"in cash; and about 95 rupees of gold and gold ornaments. Not
"having received any intelligence of them for 25 days after their
"departure, I became anxious about their safety and hired a man
"to go to Sehore and make inquiries of my correspondents there.
"I ascertained that they had never reached that place. About

Should it be thought necessary I may perhaps hereafter give a more connected history of the

" three months afterwards my younger brother Hunsraj, went in
" quest of information, and found traces of Purtapa and Sooklall,
" having been murdered near the Gola pass, a short distance beyond
" Tuppa.*
" *Question.*—Do you recollect the ungurka which your brother
" Purtapa wore when he left Indore ?
" *Answer.*—Yes, it was made of Europe chintz and lined with
" blue cotton."
The ungurka sent by Captain Sleeman, which corresponded with the above description, was shown to the witness who immediately recognised it, and was so much affected as scarcely to be able to speak. He took hold of the twisted silk cords attached to the ungurka, and said he had himself purchased them for his brother.
Hunsraj, brother of the preceding witness, being called, deposes as follows :—
" I returned to Indore from Rutlam about three months after
" my brother Purtapa was missing, and then proceeded towards
" Sehore for the purpose of inquiring after his fate. I ascertained
" that he and my relation Sooklall had stopped the first night after
" leaving Indore at Akeypoor, and the second at Peeplia. I found
" they had left Peeplia on the morning of the third day, but I
" could trace them no further. In the course of my inquiries at
" Tuppa, I was informed by a Bunya that the bodies of some
" persons had been found about three months previously near the
" Gola pass, about two coss to the eastward of the town. He said
" that a boy, the son of a Chumar belonging to Tuppa, observed a
" number of jackals and vultures near the pass, and had gone
" there in expectation of finding some dead animal and getting its
" skin. On reaching the spot, however, he found the bodies of
" two men which had been buried under a heap of stones so imper-
" fectly, that the wild beasts had afterwards dragged them out and
" almost entirely devoured them. The boy gave notice to the
" villagers, who went to the pass and buried the remains of the
" bodies. On hearing this account, I went to the Gola pass in com-
" pany with the Bunya who pointed out the spot where the bodies

* Tuppa, half way between Ashta and Rajpoogur, and a coss pucka this side of Amla. One going from Ashta descends the Ghat about a pucka coss before he reaches Tuppa.

system and of our operations for its suppression, but for the present I can only offer, in addition to the above observations, the almost literal translation of some conversations I have had with the approvers in revising the vocabulary of their peculiar dialect for the last time.   These conversations were often carried on in the presence of different European gentlemen who happened to call in, and as they seemed to feel a good deal of interest in listening to them, I thought others might possibly feel the same in reading them if committed to paper; and from that time I, for several days, put down the conversations as they took place in the the present form.

W. H. SLEEMAN,
Genl. Supt. for the Suppression of Thug Associations.

Head-Quarters,   }
Jubulpore, 8th Sept. 1835. {

" had been found. A large stone which lay near the place had " some marks of blood upon it, and on removing it I found a shoe, " which I at once recognised as having belonged to my brother, " and I wept bitterly. I took the shoe to Indore where it was " identified by the family, and as we had no doubt that our rela- " tions had been murdered, we performed their funeral rites accord- " ing to the customs of our sect."

The ungarka sent by Captain Sleeman was shown to the witness, but he said it had been made up while he was at Rutlam, and that he had not seen it before.

(Signed)   P. JOHNSTONE,
Assist. to the Resident.

The lad who had on the vest was the son of Kaleean Sing, Jemadar of Thugs, and now approver. He got it in a present from his uncle Dureean, and rather than alter so pretty a garment, he ran the risk of wearing it till he was taken.

W. H. S.

DISCLOSURES

OF

THUG INFORMERS, MADE IN CONVERSATIONS HELD WITH THEM BY CAPTAIN SLEEMAN, WHILE PREPARING HIS VOCABULARY OF THEIR LANGUAGE.

THE following conversations form the most curious and interesting portion of Captain Sleeman's book. The perfect frankness of the disclosures, the coolness with which the most atrocious villanies are confessed and justified by an appeal to their superstitions; and the coincidence of the stories of different informers with respect to facts and motives, form one of the most singular chapters in the history of the human character. The explanation of the peculiar Thug terms, which sometimes occur, will be found by referring to the Vocabulary in the Appendix.

Q.—Do you ever recollect any misfortune arising from going on when a hare crossed the road before you?

Nasir, of Singnapore.—Yes; when General Doveton commanded the troops at Jhalna we were advancing towards his camp; a hare crossed the road; we disregarded the omen, though the hare actually screamed in crossing, and went on. The very next day I, with seventeen of our gang, were seized; and it was with great difficulty and delay that we got our release. We had killed some

people belonging to the troops, but fortunately none
of their property was found upon us.

Q.—And you think these signs are all mandates
from the deity, and if properly attended to, no harm
can befall you?

Nasir.—Certainly; no one doubts it; ask any
body. How could Thugs have otherwise prospered? Have they not every where been protected
as long as they have attended religiously to their
rules?

Q.—But if there was such a deity as *Bhowanee,**
and she were your patroness, how could she allow
me and others to seize and punish so many Thugs?

Nasir.—I have a hundred times heard my father
and other old and wise men say, when we had
killed a sweeper and otherwise infringed their rules,
that we should be some day punished for it;
that the European rulers would be made the instruments to chastise us for our disregard of omens,
and neglect of the rules laid down for our guidance.

Q.—And you really believe that *Bhowanee* sends
these signs to warn you of your danger, and guide
you to your booty?

Nasir.—Can we—can any body doubt it? Did
she not in former days when our ancestors attended
to rules, bury the bodies for us, and save us the
trouble; and remove every sign by which we could
be traced?

Q.—You have heard this from your fathers, who
heard it from their fathers; but none of you have
ever seen it, nor is it true?

Nasir.—It is true, quite true; and though we
have not seen this, we have all of us seen the sacred

---

* Bhowanee or Davey, a female goddess, is the tutelary deity
of the Thugs.

pick-axe spring in the morning from the well into which it had been thrown over night, and come to the hands of the man who carried it at his call: nay we have seen the pick-axes of different gangs all come up of themselves from the same well at the same time, and go to their several bearers.

Q.—Yes; and you have all seen the common jugglers, by sleights of hand, appear to turn pigeons into serpents, and serpents into rabbits, but all know that they do it by their skill, and not by the aid of any goddess. The man who carries your pick-axe is selected for his skill, and gains extra emoluments and distinction; and no doubt can, in the same manner, make it appear that the axe comes out of itself when he draws it out by his sleight of hand.

Nasir.—With great energy—" What! shall not a hundred generations of Thugs be able to distinguish the tricks of man from the miracles of God? Is there not the difference of heaven and earth between them? Is not one a mere trick, and the other a miracle, witnessed by hundreds assembled at the same time?"

Q.—Sahib Khan, you are more sober than Nasir, have you ever seen it?

Sahib Khan.—On one expedition only.

Q.—Who were the pick-axe bearers?

Sahib.—They were Imam Khan and his brother.

Q.—From what country?

Sahib.—From Arcot. I was obliged to fly from Telingana when Major Parker and Captain Sheriff made their inroad upon us (Gurdee) and I went and joined the Arcot gangs. During a whole expedition that I made with them, Imam Khan and his brother carried the pick-axe, and I heard them repeatedly in the morning call them from the well into which they had thrown them over night, and saw the pick-axes come of themselves from the well, and fall into their aprons, which they held open *thus :*—Here he described the mode.

Q.—And you never saw any of your own gangs do this?

Sahib.—Never; I have Thugged for twenty years and never saw it.

Q.—How do you account for this?

Sahib.—Merely by supposing that they attend more to omens and regulations than we do. Among us it is a rule never to kill women; but if a rich old woman is found, the gang sometimes gets a man to strangle her by giving him an extra share of the booty, and inducing him to take the responsibility upon himself. We have sometimes killed other prohibited people, particularly those of low cast, whom we ought not even to have touched.

Q.—You are from the Delhi clans?

Sahib.—Yes, I am of the Bursote clan, and my family went to the Dunkun, three generations ago.

Q.—Do you think the Arcot and Carnatic gangs are also from the Delhi clans?

Sahib.—We suppose that all Thugs originated by descent or initiation from the Delhi clans: but I think we are wrong. I became intimate with the Arcot gangs; and some of them, about seven years ago, after my return, came and settled in Telingana, between Hydrabad and Masulipatam, where they still carry on their trade of Thuggee; but they will never intermarry with our families—saying that we once *drove bullocks and were itinerant tradesmen,* and consequently of lower cast. They trace back the trade of Thuggee in their families to more generations than we can, and they are more skilful and observant of rules and omens than we are ; and I, therefore, think that they are neither descended from the Delhi stock, nor were ever disciples of theirs.

Q.—Do you think there is any truth in their assertion that your ancestors drove bullocks ?

Sahib.—I think there is. We have some usages and traditions that seem to imply that our ancestors kept bullocks, and traded ; but how I know not.

Here a Brahman Thug, of one of the most ancient Thug families, interposed, and declared that he had seen the funeral rites of Musulman Thugs, and that the women who brought the water there chanted all the occupations of the ancestors of the deceased, which demonstrated that they were originally descended from gangs of wandering *Khunjurs*, or vagrant Musulmans, who followed armies and lived in the suburbs of cities, and in the wild wastes, and that their pretensions to higher descent was all nonsense. Several Musulman Thugs protested sturdily against this, but the arguments were too strong against them, and after a time the dialogue was resumed.

Q.—What do you think, *Sahib Khan*, am I right in thinking that we shall suppress Thuggee, or is *Nasir* right in thinking we shall not ?

Sahib.—There have been several gurdies (inroads,) upon Thuggee, but they have ended in nothing but the punishment of a few ; and, as *Nasir* says, we have heard our fathers and sages predict these things as punishments for our transgression of prescribed rules ; but none of them ever said that Thuggee would be done away with. This seems a greater and more general gurdie than any, and I know not what to think.

Q.—But tell me freely ; do you think we shall annihilate it ?

Sahib.—How can the hands of man do away with the works of God.

Q.—You are a Musulman?

Sahib.—Yes, and the greater part of the Thugs of the south are Musulmans.

Q.—And you still marry; inherit; pray; eat and drink according to the Koran; and your paradise is to be the paradise promised by **Ma**hommud?

Sahib.—Yes, all, all.

Q.—Has *Bhowanee* been any where named in the Koran?

Sahib.—No-where.

Here a musulman Thug from Hindustan interposed, and said, he thought *Bhowanee* and *Fatima,* the daughter of Mahommud, and wife of *Alee,* were one and the same person; and that it was *Fatima* who invented the use of the *roomal* to strangle the great demon *Rukut-beej-dana;* which led to a discussion between him and some of my Musulman native officers, who did not like to find the amiable *Fatima* made a goddess of Thuggee—An "Iphigenia in Tauris." The Thug was a sturdy *wrangler,* and in the estimation of his associate Thugs had, I think, the best of the argument.

Q.—Then has *Bhowanee* any thing to do with your paradise?

Sahib.—Nothing.

Q.—She has no influence upon your future state?

Sahib.—None.

Q.—Does Mahommud, your prophet, any where sanction crimes like yours; the murder in cold blood of your fellow creatures for the sake of their money?

Sahib.—No.

Q.—Does he not say that such crimes will be punished by God in the next world?

Sahib.—Yes.

Q.—Then do you never feel any dread of punishment hereafter?

Sahib.—Never; we never murder unless the omens are favourable; and we consider favourable omens as the mandates of the deity.

Q.—What deity?

Sahib.—*Bhowanee.*

Q.—But *Bhowanee*, you say, has no influence upon the welfare or otherwise, of your soul hereafter?

Sahib.—None, we believe; but she influences our fates in this world, and what she orders in this world, we believe, that God will not punish in the next.

Q.—And you believe that if you were to murder without the observance of the omens and regulations, you would be punished both in this world and the next like other men?

Sahib.—Certainly; no man's family ever survives a murder: it becomes extinct. A Thug who murders in this way loses the children he has, and is never blessed with more.

Q.—In the same manner as if a Thug had murdered a Thug?

Sahib.—Precisely; he cannot escape punishment.

Q.—And when you observe the omens and rules, you neither feel a dread of punishment here nor hereafter?

Sahib.—Never.

Q.—And do you never feel sympathy for the persons murdered—Never pity or compunction?

Sahib.—Never.

11*

Q.—How can you murder old men and young children without some emotion of pity—calmly and deliberately, as they sit with you and converse with you,—and tell you of their private affairs, of their hopes and fears, and of the wives and children, they are going to meet after years of absence, toil and suffering?

A.—From the time the omens have been favourable, we consider them as victims thrown into our hands by the deity to be killed; and that we are the mere instruments in her hands to destroy them: that if we do not kill them, she will never be again propitious to us, and we and our families will be involved in misery and want.

Q.—And you can sleep as soundly by the bodies or over the graves of those you have murdered, and eat your meals with as much appetite as ever?

Sahib.—Just the same; we sleep and eat just the same unless we are afraid of being discovered.

Q.—And when you see or hear a bad omen, you think it is the order of the deity not to kill the travellers you have with you or are in pursuit of?

Sahib.—Yes; it is the order not to kill them, and we dare not disobey.

Q.—Do your wives never reproach you with your deeds?

Sahib.—In the south we never tell our wives what we do lest they should disclose our secrets.

Q.—And if you told them would they not reproach you?

Sahib.—Some would, and some, like those of other Thugs who do tell them, would quietly acquiesce.

Q.—And be as affectionate and dutiful as the wives of other men?

Sahib.—The fidelity of the wives of Thugs is proverbial throughout India.

Q.—That is among Thugs ?

Sahib.—Yes.

Q.—And the fear of the *roomal* (*Pehloo*) operates a little to produce this ?

Sahib.—Perhaps a little, but there have been very few instances of women killed for infidelity among us.

Q.—And your children too reverence their Thug fathers like other sons, even after they have become acquainted with their trade ?

Sahib.—The same : we love them and they love us the same.

Q.—At what age do you initiate them ?

Sahib.—I was initiated by my father when I was only thirteen years of age.

Q.—Have you any rule as to the age ?

Sahib.—None ; a father is sometimes avaricious, and takes his son out very young, merely to get his share of the booty ; for the youngest boy gets as much in his share as the oldest man : but generally a father is anxious to have his son in the rank of the *Burkas* as soon as possible ; he does not like to have him considered a *Kuboola* after he has attained the age of puberty.

Q.—How soon do you let them see your operations ?

Sahib.—The first expedition they neither see nor hear any thing of murder. They know not our trade, they get presents, purchased out of their share, and become fond of the wandering life, as they are always mounted upon ponies. Before the end of the journey they know that we rob. The next expedition they suspect that we commit murder, and some of them even know it; and in the third expedition they see all.

Q.—Do they not become frightened?

Sahib.—Not after the second or third expedition.

Feringeea.—About twelve years ago my cousin Aman Subahdar took out with us my cousin Kurhora, brother of Omrow approver, a lad of fourteen, for the first time. He was mounted upon a pretty pony, and Hursooka, an adopted son of Aman's was appointed to take charge of the boy.

We fell in with five Sikhs, and when we set out before daylight in the morning, Hursooka, who had been already on three expeditions, was ordered to take the bridle and keep the boy in the rear out of sight and hearing. The boy became alarmed, and impatient, got away from Hursooka, and galloped up at the instant the *J,hirnee*, or signal for murder was given. He heard the screams of the men, and saw them all strangled. He was seized with a trembling, and fell from his pony; he became immediately delirious, was dreadfully alarmed at the sight of the turbans of the murdered men, and when any one touched or spoke to him, talked about the murders and screamed exactly like a boy talks in his sleep, and trembled violently if any one spoke to him or touched him. We could not get him on, and after burying the bodies, Aman and I, and a few others, sat by him while the gang went on: we were very fond of him, and tried all we could to tranquillize him, but he never recovered his senses, and before evening he died. I have seen many instances of feelings greatly shocked at the sight of the first murder, but never one so strong as this. Kurhora was a very fine boy, and Hursooka took his death much to heart, and turned

Byragee; he is now at some temple on the bank of the Nerbudda river.

Q.—Was not Jhurhoo, who was taken with your gang after the Bhilsa murders, and hung at Jubulpore, a brother of his?

Feringeea.—Yes, poor Jhurhoo! you ought not to have hung him; he never strangled or assisted in strangling any man!! Here the tears ran down over Feringeea's face. Strange as it may seem, I have never heard him speak of his young cousin Jhurhoo's fate without weeping, and yet all the males of his family have been Thugs for ten generations. Another brother of this Jhurhoo, is a very noted Thug leader, still at large—Phoolsa.

Q.—Do you in the Duckun send any offerings to the Brahmans of the temple of *Davey?*

Feringeea.—Never; we neither make offerings to her temples, nor do we ever consult any of her priests or those of any other temples. Our sages alone are consulted, and they consult omens alone as their guides.

Q.—Have they any written treatises on augury?

Feringeea.—None; they never consult books; they learn all from tradition and experience.

Q.—But you worship at *Davey's* temples?

Feringeea.—Yes, of course, all men worship at her temple.

Q.—No.—We *Sahib loge* never do.

Feringeea.—I mean all Hindoos and Musulmans. Here my Mahommudun officers again interposed, and declared that they never did; that it was only the very lowest order of Musulmans that did. But, unfortunately, these keen observers of passing events had seen the wives of some very respectable Musulmans at Jubulpore, during the time that the small pox was raging, take their children to her temples and prostrate them before the images of the Goddess of Destruction. The officers admitted this to be sometimes the case, but pretended that it was unknown to their husbands.

Sahib Khan and *Nasir.*—In the Duckun the greatest Nawabs and officers of state worship at the temples, and prostrate themselves and their children before the image of the Goddess when the small pox or the cholera morbus rages. We have ourselves seen them do it often.

Q.—And do they believe you Thugs to be under her special protection?

Sahib and *Nasir.*—Some of them do, and though they often try to dissuade us from our trade, they are afraid to punish us. Bura Sahib Jemadar, of Madura, had several hundred followers, and used to make valuable presents to Nawab Dollee Khan who knew how he got them, and offered him a high post with rent-free lands if he would leave off the trade. He would not.

Q.—What became of him at last?

Sahib and *Nasir.*—There was a great Decoit leader of the same name who had been committing great ravages, and orders were sent by the Nawab to the local officers to blow him away from a gun as soon as they could seize him. They seized Sahib Khan Thug, and blew him away by mistake before the Nawab got information of the arrest. In a few hours after his death a message came from the Nawab to say that he feared there might be a mistake, and when he heard that Sahib Khan Thug had been blown away, he was much grieved, but said that God must have ordained it, and the fault was not his.

Q.—Has he any sons?

Sahib and *Nasir.*—Yes. He has two; Ameen

Sahib, forty-five years of age, who has a gang of thirty Thugs, and Rajee Khan, forty years of age, who has a gang of ten Thugs, all from among their relations and connexions; and they act together and live in Omurda, Taalluk Afzulpore, in the Hyderabad territories.

Q.—What made your friends desert their old abodes in Arcot?

Sahib and *Nasir.*—Some magistrate got hold of some Thugs who turned informers, and gave them a good deal of annoyance.

Q.—Have they returned?

Sahib and *Nasir.*—Some of them have gone back, and a great many who had not been molested remained there till the annoyance was over.

Q.—What leaders came away?

Sahib and *Nasir.*—Sheikh Amed who is considered the most able leader of his day. He has sixty fully initiated Thugs (*Borkas*) who pretend to be recruits for regiments. He is thoroughly acquainted with the drill of the Company's regiments and their military terms, and can speak English.

Q.—How do you know? You do not understand English.

Sahib and *Nasir.*—He can make the gentlemen and those who speak English understand when he speaks a language we do not understand, and he tells us this is English. Other Thug leaders generally display their wealth in an ostentatious appearance that betrays them. Sheikh Amed is sixty years of age, and will go about for months cooking his own food, walking and living like the poorest man, while he can command the services of a hundred men.

Q.—Who are the others?

Sahib and *Nasir.*—Osman Khan, who has about

thirty *Borkas*, or fully initiated and able Thugs.
He is fifty years of age.

Husun Khan, who has twenty-five *Burkas*, and
is fifty-five years of age.

Sahib Khan of Lodeekar, who has thirty *Borkas*,
and is forty-five years of age.

Tipoo Jemadar, brother of Sahib Khan, who
has ten *Borkas*, and is about forty years of age.

Hoseyn Khan, the nephew of Husun Khan, who
has about six *Borkas*, and is thirty-five years of
age.

Noor Khan, who has ten, and is about forty : all
these leaders came to Telingana from the Carnatic,
about the same time, and settled near Nulganda,
about fifty cose from Hyderabad, on the road to
Masulapatam, and they operate on the roads leading to the seaports.

Q.—You consider that a *Borka* is capable of
forming a gang in any part of India to which he
may be obliged to fly ?

Sahib and *Nasir.*—Certainly; in any part that
we have seen of it.

Q.—Do you know any instance of it?

Sahib and *Nasir.*—A great number. Mudee
Khan was from the old Sindouse stock, and was
obliged to emigrate after the attack upon that place.
Many years afterwards we met him in the Duckun,
and he had then a gang of fifty Thugs of all casts
and descriptions. I asked him who they were;
he told me that they were weavers, braziers, brace-
let-makers, and all kinds of ragamuffins, whom he
had scraped together about his new abode on the
banks of the Herun and Nurbudda rivers, in the
districts of Jebulpore and Nursingpore. He was a
Musulman, and so were Lal Khan, Kalee Khan,

who formed gangs after the Sindouse dispersion along the same rivers.

Q.—Did they find the same patrons among the landholders and other heads of villages?.

Sahib and *Nasir.*—They every where made friends by the same means; and without patrons they could not have thrived. They were obliged of course to give them a liberal share of the booty.

Q.—But these men have all been punished, which does not indicate the protection of *Davey*?

Sahib and *Nasir.*—It indicates the danger of scraping together such a set of fellows for Thuggee. They killed all people indiscriminately, women and men, of all casts and professions, and knew so little about omens that they entered upon their expeditions and killed people, in spite of such as the most ignorant ought to have known were prohibitive. They were punished in consequence, as we all knew that they would be; and we always used to think it dangerous to be associated with them for even a few days. Ask many of them who are now here,—Kureem Khan, Sheikh Kureem, Rumzanee and others, whether this is not true, and whether they ever let go even a sweeper if he appeared to have a rupee about him!

Q.—And you think that if they had been well instructed in the signs and rules, and attended to them, they would have thrived?

Sahib and *Nasir.*—Undoubtedly; so should we all.

Q.—You think that a *Kuboola* or tyro could not any where form a gang of Thugs of himself?

Sahib and *Nasir.*—Never; he could know nothing of our rules of augury, or proceedings, and how could he possibly succeed? Does not all our success depend upon knowing and observing omens and rules ?

Q.—It would therefore never be very dangerous to release such a man as a *Kuboola ?*

Sahib and *Nasir.*—Never; unless he could join men better instructed than himself. Every one must be convinced that it is by knowing and attending to omens and rules that Thuggee has thrived.

Q.—I am not convinced, nor are any of the *native officers* present; on the contrary, we do all we can to put down what you call an institution of the deity, and without dreading at all the effects of her resentment?

Sahib and *Nasir.*—They may say so, but they all know that no man's family can survive a murder committed in any other way; and yet Thugs have thrived through a long series of generations. We have all children like other men, and we are never visited with any extraordinary affliction.

Q.—Tell me frankly which oath, now while you are in custody, you who are Musulmans deem the strongest,—that upon the Koran or that upon the pick-axe ?

Sahib and *Nasir.*—If we could be allowed to consecrate the pick-axe in the prescribed form, neither the Koran nor and thing else on earth could be so binding; but without consecration it would be of no avail.

Q.—Do you not sometimes make up a piece of cloth in the jail in the form of a pick-axe, and swear upon it ?

Sahib and *Nasir.*—We have heard that the Hindustan Thugs do, but we have never seen it.

Q.—Do you think it answers?

Sahib and *Nasir.*—It may with proper conse-

cration ceremonies, but we have never tried it.
Even *mud* made into the same form and consecrated would do. If any man swears to a falsehood upon a pick-axe, properly consecrated, we
will consent to be hung if he survives the time
appointed; appoint one, two or three days when he
swears, and we pledge ourselves that he does not
live a moment beyond the time; he will die a horrid death; his head will turn round, his face
towards the back, and he will writhe in tortures till
he dies.

Q.—And all this you have seen?

Sahib and *Nasir.*—Yes, we have all seen it.

Q.—Above the Norbudda, chiefs have never had
the same dread of punishing Thugs as below it;
have they?

Feringeea.—They had formerly, and have still in
many parts.

Q.—Why should they fear; have there been any
instances of suffering from it?

Feringeea.—A great many. Was not Nanha,
the Raja of Jhalone, made leprous by *Davey* for
putting to death Bodhoo and his brother Khumolee,
two of the most noted Thugs of their day. He
had them trampled under the feet of elephants, but
the leprosy broke out upon his body the very next
day.

Q.—Did he believe that this punishment was
inflicted by *Davey* for putting them to death.

Dorgha Musulman.—He was quite sensible of
it.

Q.—Did he do any thing to appease her?

Dorgha.—Every thing. Bodhoo had began a
well in Jhalone: the Raja built it up in a magnificent style; he had a chubootra (tomb) raised to
their name, fed Brahmuns, and consecrated it, had

worship instituted upon it, but all in vain; the disease was incurable, and the Raja died in a few months a miserable death. The tomb and well are both kept up and visited by hundreds to this day, and no one doubts that the Raja was punished for putting these two Thugs to death.

Q.—But Bodhoo had his nose and hands cut off before, and could have been no favourite of *Davey's?*

Feringeea.—But he was a Thug of great repute; for sagacity we have never seen his equal; people who had been robbed used to go to him as an oracle.

Q.—But he had turned informer, and was sent to Jhalone by Mr. Stockwell to arrest his associates.

Dorgha.—He went to Mr. Stockwell in a passion; his heart was not fully turned away from us then.

Q.—Have you any other instances?

Inaent.—Hundreds! When Madhajee Scindheea caused seventy Thugs to be executed at Muthura, was he not warned in a dream by *Davey* that he should release them? and did he not the very day after their execution begin to spit blood? and did he not die within three months?

Feringeea.—When Dureear the Rathore, and Komere and Patore, the Kuchwaha Rajpoots, Zumeendars, arrested eighty of the Thugs who had settled at Nodha after the murder of Lieut. Monsell, they had many warnings to let them go; but they persisted and kept them till some thirty died. They collected fourteen thousand rupees at the rate of one hundred and twenty-five rupees from every Thug. What became of their families? Have they not all perished? They have not a child left. Rae Sing Havildar, the Gwalior Subah of Nodha, took the money, but that very day his only son and the best horse in his stable died, and he was himself taken ill and died soon after a miserable death.

Nasir.—Ah *Davey* took care of you then, and why? Was it not because you were more attentive to her orders?

Zolfukar.—Yes; we had then some regard for *religion.* We have lost it since. All kinds of men have been made Thugs, and all classes of people murdered, without distinction, and little attention has been paid to omens. How after this could we expect to escape?

Nasir.—Be assured that *Davey* never forsook us till we neglected her.

Q.—Do you know of any instance of her punishing a man for annoying Thugs in the Duckun?

Sahib Khan.—A great many. The Raja of Kundul, some ninety cose east from Hydrabad, arrested all the Thugs in his Raj for some murders they had committed. For three successive nights the voice of *Davey* was heard from the top of every temple in the capital, warning the Raja to release them. The whole town heard her, and urged the Raja to comply. He was obstinate, and the third night the bed on which he and his ranee were sleeping was taken up by *Davey* and dashed violently against the ground.

Q.—Were they killed?

Nasir.—They were not killed, but they were dreadfully bruised; and had they not released the Thugs, they would certainly have been killed the next night.

Q.—Were any of you present?

Sahib Khan.—Our fathers were, and we heard it from them.- It occurred sixty years ago.

12*

Q.—And do you think that the chiefs have still
the same dread of punishing Thugs in all parts of
India ?

Sahib.—Certainly not in all parts ; because in
many they have been suffered to punish them with
impunity on account of their neglect of rules and
omens.

Morlee.—There is no fear now. They are
every where seized and punished with impunity ;
there is no resisting your *Ikbal* (good fortune).

Dorgha.—The Company's *Ikbal* is such that
before the sound of your drums, sorcerers, witches
and demons take flight, and how can Thuggee
stand.

Davey Deen.—Thuggee ! why it is gone ; there
are not fifty Aseel Thugs, (Thugs of good birth)
left between the Ganges and Jumna.

Chotee Brahman.—And not more than that number of all our old clans of Gwalior and Bundelcund ; but the Sooseas of Rajpootana have been
untouched, and much is to be done about Delhie
and Puteeala.

Q.—But Nasir and Sahib Khan think that it can
never be suppressed in the Duckun ?

Nasir.—I think it never can.

Sahib Khan.—I do not say it never can. I say
only that the country is very large ; that in every
one of the five districts there are hundreds of Aseel
Thugs, who are staunch to their oath, and attentive to their usages ; that the country is every
where intersected by the jurisdiction of native
chiefs who cannot be easily persuaded to assist.

Nasir.—Assist ! why when we go into their
districts after a Thug we are every instant in danger of our lives. I got nearly killed with all the
guard lately when close upon the heels of a gang,

and when I complained to Captain Reynolds, he told me that we must consent to bear these drubbings on account of the Company, or I could be of no use to him in such a country as that! .

Q.—And you think that all these obstacles are not to be overcome?

Nasir.—I think not.

Q.—That is, you think an institution formed by *Davey*, the Goddess, cannot be suppressed by the hand of man?

Nasir.—Certainly, I think so.

Q.—But you think that no man is killed by man's killing, " *admeeke marne se koee murta nuheen ;*" that all who are strangled are strangled, in effect, by God.

Nasir.—Certainly.

Q.—Then by whose killing have all the Thugs who have been hung at Saugor and Jubulpore been killed?

Nasir.—God's of course.

Q.—You think that we could never have caught and executed them but by the aid of God.

Nasir.—Certainly not.

Q.—Then you think so far we have been assisted by God in what we have done?

Nasir.—Yes.

Q.—And you are satisfied that we should not have ventured to do what we have done unless we were assured that our God was working with us, or rather that we were the mere instruments in his hands?

Nasir.—Yes, I am.

Q.—Then do you not think that we may go on with the same assurance till the work we have in hand is done; till in short, the system of Thuggee is suppressed?

Nasir.—God is almighty.

Q.—And there is but one God ?

Nasir.—One God above all Gods.

Q.—And if that God above all Gods supports us, we shall succeed ?

Nasir.—Certainly.

Q.—Then we are all satisfied that he is assisting us, and therefore hope to succeed even in the Duckun ?

Nasir.—God only knows.

Sahib Khan.—If God assists, you will succeed ; but the country is large and favourable, and the gangs are numerous and well organized.

Q.—So was the country we have already gone over. How many Thug leaders from Sindouse after Mr. Halhed and Mr. Stockwell's attacks came and settled in the Saugor and Nurbudda districts ?

Shiekh Inayat.—My father Hinga Jemadar and his three sons, two of whom were hung at Saugor the year before last, came to Lowa, a village between Dhamonee and Khimlassa in Saugor ; my younger brother Dhurum Khan was born after my father's death ; his mother could not, and my wife nursed him. We were joined by Monowur Musulman, Niddee and Mungoa Brahmans, Lulloo and his sons.

Q.—And how many noted Thugs and the gangs they formed are still at large.

Sheikh Inayat.—Since I was taken in 1829, these have all been seized, and have been hung or transported or are now in jail. Two of my brothers have been hung. My youngest is now here. The men whom they made Thugs have also been taken, and there are only five or six that we know of. There are Bahadur Chabukaswur, Kuseea

Kirar, Bodhooa, son of another Bahadur: these are new Thugs; but they proved themselves good ones. There are Kadir and Poosoo, adopted sons of Imamee, the son of Mirja Musulman. These Thugs are at large in the district of Seonee or Nursingpore. We know of no others.

Q.—Do you think that if we persevere, we shall be able to do in the Duckun what we have done here, and in the Dooab?

Inaent.—No doubt.

Sahib Khan.—It will be a work of greater difficulty. Half or three-quarters of these gangs were Kuboolas. In the Duckun they are almost all composed entirely of *Burkas*—men well born, staunch and able; above all the men of Arcot.

Feringeea.—And the Hindoo Thugs of Talghat upon the Krishna river?

Sahib Khan.—Yes; they are extraordinary men.

Feringeea.—They have three painted lines on their foreheads extending up from a central point at the nose. I served with them once for two months.

Sahid Khan.—Yes; they have these lines.

Q.—But do not all Hindoos in that quarter wear the same marks?

Sahib Khan.—All Hindoos put them on occasionally, but they always wear them. They and the Arcot Thugs associate and act together; but they will never mix with us of Telingana.

Q.—What are they called?

Sahib Khan.—We call them the Talghat men. What they call themselves I know not.

Q.—Sahib Khan tells tells me that the Arcot men will not intermarry with the descendants from the old Delhi clans, because they think they were orignally of lower cast?

Sahib Khan.—But we refuse our daughters to them as they refuse theirs to us; and they are in error when they suppose us of low origin.

Q.—Have you Hindoostan men any funeral ceremonies by which your origin can be learnt?

Inaent.—No funeral ceremonies; but at marriages an old matron will sometimes repeat, as she throws down the *Toolsee,* " Here's to the spirits of those who once led bears, and monkeys; to those who drove bullocks, and marked with the godnee; and those who made baskets for the head."

Q.—And does not this indicate that your ancestors were Khunjurs, itinerant tradesmen, wandering with their herds and families about the country.

Sahib Khan.—By no means. It only indicates that our ancesters after their captivity at Delhi, were obliged to adopt these disguises to effect their escape. Some pretended to have dancing bears and monkeys; some to have herds of cattle, and to be wandering Khunjurs, (Gypies); but they were not really so; they were high cast Musulmans.

Dorgha.—Certainly. I have heard this often from our wise men.

Feringeea.—You may hear and say what you please, but your funeral and marriage ceremonies indicate that your ancestors were nothing more than Khunjurs and vagrants about the great city?

Inaent.—It is impossible to say whether they were really what is described in these ceremonies, or pretended to be so; that they performed these offices for a time is unquestionable, but I think they must have been assumed as disguises.

Feriugeea.—But those who emigrated direct from Delhi into remote parts of India, and did not rest at Agra, retain those professions up to the present day ; as the Moltanies.

Sahib Khan.—True ; but it is still as disguises to conceal their real profession of Thuggee.

Feringeea.—True, and under the same guise they practised their trade of Thuggee round Delhi before the captivity, and could never have had any other.

Sahib.—I pretend not to know when they put on the disguise, but I am sure it was a disguise ; and that they were never really leaders of bears and monkeys.

Q.—Have the Talghat men the same language and usages as you have ?

Sahib.—They have the same omens and language, and observe the same rules ; but we hear that they use the round instead of the oblong grave to bury their victims, the same as the Behar men. They call it the *Chukree;* the Behar men and others call it the *Gobba.*

Q. — You call yourselves Telingana Thugs. What do you understand by the term ?

Sahib.—The country extending from Nandair to Nulgonda, which is four stages from Hydrabad on the road to Musalapatam.

Q.—How many divisions do the Thugs count in the Duckun; that is, the country south of the Nurbudda ?

Sahib.—There are five districts ; 1, Telingana ; 2, Berar, extending from Nagpore to Nandair ; 3, The Duckun, extending from Mominabad, which is fifty cose from Hyderabad on the road to Poona, to the city of Poona : 4, The Kurnatic, extending.

from Satara to Kurpakundole; 5, Arcot, extending from Kurpakundole to Seetabuldee Ramesur.

Q.—And the Thugs of these several divisions consider themselves as distinct?

Sahib.—All distinct, and called after their divisions as Telinganies, Arcoties, Kurnatekies, Duckunees, and Beraries.

Q.—Can you name the principal leaders now at large in these divisions?

Sahib.—Yes, all except those who reside in Arcot. The only leaders of that district that I know are the men already named, who occasionally go back, and always keep up their connexions with their old associates.

Q.—How is it that you Hindostan Thugs kill women with less scruple than the Duckun Thugs?

Feringeea.—To that we owe much of our misfortunes. It began with the murder of the Kalee Bebee.

Q.—Who was the Kalee Bebee?

Dorgha.—I was not present, but have heard that she was on her way from Elichpore to Hyderabad with a gold chadur or sheet for the tomb of Dolla Khan Nowab, the brother of Salabut Khan of Hyderabad, who had died just before. Shumshere Khan and Golab Khan strangled her I believe.

Q.—When was this?

Dorgha.—It was I believe about four years before the Surtrook affair in which we murdered the sixty persons at Chitterkote, among whom were some women.*

Q.—In what year did that take place?

---

* This gang of Thugs must have travelled above one hundred and sixty miles with these people before they put them to death, and been in company with them about twelve days, on the most friendly terms.

Dorgha.—I do not know; but it was either the year before, or two years before the Surgooja expedition in which the Chuleesrooh affair took place (forty persons at one time) where women were again murdered.

Q.—Do you recollect the year?

Kuleean Sing.—The Surgooja expedition took place the year that Mr. Jenkins went first from Banares to Nagpore as Resident, and the Chuleesrooh was one of the affairs. He had just arrived and was encamped near the Seetabuldee hill when our gang reached Nagpore.

Q.—Did any calamity befal you after the murder of the Kalee Bebee?

Dorgha.—I think not.

Q.—And therefore you continued to kill them?

Feringeea.—For five years no misfortune followed, and they continued to kill women; but then the misfortunes of my family began.

Q.—What relation had you there?

Feeringeea.—My father Purusram was one of the principal leaders, and the chadur they got was worth about three thousand rupees. It was cut up and divided, and my father brought home one fine slip. But the fifth year after this his misfortunes began; our family was never happy; not a year passed without his losing something, or being seized; he was seized every year some where or other.

Ghasee Subahdar was another leader, and he suffered similar misfortunes, and his family became miserable. Look at our families; see how they are annihilated; all that survive are in prison except Phoolsa and Rambuksh.

Q.—And still you went on killing women in spite

of your conviction that your misfortunes arose from it ?

Dorgha.—Yes, it was our fate to do so.

Q.—And you are worse than the Duckun Thugs, for you murder handsome young women as well as the old and ugly ?

Feringeea.—Not always. I and my cousin Aman Subahdar were with a gang of one hundred and fifty Thugs on an expedition through Rajpootana about thirteen years ago when we met a handmaid of the Peshwa, Bajee Row's, on her way from Poona to Cawnpore. We intended to kill her and her followers, but we found her very beautiful, and after having her and her party three days within our grasp, and knowing that they had a lakh and a half of rupees worth of property in jewels and other things with them, we let her and all her party go: we had talked to her and felt love towards her, for she was very beautiful.

Q.—And how came you to kill the Moghulanée. She also is said to have been very handsome ?

Feringeea.—We none of us ventured near her palankeen. The Musulmans were the only men that approached her before the murder. Madar Buksh approver strangled her.

Q.—And you think killing women has been one of the chief causes of your misfortunes ?

Feringeea.—Yes.

Q.—And of our success against you ?

Kuleean Sing.—Yes; I and my gang were arrested after the murder of Newul Sing and his daughters at Biseynee in 1820.

Q.—But Newul Sing had lost an arm, and you before told me that you suffered because you there infringed a good old rule and murdered a maimed person ?

Kuleean.—Yes; it was partly that; but was not the great gang seized by Mr. Molony after the murder of Monshee Bunda Alee and his wife and daughter at Lucknadown, three years after?

Q.—Who was that Bunda Alee. I have never been able to discover?

Kuleean.—He was the Monshee of General Doveton, who commanded at Jhalna, and he was going to his home in Hindustan to celebrate the marriage of that daughter. His wife and an infant daughter and six servants, besides the eldest daughter, were all strangled.

Q.—Was not this about the time that you and your party were arrrested, Nasir, for not attending to the omen of the hare?

Nasir.—When we were taken before general Doveton he was in Durbar, and there was a Moonshee called Bunda Alee present. He did not write down our statements, but he asked questions, and explained them to the general. Rangrow Brahman, his Kamdar, wrote them down. He took down all the stages we had made, the names of our villages, and could not find any discrepancies.

Q.—Who denounced you to the general?

Nasir.—There were two brothers going to cantonments with bullocks, one had gone on in advance, and the other we murdered. The man in advance came back for his brother, and seeing us one hundred and fifty Thugs, and not finding his brother, he suspected us of the murder. A large party of horse and foot came after us. All however made off but eighteen of the staunchest and of most respectable appearance, who remained to stop the pursuit. We pretended to have been going with our friends in search of service; and after a long examination, Moonshee Bunda Alee urged the improbability of so large a body of robbers coming so far to murder one poor bullock driver. This argument had weight; we were let go, and the bullock man sent about his business.

Q.—Was this the same Bunda Alee who was afterwards murdered, think you?

Nasir.—I do not know; I never saw him or heard of him after that time.

Q.—How long ago was it?

Nasir.—About thirteen or fourteen years ago.

Q.—Had not the daughters of Newul Sing Jemedar prevented the gang from being imprisoned?

Kuleean.—Yes. Omrow Sing, Dufadar of Captain Nicholson's corps, was then on duty at Seonee. The gang had brought on this family from Nagpore. They were Newul Sing, a Jemedar in the Nizam's service, who had lost one arm, his brother Hurbuns Sing, his two daughters, one thirteen and the other eleven years of age, the two young men who were to have been married to them on reaching home, Kuleean Sing and Aman, the brother of the two girls, a boy about seven years of age, and four servants. The house in which part of the gang lodged at Dhoma took fire, and the greater part of the gang were seized by the police, but released at the urgent request of Newul Sing and his daughters, who had become much attached to Khimolee, the principal leader of the gang, and some of the others. Omrow Sing Dufadar was a relation of Newul Sing, and he assisted in getting them released as he can now tell you. Had the gang been then imprisoned and searched we must have been discovered, as they had with them two bags of silk taken from the three carriers on their way from Nagpore to Jubulpore, whom we had murdered in the great temple at Kamtee, where the cantonments now stand.

On reaching Jubulpore part of the gang went on. Adhartal and the rest lodged in the town with Newul Sing and his family. The merchants at Nagpore finding that their men with the silk had not reached Jubulpore, and hearing of our gang having passed, sent to their correspondents at Jubulpore, who got the Cotwal to search those who were lodged with Newul Sing. Hearing of the approach of the police, Khimolee again availed himself of the attachment of Newul Sing and his daughters, and the girls were made to sit each upon one of the two bags of silk while the police searched the place. Nothing was found, and the next day they set out and passed us at Adhartal, and five days after this they were all strangled at Biseynee.*

Q.—How did you not preserve the infant daughter of Bunda Alee Moonshee for adoption?

Chutter.—Ghubboo Khan strangled the mother while her infant was in her arms, and he determined to keep and adopt the child; but after the bodies had all been put into the grave, Dhunnee Khan urged him to kill the child also, or we should be seized on crossing the Nurbudda valley. He threw the child living in upon the dead bodies, and the grave was filled up over it.

Q.—And the child was buried alive?

* This gang accompanied Newul Sing and his family from near Nagpore through Sconee and Jubulpore to Biseynee, a distance of more than two hundred miles, and were with them about twenty days on the most intimate terms, before they put them all to death. The circumstance of Newul Sing's having lost an arm made them hesitate, and one gang separated from the main body before they reached Seonee rather than be present at his murder; and there seemed no chance of their being able to separate him from the rest.

Chutter.—Yes. My brother Dulput and I were then mere children; we were seized in crossing the Nurbudda valley and never after released; he is now dead and I am the only surviving son of Ghasee Subahdar.

Q.—How was that affair managed?

Chutter.—We fell in with the Moonshee and his family at Chupara, between Nagpore and Jubulpore; and they came on with us to Lucknadown, where we found that some companies of a native regiment under European officers, were expected the next morning. It was determined to put them all to death that evening, as the Moonshee seemed likely to keep with the companies. Our encampment was near the village, and the Moonshee's tent was pitched close to us. In the afternoon some of the officers' tents came on in advance, and were pitched on the other side, leaving us between them and the village. The Khulasies were all busily employed in pitching them, Noor Khan and his son Sadee Khan and a few others, went as soon as it became dark to the Moonshee's tent, and began to sing and play upon a Sitar, as they had been accustomed to do. During this time some of them took up the Moonshee's sword on pretence of wishing to look at it. His wife and children were inside listening to the music. The *Jhirnee*, or signal, was given, but at this moment the Moonshee saw his danger, called out murder, and attempted to rush through, but was seized and strangled. His wife hearing him, ran out with the infant in her arms, but was seized by Ghubboo Khan, who strangled her and took the infant. The other daughter was strangled in the tent. The saeses (grooms) were at the time cleaning their horses, and one of them seeing his danger, ran under the belly of his horse, and called out murder; but he was soon seized and strangled as well as all the rest.

Q.—How did not the Khalasies and others who were pitching their tent close by hear these calls for help?

Chutter.—As soon as the signal was given, those of the gangs who were idle began to play and sing as loud as they could; and two vicious horses were let loose and many ran after them calling out as loud as they could: so that the calls of the Moonshee and his party were drowned.

Q.—Do you Behar Thugs ever murder woman?

Moradun.—Never; we should not murder a woman if she had a lakh of rupees upon her.

Davey Deen.—Nor would the Dooab Thugs if she had two lakhs upon her.

Gopaul.—We have never been guilty of so great a crime in the Dooab or any part east of the Ganges and Jumna where I have been employed.

Q.—But you Bundelcund men murdered abundance?

Zolfukar.—Yes, and was not the greater part of Feringeea's and my gang seized after we had murdered the two women and little girl at Manora in 1830 near Saugor? And were we not ourselves both seized soon after? How could we survive things like that: our ancestors never did such things.

Feringea.—We had no sooner buried their bodies than I heard the *chirega*,* and on leaving the ground we saw the *loharburhega ;** these were signs that *Davey* was displeased, and we gave ourselves up for lost.

* See these words in the Vocabulary.

Q.—But some of the Dooab Thugs have murdered women in your expeditions on this side of the Jumna?

Davey Deen.—That was while they were in company with the Bundelcund and Saugor men.

Gopaul.—On the other side of the Jumna and Ganges, we never have done so.

Bhikka.—How could we do so? we do not even murder a person that has a cow with him.

Q.—Had not the fourteen persons murdered at Kotree a cow with them, and were there not women in the party, and all killed?

Chotee.—We were almost all Gwalior and Bundelcund and Saugor men in that gang, but we persuaded the party to sell us the cow at Shahpore; and we gave it to a Brahman at that place, and two or three days after they were all strangled at Kotree in Huttah. I pointed out the grave to Captain Crawford, and he took up the bodies.

Q.—And you could not have strangled them if they had not parted with the cow?

Chotee.—Certainly not; nor could we have made them part with her had we not pretended that we had vowed to make such an offering at Shahpore, and were very much in want of her.

Zolfukar.—Durgha and Feringeea have been confounding cases; I have heard of the Kalee Bebee it is true, but I was not at her murder; and yet I was at the taking of the sheets intended for the Nowab's tomb. Peer Mahommud was there, so also was Kadir, then a boy; and I have heard that he has still in his family one of the slips that fell to the share of his adopted father, the great Dhurum Khan.

Feringeea.—But was not my father Purusram in that affair?

Zolfukar.—He was, and so was Ghasee Subahdar, but no Kalee Bebee was killed in that affair. There were only three persons, and they were men. We got two sheets, one green and the other red.

Kadir.—I was a little boy and that was my first expedition, and I was mounted upon a pony. The piece of the chadar we gave to a priest, and it was taken and lodged in the Sangor Malkhana, and afterwards put up to auction I believe.

Zolfukar.—The two chadars were sent by Nowab Salabut Khan, the Elichpore Nowab, for the tomb of his brother Buhlole Khan, who had died at Hyderabad. Lalmun Musulman, and Khandee and his brother Nundun Brahmans, must know all about the Kalee Bebee; they are very old men.

Khandee and *Nundun*, brothers and Brahmans, one 83 and the other 85 years of age, being sent for, deny having been present at the murder, but say they knew of it, and of the dire effects of it to the Thug fraternity.

Lalmun.—Being sent for, age 90. I remember the murder of the Kalee Bebee well; I was at the time on an expedition to Barodah, and not present, but Punna must have been there. A dispute arose between the Musulmans and the Hindoos before and after the murder. The Musulmans insisted upon killing her, as he had four thousand rupees worth of property with her: the Hindoos would not agree. She was killed, and the Hindoos refused to take any part of the booty; they came to blows, but at last the Hindoos gave in, and consented to share in all but the clothes and ornaments which the women wore. Feringeea's father, Purusram Brahman, was there; so was Ghasee Subahdar, a Rajpoot; so was Himmut Brahman.

When they came home to Murnae, Rae Sing, Purusram's brother, refused to eat, drink or smoke with his brother till he had purged himself from this great sin ; and he, Himmut, and Ghasee gave a feast that cost them a thousand rupees each. Four or five · thousand Brahmans were assembled at that feast.   Had it rested here, we should have thrived ; but in the affair of the sixty, women were again murdered ; in the affair of the forty, several women were murdered ; the Musulmans were too strong for the Hindoos: and from that time we may trace our decline.

Q.—But you are a Musulman ?

Lalmun.—True : but our family had been settled for two generations with that of Rae Sing and Purusram at Murnae ; and had adopted their notions on all points of Thuggee. We had been first initiated by them, our family not being of the clans.   Busuntee must have been present at the Kalee Bebee's murder.

Busuntee.—No ; but my brother Punna was.

Punna—Being sent for, states—I was present. She was coming from Hyderabad, and was carried in a dooly, and had twelve followers. She had four thousand rupees worth of property. The Musulmans insisted upon killing her ; the Hindoos opposed. She was killed with all her followers, and the Hindoos, after a desperate quarrel, consented to share in all but her clothes and ornaments. Madaree, who died last year in the Saugor jail, was the man who strangled her. On going home Purusram, Ghasee, and Himmut were obliged to give a feast, and deprecate the wrath of *Davey* by a great deal of Poojah. Five thousand Brahmans assembled at that feast, and all was well ; but the Sutrooh followed, and after that the Chaleesrooh.

In both these affairs the Hindoos consented to share, but they were sadly punished. Himmut, after the Surgooja affair, got worms in his body, and died barking like a dog. Kosul died a miserable death at Nodha. One of his sons has been transported from Saugor, and the other died in the jail. His family is extinct. Look at Purusram's family; all gone! And Ghasee Subahdar's also!

Q.—Did not the Hindoos assist in strangling the women in the Sutrooh (60) and Chaleesrooh (40) affairs?

Punna.—God forbid. They sinned enough in consenting to share in the booty, but they never assisted in the murder.

Q.—How did Feringeea get his name?

Lalmun.—General Perron could not make his uncle Rae Sing pay eighteen thousand rupees arrears due on account of his farm of the customs, and sent a regiment under Blake Sahib to seize him. The village was assaulted and burnt; and in her flight Purusram's wife gave birth to Feringeea, and he got his name from that event—Feringeea, from the attack of the Feringies.

Q.—And you think that much of your misfortunes have arisen from the murder of women?

Lalnum.—We all knew that they would come upon us some day for this and other great sins. We were often admonished but we did not take warning, and we deserve our fates.

Q.—What, for committing murder?

Lalmun.—No, but for murdering women, and those classes of people whom our ancestors never murdered.

Q.—They tell me that you were the best *Belha* (chooser of the place for murder) in your day. Was it so?

Lalmun.—I was thought a good one in my day, but I am now very old and blind. I was a man when even Khandee and Nunden were children!

Dorgha.—I got a bay pony from the Kalee Bebee's affair. My brother Punga, who died lately in the Saugor jail, and my father Khyroo, were there.

Q.—Are you never afraid of the spirits of the persons you murder?

Nasir.—Never; they cannot trouble us.

Q.—Why? Do they not trouble other men when they commit murder?

Nasir.—Of course they do. The man who commits a murder is always haunted by spirits. He has sometimes fifty at a time upon him, and they drive him mad.

Q.—And how do they not trouble you?

Nasir.—Are not the people we kill killed by the orders of *Davey*?

Kuleean.—Yes, it is by the blessing of *Davey* that we escape that evil.

Dorgha.—Do not all whom we kill go to Paradise, and why should their spirits stay to trouble us?

Inaent.—A good deal of our security from spirits is to be attributed to the roomal with which we strangle.

Q.—I did not know that there was any virtue in the roomal.

Inaent.—Is it not our sikka, (ensign) as the pick-axe is our nishan? (standard).

Feringeea.—More is attributable to the pickaxe. Do we not worship it every seventh day? Is it not our standard? Is its sound ever heard when digging the grave by any but a Thug? And can any man even swear to a falsehood upon it?

Q.—And no other instrument would answer, you think, for making the graves?

Nasir.—How could we dig graves with any other instruments. This is the one appointed by *Davey*, and consecrated, and we should never have survived the attempt to use any other.

Feringeea.—No man but a Thug who has been a strangler, and is remarkable for his cleanliness and decorum is permitted to carry it.

Q.—And there is no instance of a Thug being troubled by a spirit?

All.—None. No Thug was ever so troubled.

Q.—What became of Khimmolee to whom Newul Sing and his daughters were so much attached?

Kuleean.—He died in the Jubulpore jail.

Q.—What became of Ghubboo Khan who strangled the Moonshee's wife?

Chutter.—He also died in the Jubulpore jail.

Q.—What become of Noor Khan and his son Sadee?

Chutter.—Noor Khan died in the Huttah jail, and his son Sadee was lately transported from Jubulpore.

Q.—Were you not once arrested with a large gang at Kotah?

Feringeea.—Yes; we had murdered four men with bundles of clothes at Kunwas, going from Ashta to Kotah; and four days after we killed the nephew of Jeswunt Raw Lar, and his four servants, whose bodies were taken up last year. Twenty-eight of the gang were arrested; but the next day they had their faces blackened, and were released. I had fled, leaving my clothes behind, and after the release of the gang they discovered in my clothes the hilt of the young chief's sword, with his name

written under it, and some of the cloth. In trying
to overtake us they fell in with Bhimmee and Hurnagur and their gangs, and arrested forty, who
were confined for four years, and released the year
that the Lucknadown gang was arrested by Mr.
Molony,* (1823.)

Q.—Where did you go?

Feringeea.—Ashraf Khan, Subahdar Major of
Colonel Ridge's regiment of cavalry (4th Cavalry),
was at Kotah, on his way home sick, the day we
were released, and we followed him up and killed
him and all his party.

Q.—Had he not been wounded and become an
improper person to be killed?

Feringeea.—I did not go near enough to him to
see. He was sick and carried in his palankeen;
and my party having been arrested and had their
faces blackened, we could not take any part in the
murder. We got a share of the booty however.

Q.—And why did they release Hurnagur and
his party?

Feringeea.—They thought it too expensive to
feed them every day.

Q.—What is commonly the proportion of Musulmans to Hindoos?

Feringeea.—In Oude nine-tenths are Musulmans.
In the Dooab four-fifths were Hindoos. South of
the Nurbudda three-fourths Musulmans. In Bundelcund and Saugor one-half were Musulmans.
In Rajpootana one-fourth Musulmans. In Bengal,
Behar, and Orissa about half and half. This is a
rough guess, since we have no rule to prescribe or
ascertain them.

* This is a mistake of *Feringeea's*—it was the year that the gang
of Beg Khan was arrested by Major Wardlow—committed by Mr.
Fraser, and tried by Mr. Wilder, 1826.

Q.—Are the usages of the River Thugs the same as yours?

Moradun.—In worship the same. They strangle in boats and throw the bodies into the river. If they see blood, they must go back and open the expedition anew. They give the *Jhirnee* by striking on the neck of the boat three times, when the man appointed to give it sees all clear.

Q.—Have the River Thugs the same Ramasee (dialect) as you?

Imam Buksh, of Rustur in Ghazeepoor.—No, totally different. They neither understand our Ramasee nor do we theirs. They call a strangler Charud, and a Beetoo, or traveller Khan, meaning their food; as we call him our Bunij, or merchandise. When they give their *Jhirnee* they say "*pawn law*," bring paun.

Q.—Where do the River Thugs reside chiefly?

Imam Buksh.—They formerly, as I have heard my father and other old men say, constituted the exclusive population of some villages, till á Gurdee (inroad) was made upon them, and their villages were pulled down about their ears.

Q.—What was the cause of this?

Imam Buksh.—They never kill women, and there was a party of five travellers, four men and one woman, who wanted to pass across the river with them at Rajmahul. They contrived to leave the woman behind, and this led to the discovery of the murder of the men. From that time they have been scattered over the district of Burdwan, and now they live in villages occupied by other people —four or five families of them in a village.

They go in considerable parties, and have generally several boats at the ghat at the same time. The ghats most frequented by them are those of

Kohelgaum, Rajmahul, Moremukaea, an invalid station, and Monghyr; but they go on so far as Cawnpore, and even Furruckabad. Their murders are always perpetrated in the day time. Those who do the work of the boatmen are dressed like other boatmen; but those who are to take a part in the operations, are dressed like travellers of great respectability; and there are no boats on the river kept so clean, and inviting for travellers. When going up the river they always pretend to be men of some consideration going on pilgrimage to some sacred place, as Banares, Allahabad, &c. When going down they pretend to be returning home from such places. They send out their Sothas, or inveiglers, well dressed upon the high roads, who pretend to be going by water to the same places as the travellers they fall in with. On coming to the ghat they see these nice looking boats with the respectably dressed Thugs amusing themselves. They ask the Manjee (captain) of the boat to take them and the travellers on board, as he can afford to do so cheaper than others, having apparently his boat already engaged by others. He pretends to be pushed for room, and the Thugs pretend to be unwilling to have any more passengers on board. At last he yields to the earnest requests of their inveiglers, and the travellers are taken up. They go off into the middle of the river, those above singing and playing and making a great noise, while the travellers are murdered inside at the signal given by three taps, that all is clear, and their bodies are thrown into the river. The boat then goes on to some other ghat, having landed their inveiglers again upon the roads.

Q.—How many of these river Thugs do you suppose there are?

Imam Buksh.—I have never served with them but once, and cannot say; perhaps from two hundred to two hundred and fifty.

Q.—Have you ever served with the Motheeas?

Imam Buksh.—I have. They are from a class of weavers or Tantooas: their Ramasee or dialect is the same as ours; they are called Motheeas by their associate Thugs, but by other people they are known only as Tantooas. I have however seen very little of them; others here know more than I do about them; ask Bukhtawur.

Q.—Have you seen the Lodahas?

Imam Buksh.—Yes; they are descended from the same common stock as ourselves, and are Jumaldehees, and Musulmans. Their dialect and usages are all the same as ours, but they rarely make Thugs of any men but the members of their own families. They marry into other families, who do not know them to be Thugs, but their wives never know their secrets, and can therefore never divulge them. No prospect of booty could ever induce them, or any of the Bengal or Behar Thugs to kill a woman.

Q.—Where do they chiefly reside?

Imam Buksh.—They occupy some villages north-east of Durbunga on the Nepaul frontier. They emigrated from Oude when annoyed on some occasion some generations ago; part of the emigrants remained in the Goruckpore district, and have spread to that of Chupra. They have every where followed the same trade of Thuggee; and, as in other parts, all under the auspices of *Davey.* It was about five generations ago that this emigration from Oude took place. The Lodahas extend their expeditions from the city of Patna along all the roads leading through Dinjapore,

14*

Rungpoore, Titaleea, Durbhunga, Poruneea, Dibeea, Nathpore, and up to the banks of the Burhampootre, but I never served with them during more than one expedition. Bukhtawur knows more about them than I do. They cannot speak the language of the western provinces, and in consequence never go west of the city of Patna.

Q.—What castes are you forbidden to kill?

Imam Buksh.—We never kill any of the following classes:

Dhobies or Washermen.

Bharts or Bards.

Siks are never killed in Bengal.

Nanuksahees.

Mudaree Fukeers.

Dancing men or boys.

Musicians by profession.

Bhungies or sweepers.

Teylies, oil venders.

Lohars and *Burheys*, blacksmiths and carpenters, when found together.

Maimed and leprous persons.

A man with a cow.

Burhumcharies.

Kawrutties, or Ganges water carriers, while they have the Ganges water actually with them. If their pots be empty, they are not exempted.

Bukhtawur being sent for:

Q.—You are said to have occasionally gone with the river Thugs; what do you call them?

Bukhtawur.—We call them *Pungoos.* On one occasion only have I ever served with them.

Q.—What was the said occasion?

Bukhtawur.—About fourteen years ago I had been on an expedition from Chupra to Moorshedabad. We were twenty-two Thugs, under Sew-

buns Jemadar, who was a Rajpoot. Two of our
gang, Khoda Buksh and Alee Yar, had often
served with the river Thugs, and used to interest
us by talking about their modes of proceeding. On
the other side of Rajmahul we fell in with two of
these Thugs. They had two bundles of clothes,
and pretended to be going on a pilgrimage, and
had with them five travellers, whom they had
picked up on the road. Sewbuns recognised them
immediately, and Alee Yar and Khoda Buksh
found in them old acquaintances. They got into
conversation with them, and it was agreed that
Sewbuns, I, and Dhorda Kormee should go with
them, and see how they did their work, while the
rest of the gang went on along the bank of the
river. We embarked at Rajmahul. The travellers sat on one side of the boat and the Thugs on
the other, while we were all three placed in the
stern, the Thugs on our left and the travellers on
our right. Some of the Thugs dressed as boatmen
were above deck, and others walking along the
bank of the river, and pulling the boat by the goon,
or rope; and all at the same time on the look out.
We came up with a gentleman's pinnace and two
baggage boats, and were obliged to stop and let
them get on. The travellers seemed anxious, and
were quieted by being told that the men at the rope
were tired, and must take some refreshment. They
pulled out something and began to eat; and when
the pinnace had got on a good way they resumed
their work, and our boat proceeded. It was now
afternoon, and when a signal was given above
that all was clear, the five Thugs who sat opposite
the travellers, sprung in upon them and with the
aid of others strangled them. They put the roomal
round the neck from the front, while all other

Thugs put it round from behind; they thus push them back, while we push them forward. Having strangled the five men, they broke their spinal bones, and pounded their private parts; and then threw them out of a hole made at the side into the river; and kept on their course, the boat being all this time pulled along by the men on the bank.

The booty amounted to about two hundred rupees. We claimed and got a share for all our party; and Sewbuns declared that we were twenty-nine, while we were really only twenty-three, and got a share for that number; he cheated them out of the share of six men.

We landed that night and rejoined our gang, and operated upon the roads leading along the river Ganges till we got to the Mormukaeea ghat where there is an invalid station—about four cose the other side of Bar. Here we fell in with the same party of *Pungoos*, or river Thugs, who had three travellers with them. I did not join them this time, but Sewbuns with two other members of our gang went on board, and saw them strangled. What share he got I do not know.

Q.—Where do they reside?

Bukhtawur.—They reside about Beerbhoom, Bancoora, Kulna-Kutooa, Sewree and other places in the district of Burdwan, which is a very large district. Kulna and Kutooa are two distinct towns on the Bhageeruttee river, half way from Calcutta to Moorshedabad, though we always join their names together in speaking of the place. Thugs do not live in these or any other towns, as they are there always liable to be a good deal annoyed by police questions, but in small villages around about them.

Q.—What do you call police questions?

Bukhtawur.—Questions about who's come; who's gone; who's born; who's died; what's your occupation; whence your income, and so forth. These questions annoy Thugs a good deal, and oblige them to share their incomes with the police men as well as with the Zumcendars.

Q.—What's your age?

Bukhtawur.—Between sixty and seventy.

Q.—Was your father a Thug?

Bukhtawur.—No; I am the first of my family, but Iman Buksh is an hereditary Jumaldehee Thug. I was taught the trade by Manickrae Rajpoot, a Jemadar of Thugs. Both he and his son Kishun are now dead. Manickrae had lived with several families of Thugs in the village of Seesooa in Beteea, but a native collector came and gave them a good deal of annoyance, and they went to a small village near Julloo, ten cose this side of Junuckpore. I live in Pherirdaha, from Goruckpore sixteen cose east, from the great Gunduk river nine cose west, and from the little Gunduk one cose east.

Q.—Does not the Rajah of Beteea encourage the residence of Thugs?

Bukhtawur.—Not now; he is afraid, and tries all he can to find them out and expel them; but he has got the most expert thieves in India; they will steal the bullocks from your plough without your perceiving them.

Q.—Have you ever served with the Lodahas?

Bukhtawur.—Yes. I have often served with Jhoulee Khan Jemadar. He lives thirty cose from Durbhunga on the frontier, and has thirty good Thugs. He is ostensibly a mere cultivator. He is called Jhoulee Khan the fair. There is also the black Jhoulee Khan, who has fifteen good Thugs,

and holds a village in farm as a Zumeendar, though
he is not so great a man as the other.   Their followers are all hereditary and well trained Thugs.
Jhubbun Khan, another leader of great note, lives
near them.   They reside in five or six villages
within a few cose of each other, and are about
fifty families of Thugs, most of them Musulmans,
but there are some Rajpoots and some Tantooas,
or weavers.   These fifty families have perhaps
from two hundred to two hundred and fifty Thugs.

Q.—Are your gangs never arrested in that quarter ?

Bukhtawur.—Sometimes : about ten years ago
a gang of seventeen were arrested near Durbhunga ; four were hung, and twelve transported.

Q.—How was that managed ?

Bukhtawur.—Gobind Rawut, son of Peearee
Rawut, and Gheena Khan Jemadars, and a gang
of fifteen Thugs had strangled and buried four
travellers.   Syfoo and Gheena Khan had married
two sisters, and Syfoo gave himself airs, and
demanded a coral necklace that was taken from
one of the travellers.   Gheena refused to give it ;
a quarrel ensued, and Syfoo, in a passion, went to
the Thanadar at Durbhanga, brought him and his
guard down upon them at night, and seized the
whole gang.   But Syfoo had not seen the grave,
and he made the Thanadar tie up his cousin, Peer-
buksh, a boy, throw him down, draw his sword,
and pretend to be about to cut his throat.   The boy
got alarmed, confessed, and pointed out the grave.
The bodies were taken up, the prisoners sent to
Mozuffurpore, and the four men who strangled
them were hung ; twelve, including the two leaders,
were sent to the black water.   Syfoo was released,

but died on his way home. How, we could never discover.

Q.—Did he die because he disclosed?

Bukhtawur.—No doubt.

Q.—That is, some of his old associates killed him?

Bukhtawur.—No; had he been killed by them we should have discovered it. In those days a man who peached was either killed by his old associates, or by *Davey.* They were only rare and solitary instances; now we do not fear, as we are many and become servants of government. Syfoo must have perished for his treachery, but he was not killed by any of us.

Q.—Where were the four men murdered?

Bukhtawur.—About half a cose east of the Kolesuree river, a sacred stream, about two cose east from Durbunga.

Q.—What year was it in?

Bukhtawur.—I don't know; about ten years ago.

Moradun of Arah.—It must have been after the siege of Bhurtpore, for I saw Gheena Khan that year on an expedition. He resided near Jugtowlee in Chupra, not far from Bukhtawur's village of Phurindha.

CONVERSATION RESUMED WITH THE DUCKUN AND HINDOS-TANEE THUGS.

Q.—If *Davey's* displeasure visits all who punish Thugs, how is it that you all escape so well?

Moradun.—*Davey's* anger visited us when we *were seized.* That was the effect of her resentment; she cast us off then and takes no notice of us now.

Q.—And if you were to return to Thuggee, she would still guide and protect you?

Moradun.—Yes, but what gang would now receive us?

Q.—And are you not afraid to assist in suppressing Thuggee?

Moradun.—No; we see God is assisting you, and that *Davey* has withdrawn her protection on account of our transgressions. We have sadly neglected her worship. God knows in what it will all end.

Q.—True, God only knows; but we hope it will end in the entire suppression of this wicked and foolish system; and in the conviction on your part that *Davey* has really had nothing to do with it.

Nasir.—That *Davey* instituted Thuggee, and supported it as long as we attended to her omens, and observed the rules framed by the wisdom of our ancestors, nothing in the world can ever make us doubt.

Q.—Do the five divisions you mention in the Duckun comprise, geographically, all the country south of the Nurbudda river?

Sahib Khan.—No, there is a sixth, Khandiesh; but we know of no Thugs in that country; and a seventh, the Concan along the Malabar coast; we know of no Thugs in that country either.

Q.—Are there no Thugs in these two districts think you?

Sahib.—There may be some, but we do not know of any.

Feringeea.—Our gangs from Hindostan used often to go through Khandiesh in our expeditions, but we never heard of any Thugs who resided there: many may have emigrated into that quarter from others since this pursuit began.

Q.—You got some valuable prizes in Khandiesh latterly ?

Chotee.—There was the Choupura case on the Taptee river, in which we got 25,000 rupees in 1826.

The Dholeea and Malagaum case in which we got twenty-two thousand rupees worth of gold in 1827. The Dhorecote case in which we got twelve thousand rupees in 1828, and the Dhoree case in 1829, in which they got seventy-two thousand rupees worth of pearls, and ten thousand rupees worth of gold, though they could not keep it all. These were our prizes in Khandiesh.

Q.—You were not in the Dhoree case ?

Chotee.—No, but I was in all the others. I was in arrest with Dhun Raj Seth's Agent at Alumpore, trying to recover some of the Spanish dollars taken from him at Burwaha ghat, when that occurred ; but I sent part of my gang that year with Feringeea's, and they fell in with the Dhoree case men as they were coming back with the pearls.

Feringeea.—Yes ; some of Chotee's men were with me in the Ranjuna case, which took place in March, 1829 ; and we soon after fell in with some of our friends coming home with their pearls from the Dhoree case.

Q.—But the Dhorce case and Burwaha ghat case must have taken place within a few days of each other in February, 1829 ; the Dhoreo case took place on the 6th, and the Burwaha ghat case, on the 1st of that month. We have the records of the dates from Indore ?

Chotee.—Your records must be wrong. The Dhorecote case, in which I was present, occurred fifteen days after the Burwaha ghat case, for I was taken up on the suspicion of being present in the

Burwaha ghat case, and it was the year after that
the pearls were taken at Dhoree.

Feringeea.—Yes; Chotee was with Dhun Raj
Seth's man Bearee Lal when we went on the
Ranjuna expedition and met the pearls.

Moklal.—He was arrested soon after our party
got the Spanish dollars at Burwaha ghat, which
was fifteen days before his party took the gold at
Dhorecote.

Q.—How many Spanish dollars did you get?

Moklal.—We got forty thousand rupees worth,
but a great part had been beaten up.

Feringeea.—But none of us got so fine a prize as
Bowanee the Sooseea and his gang of Rajpootana
got in Khandiesh. They carried off clear in one
affair above two lakhs of rupees worth of property
coming from Bombay to Indore.

Q.—How did you manage the Burwaha ghat
affair?

Moklal.—It gave us a great deal of trouble, as
the dollars were laden on camels. They went fast,
and, afraid to appear near to them in a body, we
several times lost all trace of them. We first fell
in with them at Borhanpore. Ours was only one
of three great parties that went from Bundelcund,
Gwalior and Saugor that year to Khandiesh; and
it consisted of about one hundred and sixty Thugs,
concentrating upon the treasure party. At Burwaha ghat, on the Nurbudda river, we found them
disputing with the custom-house officers about the
payment of duties; and stating the hardship of
being obliged to expose the value of their charge
in an unsettled country. We paid duties for ourselves and our six ponies; and, leaving a few
scouts, passed over the river, and went on to the
small deserted village of Naen, in the midst of a

jungly waste. Here we waited till the treasure party came up, consisting of eight men, mounted on camels and armed with matchlocks, and a merchant, by name Futteh Alee, who had joined them on the road in the hope of being more secure in their company than alone. It was about nine o'clock in the morning when they reached the place. The signal was given, we rushed in upon the camels, seized them by their bridles, and made them sit down by beating them with sticks. The men were seized and killed; some strangled, some stabbed with spears, and some cut down with swords. Futteh Alee was pulled off his pony and strangled. We transferred the treasure to our ponies; threw the bodies into a ravine, and went on for three days without halting any where, as we knew we should be immediately pursued. After we had got beyond danger we rested and divided the booty, setting aside the proper share for the temple of *Davey* at Dindachul, near Mirzapore.

Dhun Raj Seth sent his agent, Bearee Lal, to the Resident at Indore, and the agent of the Governor General in Bundelcund to recover his dollars. He got a good many of the principal Thug leaders arrested; they were sent by the agent in Bundelcund to the Resident at Indore, who sent them back to the agent, who made them over to the native chiefs, in whose jurisdiction they resided, with orders to make good the money. These chiefs told us to make good three-fourths of the money taken at Burwaha ghat by a general contribution. We agreed to do so and were let go; some paid out of the fruits of former expeditions, others borrowed in anticipation of future success; and those who had neither money nor credit pledged themselves to pay part of their future earnings. To this Bearee Lal agreed, and sent them on expeditions, retaining Chotee, Bukut and other Jemadars of great influence about his person. He got a good deal of money by procuring the release of all the noted Thugs then in confinement at different places. He got nine thousand rupees for the release of Dhurum Khan Jemadar from Gwalior, on the pretence that he was engaged in the affair when he had been in prison long before. He had got a great prize of jewels from some men killed near Kotah, and his family could afford to pay. Such was Dhun Raj Seth's influence that he could get a gang released from prison in any part of India; and for some time his agent Bearee Lal had always half a dozen of the principal Thug leaders about his person, and used to attend all our marriages and festivals. What his master got, we know not, but he got a great deal of our money.

Q.—What became of him after our operations began?

Moklal.—He ran off to his master at Omrowtee: we returned to our homes and got all arrested.

Q.—Are there any Thugs in Guzerat?

Moklal.—We think not. We have often gone through Guzerat in our expeditions of late years; particularly since your operations commenced, and have penetrated beyond Joonagur up to the shores of the ocean, but have never become acquainted with any Thug residing in Guzerat. There are numbers in Rapjootana. The Thugs of Deogur Mudara are to Oudeepore, what the Sindouse and Murnae men were to Etawa and Gwalior. In Joudhpore there are ten villages occupied by Thugs; and they are scattered all over Jypore, and are still very numerous about Ojeyn and Pertabjur in western Malwa.

Q.—But you think that a number of the members of your old gangs who have escaped-us may go and settle in Guzerat and Khandiesh?

Moklal.—Certainly some of them will. Is not Rambuksh for whom you offered five hundred rupees reward gone to that quarter?

Q.—And they will raise new gangs there you think? —

Moklal.—Certainly, if left undisturbed for a time

· *Q.*—Who were the leaders in the Burwaha gha affair?

Moklal.—Roshun, who was hung at Saugor, 1832.

Dhurun Khan, the stutterer, hung at Saugor, 1832.

Maharaj Partuk, who drowned himself at Saugor, 1832.

Persaud, hung at Saugor, 1832.

Lal Mahommud, approver.

Bukhtawur, who died at home.

Bukut, the son of old Khadeea approver, who is still at large and a Jemadar.

Q.—How did you manage the Dholeea and Malagow affair?

Feringeea.—Our gangs concentrated at the village of Jokur, between Dholeea and Malagow, in Khandeish, amounting to two hundred and fifty Thugs under myself.

Makun, who was hung at Indore, 1829.

Gunga Deen, who was hung at Indore, 1829.

Chotee, approver.

Maharaj Partuk, drowned himself at Saugor.

Sheikh Nungoo, dead.

Persaud, hung at Saugor 1832, and others,

15*

We left Jokeer for Malagow with two travellers, whom we had killed before daylight and were resting at a well two cose north of Malagow, when we heard after sunrise, the *Chimmama* on the right. I proposed, according to all the recognized rules of augury, to go back to Jokur immediately. To this proposal they would not consent, and we went on to Malagow, where I proposed that we should halt and avert the threatened evil by a sacrifice. This was overruled by a party who supposed that it might be as well averted by quitting the high road to Kopurgow, and diverging to the right upon that of Chandore. I went on with them four cose to a village, whose name I forget, but at night determined to obey the omen, and came back with my gang of twenty-five Thugs to Malagow, where I found a gang of one hundred Thugs under the following leaders :

Omrow, hung at Indore, 1829.

Bhimmee, approver.

Budoloo, hung at Saugor, 1832.

Bukut, approver.

Kunhey Aheer, killed in Joudpore, 1833.

Hinder Benguna, approver.

They had with them four treasure bearers from Poona on their way from Indore, whom they intended to kill on the way to Dholeea. I joined them and we went on to the village of Jokur, and were joined on the way by three other travellers, whom we could not shake off. Hinder Benguna's son Chiddee had quarrelled with his father, and gone off to join Chotee's party on the Chandore road with Gurhoo, who went to see two of his brothers who were with them ; and they having let out the secret of the treasure bearers, Chotee came off as fast as he could with Maharaj and a party of forty, and joined us during the night at Jokur.

Omrow's party was composed chiefly of Kuboolas, fellows of all casts, whom he had scraped together to make up a gang for this expedition, and we insisted upon his sending thirty of the rawest of them in advance from Jokur in the afternoon. There were at least two hundred men that night at Jokur on their way back from Hindostan to their regiments; but we watched the treasure bearers closely, and when they set out, we followed; and at a bowlee, a mile or two on, we closed in upon them and put them to death. We had not been able to shake off the other three travellers, and were in consequence obliged to put them to death also, some of the bodies were thrown into the bowlee, and the others were slightly buried in a field close by.

Chotee claimed a share for that part of their gangs which had gone on to Chandore, as well as for that which had come with him; and Omrow claimed an equal share for all the thirty Kuboolas whom he had consented to send on in advance, that they might not by their blunders frustrate our designs upon the treasure bearers. After a good deal of dispute it was settled that those who were actually present, should all share alike without distinction of rank or office; and that those who belonged to absent parties might share what they got with them or not as they pleased. According to this arrangement each man got of gold one hundred and twenty-five rupees worth. Omrow's seventy men afterwards shared with the thirty Kuboolas: and Chotee's party went and shared what they got with the men at Chandore.

Q.—And you think the *Chimmama* was sent to

you by *Davey* to induce you all to stay and share in this booty?

Feringeea. — Undoubtedly; every one now admits it, but at the time they were all mad!

Q.—Why did they not diverge immedietely from the Malagow road?

Feringeea.—It is all a horrid Jungle, and there is no road right or left till you get to **Malagow.** We had intended to go the straight road to the Kopurgow through Malagow.

Q.—Who were the three travellers that joined you?

Feringeea.—Two were weavers, and one a dawk hurcara.

Q.—How was the Dhoree affair managed.

Feringeea.—We were a gang of about one hundred and fifty Thugs from Hindostan; in the month of January, 1829, near Chopra, on the bank of the Taptee river, under Khoseeala, alias Rymoo, executed afterwards at Dholeea in Khandiesh. Bhujjoo, executed at Saugor, 1832, and Persaud Musulman, executed at Indore, 1829, when the seven treasure bearers came up on their way from Bombay to Indore. We followed them with a select party from all the gangs on the Dhoree, and thence through the Dholeebaree pass, where they spoke with Dusrut Naek, the officer of the police guard, stationed at that pass. While they rested here, one of the seven, without our scouts perceiving it, went on in advance towards Godurghat, which is about four cose distant. When they had left the guard we continued to follow, and on passing the guard we were questioned, by Dusrut Neak, and we told him that we were government servants on our way home on furlough. About half way between this pass and Godurghat we came up with the treasure bearers, and strangled them; but to our surprise we found only six instead of seven. Heera and three others were instantly sent on after the other but they could not find him, and we hastily threw the bodies into a nalah and made off with the booty.

The man who had gone on in advance, finding that his companions did not come up so soon as he expected, returned to look after them, and met a traveller, who told him that he had seen some dead bodies in a nalah by the side of the road; going to the place described he found that they were the bodies of his companions, and reported the circumstance to Dusrut Neak, who sent information to Captain Hodges, the acting magistrate in Khandeish, and set out with all his men in pursuit of us. Captain Hodges with his mounted police, succeeded in seizing thirteen or fourteen of our party who had separated and lost their road in the jungles. They had with them the greater part of the booty, which we in consequence lost. Of these men four contrived to get released, and the rest were either hung at Dholeea or sent to the black water. Only three of the bags of pearls were brought off, one by Purumna, who honestly shared it on his return with the rest of the gang who escaped; and two by Bhujjoo, alias Sooper Sing and Rae Sing, who were lately hung at Saugor, and who could never be prevailed upon to give up any share.

Q.—When you have a poor traveller with you, or a party of travellers who appear to have little property about them, and you hear or see a very good omen, do you not let them go, in the hope that the virtue of the omen will guide you to better prey?

Dorgha, Musulman. — Let them go! never, never; *kubhee nuheen, kubhee nuheen.*

Nasir, Musulman, of Telingana.—How could we let them go? Is not the good omen the order from Heaven to kill them, and would it not be disobedience to let them go? If we did not kill them, should we ever get any more travellers?

Feringeea, Brahmun.—I have known the experiment tried with good effect. I have known travellers who promised little let go, and the virtue of the omen brought better.

Inacnt, Musulman.—Yes, the virtue of the omen remains, and the traveller who has little should be let go, for you are sure to get a better.

Sahib Khan, of Telingana.—Never! never! This is one of your Hindostanee heresies. You could never let him go without losing all the fruits of your expedition. You might get property, but it could never do you any good. No success could result from your disobedience.

Morlee, Rajpoot.—Certainly not! the travellers who are in our hands when we have a good omen must never be let go, whether they promise little or much; the omen is unquestionably the order, as Nasir says.

Nasir.—The idea of securing the good will of *Davey* by disobeying her order is quite monstrous. We Duckun Thugs do not understand how you got hold of it. Our ancestors were never guilty of such folly.

Feringeea.—You do not mean to say that we of Murnae and Sindouse were not as well instructed as you of Telingana?

Nasir and *Sahib Khan.*—We only mean to say that you have clearly mistaken the nature of a good omen in this case. It is the order of *Davey* to take what she has put in our way: at least so we, in the Duckun, understand it.

Q.—How did you manage the Shikarpore affair?

Inaent.—Our gang consisted of one hundred and twenty-five Thugs under,

Noor Khan, hung this year at Jubulpore.

Bhudae, lately arrested at Kotah.

Gholab Khan, hung at Saugor 1832.

Hyput, aprover.

Other Jemadars and myself were encamped in the grove near the town of Sehora in this, the Jubulpore district, in March, 1816, when the Resident of Nagpore passed on his way from Nagpore to Bundelcund.* We had heard of his approach with a large escort and determined to join his party in the hope of picking up some travellers, as in the time of the Pindaries, travellers of respectability generally took advantage of such opportunities to travel with greater security. Our gang separated into small parties, who mixed themselves up with the Resident's parties at different places along the road, without appearing to know any thing of each other; and pretended to be like others glad of the occasion to travel securely. When the Resident reached Belehree some of our parties stated, that, as the Resident was going the western road by Rewah, they had better go the northern by Powae, as there was no longer any danger from Pindaries, and, by separating from so large an escort, they should get provisions much cheaper; that water was now becoming scarce on the western road, and was always made dirty by the elephants and camels. Other parties pretended to argue against this, but at last to yield to the strong reasons assigned. We had by this time become very

* This was Major Close, on his way from Poona to Gwalior, to take charge of his office as Resident, in 1816.

intimate with a party of travellers from Nagpore,
consisting of eighteen men, seven women, and two
boys. They heard our discussions, and declared
in favour of the plan of separating from the Resident's party, and going the northern road through
Shikarpore and Powae.

On reaching Shikarpore, three cose this side of
Powae, we sent on Kunhey and Mutholee to select
a place for the murder, and they chose one on the
bank of the river in an extensive jungle that lay
between us and Powae. We contrived to make
the party move off about midnight persuading
them that it was near morning; and on reaching
the place appointed they were advised to sit down
and rest themselves. All our parties pretended to
be as much deceived as themselves with regard to
the time; but not more than half of the travellers
could be prevailed upon to sit down and rest in such
a solitude. The signal was given, and all, except
the two boys, were seized and strangled by the
people who had been appointed for the purpose,
and were now at their posts ready for action. The
boys were taken by Jowahir and Kehree, who
intended to adopt them as their sons; and the
bodies of the twenty-five persons were all thrown
into a ditch, and covered over with earth and
bushes. On seeing the bodies thrown into the
ditch, Jowahir's boy began to cry bitterly; and
finding it impossible to pacify him or to keep him
quiet, Jowahir took him by the legs, dashed out his
brains against a stone, and left him lying on the
ground, while the rest were busily occupied in
collecting the booty. Going on to Powae we purchased five rupees worth of sugar to celebrate this
event; and without halting we went on to the
village of Choumooka in Punna. After resting till

midnight we went on to Tigura, in Jytpore, where
where we ate the sugar, and then set out the same
day for Huttah.

A fisherman going to the river to fish, soon after
we had left the scene of the murders, found the
body of the boy lying by the stone against which
his head had been beaten ; and he gave information to
Thakur Burjore Sing of Powae, who proceeded to
the place with some of his followers, and discovered all the other bodies lying in the ditch. He
collected all the men he could, and following our
traces which were still fresh, he came up with us
as we were washing ourselves in a stream within
the boundaries of the village of Tigura. We formed
ourselves into a compact body, and retired upon
the village of Tigura. The Thakur repeatedly
charged in upon us, and seeing Hyput Jamadar
pierced through the chest with a spear, and Bhugwan receive a sabre cut in the face, we dispersed
and made for the village of Tigura in the best way
we could. The villagers all came to our support,
and defended us against the Thakur ; but he had
already secured Husun Khan, who afterwards died
at home, Imam Buksh, alias Kosula, who was
hung in Khandiesh in 1829, Shumshera, who was
hung at Saugor in 1832, and Bahadera, who is
now in service at Hingolee.

The Tigura people tempted by the promise of
part of our booty, protected us all that day and
night ; and in the morning escorted us to Simareea,
where a promise of all the booty that we had left,
secured us a safe retreat till the pursuit was over,
in spite of all that the Thakur could say or do.

The Thakur took all his prisoners to the governor general's agent, Mr. Wauchope, before whom
Bahadera confessed, and stated all the circumstan-

ces as they occurred; but being afterwards told that it was the practice of the English to hang all who confessed, and to release all who denied, he soon denied stoutly all that he had said, and pretended to know nothing at all about the murders; and being made over to the magistrate, they were all released for want of evidence. Ram Buksh Tumbolee came from Nagpore to the Agent, Mr. Wauchope, in the hope of recovering his child, who was the boy that was killed by Jowahir.*

Q.—What became of Jowahir?

Inaent.—He was the Jowahir Kusbatee the Brahmun, who was hung at Saugor, 1832. He had settled on the Norbudda river.

Q.—What became of Kehree?

Inaent.—Kehree was the father of Sewa, approver, and he was hung at Jubulpore in 1831. He named the boy Gunesha, and kept him at home to look after his cattle. Kehree's widow is now here with her son Sewa; and I heard her some time ago lamenting the death of Gunesha, and performing funeral ceremonies. The boy was a Brahmun and died at Kehree's home.

Q.—Where is Bahadera?

Inaent.—The last time I saw him was about ten years ago, when he was a Sipahee in the 1st battalion of a brigade of five battalions at Aurungabad. He had given up Thuggee, and never, that we know of, returned to it; but he was still our friend.

Q.—You told Mr. Johnstone the traveller, while he was at Saugor, that the operations of your trade were to be seen in the caves of Ellora?

Feringeea.—All! Every one of the operations is to be seen there: in one place you see men

---

* This is all strictly true.

strangling : in another burying the bodies; in another carrying them off to the graves. There is not an operation in Thuggee that is not exhibited in the caves of Ellora.

Dorgha.—In those caves are to be seen the operations of every trade in the world.

Chotee.—Whenever we passed near, we used to go and see these caves. Every man will there find his trade described, however secret he may think it; and they were all made in one night.

Q.—Does any person beside yourselves consider that any of those figures represent Thugs?

Feringeea.—No body else; but all Thugs know that they do. We never told any body else what we thought about them. Every body there can see the secret operations of his trade, but he does not tell others of them; and no other person can understand what they mean. They are the works of God. No human hands were employed upon them. That every body admits.

Q.—What particular operations are there described in figures?

Sahib Khan.—I have seen the Sotha (inveigler) sitting upon the same carpet with the traveller, and in close conversation with him, just as we are when we are worming out their secrets. In another place the strangler has got his roomal over his neck, and is strangling him; while another, the Chumochee, is holding him by the legs. These are the only two operations that I have seen described.

Nasir.—These I have also seen, and there is no mistaking them. The Chumochee has close hold of the legs, and is pulling at them *thus*, while the Bhurtote is tightening the roomal round his neck, *thus!*

Q.—Have you seen no others?

Feringeea.—I have seen these two, and also the Lughas carrying away the bodies to the grave, *in this manner*, and the sextons digging the grave with the sacred pick-axe: all is done just as if we had ourselves done it; nothing could be more exact.

Q.—And who do you think could have executed this work?

Feringeea.—It could not have been done by Thugs, because they would never have exposed the secrets of their trade; and no other human being could have done it. It must be the work of the Gods: human hands could never have performed it.

Q.—And supposing so, you go and worship it?

Sahib Khan.—No. We go to gratify curiosity, and not to worship; we look upon it as a Mausoleum, a collection of curious figures cut by some demons, who knew the secrets of all mankind, and amused themselves here in describing them.

Hurnagur.—We Hindoos go for the same purpose. We never go to worship. We consider it as a Pantheon of unknown Gods.

Q.—Relate the circumstances of the Chaleesrooh affair?

Kuleean Sing.—In the year that Mr. Jenkins went as Resident to Nagpore through Benares and Sumbulpore, this affair took place. He had just encamped near the Seetabuldee hill when we passed through Nagpore. (February, 1807.)

Dorgka.—The roads from the Duckun across the Nurbudda, had become so unsafe from the Pindaries that all travellers from Poona, Hyderabad, and Nagpore, going towards the Ganges, went by way of Surgooja and Sumbulpore; and several of

our gangs that went from Bundelcund and the
Dooab to that road came back with immense booty
for several years. In the rains preceding this affair
it was determined that all the gangs should take
that direction; and we accordingly set out. There
were more than forty Jemadars of note; among
them Bukshee Jemadar, whose head Doctor Spry
sent to England, and Ghasee Subahdar; and many
others of equal note. We set out from our respective homes after the Dushera in October, (1806)
passed through Mirzapore, in order to make our
votive offerings at the temple of *Davey* at Bindachul, and rendezvoused at Ruttunpore in the Surgooja district, where we were assembled above six
hundred Thugs. From Ruttunpore we went to
Tukutpore, where we murdered a good many
travellers who took up their quarters in our several
places of encampment. All pretended to have been
on furlough and to be returning from Hindostan to
different armies in the Duckun, with some of our
relations and friends as young recruits. On the
third day a female of rank came up. Her husband
had been an officer in the Nagpore service, and
being left a widow by his death at Nagpore, she
was on her way home to her friends with her
deceased husband's brother. She occupied a tent,
and was accompanied by a slave girl, and had
twelve armed men as a guard. She left Tukutpore the morning after her arrival, and was followed
by a detachment from every one of our gangs,
making a party of one hundred and sixty Thugs,
under some of our best leaders. For several days
they followed them without finding a convenient
opportunity of disposing of them, till they reached
the village of Choora, between which place and

16*

the village of Sutrunja the road passed through an extensive jungle, without a village on either side for many miles. Leaving this place in the morning they put the whole party to death, and buried their bodies in a nalah. I did not go with this party.

When they set out after the widow, we all proceeded towards Nagpore; and on reaching Lahnjee, a party of sixty Thugs remained there, while the rest went on towards Nagpore. I remained with the sixty at Lahnjee, and two days after the main body had left us, a party of forty travellers came up on their way to the Ganges; thirty-one men, seven women, and two girls. The greater part of these people were from Ellichpore; the rest from Nagpore. Our Jemadars soon became intimate with the principal men of this party, pretended to be going to the same parts of India, and won their confidence; and the next day we set out with them, and in four days reached Ruttunpore, where we met the party of one hundred and sixty Thugs returning after the murder of the widow and her party. They did not, however, appear to be known to us. Soon after, two hundred of the main body, who had gone on towards Nagpore from Lahnjee, came up, having heard of the forty travellers soon after they left us; and all pretended to be going the same road, without appearing to have any acquaintance with each other. It was, however, agreed that sixty, of the one hundred and sixty, should go on and rejoin the party who had proceeded to Nagpore, leaving three hundred and sixty to dispose of this party.

From Ruttunpore, we proceeded with the party of travellers to the village of Choora, whence we sent on people to select a proper place for the murder. They chose one not far from that in which the widow and her party had been put to death. Durroo and Sheera were sent on to the village of Sutrunja to see that all was clear in front; and about a watch and half before daylight we set out with the travellers, leaving scouts behind to see that we were not interrupted from the rear. By the time we reached the appointed place the Bhurtotes and Shumseeas had all on some pretext or other got close by the side of the persons whom they were appointed to strangle; and on reaching the spot the signal was given in several places at the same time, and thirty-eight out of forty were seized and strangled. The daughter of Gunga Tewaree was a very handsome young woman, and Punchum, one of our Jemadars, wished to preserve her as a wife for his son Bukholee. But when she saw her mother and father strangled, she screamed, and beat her head against the stony ground, and tried to kill herself. Punchum tried in vain to quiet her, and promised to take great care of her, and marry her to his own son who would be a great chief; but all was in vain. She continued to scream, and at last Punchum put the roomal round her neck and strangled her. The widow of Alfie's brother was strangled, but her daughter, a girl about three years of age, was preserved by Kosul Jemadar, who married her to his own son Hunnee Rae Brahmum, by whom she had two sons, one of whom is still living, and about ten or eleven years of age. Since the death of Kosul and Hunnee Rae she has lived with her husband's mother.

We buried all the bodies in a nalah, and got property to the value of about seventeen thousand rupees, which we took on with us and divided at

Sutrunja.   After this affair we returned home through Rewah and Chitterkote, the place where we had murdered the sixty persons at one time about two years before.   The widow of Hunnee Rae often heard, after she grew up, of the Chalees-rooh affair in which her mother and uncle were strangled; and she has herself told you all she knows about it.

Q.—What became of Punchum?

Dorgha.—Punchum died before we reached home.

Q.—Had Punchum any sons?

Inaent.—Punchum had Chunderbhan, who died on a Thug expedition; Bhugholee, hung at Gwalior by Jacob Sahib; Jowahir who died in Gwalior; Odeebhan hung in Khandiesh, 1829—and Mollo who died in the Nursingpore jail.

Q.—And Kosul, what became of him?

Dorgha.—Kosul Subahdar died at his home: he had two sons—Ajeeta who was transported from Saugor, 1832, and Rawut Rae who died last year in the Saugor jail.   Hunnee Rae was the son of his brother, but he had adopted him.

Q.—How long had you given up Thuggee before you were seized?

Dorgha.—Soon after the Moghalanee affair 1821. Saugor and all the countries along the Nurbudda through which we used to pass in going to the Duckun were taken by the Company, and as we were constantly liable to be detained and asked a number of questions, I thought I had better give up Thuggee, otherwise I and my children might some day get hung or sent to the black water.   I accordingly entered the service of Bebee Knox, who resides in the Orderly Bazar at Cawnpore, and has some thirty-two villages purchased at auction, and thirteen bungalows at that station. I became one of her confidential servants, and was employed in bring her rents from her native collectors of the villages. Colonel Knox died, I believe at Futtehgur, about the year that Saugor was taken, but I never saw him. I had served her for nearly twelve years when you sent for me, and she and all the people had become attached to me, and you know what difficulty you had to get me away.

Q.—And during this time you never went on Thuggee?

Dorgha.—Never.

Q.—But your brother Kohman went, though he was in the same service.

Dorgha.—True he went, but it was very seldom that he could be persuaded to join the gangs. He went only after long intervals, and was never long absent at a time.

Q.—I thought Hindoos never strangled women. How came Punchum to strangle this girl?

Feringeea.—Punchum was my mother's brother, and he never strangled her!

Q.—Who did?

Feringeea.—I have heard that it was Bhugwan Kachee, a slave or disciple of his.

Punna.—But is not the act of the slave the act of the master? and did not Bhugwan strangle her by Punchum's order?

Feringeea.—Well, but how was Punchum punished! did he not die before he could reach home; and was not his son Bughola hung the November following, with twenty others, whom Jacob Sahib strung up at Kalapaharee in Gwalior? and was not Bhugwan hung with him—and what a horrid death did Himmut **die**? He was eaten alive by the worms!

Dorgha.—I myself saw Punchum strangle the young woman. Bhugwan may have assisted.

Q.—How did Jacob Sahib seize and convict this gang?

Dhorgha.—After the Surgooja affair in the month of October, a body of thirty or forty Thugs from Murnae and Sindouse, on passing near Kala-paharee, murdered three men; and soon after one of the party flogged a boy whom he had picked up some where and adopted: the boy went off to Jacob Sahib, told of the murder, and pointed out the bodies; and he seized them, and hung up twenty-one at four different places along the road.

Ameer Alee.—I. was with that party. It was some years after the Surgooja expedition. I forget the name of the boy, but he belonged to Bukshee Jemadar, whose head is gone to Europe. I was employed to go forward and back with messages from the arrested Thugs to their families and friends. Large sums were offered to Jacob Sahib for their ransom, but he would not let them go: one day I found some of them hanging upon trees, and got too much frightened to return.

Q.—You were in the Chitterkote, or as you call it, the Surtrooh (sixty soul) affair. Pray tell me what you recollect of it?

Dorgha.—After the capture of Gawilgur by General Wellesley (Duke of Wellington*) it was restored to the Nagpore Rajah, who appointed Ghureeb Sing to the command of the fortress. Anxious to get some good soldiers from Hindostan

---

* Gawilgur was taken December, 1803. This affair must have taken place 1805.

to garrison it, he sent his younger brother Ghyan
Sing, with a number of followers, and a large sum
of money, to raise them in the Oude country and
districts between the Ganges and Jumna rivers.

Ghyan Sing and his party passed through Nagpore, and came to Jubulpore in the month of June,
while we were there concentrated from the different parts into which we had extended our expeditions that season. His party consisted of fifty-two
men, seven women, and a Brahmun boy, then
about four years of age. Some of our gangs
lodged in the town, some in the cantonments,
among the troops, and some were encamped at the
tank of Adhar, two or three miles from the town
on the road to Mirzapore. As soon as we heard
of the arrival of this party from the Duckun, every
party of Thugs deputed some of its most respectable members to mix with them in the town, and
win their confidence. At first they tried to separate them into different parties to proceed by
different roads, but though they had collected
together at different times and places on the road,
it was found impossible to separate any part of
them from Ghyan Sing; and we agreed to unite
all our gangs, and to lead the party by the most
unfrequented roads till we might find a place convenient for the murder of the whole at once.

On reaching Sehora we persuaded them to quit
the high road through Belehree and Myhere, and
take that through Chundeea and the old fort of
Bundoogur, which leads through very extensive
tracts of jungle, and uninhabited country. We
went with them through all this country however
without finding what we considered a fitting time
and place, and reached Rewah winning more and
more upon their confidence every day. From

Rewah we went to Simareea, and from that place
to a small village half way to Chitterkoke, called
by us the Burwala Gow, from a large Bur tree
that stood near it.   Thence we sent on people as
usual to select a place for the murder, and they
found one about two cose and a half distant, in a
very extensive jungle, without a human habitation
for many miles on either side.   We persuaded the
party to set out soon after midnight; and as they
went along we managed to take our appointed
places, two Thugs by every traveller, and the rest
in parties of reserve at different intervals along the
line, every two managing to keep the person they
were appointed to kill, in conversation.   On reaching the place chosen, the signal was given at
several different places, beginning with the rear
party and passing on to that in front; and all were
seized and strangled except the boy.   It was now
near morning, and too late to admit of the bodies
being securely buried; we made a temporary
grave for them in the bed of the river, covered
them over with sand, and went on with the boy
and the booty to Chitterkoke, intending to send
back a large party the next night, and have the
bodies securely buried.   The rains had begun to
set in, and after the murders it rained very heavily
all the day.   The party however went back, but
found that the river had risen and washed away
all the bodies except two or three, which they
found exposed, and pushed into the stream to follow the rest.*

Q.—What became of the boy?

Dorgha.—He was brought up by Mungul Brahmun, the brother of Laljoo, and having taken to

---

* This is a very correct statement of the case.

the trade of Thuggee, he was last year sent to the black water from Saugor.

Q.—What became of Mungul and Laljoo?

Dorgha.—They both died in a village in Bhopaul where they had settled.

Q.—Chotee—You were with the party arrested by Major Henley in March, 1832, I believe?

Chotee.—Yes: we had killed five Sipahees a little on this side of Ashta, and having put them into a temporary grave, we went on, leaving nine men to bury them securely the next night. They were seized, and a party was sent after us. We were all taken, a party of sixty-three, and brought to Sehore where we were detained some days, and then sent to Mr. Maddock at Saugor. He sent us to Mr. Robinson at Cawnpore, where we were all released immediately.

Q.—Were the bodies discovered?

Chotee.—I believe so, but it was not for that affair that we were arrested. Bechoo and his party had killed three months before a Jemadar of Hurcaras, whom the Nowab of Bhopaul had sent to escort his gang from the city of Bhopaul to Major Henley's camp. They strangled him on the road, and made off. We could tell Major Henley nothing about this affair, and he sent us out of the country.

Q.—Thakur Persaud was with that gang I believe?

Thakur Persaud.—Yes, I was in that gang with Bechoo. We were a party of about forty Thugs, and in the city of Bhopaul we were taken up by the Nowab's people on suspicion and sent to Major Henley the Agent, who lived three stages off at Sehore. He was at the time out on his circuit. One Jemadar of Hurcaras was sent with us, and

at a place about a cose and a half from the village
of Kuttora he was strangled by Hindoo Aheer
Jemadar, who was hung at Indore 1829, and his
body was thrown into a nalah where it lay concealed in the long grass.   We went on to Sohud,
about eighteen cose from Ojeyn, where we murdered four people, and got a booty that gave to
each man a quarter of a seer of gold: it was
fifteen years ago.

Q.—Were you not of the party arrested by
Captain Waugh at Kotah in the beginning of 1822 ?

Hurnagur.—Yes, we had killed two Suraffs at
Patun, and were forty-four of us arrested in the
beginning of that year, a day or two after Feringea's gang had been released with their faces
smutted over.   Our affair of the Suraffs had not
been discovered, and we were arrested on the sup-
position that we were part of his gang who had
been concerned in the murder of the cloth merchants at Kunwas.   We were made to work on
the roads about Major Caulfield's house at Kotah
for four years and half, when he ordered us to be
released.   There were two Koeleea Thugs confined with us at the same time—Imma Khan and
Soobratee.

Q.—What has become of all these forty-four
men ?

Hurnagur.—There are only seven surviving
and still at large.   Some have died, some been
hung, some sent to the black water, and some are
here in prison.   Bhimmee Jemadar has told Mr.
McLeod all about them.   He has put all their
names in a book.

10th JULY, 1835.—PRESENT, FERINGEEA BRAHMUN—AND
MUDAR BUKSH, DORGHA, KAEM KHAN, MUSULMANS.

Q.—Where did you fall in with the Moghulanee?

Feringeea.—My gang consisted of about fifty
persons, and returning from Joudpore to Chourcoo
we fell in with the Moghulanee. It was the year
before Ashraf Khan Subahdar Major and his
party were murdered.* We came on to Madhoorajpore, where we fell in with the brother of a
Kuptan in the Kuroulee Rajah's service, bringing
from the Po'kar fair a fine young horse for the
Rajah. We set out before daylight with him and
his party, put them to death and buried their bodies
about a cose distant, and came on nine cose to
Charsoo.

Q—And what became of the young woman?

Feringeea.—We left her behind as we had no
designs upon her; but she followed, and lodged in
the Surae while we encamped on the bank of the
Tank. The next day we came to Duolutpore,
where we lodged with some of our Sooseea Thug
friends, and the Moghulanee still followed, and
lodged in the Bazar. Six of our Sooseea friends
joined us here, and came on with us to Lalsont.
I had tried to shake off the Moghulanee, but soon
after our arrival she came up.

Q.—Where did you fall in with the Musulman
party?

Feringeea.—At Lolsont. Baz Khan, Zalim,
Bhimmee, Dorgha and their gangs, amounting to
one hundred and twenty-five Thugs, came up from
Ameergur.

Q.—What had you been doing at Ameergur?

* Ashraf Khan was murdered 1822, February.

Dorgha.—We were a large gang on our way from Ajmere to Neemuch, and having killed a good many people on the way, we reached Ameergur with a Musulman traveller, who had joined us during the last stage. Two shop-keepers came up from the Mow cantonments and lodged in our camp, and about nine o'clock at night they were all three strangled, and their bodies were wrapped up like bundles of cloth and taken by five *Lughas* to the Jheel, to the south west corner of the Fort. We were encamped on the west side. It was a moonlight night in March, and some people on the bastion saw them, and came down to see what they were about. Two out of the five men ran into our camp, and three fled in the opposite direction. The four men from the Fort, without examining the bundles, followed the two men into our camp, and demanded the thieves. They were four Meena police men, and they declared that they had seen five men making off with bundles of clothes, and as they ran into our camp, they insisted upon our giving them up. I addressed those about me in Rumasee and proposed to strangle the whole four. Punna, approver, and Molloo, lately transported, seconded me, and our roomals were ready, when the Jemadars said that it could be of no use, as others must have seen the *Lughas* at the same time, and we should have them down upon us before we could dispose of the bodies. I then told the Meenas that I could not believe them unless they showed me the bundles. They offered to do so, and we proceeded on half way to the spot, which gave the gangs time to get ready to be off, when I pretended that I was afraid to go with them alone, and would go back for my sword, and a friend or two. They went on to the bundles, and I returned to our camp.

We all made off by different roads having agreed to re-unite at Chouroo, and travelled all night and all the next day; as we met a regiment of cavalry soon after leaving camp, on their way from Ajmere to either Neemuch or Mow. We were all re-united at Chouroo five or six days after, and there we rested and divided the booty. Molloo pretended that he had thrown away in his flight all the valuables that he got from the two shop-keepers; but we suspected him. The booty acquired from eight men murdered by our different parties in their flight, was here divided with what we got from the Musulman at Ameergur.

Q.—But where did you fall in with Feringeea and the Moghulanee?

Dorgha.—We fell in with them at Lalsont and came on with them to Somp.

Q.—Who were with her?

Dorgha.—She had an old female servant, mounted upon a pony, one armed man servant, and six bearers for her palankeen. From Somp we sent on men to select a place for the murder, and set out with her before daylight; but the Belha, in the dark, lost the road, and we were trying to find it when the young woman beuame alarmed, and began to reproach us for taking her into the jungle in the dark. We told Feringeea to come up and quiet her, but dreading that some of her party might make off, the signal was given, and they were all strangled.

Q.—What did you get from them?

Dorgha.—Six hundred rupees worth of property.

Q.—And was this enough to tempt so large a gang to murder a beautiful young woman?

Dorgha.—We were very averse to it, and often

17*

said that we should not get two rupees a piece, and that she ought to be let go; but Feringeea insisted upon our *taking* her.

Q.—How did you advise the murder of a young woman like this?

Feringeea.—It was her fate to die by our hands. I had several times tried to shake them off before we met the Musulmans, and when we came to Lalsont I told her that she must go on, as I had joined some old friends, and should be delayed. She then told me that I must go to her home with her near Agra, or she would get me into trouble; and being a Brahmun while she was a Musulman, I was afraid that I should be accused of improper intercourse, and turned out of cast.

Q.—But you might have gone another road?

Dorgha.—He could not, as he had before told her that he was going to her village of Ateer near Agra; and had he left her, she might have suspected us, and got us all seized as bad characters. Khoda Buksh was placed by her as Sotha, and she told him that the young Subahdar, meaning Feringeea, should go to her home with her.

Q.—Why did she call him Subahdar?

Dorgha.—We all called him Subahdar at that time, because his cousin, Aman, was one of our Subahdars; and because he was a handsome young man, and looked like a man of rank, which was useful to us.

Q.—Had any thing improper taken place between him and the young woman?

Dorgha.—Certainly not, or we could never have killed her; but he had a good deal of conversation with her, and she had taken a great fancy to him. She was very fair and beautiful, and we should never have killed her had he not urged us to do so.

Khoda Buksh who died lately in the Saugor jail, and whose brother Rostum is with Mr. Wilson, told us that we must either kill her or let Feringeea go on with her. He would not consent to this, and we agreed to kill her.

Q.—Who strangled her?

Dorgha.—Madar Buksh, while Khoda Buksh held her down, and Feringeea assisted in pulling her from her palankeen.

Feringeea.—Dorgha knows this to be false and that I was not in sight at the time.

Dorgha.—I know we called you to pacify her when she got alarmed, and I think I saw you assisting.

Q.—Did you strangle the young woman?

Madar Buksh.—I did.

Q.—Did Feringeea assist?

Madar Buksh.—No.

Q.—You were then a young man, and she was a beautiful young woman: had you no pity?

Madar Buksh.—I had, but I had undertaken the duty, and we must all have food. I have never known any other means of gaining it.

Feringeea.—We all feel pity sometimes, but the goor of the Tuponee changes our nature. It would change the nature of a horse. Let any man once taste of that goor, and he will be a Thug though he know all the trades and have all the wealth in the world. I never wanted food; my mother's family was opulent, her relations high in office. I have been high in office myself, and became so great a favourite wherever I went that I was sure of promotion: yet I was always miserable while absent from my gang, and obliged to return to Thuggee. My father made me taste of that fatal goor when I was yet a mere boy; and if I were to live a thousand years I should never be able to follow any other trade.

Q.—Did you hear any thing about the bodies and the men from the fort of Ameergur?

Dorgha.—We heard afterwards from travellers that they were taken to Neemuch, and charged themselves with the murder and punished.

Q.—And you went after this into service at Cawnpore?

Dorgha.—Yes; I took lands at rent in the village of the Bebee and entered her service?

Q.—Who was this Moghulanee whom you killed?

Feringeea.—She had belonged to the family of Akoo Meean, the brother of Nowab Ameer Khan, but having eloped she went to the Neemuch cantonments, whence she was now on her way to the village of Ateer near Agra.

Q.—You Kaem Khan, were with Rostum and Khoda Buksh in the Dhosa affair. Relate what you recollect of it?

Kaem Khan.—We were on our way from Madhoorajpore to Gwalior, a gang of about forty Thugs in the month of March, ten years ago, when we fell in with Bunseelal, the son of Bhujunlal, and Cotwal of Sopur. He was a lad of about seventeen years of age, and had with him two Brahmuns, one Rajpoot Sepahee and a servant of the Jat cast, and was going to Rewaree to fetch his bride. One of the Brahmuns had come from Rewaree to accompany him. They came and took up their quarters in the same Surae with us, and we pretended to be going the same road. The next morning we went on with them to Lolsont, where we again lodged together in the Surae of Kosul Bhuteeara. The following day we went on to Ramgur with them, and thence Bikka Jemadar went on to select a place for the murder, but he came back without finding one that pleased him, and the day after we went on together to Dhosa. We had now become very intimate with the boy and his party, who told us all their secrets. The boy lodged in the shop of a Buneeh who had been long in league with us, while we lodged in the Surac at Dhosa, and in the afternoon Bikka went on again to select a bele. He chose one in the bed of a nalah a cose and a half distant, and the five stranglers having been appointed, we set out with the boy and his party long before daylight the next morning. On reaching the place appointed, they were persuaded to sit down and rest themselves. The boy sat with one of the Brahmuns upon a carpet that we had spread for him, and the other three attendants sat down upon the sand at a little distance from them. A *Shumseea* took his seat by the side of each of the five, and the *Bhurtotes* stood each behind his intended victim. The signal was given by Rostum Khan, and all five were immediately strangled, the boy himself by Bhikka Jemadar, who is still at large, while his hands were held by his brother Chunda. The bodies were buried in the bed of the nalah. While they were strangling them, the fine mare on which the youth rode ran off, and while we were engaged in recovering her, Chunda made off with a purse of gold Mohurs, which he found in the boy's waist-band.

Q.—Did you not return to Doosa soon after and heard the boy's friends searching for him ?

Kaem Khan.—Yes ; we came back to Doosa some time after and heard from our friends the shop-keepers, that the bodies had been dug up by

Jackals, and that the friends of the murdered youth were then at Doosa inquiring about him. Going to Surae we found the uncle of the youth sitting on a Chubootra in front of the door, weeping and lamenting the loss of his nephew.

Q.—Did not the father die of grief soon after?

Kaem Khan.—Yes. He could never be persuaded to eat any thing after he learnt the fate of his only son, and soon died. This we afterwards learned from the people of Sooper who still recollect the circumstance of the loss of the son and death of old Cotwal.*

PRESENT THUKOREE, FERINGEEA, DORGHA, INAENT, LALMUN, KHARUDEE, NUNDUN.

Q.—You were, I believe, Thukoree, among the Thugs arrested after the murder of Lieut. Monsell in the end of 1812?

Thukoree Aheer.—I was, and we were kept in prison thirteen months and horribly maltreated.

Q.—What made them maltreat you?

Thukoree.—To get money from us.

Q.—Then those who paid were of course well treated and released?

Thukoree.—Not so; those who could not pay were beaten in hopes that their friends would in time pay; and those who paid, were beaten in hopes that their friends would be made in time to pay more.

Q.—I understand that some forty Thugs died from the beating, and confinement?

Thukoree.—No; not from the beatings; forty or more died, but they were all killed by a great

* All that is here stated is strictly true.

demon that every night visited our prison and killed or tortured some one.

All.—Yes; that demon is well remembered to this day, we have all heard him a hundred times described by the survivors.

Thukoree.—I saw him only once myself. I was awake while all the rest were asleep; he came in at the door, and seemed to swell as he came in till his head touched the roof, and the roof was very high, and his bulk became enormous. I prostrated myself, and told him that " he was our Purmesur, " (Great God) and we poor helpless mortals depend- " ing entirely upon his will." This pleased him, and he passed by me; but took such a grasp at the man Mungulee, who slept by my side, that he was seized with spasms all over from the nape of the neck to the sole of his foot.

Q.—Was this the way they all died ?

Thukoree.—Yes; this was his mode of annoying them, and but few survived. They all died like Mungulee. They had rheumatic pains and spasms all over, and the prison was for a long time visited by him every night.

Q.—Was it in the cold and rainy season ?

Thukoree.—We were in more than a whole year, but this spirit came most often in the cold and rainy weather.

Q.—Who seized you ?

Thukoree.—We were seized by Komere and Puhar, *Kuckwahas,* and Dureear the *Rathore,* Zumeendars.

Feringeea.—Yes; and not a soul of their families are now left to pour the libation at their funeral obsequies !

Thukoree.—Yes; they were severely punished afterwards for giving us so much annoyance.

Q.—By whom ?

Thukoree.—By *Davey.*

Q.—How many were you ?

Thukoree.—We were one hundred and thirty-three seized, at the requisition of the Mynporee magistrate, who might have had the whole if he liked, but he wanted only four, and four were sent to him ; but the only evidence against them was Aman, the father of Birjee, who died here in jail after the Lucknadown murders, and he became so much frightened that he let the cup of Ganges water fall out of his hands before the magistrate, who did not in consequence believe him ; and they were all four released, though they were all present at the murder of Lieutenant Monsell. One was Ruttce Ram, who was hung at Indore 1829, and for whom you paid a thousand rupees ; Bukut hung at Saugor 1832; Deena, the father of Munohur, approver, and Hurnam a Zumeendar of Murnae. 129 were kept in confinement, and for each of these men 129 rupees were taken. They got above sixteen thousand rupees. Fourteen thousand of them were paid to the Subah of Nodha Rae Sing, Havildar. The very day that the money was paid into his treasury, his son and a fine horse of his died, and he was himself taken ill. He was summoned to Gwalior, and when he offered the money to Doulut Rae Scindheea, the Bala Bae, the daughter of Madhajee Scindheea, whom he used to consult on all public affairs, told him that her father owed his death to the execution of some of these strange people at Muthura ; and that he had better not meddle with the money that Rae Sing had so foolishly extorted from them ; that it was money acquired by murder, and that those who got it seemed to be under some supernatural influence.

Doulut Rae told Rae Sing to give away all the money in charity, and release the survivors. He did so, but it was too late; his sickness and misery continued and he died. Doulut Rae was the adopted son of **Madhajee Scindheea**; Bala Bae was his real daughter, and a very wise and good woman.

Q.—What made you all go to Nodha?

Thukoree.—Mr. Halhed attacked our villages, and after Lieutenant Monsell had been killed, we did not think ourselves any longer safe. Aman Sing, called the Raw Sahib, was the chief of Nodha, and he would have protected us, as there had been a compact between us and his family; but he had been removed, and **Rae Sing** sent us the Amil.

Q.—What were the villages you occupied in Sindouse, and Murnae?

Thukoree.—We occupied sixteen out of the fifty-two villages of Sursaedhar, and the sixteen villages of Sindouse, most of which we formed and peopled. All these villages are situated in the Delta of the Sinde and the Koharee rivers, near where they join and flow together into the Jumna.

Q.—Whence did you come to occupy these villages?

Thukoree.—The Bursotes and some other of the original **Mahommadan** clans, after trying to establish themselves at Agra, came to Akoopore in the Dooab, and were protected in their vocations for forty years by the Gour Rajah; but he demanding too great a share of the booty, they left his country, and came to Himmutpore on the bank of Jumna, and took up their abode under the protection of the Sengur Raja Juggummum Sa, from whom the fort and town of Juggummunpore derive their name.* He became in time too exorbitant in his demands for a share of the booty, and family after family left his territory, and established themselves in the Purheear, on Sindouse purguna—some occupying old, and some forming new villages, and in time they constituted the entire population of the greater part, cultivating all the lands themselves, and extending their expeditions annually into distant countries. At all these different seats the old clans made new converts from all casts of Hindoos, Brahmuns, Rajpoots, cowherds, shepherds, and others.

Feringeea.—My ancestors were not among the people who came this way to Sindouse. The fort of Sursae was held by Rajahs of the Meoo cast, whence the term Mewatee. The Brahmuns of the village of Tehngoor served them as household priests; and when one of these Meeo Rajahs went to wait upon the Emperor at Delhi, some of these Brahmuns accompanied him, and there they were initiated in the mysteries of Thuggee; and on their return they introduced it among their friends at Murnae and other places in the Sursae or Omuree purguna. Our great progenitors Seeam and Asa went to Murnae to seek employment about seven generations ago, and were there married into the Tehngoorea families, and became initiated in the mysteries of Thuggee, and from that time it has descended without interruption in the family. Every male as he became of age, became a Thug.

Q.—Is this true Kharndee?

---

* From Juggummun Sa there have been, it is said, Pem or Pertab Sa his son, Somere Sa, son of Pem Sa, Rutun Sa, son of Somere Sa, Rukut, son of Rutun, and Muhepat Sa, son of Rukut—the present Rajah, who holds his estate under the Rajah of Jhalone.

Kharndee and *Nundun.*—This has been believed
ever since we can remember, and the Kusbatee
and Porasur Brahmuns in the same way married
into Tehngoorea and Kunouj families, and became
Thugs like themselves.

Thukoree.—The Tehngooreas and Kunouj Brahmans did not certainly come with the emigrants
from Agra. They were in Sursae long before, but
how they got there I know not.

Feringeea.—There was a Rajah of Kuchwaha
who has since become a god. His image is still
worshipped in our village of Murnae. He was the
Rajah of Lahae, and had three sons, Ruttun Sing,
Anoord Sing, and Mehngoo. Mehngoo came to
Roragow, one of the fifty-two villages of Sursae,
and having invited all the Meeo chiefs to a feast
he got them all put to death, and established himself as Rajah, and from that time it became a
Kuchwaha Rajpoot Raj. The Tehngoor Brahmuns served them as they had served the Meoo
Rajahs as household priests. Rutun Sing reigned
over Lalae, Mehngoo over Sursae, and the third
brother over Amaen.

Q.—How came the tax of 24 rupees 8 anas to
be first imposed upon you?

Thukoree.—Thugs had always been obliged to
make occasional presents to the chiefs and heads
of villages under whose protection they resided,
but there was never any fixed rate of payment.
The handsomest horse, sword or ornament, that
they got in an expedition was commonly reserved
for the most powerful patron of the order. At last
two of the ancestors of Feringeea, Hirroulee and
Rae Sing in an expedition to the south across the
Nurbudda river got a booty worth some hundred
and forty thousand rupees. Rae Sing had secreted

one of the diamonds which weighed a rupee, and
in the division of the spoil on their return home a
quarrel ensued. In his rage Rae Sing said to
Hirroulee, " that a man who could not keep his
" mother from the embraces of a tanner of hides
" might be contented with what others chose to
" give him."   Hirroulee had no arms on, but calling upon his friend Telokee Rajpoot for vengeance,
he stabbed Rae Sing in the belly with his spear.
His bowels burst out, but we got a silver plate
applied to the wound and Rae Sing recovered;
but was for a long time obliged to wear the silver
plate.   Rae Sing went to the Rana of Gohud,
from whom he got the farm of the customs for one
hundred and thirty thousand rupees a year, and
the farm of the purguna of Omree or Sursae at
sixty thousand.   He induced the chief of Gohud to
invade Sindouse, which was burned to the ground,
and from that time the Thug families were made
to pay every three years a tax of twenty-five
rupees each. Rae Sing sold the large diamond afterwards for sixty-five thousand rupees; and the rest
of the booty was estimated at sixty-seven thousand.

Hirroulee went off to the Rajah of Rampoora,
Kuleean Sing, and gave him a present of four
thousand rupees to espouse his quarrel. He got in
return the village of Koorcha, granted in rent-free
tenure, and built there a fine well that still goes by
his name.

Q.—And had Hirroulee's mother gone off with
the Chumar?

Feringeea.—It is too true; she went off with
the Chumar, and that crime has accelerated the
ruin of our family.

Q.—When were the Sonars murdered at Murnae ?

Dorgha.—When Rae Sing and Hirroulee brought home the great booty, they sent Dorgha and another Sonar as usual to fetch merchants from Oude to buy it. They came with two merchants and bought a good deal, but Hirroulee's wife wanted to see how we killed people as she had heard a good deal about it, and they were all four strangled for her entertainment I have heard.

Lalmun.—Not so ; I was present on that occasion ; Hirroulee had been dead some time, when the Sonars and two merchants came to buy some of her jewels, which Hirroulee had secreted. They said they had ready money in order to tempt her to sell them cheap, and the widow persuaded some of her friends to kill them. They were strangled and buried, but instead of seven thousand rupees, which the widow expected, we got only seven hundred. The families of the Sonars made a great noise when they could not be found. Kuleean Sing Rajah, of Rampoora, came, and found the bodies, plundered the widow and turned her out naked, and levied a fine from all, saying that now we had begun to murder at home as well as abroad, we were no longer deserving of favour.

Inaent.—I saw the widow afterwards begging her way through Saugor, and she died of starvation at Sehwas in Bhopaul.

Thukoree.—When Sursae and Sindouse came under Gwalior, the Gwalior amil continued to levy the tax upon the Thugs through Laljoo Choudhuree the Zumeendar. He divided them all into families, and each family was rated at twenty-four rupees eight anas every three years, upon which he as collector, got a per centage. But

18*

in his accounts rendered to the amil he inserted, as one family under the ostensible head, many branches who had separated and from whom he levied the tax separately. He therefore collected a great deal more than he accounted for. Laljoo after the murder of Lieut. Monsell, was imprisoned in the Bareilly jail, and was succeeded in the Zumeendaree of Sindouse by his son Suntokerae. The purguna of Sindouse came under the Company's government, but that of Sursea continued under Gwalior.

Sheikh Inaent.—After the attack of Mr. Halhed we thought that part of the country very unsafe, and a great many come off to Bundlecund, and the Bhopaul and Nurbudda districts.

PRESENT INAENT, DIBBA, MIHRBAN, BHEEKUN KHAN AND OTHERS.

Q.—Tell me all you recollect about the expedition in which you were seized, Inaent?

Sheikh Inaent.—After the Dusehra of 1829, several gangs united from different points at the village of Kohpa, between Jubulpore and Banda, about forty from the districts of Futtehgur and Cawnpore under Rambuksh, Mihrban and others, twelve under Bhola Buneea from Jhalone, and twenty-five under myself from Jhansee. We intended to operate that season upon the great road from Mirzapore to Jubulpore, and strike off to that between Saugor and Calpee when necessary. We came on to Shahnagur, and there leaving the main body I came on with Rambuksh, Bhola, and fifteen other Thugs to the village of Pureyna to search for *Bunij*. Here we met two shop-keepers, two blacksmiths and a Musulman trooper, on their way from the Duckun to the Dooab; and having won their confidence in the usual manner we sent them on to our friends with four of our party, and a message to say that they would find them worth taking; at night we rejoined the main body and found Dibba Jemadar entertaining the travellers. We set out the next morning intending to put them to death on the road to Biseynee, but we found so many parties of Brinjaras encamped and moving along that road that we could not manage it. The next morning we went on with them from Biseynee, and at a nalah in the jungle three cose distant we killed them at about eight o'clock in the morning. The bodies were buried under some stones where your people afterwards found them. We returned through Biseynee to Shahnagur, and thence came in upon the great road to Mirzaporee at the village of Sewagunge. In the evening four travellers came up on their way from Jubulpore to Banda, and were persuaded to pass the night with us on the bank of the tank. We were preparing to go on with them after the third watch with the intention of killing them on the road, when we heard the *Duheea* (the call or cry of the hare) a dreadful omen, and we let them go on unmolested.

Soon after four Sipahees of the 73d regiment, came up and sat down at the fire to warm themselves. The regiment was on its march from Jubulpore to Banda, and the four Sipahees were a little in advance of it. After some conversation they went on, and we prepared to set out, having thrown into the fire some clothes and a churee (a painted stick as a badge of office) belonging to the trooper whom we had murdered. While we were preparing, the two men whom you had sent on with the regiment, Dhun Sing and Doulut, came up and sat down to warm themselves.* We over-heard Doulut say to Dhun Sing "this stick and these clothes must have belonged to murdered men, and these must be some of our old friends, and a large party of them," and both seemed to be alarmed at their situation as they were then alone. I made a point of being the last off, and my brother Sheikh Chund, who was lately hung, had already mounted his horse, and I had my foot in the stirrup when they saw part of the advanced guard and immedi-ately made a rush at our bridles. We drew our swords but it was too late. Chand Khan jumped off his horse and made off, both fell upon me, and I was secured. Had Doulut and Dhun Sing called out Thugs, the guard might have secured a great part of the gang, but they appeared to be panic struck, and unable to speak. By this time the regiment came up, and finding some of the remains of the troopers' clothes on the fire, the European officers found it difficult to prevent the Sipahees from bayonetting me on the spot. I put on a bold face, and told them that they ought all to be ashamed of themselves to allow a native gentleman to be thus insulted and maltreated on the high road, and that nothing but the dread of the same ruffianly treatment had made my friends run off and leave me. I had three brothers in that gang; they were all afterwards taken; two have been hung and the third is here.

* Dhun Sing and Doulut were two approvers whom I got from Mr. Maddock at Sehore in 1828, and sent off with Lieut. James Sleeman, of the 73d, on his march from Jubulpore to Banda with his regiment, in the hope of meeting with these gangs on the great roads to Mirzapore. I was then in the civil charge of the district of Jubulpore.—W. H. S.

Q.—What did you do after Sheikh had been taken?

Bheekun Khan.—We Musulmans of his gang took the road to Biseynee through Belehree; the Dooab men went off on the road to Mirzapore, and Bhola and his party went to their homes. While we were resting at a village two cose on the other side of Beleheree, in this district, two carriers of Ganges water, two tailors and a woman came up on their way to Banda, and having rested and taken some refreshments with us, they went on in our company to Shahnagur, where we passed the night, and the next day we went on together to Biseynee, where we fell in with two other travellers on their way to Banda. These two men we found so poor that we tried to get rid of them, as they might be some obstacle to our designs upon the five, and could yield us nothing. We tried to get off without waking them, but in vain; they got up and we tried to persuade them that it was too soon for them to set out, but in vain. We then sent four of our party with orders to take them along the high road while we struck off on the bye path by which we usually took our victims on that road. They soon after got alarmed, and insisted upon being taken to the main body which they had seen strike off to the right. The four Thugs were obliged to consent, and they soon overtook us. It was now determined that they also should die, and six of our party were desired to attend them and move on a little faster than the main body to the nalah in the jungle, where we usually killed people. We slackened our pace, and as soon as the six men reached the nalah they put the two men to death, and concealed their bodies till we came up, when the other five persons were strangled; and the bodies of all seven were buried under the stones near the place where we had buried the five men whom we killed in our advance, and where we the next year killed the five Byragees and the Sipahee. All these eighteen bodies I pointed out to Chundee-deen, Subahdar of the 4th regiment, whom you' sent with me from Saugor in 1832.* From the two poor men we got only one rupee; but from the others we got two hundred; and in the division Chand Khan and Dulele, who have been hung at Saugor, took the share of their brother Seikh Inaent who had been arrested by the 73d regiment.

Q.—Is this true?

Sheikh Inaent.—I believe so; they gave my share to my wife.

Q.—And what did you Dooab Thugs do in your flight?

Dibba.—We did not rest till we had got thirty miles in advance of the regiment on the Mirzapore road. We then halted and spent the night at a small village, and were going on again the next morning when we fell in with four Gosaens, a Brahmun and a Rajpoot, on their way from Hy-drabad to Mirzapore. They went on with us to Omurpatun in Rewa, whence we set out with them before daylight, and on reaching the place that had been chosen the evening before they were all six strangled. It was about an hour before daylight. After we had examined the booty and made the grave, we went to take up the bodies, but one of the six got up and tried to run away. He had got off about a hundred yards when he was overtaken and strangled again.

Q.—Did he not call out?

* These bodies were all taken up by the party under the Subahdar.

Miherban.—Yes; but he had been so much hurt in the neck the first time that he could not be heard at any distance; and we had no sooner brought his body back and put it down among the others, than we heard the servants of Captain Nicolson coming up.* The Captain was coming from Mirzapore, and was to encamp that day at Omurpatum. As soon as we heard his servants coming up we all made off, leaving the bodies unburied; a white pony belonging to Esuree Jemadar got loose and ran towards the servants, who called out to know whose it was; and thinking they must come up before we could dispose of the bodies we made off and left the pony behind us. Whether they discovered the bodies or not I do not know; but the people of the town must have seen them.

Q.—Had the man been able to raise his voice, the servants must, you think, have heard him?

Miherban.—Certainly. They were within hearing at the time.

Q.—Who strangled the man who attempted to run off?

Miherban.—Dibba and two of his men went after him, and strangled him.

Dibba.—That is not true. Persaud, who is now with Mr. Wilson, and Dojja, who is still at large, cut him down with their swords. We did not strangle him.

Q.—Did not part of your gangs after the arrest of Sheikh Inaent proceed and join that of Feringeea between Saugor and Bhopaul?

Zolfukar.—When Inaent was seized I was with a gang of twenty-four Thugs at Shahnugur coming

* Captain and Mrs. Nicolson came that morning to Omurpatam, on their way from Mizarpore to Jubulpore.

up with the others. Mahumud Buksh was with another of seven at Biscynee. Bhola Buneea in his flight came up and told us of Inaent's arrest. We went as fast as we could through Saugor towards Bhopaul, and at Sehora we fell in with Feringeea coming from Bhopaul with a gang of forty Thugs. He returned with us and we proceeded to Bhopaul without killing any person. From Bhopaul we retraced our steps towards Saugor, and at Omaree fell in with the Farsee and his servant and two Buneeas whom we killed. But before we killed them we had fallen in with a gang of eighteen Lodhies from the Dooab, and having shared in the booty, they left us to operate upon the Seronge roads. We had also fallen in with Noor Khan Jemadar and his gang of seven men, and they also shared in the booty of the Farsee.

After the Lodhies left us, we came on to Bhilsa where we fell in with three men and two women, whom we killed near Manora, Ramdeen Sipahee of Bhopaul and his mother on their way home to Banda, a bearer, his wife and brother. Coming on to Baghrode we fell in with two men who told us that three of their companions had been plundered by robbers, and were behind. We came on to Bahadurpore with them, and killed them between that place and the village of Mirzapore. We had left people to detain the three who were coming up as we thought they could have nothing left after the robbery. They asked after their two companions, and we told them that they were pushing on as fast as they could for Saugor.

We now struck off upon the Hoshungabad road, and at Belehra met Mahamud Buksh's gang of seven Thugs, and went on to Raneepore, where we killed two men, and another at Kurbeya Khera.

Here to our great surprise and consternation, my mare dropped a foal, and we all came under the Eetuk, all contaminated alike; we separated to return home. I with a party of about thirty came through Bishunkera, Bhopaul, Bhilsa and Saugor home.

Mahamud Buksh.—Near Bagrode three bearers and a Bhistee came up while we were washing ourselves in the stream, on their way from Bhopaul to Saugor, and told us, in the course of conversation, that they had seen your guard seize a number of people very like us near Bhilsa. We knew it must be Feringeea's party, and fearing that these men would get us also seized on the road, we killed them and got home all safe.

Feringeea.—We were bathing at a river four cose this side of Bhilsa when I heard directly over my head the *Chireya.** I was much alarmed, and Kurhora, who is an excellent augur, told me that I ought to take the gang back on the Gunj Basoda road immediately after so bad an omen; but I determined upon coming on towards Saugor two cose to the village of Murue. On reaching this place I tied my horse to a tree, and went into the village to talk with the Putel, leaving the gang near the horse. While talking with him I heard a great uproar and saw my horse running towards the village, and on going to catch him, saw your Nujeebs seizing and binding my gang. There were forty, but they secured only twenty-eight. I made off as I was half dressed and got home, and twelve of my gang escaped. Had I attended to Kurhora's advice you would have had none of us, another proof of the efficacy of omens if attended to. My

* See Vocabulary,—*Chireya.*

adopted son Húrreea, and Mahadeo pointed out the bodies of most of the people whom we murdered in that expedition; the rest were taken up by Zolfukar himself last year.

Mahamud Buksh.—It was a very unfortunate expedition. At Biseynee we fell in with some travellers, and should have secured them, but when Zolfukar came up, Bhola, who is always talking, could not help saying in *Ramasee*—"After all we "shall not go home without something to please "our wives and children." The travellers heard, suspected our designs, left our encampment on the bank of the tank, and went into the village. This was our first banij (merchandize) and to lose it thus was a bad omen: it was in fact like being seized.. Then came the murder of the women at Manora, and to crown the whole, *the foaling of Zolfukar's mare which brought us all under the Eetuk.* Every think seemed to go wrong with us that season, and I often proposed to return home and open the expedition anew, but I was unhappily over-ruled.

Q.—How did the guard of Nujeebs pass without seeing you?

Mahamud Buksh.—We have never been able to understand. We came the direct road to Saugor and they passed us on that road in advancing to Bhilsa. We never saw them, nor did they see us.

Q.—How did you afterwards allow yourself to be taken?

Feringeea.—Having lived among the clans of Rajpootana and Telingana for years together, I should have gone off to some of them, but you had secured my mother, wife and child. I could not forsake them—was always inquiring after them, and affording my pursuers the means of tracing me. I knew not what indignities my wife and mother might suffer. Could I have felt secure that they would suffer none, I should not have been taken.

Q.—You were in General Ochterlony's service for some time. How did that happen?

Feringeea.—My cousin, Aman Sing Subadar, after the death of his brother, Dureear, and my father, Purusram, became our guardian. His mother was one of the first families in the country, and her sister's son, Jhundee alias Gunga Sing, had the command of two regiments at Kotah. Having no sons of his own, he asked Aman to give him either me or Phoolsa, the son of Dureear, for whom you have offered two hundred rupees, for adoption, as he had great wealth and no child to leave it to. He suspected Aman to be a thief, but knew not that he was a leader of assassins, or he would have had nothing to say to us.

Q.—But did not Aman's mother know that he was so?

Feringeea.—Not till long after she was married, and from that time she was never suffered to visit her sister. Phoolsa would not consent to live with Gunga Sing Kuptan, nor should I, had I not had a dispute with Aman while out on a Thug expedition. I went to him, and he became very fond of me, and got me made a Subahdar in the grenadier company of the Buldeo regiment. I could not live without some of my old Thug friends, and got Rambuksh my cousin, for whom you have offered five hundred rupees, enlisted and made a Havildar on my own security for his good conduct. He was always a very loose character, and when Gunga Sing went to Oudeepore with his two regiments as the body guard of the young Queen, who was the daughter of the Kotah Chief, Rambuksh seduced a young widow, the daughter of one of the most respectable bankers of the city, who became pregnant. As soon as the intrigue was discovered, she pounded and ate the diamond of her own ring, or something of the kind, and died, and Rambuksh was obliged to fly to save his life, which was demanded by her family of the chief. Having given security for his good conduct, I thought my own head in danger, and fled to Boondee, where I contrived to get into the service of Major Tod, recommended to him by the post master as a young man of high birth and great promise. On going to meet General Ochterlony at Bheelwara soon after, he recommended me to him, and he made me Jemadar of Hurcaras. I attended him to Delhi and to Ajmere, whence he sent me in charge of the post office peons to Rewaree. From this place I was sent with four peons to attend a young lady of the General's family from Delhi to Calcutta. Her escort consisted of a Havildar, a Naek, and twenty Sipahees, under the command of Bhowanee Sing, Jemadar of the local regiment. We reached Muthura without any accident, and lodged in Colonel Gunge. At night Bhowanee Sing was caught in an awkward position with one of the young lady's women, and dreading the vengeance of the general, he and all his guard fled. He roused me, told me what had happened, and advised me to go off with him and try our fortunes with Runjeet Sing. This I declined; but hearing that my cousin Aman Subahdar had gone that season with his gang into Rajpootana, I started, and passing through Hindone and Beeana, joined them at Kuraulee, after having been absent from him some years. It was, I believe the year after I rejoined Aman that my gang was arrested at Kotah, and that we killed Ashraf Khan, the Subahdar Major of the 4th cavalry and his party. From that time till I was taken, or about ten years, I was always out with my gang except in the season of the rains; and for several even of these seasons we were out in Rajpootana, where the rains offer little impediment. Indeed in the western parts of Rajpootana Thugs have an advantage in the rainy season, as at the other seasons the most wealthy travellers move along in wheeled carriages, and cannot be so easily managed as on foot or on horseback, to which mode of travelling they are obliged to have recourse in the rains.

Q.—Is Gunga Sing still living?

Feringeea.—No, I have just heard from Jowahir, one of the Thugs whom Lieutenant Briggs has sent in, that he died four years ago at Oudeepore.

Q.—Did your wife know that you were a Thug?

Feringeea.—Neither she nor her family knew it till you seized her and had her brought to Jubulpore, where she found poor Jhurhoo and the other members of my gang taken at Bhilsa. Her family are of the aristocracy of Jhansee and Sumtur, as you may know.

Q.—Do not the Brinjaras often perpetrate murder in their encampments?

Feringeea.—Just before the twenty-six of my gang were taken by you at Bhilsa, and before Zolfukar joined us, we were cooking our dinner in the afternoon at a village three cose this side of Sehore, when five travellers came up on their way to Bhilsa. We tried to prevail upon them to wait for us, but they went on, saying they should spend the night at Hirora, a village four cose further on. We made sure of securing them at Hirora, and remained

19*

where we were to dine. We reached Hirora about nine at night, and searched all the village in vain for the travellers. We knew that they must either have suspected our designs, or been disposed of by other Thugs on the road; and I recollected that about three miles from Hirora we had passed a Brinjara encampment. In the morning I went back with a few followers, and there found a horse and a pony that we had seen with the five travellers. "What have you done with the five travellers, my "good friends. You have taken from us our mer- "chandise?" "Bunij," said I in Rumasee. They apologized for what they had done; said they did not know we were after them, and offered to share the booty with us; but I said we had no fair claim to a share, since none of our party were present at the *loading*—(killing). We left them and came on to Bhilsa where we met your party of Nujeebs.

Q.—And these Brinjaree Thugs are rarely seized or punished?

Sahih Khan, of Telingana.—How can their deeds be known. They do all their work them- selves. They live in the desert and work in the desert. We live in villages, and cannot do our work without the convenience and support of the farmers who hold, and the influential men who occupy them. Local authorities of all kinds and degrees must be conciliated by us; but these men are relieved from all this cost and trouble by fore- going the pleasure of other men's society, and the comforts of a fixed habitation. They are wiser men than we are!

Morlee.—I was one day walking with some of our party near Jeypore by an encampment of wealthy merchants from the westward, who wore very high turbans. I observed to my friends as we passed "what enormous turbans these men wear!" using our mystick term *Aghasee*.   The most respectable among them came up immediately and invited us to sit down with them, saying, "my "good friends, we are of your fraternity, though " our *Aghasees* are not the same." They told us that they were now opulent merchants, and independent of Thuggee, the trade by which they had chiefly acquired their wealth ; but that they still did a little occasionally when they found in a suitable place a Bunij worth taking ; but that they were now beyond speculating in trifles! We were kindly entertained, and much pleased with our new friends, but left them the same day, and I have never met any men of the kind since.   The common Moltanee Thugs, who strangle men with the thongs which they use in driving their bullocks, we have often met. They are to be found all over India, but abound most to the north-west.

Q.—What—among the Sieks?

Morlee.—Yes ; but they are not themselves Sieks. They are what we call Moltanee Thugs chiefly.

Q.—Have you ever known a Sick Thug?

Morlee.—Never.   I never saw a Siek take to Thuggee.

Sahib Khan.—I know Ram Sing Siek : he was a noted Thug leader ; a very shrewd man. He resided and still resides at Borhanpore, and used to act with Ram Sing (who was hung here at Jubulpore last month) and Rama Dheemur, and Mohun Sing, son of Pahar Sing of Poona.   He served with the celebrated Sheikh Dulloo as a Pindaree for some years after he had become distinguished as a Thug, but returned to Thuggee, and acted with his old associates for two years about Borhampore, when he went off again and joined Sheikh Dulloo.   He sold

Dulloo a very fine horse, for which he could never get payment; and as he wanted money he got annoyed. A large reward had then been offered by the Company for Dulloo's head. He left him for a month or two, and on coming back, Dulloo who was annoyed at his importunity, instead of advancing to embrace him as usual, merely got up from his charpae (couch) and put one foot upon the floor keeping the other upon the couch. That slight decided his fate. Ram Sing had been long thinking of the reward, and he now determined to win it. He killed Sheikh Dulloo either that night or the night following, and took his head to Colonel Seyer at Elichpore. The colonel said that he was sorry so brave a man should have been killed in so cowardly a manner, and sent Ram Sing to get his reward from Dhunraj Seth at Omrowtee. Dhunraj knew that Ram Sing was the Thug who had murdered a party of his treasure bearers. He arrested him, and soon after got hold of his friends Pahar Sing, his son Mohun Sing, and Rama Dheemur. They soon after made their escape from prison, and Ram Sing is now at his old trade in Berhampore. He never either got paid for his horse, or for the murder of Sheikh Dulloo.*

Q.—How often had you been on Thuggee before you saw a murder?

Sheikh Inaent.—It was on my return from the

---

* *Extract of a Letter from Lieutenant Graham, Assistant Magistrate in Khandeish, to the address of Captain W. H. Sleeman, dated the 5th November, 1835.*

"Of the other Thugs mentioned as residing about Borhampore, Ram Sing died at Dhoobo, four years ago; he was the person who murdered the famous Pindarra Chief Shaikh Dullah, on whose head a reward of 15,000 rupees was placed."

(True Extract)

W. H. SLEEMAN, *General Superintendent.*

first expedition which I made with my father to the Duckun, when I was fifteen years of age, and about thirty-five years ago. We were a gang of about eighty or ninety Thugs under my father Hinga and some of the Duckun chiefs, lodged in the Maasoleum outside of the town of Elichpore. Two of our leaders, Gumboo and Laljoo, on going into the Bazar fell in with the grooms of the Nawab Subjee Khan, the uncle of the Nawab of Bhopaul Wuzeer Muhommud Khan, who told them that their master had been with his son and his two hundred horse in the service of the Nizam at Hydrabad; and having had a quarrel with his son he was now on his way home to Bhopaul. They came back and reported; and Dulele Khan and Khuleel Khan and other leaders of fame went and introduced themselves to the Nawab, pretending that they had been to the Duckun with horses for sale, and were now on their way back to Hindostan. He was pleased with their address and appearance, and invited them to return the next day, which they did; and the following day he set out with as many of our gang as it was thought safe to exhibit. He had two grooms, two troopers, and a slave girl, two horses and a mare with a wound in the neck, and a pony. The slave girl's duty was to prepare for him his daily portion of subzee, and he told us that he had got the name of Subzee Khan from the quantity of that drug which he was accustomed to drink.

We came on together three stages, and during the fourth stage we came to an extensive jungle this side of Dhoba, and in the Baitool district; and on reaching a nalah about nine o'clock Khuleel said, " Khan Sahib, we have had a fatiguing jour-" ney, and we had better rest here, and take some

" refreshment." " By all means," said the Nawab,
" I feel a little fatigued and will take my Snbzee
" here." He dismounted, laid his sword and shield
upon the ground, spread his carpet and sat down.
Dulele and Khuleel sat down by his side while the
girl was preparing his potion, of which he invited
these two men, as our supposed chiefs, to partake ;
and the grooms were engaged with the horses, and
the troopers were smoking their pipes at a distance.
It had been determined that the Nawab should be
first secured, for he was a powerful man, and if he
had a moment's warning he would certainly have
cut down some of the gang before they could
secure him. Laljoo also went and sat near him,
while Gomanee stood behind and seemed to be
much interested in the conversation. All being
now ready the signal was given, and the Nawab
was strangled by Gomanee, while Laljoo and
Dulele held his legs. As soon as the others saw
the Nawab secured they fell upon his attendants,
and all were strangled, and their bodies were buried
in the bed of the water course. On going back to
Elichpore, Gomanee sold the Nawab's shield for
eight rupees, but it was worth so much more that
the people suspected him, and came to our camp
to search for him. Our spies brought us timely
notice and we concealed him under the housings
of our horses.

Q.—What was the cause of the quarrel between
him and his son ?

Inaent.—The son in a passion had drawn his
sword and cut the Nawab's favourite mare over
the neck. A quarrel ensued, and he left his son

in charge of the squadron of horse to return to Bhopaul.[*]

Q.—And this was the first murder you ever witnessed?

Inaent.—This was the first, and it made a great impression upon my mind, and you may rely upon the correctness of what I state regarding it.

* Reference having been made to the Court of Bhopaul through the Political Agent; this story is found to be quite true.

END OF VOLUME I.

THE

THUGS

OR

PHANSIGARS OF INDIA:

COMPRISING A

HISTORY OF THE RISE AND PROGRESS

OF THAT

EXTRAORDINARY FRATERNITY OF ASSASSINS;

AND A

DESCRIPTION OF THE SYSTEM WHICH IT PURSUES, AND OF THE

MEASURES WHICH HAVE BEEN ADOPTED BY THE SUPREME

GOVERNMENT OF INDIA FOR ITS SUPPRESSION.

Compiled from Original and Authentic Documents published

By CAPTAIN W. H. SLEEMAN,

SUPERINTENDENT OF THUG POLICE.

VOL. II.

PHILADELPHIA :

CAREY & HART.

1839.

CONTENTS.

HISTORY

OF THE

THUGS OR PHANSIGARS.

DISCLOSURES OF THE INFORMERS.

—

PRESENT INAENT, DIBBA, MIRHBAN, BHEEKUN KHAN AND OTHERS.

Q.—What gangs were in the Dhooma affair?

Inaent.—There were a great many both from Hindostan and the Duckun. We had concentrated at Chourae in the Seonee district between this and Nagpore, and were at least three hundred Thugs, and had just performed the concluding ceremonies of the festival of the Mohurrum, when a party of about twenty-seven persons, decoits I believe, came up on their way from the Duckun to Hindoostan. They had four ponies laden with rich booty which they had acquired in an expedition to the south. The following day they came on to Chupara, and we followed. They lodged in the town, we outside. Bodhoo Jemadar Musulman, calling himself Kour Khuluck Sing, and pretending to be a Hindoo of rank, went to the party and told them that the road from Chupara passed through an extensive

and very dangerous jungle,* and begged that for
security we might unite our parties, as we were
merchants and government servants, and not very
well armed.   They agreed, and the next morning
one hundred and twenty-five of our gang went on
with them, while the rest came by another road,
all agreeing to rendezvous at Nutwara, in the valley of the Nerbudda.

I was with the 125, and on reaching two trees
in the jungle sacred to the two saints Chittureea
and Kunkureea, and on which people tie pieces of
cloth as votive offerings, the signal was given, and
sixteen of the decoits were strangled and eleven
cut down with our swords.   We took the bodies
into the jungle near the road, and without burying
them, made off with the booty, and rejoined our
friends at Nutwara.   The booty consisted of gold,
silver and cloths, to the value of thirteen thousand
rupees.   We went on to Kutungee, divided the
booty, and separated.   The Duckun Thugs returned home, and we came with a party of eighty
to Jubulpore, and encamped in the Beohar's grove
which you see yonder, where we had a grand
Natch (ball).

While engaged in our feast, we heard that the
Subah of the district was sending troops to seize
us, and we made off.   When the signal for the
murder was given a boy happened to be unper-
ceived at a distance from the rest, and hearing
their screams, he got up into a tree, and saw the
whole affair without our seeing him, as it was daylight.   After we had come on, he descended, came
on to Jubulpore, and found some of our party selling

* This extensive jungle was one of their "Matabur Beles," or
favourite places of murder, where they used every year to kill a
great many travellers.

some of their gold lace in the Bazar, and denounced
us to the governor. We all denied any knowledge
of the affair of course, but the Subah got hold of
the adopted son of Khuleel Jemadar, tied him up
to a tree, and gave him a severe flogging. Khuleel protested against this,.and said he had better
send for swords and have us all cut to pieces at
once. The Subah would not listen, and at last the
boy confessed. The seven leaders were confined
in the fort. The others all in the Beohar's house,
but after having been made to disgorge all their
property, they were all suffered to escape, except
three leaders, Hinga, my father Kuleel, and Murdan: the two latter were sent to Nagpore, where
the Rajah released them. My father Hinga had
broken his back in jumping over the fort wall, and
Murdan sprained his ankle.

Q.—Were you all taken in the grove?

Inaent.—No. We had got off on the Saugor
road to Kutungee, but the Subah sent a squadron
of horse after us, and we were all brought back.
It was commanded by Khan Mahomad, the present
Cotwal of Saugor. Nasir of Telingana was in this
affair.

Q.—Is this true?

Nasir.—All true; and I was obliged to give the
chief officer at Kutungee a fine horse, and some
other valuable articles that I had picked up on this
expedition, as I found he was an old acquaintance
of mine, and well disposed towards us as long as
be was well conciliated in this way. I had got far
off with my gang before the Subah's party came
up after the rest.

Inaent.—Purumsook was then master of the
Adalut here, and all our property had to pass

through his hands.   He was an old friend of ours, and must recollect the circumstance well.*

Q.—What makes you think the party were decoits?

Inaent.—Some decoits from the west, who have been confined for fourteen years in the Saugor jail, told us while we were there last year, that a party of theirs had been killed about that time near Chupara on their way back from the Duckun.   They must have learnt it from the boy who escaped.

Q.—Were Bodhoo's nose and hands cut off before this affair?

Inaent.—No—A year or two after at Seronge. He went to Stockwell Sahib who sent him to Jhalone, where the Raja put him to death, by making elephants walk over him.   A very dear man was Bodhoo!

Q.—What were the circumstances that made you fly to the Carnatic?

Sahib Khan.—It was about twelve years ago that my own gang of fourteen, and another of twenty-five under Jumal Khan, Seodeen, and Fukeer Mahommud, in an expedition between Aurungabad and Elichpore, joined in the murder of a Subahdar, his servant, and two Rajpoots at a Bowlee near Chandae.   The bodies were tied up in blankets and thrown into the Bowlee.   Going on towards Jhalna we fell in with a Marwaree taking turbans for sale to Jhalna, and near Phaleegow we strangled him; but getting only a rupee each, we agreed to go on and wait in the Jhalna canton-

---

* Purumsook, who is now a kind of attorney at Jubulpore, being referred to, confirms all this, but denies the *friendship.* He sold the property he says for the then government, and not for himself or the Thugs. He was a kind of *Deputy Chief Justice* at the time, and in league with all these gangs.

·ments till we could find a *Bunij* more worth taking. We had however no sooner came to this resolution, after discussing over our plans on the bank of the river, than we heard the dire *Chimmama* on our right. We all started up, and with my gang I instantly retreated. Jumal Khan however ventured to take his gang on towards Jhalna in spite of this warning. We came to Omrowtee where we celebrated the Mohurrum, after. which I returned to my home at Nandair, where I heard that Jumal, on reaching Jaferabad, had got drunk in a spirit shop and been seized with the Subahdar's Dooputta upon him, by some of Captain Sherriff's runners. He gave information against Syud-alee, and he against others, till fourteen of his gang were arrested. The four bodies were taken out of the Bowlee, and parties were sent off to Major Parker, who commanded at Hingolee, with information against me and my gang. I kept myself well informed of all these proceedings, and continued to cultivate my fields. Eleven of Jumul Khan's gang having been hung, and seeing no longer any chance of escape at home, I fled. My wife and children, and my brother Bureea, and brother-in-law Chand Khan, were seized and taken to Major Parker, who released the women and children. I went first to my uncle Towukul Sah, a celebrated Fukeer and Thug, but not yet suspected, and fearing to implicate him, I proceeded soon after to Golburga to my cousin Sahib Khan Jemadar. I found that he, Rusool Khan, and other Thugs of his party had been seized and taken to Hydrabad. As soon as the women saw me, they wept bitterly, and having heard the tale of my misfortune, his wife took me the next day to Ochergee, eight cose distant, in hopes of finding some Thugs with whom

I might serve and earn my bread. They were absent on an expedition, and I left her, and went to Muhcenkulga, where I met Lungotee Jemadar, an old follower of my father's. He made me dine with him; and after dinner he told me that he intended to take the auspices in a few days, and if the omens proved favourable, should take out his gang, and me with them. I told him that I should be glad to join him, but that I would not consent to recognise him as my chief, by paying him the fees of office, as Jemedar, like the other members of his gang. He said he would take me on no other conditions. I expostulated with him, and as Peer Khan, the brother of Chand Khan, was with me, I said that he must set aside both our shares before the general division; and asked him whether he had so far forgotten the obligations he owed to my father, who had initiated him, as to have the impudence to demand tokens of subjection from the son. "Give us," I said, " our shares " separately, and then divide the spoil with your " gang, and take your fees as leader, for I will " never consent to pay you any." He said it would be a bad precedent, and lower him in the estimation of his followers; and having refused to join him on any other terms, I proceeded to Korergee, where Sahib Khan, the husband of my sister, resided and served in the gang of Nubee Sahib Jemadar. On our way we spent one evening at Hidjgeera with the families of Baba Jemadar, and eleven Thugs of note, who had been for some time in prison at Amba, and are now with Captain Reynolds. On reaching Korergee we found my brother-in-law, who had been sent home by Nubee Sahib with a booty of seven thousand rupees. Nubee Sahib being absent on an expedition, he

recommended me to go to the great leader Sahib
Khan of Kakurmulla. I did so, and found his
brother Sooltan at home. I told him the story of
our misfortunes, and he consoled me, and told me
that though Thugs were getting seized all round
them, they were as yet secure, and had still a few
hundred good men for work. Sahib Khan soon after
returned from market, received me very kindly and
made me dine with him. While at dinner, however, we heard the *Orutputholee,** which is considered a very bad omen in the south, and Sahib
Khan told me that I ought immediately to return
to my home after such an omen; but as this was
impossible under present circumstances, I must
leave his house, sleep in another village, and return
in the morning. I and Peer Khan did so. We
remained with him six weeks, and were so kindly
treated that we forgot all our misfortunes. He
consented to comply with my conditions, and not
to exact from us two his fees as leader. With a
gang of sixty Thugs we proceeded a cose to the
village of Dewurnatjee, where we waited eight
days for favourable omens. Having got them,
sixteen old men and boys were sent home, and the
expedition was opened by forty-six. It is the custom
in the Carnatic to take out all the old men and
boys on the first stage where the auspices are
taken, and when the omens are favourable to send
them back. When they get booty they take what
is necessary for the subsistence of the gang, and
send all the rest to the house of the leader, where
it remains till the gang returns, when it is divided,
and the boys and old men who are sent back, have
an equal share of it with the others who go on.

* See Vocabulary—*Orutputholee.*

The same custom prevails among the Thugs from Arcot who are said to have taken it from them.

We proceeded to a village near Dharwar which we reached in eight days, and there met the *great Sheikh Ahmed*, the Thug leader from Arcot, with his gang of fifty. Going on to Dharwar together, the two leaders divided the whole into two separate gangs, one under these two leaders to operate on the road to Poona, and the other under Nathoo, and Sirjee Khan,* the brother of Sheikh Ahmed, and Sooltan, the brother of Sahib Khan, towards Naggur. We were all to rendezvous at Echora at the end of a month.

After killing a good many travellers and getting a good deal of booty, which was all sent as taken to the house of Sahib Khan, we all re-united at the appointed place, and remained together two days, when our division took the road to Naraenpath, and the other that to Dharwar. On the bank of the Bhimra river we got a prize of twelve thousand rupees worth of silk from six men, and returned home. Seven days after our return, seven of the other division came and reported that in a drunken brawl at Dharwar, the secret of their proceedings had been disclosed, and all the division, except themselves, arrested; and as a good many had turned King's evidences, we might soon expect a guard down upon us.

Having heard that my cousin and his gang had been released at Hydrabad and come with their families to Korergee, I went and joined them; and Sahib Khan left his house at Kukurmulla in charge of his brother Meean Sahib, who was not suspect-

*This man has, I believe, been made over to Lieutenant Elwall by the authorities at Sattara, where he has been in prison ever since this expedition, Sept. 1835.   W. H. S.

ed, and concealed himself with an old friend in our
neighbourhood.   A guard came from Dharwar,
seized Meean Sahib, and so maltreated him in
order to make him point out his brother, that he
threw himself into a well and was killed.

Alarmed, I and my cousin and his party, with
all their families, went to Golburga, and leaving
the women and children there, with a small gang
went to Hydrabad, for we had now nothing to
subsist upon.   Near Bamnabad we found a traveller washing himself in the stream.   He was strangled and his body left upon the sand.   The rains
had now set in, and going on beyond Akelee we
found a traveller waiting on the bank of a river for
some one to assist him over.   He was persuaded
to go up the stream a little off the road for a better
ford, and there strangled.   We went to Hydrabad,
and thence came back through Akelee to Nowta
Moshturee, killing two men on the road; and here
we met Sheikh Ahmed, the great Arcot leader,
with a small party of twelve.   He told us that
Sahib Khan had been arrested,* and all the booty
of our late expedition taken by the government
guards.   The next morning he left us for Hydrabad; and on our way to Golburga we for three
successive days continued to fall in with small
parties of Sheikh Ahmed's gang following each
other at long intervals.   My cousin and his party
changed their abodes from Golburga to Ertalee in
Bedur; and taking my family I went to Kunkee
and entered into the service of Dhurumdass, the
Amil on the part of Chundoolal the minister.   He

---

* Sahib Khan and his brother Sooltan have been just made over
to Lieut. Elwall, having been ever since the event here described,
prisoners in the fort of Sattara, in the Poona territory, Sept. 1835.
W. H. S.

employed me to make the collections of two villages for him, and I resolved to leave off Thuggee
at least for a time. Taking the collections to
Hydrabad, two years after this, I met Sheikh
Ahmed, who asked me *how many Thugs I had
with me.* I told my story, and he mentioned that
our old friend Sahib Khan of Kakurmulla, was
confined in the Fort of Sattara, but that he would
effect his release whatever it might cost him. He
soon left me, and I could perceive that he distrusted
me. One of his followers, however, Hoseyn Khan,
told me that they had now all established themselves comfortably about Nulgonda on the road to
Masulipatum ; and in return I bid him tell his chief·
that he need not fear me.*

* *Extract from the Narrative of the last Thuggee Expedition of
Sahib Khan Jemadar, taken before Lieutenant Elwall at Sholapore,* 29th *Sept.* 1835.

About eight or nine months after this time, deponent and Mukhdoom Sahib, Sahib Khan Ruhmutwallah and Mooheendeen Jemadar, with forty followers, set out on a Thuggee expedition towards
the Carnatic, and halted for the night at the village of " Gurnullie."
On the same day Sheikh Ahmed Arcottee, Jemadar, with Guffoor
Khan his brother, and Osman Khan Jemadar, with their followers,
arrived at the village of " Goburargee," about two coss from " Gor-
nullie," and both parties starting in the morning met on the road
to the Carnatic and went on together, and after four days arrived
at Jubulpoor in the Company's territories, where we passed the
night, and having consulted together, agreed to divide into two
bodies, and it was settled that from my followers Mukhdoom Sahib
Jemadar, Sahib Khan Ruhmutwallah, and Mooheendeen Jemadar
and sixteen sepoys, should accompany the Arcottees, and Sheikh
Ahmed Jemadar and sixteen Arcottee followers, accompanied me
towards Poonah, while the other party went towards the Carnatic.
After three days deponent arrived at " Eroor" on the Krishna river
where there was a fair. Deponent staid there, and Sheikh Ahmed
went on towards Jokul, and about two coss from " Eroor," fell in
with two Hindoo Jewellers who were seated on the bank of a stream
drinking water. Having found out what the travellers had with
them, they strangled them, and buried the bodies carelessly.

Q.—But you have not told me why Sheikh Ahmed left Arcot?

Deponent arrived while they were burying them. We got from the murdered travellers a dabba of pearls and other jewels, which were of large value, and sent them home in charge of four of our men. We arrived ourselves in three days at Sangolee on the Punderpore road, at the same time with four Hindoo traders with a pony load of cloth, who were going from Jaulna to Kolapoor, and Sheikh Ahmed having insinuated himself into their acquaintance went on with them to " Walmurra," where they halted near a Hindoo Dewul. Deponent also came there and joined Sheikh Ahmud in the evening and we staid the night there. In the morning Sheikh Ahmed and the others went on with the Beiparies, and about a mile from the place, in a dry nullah, strangled the travellers and buried their bodies. I came up after the murder. We got from the travellers the following property : 13 embroidered Doputtas, 9 silk scarfs, embroidered, 45 Rs. weight of gold thread, and 156 turbands, which we sent home with six men, and went on to Mirich T'aj Gaon, when the fair of " Khoja Shumna Mearun Sahib" was being held; we saw the fair and then went towards home, and arrived at a village on the Krishna river, where four Hindoo traders, in the service of some Saokar, with three bullocks laden with silk, had put up. We staid there, and the next morning the Jemadar Sheikh Ahmed, went on with the Beiparies, and about a coss from thence, in a dry nullah, murdered and buried them, and taking the property went towards home. Sheikh Ahmed Jemadar took half the silks home with him to Chilmullah, in the Nizam's country, and the rest I took with me.

The other party which separated from us at " Jaulpar" and went towards the Carnatic, having reached Anegra in the Dharwar district, halted there. At this time in the cantonment of Hooblee a Decoittee had taken place, and the police seeing the Thugs there, suspected them, and they were immediately seized and taken to Dharwar. The Aumil then inquired concerning the Thugs; and one of the Arcottee followers named Mahumud Khan, confessed and told that Sheikh Ahmed Jemadar lived at Chilmullah, and Sahib Khan Jemadar (deponent) at Kukurmullah, and that the persons seized were the followers of the two Jemadars. I, hearing that search was making for me and Sheikh Ahmed, left my home and went and staid at the village of Neem Nullie. In the mean time the Sircar's people, by order of Mr. J. Munro, came to my house, and ordered my brother Meean Khan to tell where I was; he said that I had left the village. They thinking he was speaking falsely, began to kick and beat him till he said he would tell where his brother was, and taking the police people with him outside the

Sahib Khan.—I have never been to Arcot, and met them for the first time near **Dharwar**. They used often to talk of Arcot, and of their having been

village into a garden where there was a Baolee, he watched his opportunity and threw himself in and was drowned. My other followers being frightened fled the village and came to me at Neem Nullie, and about fifteen days afterwards the police, having got information of our being there, came and seized us, and took us before Mr. John Munro at Mungolee. The undermentioned property was seized in my house and sent in by Gobind Sobhajee Pundit and Dewan Ramchand Rao, Moonsifdar of Koolkunundghee:

List of Property, viz.

Silk, ...bundles,..	No. 3	Daul,.................	No. 5
Gold Thread or Kuliabut-		Swords or Tulwars, &c...	14
too, ...bundles...	4	Musquets,..............	2
Buttooah, wt. several stones,	1	Doputtah, ...	13
Dabba with Pearls,.......	1	Silk Scarfs or Sowla,.....	9
Horses, ...:	3	Turbands,..............	156

The three horses were sold and their price was given to my father and family, and afterwards Nursing Ba Ressuldar was ordered by the gentleman to give them their ornaments and brass vessels, &c. as also a quantity of grain of different sorts, of the value of about 100 Rupees; about this time Mr. John Munro was shot at the fight of Kittoor, and the Ressuldar sent myself, my brother *Sheikh Dawoll* and Sona Khan, Sheikh Emam Sahib and Sheikh Hoossein, followers of Sheikh Ahmed Arcottee Jemadar, (in all five persons) to Pando Rung Subahdar at Beejapoor, but the jewels, &c. were not sent. We were kept twenty days there, and then sent to Sattara, where we have been imprisoned for twelve years; when we had been there about three months, Aproop Khan, Mean Khan, and Gurd Sahib Khan, living at Naghnee, were seized, and sent to the Rajah by the Ressuldar at Mungolee; about six years after this, Mooheeodeen, a relation of Gurd Sahib Khan, living at Naghnee, in Ulmullah, procured the release of the six others by paying six hundred rupees to the Rajah's people, and I and my brother remained in prison till we were sent here.

(True extract)
(Signed) T. ELWALL, *Asst. Agt. Governor Genl.*
(True extract)
W. H. SLEEMAN, *General Superintendent.*

obliged some years before to leave it by a hot pursuit kept up by some active magistrate. Sahib Khan of Kukurmullah told me that while he and his gang of sixty men were one day cooking their food on the bank of a river near Kukurmullah, they saw these people come down to the river to fish. They soon perceived that they understood their mystic terms, and got into conversation with them. The two chiefs had an interview in which Sheikh Ahmed explained how he had been obliged to leave Arcot, and seek an asylum, which he did not much like, in a village in the neighbourhood. Sahib Khan prevailed upon him and all his party with their families to come with him; and having introduced him to the Rajah of Shorapore Bedur, as a great Thug leader, the Rajah got them established in his neighbourhood in the town of Chichurmulla. Shiekh Ahmed is the wisest man I know. He has great wealth, but he keeps it concealed in the woods. When danger approaches, he scatters his gang, and wanders alone with his wife till it is past or till he finds another secure abode, when he transfers his wealth to the woods about it. His followers have wonderful confidence in him, such as I have never seen in the followers of any other leader.*

---

* *Extract from the deposition of Sheikh Sakiban, lately arrested at Hingolee, before Captain Reynolds, 27th October, 1835.*

The Arcottee Thugs are proverbially wary and alert, among all the Thugs of the Dekhan, and their rules and regulations are very strict. They do not allow of indiscriminate strangling. The stranglers are regularly instructed in the use of the handkerchief, and no one is permitted to use it, until he has practised, and until the omens which are looked for at his initiation, are considered favourable. The Arcottees will not strangle women, nor shoemakers, dhers, barbers, goldsmiths and washermen. If the first travellers met with on an expedition have a cow with them, they are spared,

Q.—What became of your brother-in-law Chand Khan and your brother Bureca?

even if it is known they have treasure in their possession. The Hindustance and Dekhnee Thugs by not attending to these rules, and strangling shoemakers, barbers, and all sorts of people, have brought down retribution on the heads of all the Thugs in India. All the Arcottee Thugs that I have met with, adopted the dress and appearance of Sepoys of the regiments of infantry and cavalry. They wear the checkered loongees and short jackets like Sepoys, carry canes in their hands, and being very fond of beetlenut and paun, every man has a small bag in his possession for holding the ingredients. They frequently represent themselves to be Sepoys going on leave or removed from one station to another, and even make themselves acquainted with the names of European officers in order to pass more easily through the country. They make themselves *knapsacks*, (the word made use of by the deponent) and carry their clothes in them. The Jemadars take on themselves the semblance of merchants, and pretend to be going to make purchases of goods, or to be conveying merchandize for sale. They always have four or five of the gang in personal attendance on them, to give them the hookah, cook their victuals, and clean their ponies. These men march in company with the Jemadar, while the other Thugs move along the road in twos and threes, and only collect on the occasion of the perpetration of a murder. They can only be arrested by having parties of approvers stationed on all the great roads of the Carnatic. The police, though it is very vigilant, has not the means of preventing cases of Thuggee, and even if Thannahs of police peons are posted along the roads, the Thugs will manage to murder close to them. I will give an instance in proof of this. Sheikh Ahmed Arcottee Jemadar came into the southern Mahratta country and strangled some treasure carriers in charge of 16,000 rupees, at the Salpa Ghat. There is a Chowkee placed on the Ghat now, and if the peons are asked, they will state the Chowkee to have been placed there in consequence of this murder. But this has not had any effect in diminishing the number of murders perpetrated at this very Ghat, where I am sure a hundred skulls of murdered travellers might be dug up any day. The Thugs will be first to go out, beg the protection of the Police Chuprassees on the roads they travel on, pretending great dread of robbers, and then will perpetrate a murder close to the road which the police is supposed to guard.

The Arcotte Thugs usually start on their expeditions during the first seven days after the festival of Dewalee and Hulee; and if they have had favourable omens, they have no doubt taken to the roads before this time. It is very probable that Dawulgee Jemadar

Sahib Khan.—They made their escape from Hingolee, and are still on the roads some where.

of Binsee has heard of the seizures at Sholapore, and therefore will not come northward this year, and as this is his usual season of setting out, he will certainly proceed towards Bangalore and Seringapatam, or perhaps by Bellary towards Cuddapah. When I was at Binsee, this time last year, Dawuljce and his gang were intending to make an excursion into the Mysore country. They had a short time previously been as far as Hurryhur, but had turned back in consequence of the omens being inauspicious. The Arcotte Thugs do not now come into the Dekhan so much as formerly. Indeed since the time of the arrest of my brother-in-law, Sahib Khan Jemadar, and his companions, by Mr. Munro, which is about twelve years ago, they have never made their appearance north of Dharwar. When the great arrest of Thugs took place in the zillah of Arcot, by Mr. Wright, during my youth, great numbers of Arcotte Thugs fled from that part of the country, and settled first in the Sorapoor Talooka under the Hydrabad government. I have heard that Sheikh Ahmed, Ladeekur Sahib Khan, Oosman Khan, Chabriah Einaum, Hoonoorgah and other Jemadars, who were the leaders of the party that came first to Sorapoor, agreed to pay the Sorapoor Rajah 2,000 rupees a year for his protection. The party consisted of fifty or sixty Thugs, whose numbers were afterwards increased by stragglers from Arcot, and the families of the Thugs who followed them. All these Thugs remained in the Dekhan until Mr Munro commenced his seizures, when they left their habitations under the guidance of Sheikh Ahmed Jemadar, and passing through the Hydrabad country settled somewhere fifteen days journey beyond it towards Masulipatam. They afterwards obtained on three occasions 14,000, 7,000, and 3,000 rupees of treasure by the murder of the carriers. This is within the last 8 or 10 years. They then went and settled near Nundyal in the Cuddapah district. About two and a half years ago, Einaun brother of Tippoo Jemadar, a relation of my own, went from Binsee where I was at the time, to Nundyal, to see Sheikh Ahmed Jemadar. When he returned, he informed us that Sheikh Ahmed Jemadar had a short time previously been out with his gang, and had strangled four Gollah peons carrying treasure; and that each Thug had received 9 tolahs of gold, and 300 rupees as his share of the booty. During the time of Sahib Khan Jemadar's confinement at Sattara, Tippoo Jemadar, brother-in-law of Sheikh Ahmed Jemadar, was also detained along with him; and Arcottee Thugs were in the habit of coming to gain intelligence regarding him and his companions, and by that means we were kept acquainted with the proceedings of the gangs to the south.   (True Copy)

W. H. SLEEMAN.

They came to me when I was on my way to Kunkee and had resolved to give up Thuggee, and
told me of their escape.

DAVEY DEEN—BHIKHA—DOJJA—KHODA BUKSH—FERINGEEA
—ZOLFUKAR—DORGHA—KAEM KHAN.

Q.—You were among the men arrested by Mr.
Wright, were you not, at Cawnpore?

*Extract. Deposition of Myan Khan, alias Lungotea, Jemadar of
Thugs, lately arrested, taken before Captain Reynolds at Hiz-
golee on the 31st of October, 1835.*

I will state the names of such of the Arcottee Jemadars of Thugs
as I am acquainted with.

Oosman Khan Jemadar, a man of a robust habit of body. I met
him last upwards of four years ago on the Kurnool road, beyond
Hydrabad, with a gang of 50 Thugs. He resides at Mulhar, some
where in the vicinity of Bellary.

Sahib Khan Ladeekun Jemadar, a relative of Oosman Khan
Jemadar, whom he follows.

Sheikh Ahmed, son of Dawuljee Jemadar, formerly had a gang
of 50 Thugs. I have not seen him since the time Mr. Munro
arrested Thugs in the Zillah of Dharwar, but have occasionally
heard of him.

Chabreah Emaum Jemadar, and his brother Hoonoorgah, had
formerly a gang of 30 Thugs. I have not seen them since the
time of Mr. Munro's arrests, but within the last two years I have
heard that they were residing in the jurisdiction of some Rajah
near Bezwarah, on the road from Hydrabad to Masulipatam.

Tippoo, the brother of Sheikh Ahmed, in whose company he is.
I have not seen him since the time abovementioned.

In former times, all these Jemadars, with as many hundreds of
Thugs, resided in the Arcot and other adjacent Zillahs; but about
20 or 22 years ago, Sheikh Ahmed Jemadar, with a party of sixteen
Thugs and four women, came to the Oorus of Peer Dustgeer, which
takes place at the village of Neelor, in the Pergunnah of Gool-
burgah, where he met me and Khooddoo Jemadar, who had also
come to attend the Oorus. Sheikh Ahmed informed us that he
was an inhabitant of the Arcot Zillah, and that a great misfortune
had befallen the Thugs of that part of the country, for as the English gentleman had commenced arresting them, there was no
dwelling place left for them there; he therefore wished to settle

Bhikka.—Yes, I was among them; he got about a hundred, and put them all into one old jail at Bithore on the information of Munsook Brahman

himself elsewhere. We further heard from Sheikh Ahmed that his father Dawuljee Jemadar of Thugs, had been apprehended, and was then in confinement either at Vellore or Bangalore. In the end, Sheikh Ahmed and his gang went into the Sorapoor District and had an interview with the Rajah through the intervention of Khoddoo Jemadar, and then fixed his residence in the village of Bullondghee. In the course of a year, nearly 100 Thugs were assembled at Bullondghee and the neighbouring villages, in consequence of the relatives of the others coming up from the Carnatic to settle there. I have heard that they paid large sums of money yearly to the Sorapoor Rajah. Some years after, the Thugs having amassed great wealth, the Rajah demanded a fine from them. They therefore left Bullondghee and took up their abode at the village of Chinmullah, the Jageer of Raheer Patail, in the Afzoolpoor Pergunnah. During this interval the Thugs used to go out for "*Rozgar*," in the direction of Kurnool and Cuddapah, and on the road to Masulipatam.

Several years afterwards, Sooltaun Khan Jemadar, the brother of Sahib Khan Jemadar of Kukermulla, (now an approver at Sholapoor) was apprehended at Annygherry, and a Thug of his gang named Mahomedea, confessed his guilt and pointed out the places of residence of the Thugs. He was sent to Mr. Munro, the magistrate of Mungolee, in the Dharwar Zillah, who commenced arresting Thugs according to his evidence. Nearly 40 or 50 Thugs were seized, from among whom Sahib Khan Jemadar of Kukhermulla, Chunneeka Sahib Khan and others were sent to Sattara; and Mahomedea, Lumboo Burreah, Giddoo Burreah and others to Dharwar, and there detained in confinement. Dreading lest they should be arrested, Sheikh Ahmed Jemadar and the Arcottee Thugs, with their wives and families, left their homes in the Dekhan, and went to Hyderabad, from whence part of them proceeded on the Masulipatam road and the remainder on the Kurnool road, and fixed their residence in the vicinity of those places. Since that time the Arcottee Thugs have not again visited the Dekhan during their Thug expeditions. They range through the country bordering on the sea coast, by Masulipatam, Rajumundry and Chicacole; or move by way of Madras up to Seringapatam, and then back again to their own abodes.

The Arcottees are generally hereditary Thugs, by caste Musulmans, are great eaters of Beetlenut, usually wear Loongies like Sepoys, and often represent themselves to be in the Company's service, in order to secure themselves from molestation on the road.

and others of our gang.   They told us if we told
the truth and proved our story, we should have
favour, and many did so; but the people about

They bury the bodies of their victims securely, lest the secret of
Thuggee should be divulged, and are much more deceitful than the
Dekhnee Thugs, so that rich travellers and Sahookars place confidence in them on account of their respectable appearance. Their
manner of strangling with the handkerchief, mode of burial, and
other rites, are similar to those of the Dekhnee Thugs, though there
is some difference in the slang language of the Arcottees. They
generally use the Hindustanee language in common conversation,
though they also speak the Tamul.

I recently obtained intelligence of Sheikh Ahmed Jemadar and
other Arcottee Thugs in the following manner.   There was an
Arcottee Thug named Kasim, who formerly came and resided with
Sheikh Ahmed Jemadar, in the Afzoolpoor District. He contracted
a marriage in the village of Bullondghee, but when Mr. Munro
began to seize Thugs, Kasim and his wife fled the country, in company with Sheikh Ahmed.   About two years ago, Kasim's father-
in-law named Ismael, left Bullondghee in search of his son-in-law.
After some time Ismael returned, bringing with him both Kasim
and his wife, and they took up their residence at the village of
Gour, in the Afzoolpoor Pergunnah, where they were both residing
at the time of my arrest, about three months ago; and if they are
seized they will be able to give correct intelligence regarding the
place of abode of the Arcottee Thugs.   I heard from Ismael and
Kasim that Sheikh Ahmed, Mahomed Koosain, and Emaum Sahib
Arcottee Jemadars, with sixty followers, were living in some
villages four or five koss on this side of Bezwarah, on the Masulipatam road, appertaining to some Hindoo Rajah Zumeendar, beyond
the Hydrabad Territory.

There is also a female named Jugdumah, who is a Jemadarnee
of Thugs, with a party of upwards of 200 persons, who reside in
certain villages belonging to some Rajah, situated three days' journey on this side of Bangalore.   The Thugs of her gang proceed on
expeditions towards Masulipatam and Chicacole. Jugdumah is
about 50 years of age, and has two sons named Sirdar Khan and
Burree Khan, besides her own two brothers.   She exercises the
authority of Jemadarnee herself, but sends her sons and brothers
in charge of the gang; she has amassed great wealth by the practice of Thuggee.

(A true Translation)
(Signed)   P. A. REYNOLDS, *Supt.*
(True Copy)

W. H. SLEEMAN.

Court soon told us we were fools, for those who confessed were sure to *swing,* while those who denied were equally sure to get off. A Daer Saer Sahib (Judge of Circuit) came from Bareilly and examined us, and went back; another came, and as soon as he got back he sent an order for our release. Ramdeen, who was hung last year at Cawnpore, and Kesuree Subahdar, who was hung here this year, were kept in for a short time longer.

Q.—Was that Ramdeen your brother?

Davey Deen.—Yes, my eldest brother and father of Heera, approver, who is with Mr. Wilson.

Q.—How long was this before Mr. Stockwell's proceedings?

Davey Deen.—The *Istakole Kee Gurdee,* (the Stockwell inroad) took place very soon after. Dojja was one of the men arrested.

Dojja.—Yes; Stockwell and Perry Sahibs scraped together some two hundred of us at Mynporee, but a Daer Saer Sahib came from Bareilly, and released all for whom the Zumeendars would give security. The twenty who could not get it were retained.

Davey Deen.—Yes, I remember. Mr. Stockwell and Perry went down in the same buggy to the Sahib and told him that they had secured us at much cost and trouble, and that we were all *aseel, thorough-bred Thugs;* but he said it would not do to keep us upon mere general report, particularly if the Zumeendars would vouch for us. He went to Calcutta, and six months after came back and caused us all to be released, by an order from the Sudur, except eighteen.

Dojja.—But they got hold of me again two years after, and kept me in for fifteen years doing all kinds of work.

Khoda Buksh.—Mr. Stockwell seized me and six others at Oureya, and we were sent to Bithore and kept at Rabukaree, with some hundred of the Thugs, for more than six months, when Rehlee Sahib ordered us seven to cut muttee (work on the roads) for a year, after which we got off. Cheynooa Brahman and his brother Holosee are still at large. Munsa was hung here the other day. Bhowanee died in the Saugor jail, and Doulut Brahman died at home. Ramah Lodhee is here one of the approvers.

Q.—It was not your relation Ashraf Jemadar, who is still at large, among the number?

Khoda Buksh.—No, he was not with us.

Feringeea.—Ashraf never got the rank of Jemadar of Thugs.

Zolfukar.—You mistake, he is a Jemadar.

Feringeea.—None but his own relations ever called him so.

Q.—But I find him entered as a Jemadar in the book?

Feringeea.—You may write him down a *king* in your book if you please, but he was no Jemadar of ours.

Zolfukar.—Had he been a Brahman like yourself, instead of a Musulman, you would have thought him so.

Q.—But how did the Zumeendars venture to give security for you all; they must have known you to be Thugs?

Davey Deen.—They knew us very well, but they had then confidence in us; they thought we should keep our own secrets, and if we did so, no one else would be able to convict us and get them into trouble.

Zolfukar.—Yes; there was then something like

religion and good faith (Dhurum Eeman) among us, and we found friends every where. Where could we find them now?

Davey Deen.—When I and my brothers were seized by Mr. Moncton, the Zumeendar would have given any security for us.

Feringeea.—When Madhoo was seized by Mr. Benson and sent to Saugor from Etawa, they would have given ten thousand rupees security for him.

Kuleean Sing.—When our gang was arrested at Hoshungabad, was there not a scramble among the Hill Chiefs and Zumeendars to get us released upon their security? Did not many both there and at Jubulpore, who had never seen us in their lives, make their agents offer any security that could be demanded for our future good behaviour.

Q.—And why did they do this? They no doubt thought you very innocent and respectable men under misfortunes?

Kuleean Sing.—Not at all. We managed to persuade them that we could, by being allowed to follow our old trade under their protection, be made a new source of revenue to them. We told them that we would pay for the little land we might cultivate in their villages more than fifty times its value.

Chotee.—Did not the Khyrooa chief stand a long seige from his master, the Jhansee Rajah, before he would give up eight or ten of us?

Kaen Khan.—And was not the Maharajah of Gwalior obliged to send two large guns and a great force against Bhumma Zumeendar of Bahmanpora before he would give us up; and were not several lives lost in the action, which continued from daylight till nine in the morning. Bhumma was very fond of us, particularly of our Jemadar Gholab Khan, whose father had been hung the year before at Saugor, and who is now an approver with Mr. Thomas, and he said he would rather die than give us up: but poor man he had only sixteen muskets to fight with, and had got into disgrace at Court by not paying his rents! The Lord Sahib (Lord William Bentick) must have heard the guns, for he and the Rae Sahib were encamped only a few miles off at the time.

Dudoo Nujeeb.—Yes, and you strangled Larroo, the poor female spy,* whom we sent in to look after you. We heard it afterwards from a dancing girl of the place: and we had much trouble to get you after all, for the Amil would not give up the five Thugs whom he had secured, unless we gave him a receipt for the ten who had got away also, saying, "there had been trouble and fighting enough for fifty Thugs." This we refused to do however.

Kaem Khan.—I know nothing about Larroo's death. She must have been killed some where else.

Q.—What gives a man the rank of Jemadar?

Dorgha.—A man who has always at command the means of advancing a month or two's subsistence to a gang will be called so; a strong and

---

* There is no doubt that this party did strangle this woman, the wife of Peer Buksh approver. She had traced them to the village before, and now accompanied the guard sent to arrest them. She entered the village alone and was never after seen. They will not acknowledge that they killed her. A Nujeeb and trooper who entered the village in the disguise of Fukeers, to verify Laroo's information the first time, had a very narrow escape. They were obliged to plunge into the river Chumbul, and remain up to their chins in water, a whole night, while the Thugs and villagers were searching every bush on the bank.

resolute man, whose ancestors have been for many
generations Thugs, will soon get the title, or a very
wise man, whose advice in difficult cases has
weight with the gang; one who has influence over
local authorities, or the native officers of courts of
justice; a man of handsome appearance and high
bearing, who can feign the man of rank well—all
these things enable a man to get around him a few
who will consent to give him the fees and title of
Jemadar; but it requires very high and numerous
qualifications to gain a man the title of Subahdar.

2nd September, 1835.

Q.—What age are you?

Shumshera.—I am about twenty-four.

Q.—Where do you reside?

Shumshera.—My family have resided in the
village of Chorkeya, twenty cose north-east from
Ghazeepore and in that district, for three or four
generations, but my father absconded, and his
creditors became very importunate for the payment of the money he owed, and I and my brother
Runjeet, who is now in the Ghazeepore jail, were
obliged to go and reside in the village of Bhoraj-
pore, six cose north from Chupura. Four months
after this we were both seized by Mr. Smith and
brought to Ghazeepore two years ago next October.

Q.—I understand you have served with the
river Thugs of Bengal?

Shumshera.—On one occasion only. I had been
on one expedition with Dilawur Khan and one with
Futteh Khan, and after these I went with Bhowur
Khan and Moradun, two Lodaha Thugs, and
joined Jhoulee Khan the fair and Gholamun.

Jhouleee Khan had a man to carry his bundle by
name Nathoo, as he was to act this season with
Jypaul Kaet, a Jemadar of the Bongoos, or river
Thugs. He acted as their Sotha, or inveigler, this
season. We joined Jypaul at the Mormakeya
Ghat, where he had two boats at the different
ghats, two and three cose from each other. Jhoulee Khan brought two *Beetoos* to the boat which
Jypaul commanded in person, and Bhowur Khan
and I embarked with them. As soon as we had
all got on board, Jypaul said in Rumasee, " let the
Boras (Thugs) separate themselves from the *Beetoos,*" and we did so, leaving the two travellers
together. Four men were on the bank pulling
along the boat, one was at the helm, acting at the
same time as the *Bykureea* or spy, and seven of
the gang were below with us and the travellers.
We had got on about a cose when the *Bykureea* at
the helm, seeing all clear, called out " Bhugna ko
pawn do," give my sister's son pawn. This was
their mode of giving the *Jhirnee*, or signal, and
the two Betoos were strangled. After strangling
them, they broke their spinal bones *thus*, by putting
their knees upon their backs, and pulling up their
heads and shoulders. After doing this they pushed
them out of a kind of window in the side. Every
boat has two of these windows, one on each side,
and they put the bodies out of that towards the
river. They break the spinal bones to prevent all
chance of the people recovering and giving evidence against them. We generally stab the dead
bodies through on both sides under the arm pits ;
but they are afraid to cut or stab the body lest
there should be signs of blood upon the water as
the corpses pass other boats that are following them
on the river.

Q.—What booty did you get?

Shumshera.—We got only sixteen gundas of pice (64), two brass lotahs, and the old clothes which the two men wore. It was hardly worth dividing. But coming on near Monghere, Jhoulee Khan, with whom we had landed and gone along on the road near the river, inveigled another man, a Beetoo from Bengal going to Guya on pilgrimage, who yielded sixteen gundas of *rupees*, and we six got fifteen of them among us—at least Jhoulee Khan shared only fifteen with us.

Q.—How was he disposed of?

Shumshera.—In the same manner as the others I believe, but I did not go on board this time. Jhoulee Khan and Bhowur Khan embarked with him and brought back our share of the booty. After this affair I left them near Monghere, as I got very little and grew melancholy, as there were no Thugs of my own clan or district. They were all *Bungoos* and Loduhas.

Q.—What became of Jvpaul's other boat?

Shumshera.—It waited for other passengers, and we did not see it again, as the boats go on from Ghat to Ghat without returning till they reach the end of their voyage up the river.

Q.—Were your father and grandfather Thugs?

Shumshera.—I believe so. I learnt so from others, but I never was taken out with them on Thuggee. I was taught by Dilawur Khan Jemadar, of Choubar in Chupra, son of Choramun; he has two brothers, Dokkee and Futteh, and all three are very noted Thugs, but they are also cultivators.

Q.—But how could you be ignorant of your father being a Thug when he used to go every season on Thuggee?

Shumshera.—He and my uncle Dondee used to

say that they had been in service, and we never
heard them say any thing of Thuggee. I should
have known nothing about it had I not been taken
out by Dilawur, Futteh Khan, and afterwards by
Jhoulee Khan the Fair, who told me that I was of
a very high Jumaldehee family of Thugs, the clan
from which he and all the Lodahas sprung.

Q.—How are the River Thugs not suspected by
the people who live on the banks of the river?

Shumshera.—They are very well known by the
Goreyts (police-men), and some other people of
the small villages along the banks of the Ganges;
they sometimes keep their boats near these villages
for several days together. The two lotahs taken
from the two men whose murder I have described,
were given to the Goreyt of the village of More,
whom Jypaul after the murder sent off for eight
annas worth of spirits. These Thugs never keep
any part of the booty but the money, lest it should
bring them into trouble. The clothes of the two
men were thrown into the river. The principal
men of the gang, or the shrewdest of them, go
along the roads, each having a servant carrying
his bundle and proceeding towards the Ghat where
his boat is to be found, whether going up or down
the river. When a traveller overtakes him, he
learns whither he is going, pretends to be ignorant
of the road, to be going to the same place with the
traveller, but to be entirely unacquainted with it,
and anxious to have somebody to instruct him. If
the traveller had not intended to go by water, the
Thug soon pretends to be much tired, and wishes
that he were near a boat. The traveller expresses
the same wish, and they agree to diverge from the
road to the river. Coming to the Ghat the Thug
pretends that he is a good hand at a bargain, and

is allowed to agree for a passage for both. He beats down the master of his own boat, after a good deal of disputing, to half price, and the Betoo is much pleased and expresses his gratitude; they embark, and the Betoo is killed as soon as they get away from other boats. If the Betoo suspects or dislikes the first man, he soon falls in with the inveigler of another boat who learns it by a sign, and pretends to enter into the Bectoo's feelings and anxiety to throw off the first, who on some pretence remains behind, while his friend takes on the traveller to the other boat further on than his own, where he is disposed off. They are much more numerous than we are. I have not heard of more than about thirty families of Motceas, and the Lodahas are not much above two hundred men, but the Bongoos are very numerous I have heard.

Q.—What do they consider the best season for their work?

Shumshera.—The months of November, December, January, and February. In March it becomes too hot, and in the rains the river is considered to be too rapid, and the boats cannot be pulled along the banks.

Q.—Was your brother Runjeet a Thug?

Shumshera.—Never; he never went on Thuggee, and used often to admonish me against going, but I did not attend to him.

IMAM BUKSH AND BUKHTAWUR ARE SENT FOR.

Q.—How was it that this lad's father, Madar Buksh, an old and noted Thug, did not initiate him himself?

Bukhtawur.—His father used to drink very hard,

and in his fits of intoxication he used to neglect his *prayers*, and his *days of fast*. All days were the same with him. This lad, Shumshera, was always sober and *religiously disposed*, and separated from his father, living always with his uncle Dondee, who was a very worthy and good man.

Q.—But he was a Thug also?

Bukhtawur.—Yes, he was, but he did not tell this boy so.

Q.—This lad says the Bongoos are known to the villagers on the bank of the river?

Bukhtawur.—He is a mere boy; if they were known to the villagers, how could they escape so well. They rarely keep their boats near villages; but when they do, they conciliate the Goreyts and other police men that they may not ask questions.

Q.—They never keep any thing but money he says?

Bukhtawur.—Rarely. They throw every thing else away in order to keep clear of the Custom-house searchers who are very numerous in that quarter.

Q.—He tells me that Jhoulee Khan the Fair has become a river Thug?

Bukhtawur.—Yes, for the last seven years Jhoulee has taken to the river; he bought a boat or two with some of them, and being a very clever man he makes one of their best inveiglers I hear.

Q.—And his namesake? Jhoulee Khan the Black?

Bukhtawur.—He keeps to the roads, and he has villages to take care of. He rented two villages from Dolar Choudhuree, who is a Rajah without a *Tiluk*, whose son-in-law demanded from him the rent rather harshly; Jhoulee was a proud man, and gave him a drubbing with his shoe, and the

Rajah got him seized and sent to Mozufferpore as a Thug. He was twelve years in prison, and has been at large for the last ten years, reporting himself to the police in person every eight days, while his brother, Tulwur Khan, leads out his gang on the roads. They are both very great men, but Jhoulee Khan the Fair is the greatest. He knows every Thug in Bengal, whether on the river or the land.

Q.—Were not some of your family lately hung at Ghazeepore?

Imam Buksh.—Yes. My two brothers, Khuda Buksh and Peer Buksh were hung in September, two years ago. I am the oldest and last.

Q.—And how did you escape?

Imam Buksh.—They were taken in the fact (literally "Lash-ke-uper," upon the bodies,*) but I was taken afterwards at home. They offered to release me on security, and when I was ready to give it, they sent me off to Saugor.

W. H. SLEEMAN,
Genl. Supt.

* The bodies in this case could not be found I believe by the magistrate of Ghazeepore, but the evidence was sufficiently clear without them.

APPENDIX.

THE RAMASEEANA,

OR VOCABULARY

OF THE

THUG LANGUAGE.

PREPARED BY CAPTAIN WILLIAM H. SLEEMAN, SUPER-
INTENDENT OF THE THUG POLICE.

Aulae—A Thug, in contradistinction to Beetoo, any person not a Thug. When Thugs wish to ascertain whether the persons they meet are Thugs or not, they accost them with "Aulae Khan Salam," if Musulmans; and "Aulae Bhae Ram Ram," if Hindoo. This to any one but a Thug would seem the common salutation of "peace to thee, friend," but it would be instantly recognised by a Thug. Any man that should reply in the same manner would be quite safe.

Adhoreea—Any person who has separated himself from a party whom the Thugs have murdered or intend to murder, and thereby escaped them.

Ae ho to Ghyree Chulo—"If you are come, pray descend." The phrase most commonly used as the J,hirnee or signal for putting people to death, when every thing has been prepared for the purpose.

Agasee—A turban. A Thug never moves out

without his turban, except in Bengal perhaps. If a turban is set on fire, it threatens great evil, and the gang must if near home, return and wait seven days; if at a distance, an offering of goor is made, and the individual to whom the turban belonged, alone returns home. If the turban falls off it is an omen almost as bad, and requires the same sacrifices.

Agasee—Is also the term given for the cry of the kite. Heard in the day time, it is of little importance, and interpreted according to their rules for the Thibaoo and the Pilhaoo: but heard during the Kootub, or interval between the first watch and daybreak, it is called the Kootub Agasee, a dreadful omen. If in camp, they get up and fly immediately, leaving untouched any person they may have inveigled, however wealthy. If they hear it after dark, but before the end of the first watch, they are not alarmed, as they consider the threatened evil to pass away in their sleep; literally the " omen gets suffocated under their sides as they turn in their sleep." It is the same with almost all bad omens that take place between evening and the end of the first watch.

Ardal—Among the Duckun Thugs, is the same as Adhorcea among those of Hindoostan.

Agureea—Descendants of the Thugs, who, after their expulsion from Delhie, resided for a time in the district of Agra, and thence spread over India; in contradistinction to those who went to different parts of India, without resting at Agra. The Bubleems and Tundels, two of the seven original clans of Musulman Thugs, did not rest at Agra; and they are excluded. Their tradition is, that one of the Emperors of the house of Gouree expelled them all from Delhie, after the murder of a Cheyla, or slave of his, who had been long in league with them, but was murdered in consequence of a threat to betray them, made with a view to extort more money than they thought reasonable. The Emperor had them all marked on the posteriors with the stamp of the copper coin of the Empire.

Ansoolore—Literally, " tear drops." Any shower of rain that falls before or after the four usual months of June, July, August and September. If it falls during the first day and night after entering on an expedition the gang must return, and open it anew. It is always a bad omen, and requires some sacrifices. See also Rukutbondee, or blood dropping. The Duckun Thugs call this shower Now.

Agasee Birar—Term among the Duckun Thugs for thunder. If it thunders while opening an expedition, and heavy rain falls, it is of no importance. If little or no rain falls the omen is bad, and they must suspend operations : after the expedition has been opened it is of no importance.

Ankura—One thousand of any thing.

Awk,hur—Any person maimed or deprived of the use of his limbs. In this sense it is peculiar to Duckun Thugs. Among Hindoostanees it signifies any bad omen. If they meet with such a maimed person on the road, the first day after they enter on an expedition, the gang must return, and open it anew. They never kill such maimed persons. There have been instances of it, but they are all supposed to have been followed by great calamities.

Anhur—Any metallic utensil for eating, drinking, or cooking.

Anjuna or *Anjruhna*—To sleep or pass the night.

Aentha—Silver money.

Angjhap—A term used by the Thugs of the
Duckun for Rehna, or a temporary burial of bodies.

Ard,hul—Any bad omen; the same as Khurtul.
Both terms are confined to Duckun Thugs.

Balmeek—The author of one of the three
Ramaens (or histories of the rape of Seeta, the
wife of Ram, one of the incarnations of Vishnoo)
which after its author is called the Balmeek Ramaen. The Thugs consider Balmeek to have been
of their profession; but, though they quote his
name with reverence, they do not, I believe, invoke
it in their offerings and sacrifices. A sketch of
his life is given in each of the three Ramaens.
His name was Dojadh,un, and he is said to have
been a Brahmin by birth; to have been born at
Kunoje in the latter end of the Sutjoog, or golden
age; to have lost his parents when he was five
years of age, and soon after to have joined some
gangs of Bheel robbers, who, armed with bows and
arrows, infested the roads about Chutterkote; to
have married one of their daughters, and to have
become the most noted robber and murderer of his
day. From this course of life he is said to have
been reclaimed by a miracle. Seven celebrated
saints, at their holy place of abode, learned by
inspiration that a Brahmin was thus disgracefully
employed, and proceeded to the place to admonish
him. He saw them approach, and as usual bent
his bow, and demanded their money or their lives.
" Why do you, a Brahmin by birth, follow this
" horrible trade, and rob and murder innocent
" travellers?" " I have a wife and children whom
" I love, on the top of yonder hill; they want food,
" and I must provide it for them." " Go and ask
" those you love, and for whom you provide food
" by the murder of innocent men, whether they

" are willing to share with you in the crimes as
" well as in the fruits." " And in the mean time
" you will make off. Many a traveller has tried to
" escape me by similar tricks, but I am not to be
" deceived." " We swear to remain till you re-
" turn." He went to his wife and children and
asked the questions. They told him that they
shared in what he brought to them, but he must be
alone answerable for the means by which he
acquired it. He returned to the saints, with a con-
trite heart, and implored their instructions. They
told him to tarry where he stood till they should
return, and continue to repeat the words, " Mura,
" Mura, Mura," dead, dead, dead, which was
familiar to him; knowing that he would in time
convert it into Ram, Ram, Ram, God, God, God;
and thinking that his soul was not yet fitted to
repeat the holy name. He soon made the expected
change, and continued to repeat Ram, Ram, Ram,
for twelve thousand years, when the seven saints
returned. Nothing but the bones remained, but
they were erect, and repeating the holy name of
Ram. White ants had built their hill over them,
but on hearing their voice the skeleton assumed a
form of godlike beauty, and burst forth, as it is
said, like the sun from behind a dark cloud. He
became a man after God's own heart, and wrote
his Ramaen by inspiration. Balmee signifies ant
hill, and the *k* affixed signifies, born of, and his
name was changed from Dojadhun to Balmeek.

Bajeed—Safe, free from danger. When the
Thugs have got their victims at the place where
they intend to murder them, if the spies placed
around, see all clear, they call out one of the following names, and the work of murder goes on.
Bajeed or Bajeed Khan, Deo or Deomun, or Deo-

seyn. If the spies see a stranger approach and apprehend danger, they call out Sheikh Jee, or Sheikh Mahummud, or Luchmun, or Luchmun Sing, or Lechee Ram, or Gunga Ram, and the Thugs suspend operations. When one part of the gang advances with the travellers they intend to kill, and on the road meets other travellers, whom the party in the rear may conveniently murder, they tell them to bid their friends Bajeed or Bajeed Khan, and Deo, or Deoman, or Deo Sing, to make haste and overtake them. As soon as the gang behind hear this message they may fall upon and murder them, understanding by the signal that in advance the road is clear.

Baee or Dubaee—A frequented road.

Bae hojana—To become public; viz. the bodies of victims or other traces of their proceedings.

Byd,ha—A man who has lost a limb or any member of his body. If they meet such a person during the first day of their expedition it is a bad omen, and requires sacrifices. Also any thing unbecoming the cast or condition of the person, and likely to lead to suspicion and danger. They seldom murder any person who has lost a limb, and attribute much of our success against them on the Nerbudda river, to the murder of Newal Sing, who had lost an arm, and his family at Biseynee in 1820.

Bagh—Bagdena—Same as Phooldena, parole of rendezvous or meeting.

Bugureea—A class of Thugs who reside chiefly about Sooper, in the Gwalior territories. They are called also K,hokhureeas, and have followed the trade several generations, since their intermarriage with the emigrant Thugs from Delhie through Agra, or Agureeas.

Boguma—An old garment.

Bugiana—To become aware of the designs of the Thugs upon one.

Bugna—The same.

Bājunee—A gun.

Boj,ha—The Thug who takes the bodies of the murdered persons to the grave.

Bojhae—The office of the Bojha.

Bukote—A strangler; same as Bhurtote.

Buk,h—The word made use of by the Thugs when calling to each other to assemble after having been separated by accident or design. Buk,h, Buk,h, Buk,h, or come, come, come.

Bahleem—One of the seven original Thug clans. There are scarcely any of this clan to be found north of the Nerbudda.

Beyl—The place chosen for burying the victims.

Beegha—Term among the Thugs of Behar and Bengal for a share of the spoil. From every booty they first set aside ten per cent. for the leaders, and five for the stranglers, however few or many the remainder is divided into Beeghas, or shares. Their proportions are 1.2 for jemadar or leader; 1.14 for a man who has attained the rank of strangler; 1 for a person who has not attained that rank.

Beelha—A great enemy of Thugs: also a leper, or man deprived of his nose or ear; or any person much emaciated by sickness.

Beetula.—A dog. Term peculiar to the Jumaldehee, Lodaha and Moteea Thugs of Behar and Bengal.

Bykureea—The spy or scout. Term used by the Bongoos, or river Thugs, the Jumaldehees, Lodahas, and Moteeas for Tilha.

Bykuree kurna—To act as a spy or scout; or Bykuree " dek,hna," to look out.

Beyl,ha—The person who chooses the place for murdering.

Beylhae—The office of choosing the place.

Beel Grain—Term peculiar to Duckun Thugs.

Bhalee or *Bhaloo*—The call of the jackal. There are three kind of calls from which the Thugs draw omens. The Bhalee, which they also call Burhohee, is the call of one jackal. The second is the general clamour of jackals, which people call their lamentation. This the Thugs call Raureen. The third, the Ekareea, or short call of a jackal, in which he seems to be cut short after an effort or two. Any one of these calls heard during the day threatens great evil, and the gang quits the country in which they hear it, leaving untouched any persons they have inveigled, however wealthy. The Ekareea is bad either by night or by day. The other two calls, when heard by night on opening the expedition, are interpreted according to the ordinary rules for the Thibaoo and Pilhaoo.

Bileea—A brass cup; technically a place for murdering or burying the victims.

Bileea-Munjuna—Literally, to clean the brass cup. To choose the place for murder.

Bilgaree—An extensive jungle or waste, very convenient for the purpose of murder.

Bhimjodha—The bird Chirrah Q. V. peculiar to some classes of Thugs.

Banee—Blood.

Baean Geedee Sona Leedee—A proverb of the Thugs. "A jackal crossing from right to left brings gold." If a jackal crosses the path of the Thug from the right to the left it promises good fortune. If from left to right bad.

Bungoo—The river Thug of Bengal. These men live chiefly in the district of Bhurdwan, on the banks of the Hoogly river. They move up and down the Ganges during the months of November, December, January, and February, always pretending to be going to or coming from holy places, such as Bunares, Allahabad, &c. &c. They inveigle people on board their boats, strangle them and throw them into the river, having broken their spines to prevent the chance of their recovering. The leader of the gang has commonly his own boat, but he sometimes hires it for the season, and the owner of the boat gets the share of one man. The boats have a hole on each side through which they throw the bodies into the river; but they never stab or cut them, lest there should be signs of blood in the water to attract the attention of people in the boats by which they float on their way down the river. This class of Thugs is very numerous; from two to three hundred.

Bhans lena—To steal or defraud each other in the division of booty: peculiar to Duckun Thugs; same as Kootkurna among Hindoostan Thugs.

Bhontee—Calling of the kite while flying. It is a bad omen. If they see the dung of a kite falling in the air, it is considered to promise a valuable white booty, in silver or cloth.

Binderee—A sword.

Bindoo—A Hindoo.

Bunasna or *Bunas Juna*—To lose any thing, but particularly the road.

Bunij—Literally merchandize or goods; technically a traveller or any other person whom the Thugs consider worth murdering. He is their stock in trade.

Bunij Ludhna—Literally, to load the goods; technically, to murder the travellers.

Bunjaree—A cat. If a cat comes to them at their lodgings at night it promises good fortune.

Bungur—A Thug term peculiar to Duckun Thugs.

Buneana—To stain with blood a cloth or any other thing.

Bunar—Same as Baee. Bad news, untoward discovery of the Thugs' proceedings: also a road become unsafe for Thugs.

Bhurtote—A strangler.

Bhurtotee—The office or duty of strangler. Thugs seldom attain this rank or office till they have been on many expeditions, and acquired the requisite courage or insensibility by slow degrees. At first they are almost always shocked and frightened; but after a time they say they lose all sympathy with the victims. A Thug leader, of most polished manners and great eloquence, being asked one day in my presence by a native gentleman, whether he never felt compunction in murdering innocent people, replied with a smile, "Does any " man feel compunction in following his trade; and " are not all our trades assigned us by Providence." The native gentleman said, "How many people " have you in the course of your life killed with " your own hands at a rough guess?" "I have " killed none!" "Have you not been just describing " to me a number of murders?" "Yes; but do " you suppose I could have committed them. Is " any man killed from man's killing? Admee ke " marne se koe murta. Is it not the hand of God " that kills him? and are we not mere instruments " in the hand of God?" They are first employed as scouts; then as sextons; then as shumseeas or holders of hands; and lastly as Bhurtotes. When a man feels that he has sufficient courage and insensibility for the purpose, he solicits the oldest and most renowned Thug of the gang to make him his cheyla, or disciple.· The Thug agrees to become his gooroo, or spiritual preceptor, and when the gang falls in with a man of respectability but not much strength, fitted for the purpose, he tells the gooroo that he is prepared, with his permission, to try his hands upon him. While the traveller is asleep with the gang at their quarters, the gooroo takes his disciple into a neighboring field followed by three or four old members of the gang. On reaching the spot chosen, they all face to the direction the gang intends to move, and the gooroo says, "Oh Kalee, Kunkalee, Bhudkalee. Oh " Kalee, Mahakalee, Calcutta Walee.* If it seem-

---

* The Thugs, and I understand all other Hindoos, believe Kalee to have first appeared upon the earth in Calcutta. They believe also that after she had, through the means of the Thugs created by her for the special purpose, destroyed the great Demon "*Rukut beej dana*" at Bindachul, on the eastern extremity of the Vindeya range, she carried the body to Calcutta and there buried it where her temple now stands. That place they consider to be her favourite seat where she *works more miracles* than in all the rest of India. They have got a notion that in Calcutta even the Christians attend her worship, and make offerings to her temple; and I believe the priests have always actually made offerings to her image on great occasions in the name of the Hon'ble Company out of the rents of the land with which government has endowed the temple. European gentlemen and ladies frequently attend the nautches and feasts of her great days in the *Durja Pooja ;* and as these feasts are part of the religious ceremonies, this innocent curiosity is very liable to be misconstrued by people at a distance from the scene, and should not therefore be indulged. The Hindoos have a verse which they often repeat in their invocations. " *Kalee! Calcutta* " *walee! tera buchun na jawe Khalee. Oh Kalee, great goddess* " *of Calcutta, may thy promise never be made in vain."* She is said to delight in the name of *Kunkalee,* or man-eater, and to be always drinking the blood of men and of demons. The term means, I believe, the same thing as *Kunkalin.* They all believe Kalee to have been extremely black, and to have had features so terrifically hideous that no mortal man could dare to look upon them.

" eth to thee fit that the traveller now at our lodging
" should die by the hands of this thy slave, vouch-
" safe us the Thibaoo." If they get the auspice on
the right within a certain time (half an hour), it
signifies her sanction; but if they have no sign, or
the dhilhaoo, (or sign on the left,) some other Thug
must put the traveller to death, and the candidate
for honour wait for another time.

Davey's sanction having been conveyed in the
Thibaoo, they return to their quarters, and the
gooroo takes a handkerchief, and, facing to the
west, ties the knot in one end of it with a rupee or
other piece of silver inserted. This knot they call

When Kalee or Parbuttee appears in company with her husband,
Siwa or Mahadeo, she is represented as beautiful and fair, and is
commonly called *Gouree*, or *the fair*. It was only when she came
to destroy demons, or as the Goddess of war, that she is supposed
to have put on these hideous shapes. In a beautiful piece of sculpture at Beragur on the Nerbudda river, she is represented as seated
on a bull behind her husband, whose dress and ornaments are, as
usual, composed of snakes, very gracefully twisted and suspended
around him. This piece of sculpture is called *Gouree Shunkur*,
after her name *Gouree*, and that of Mahadeo, *Shunkur*; and it is
so much superior to any other they are accustomed to see, that the
people, from the most learned to the most unlettered, implicitly
believe that the God and Goddess came here, mounted as they now
are, on a visit to the Nurbudda, from the mountain *Khylas*, and got
their earthly parts turned into stone as a memorial of their visit,
and will some day resume them.

The whole is cut out of one block of lava from a dyke in the
marble rocks through which the Nurbudda flows beneath the
temple which is consecrated to them. The wall of the court in
which the temple stands is lined all round by the statutes of some
three scores *Jognies*, or petty goddesses, who attend upon Parbuttee,
about the size of life, cut out of rocks of different kinds, with
various faces and in various attitudes, and all mounted upon different *Bahuns*, or vehicles of birds and quadrupeds. They are all
sadly mutilated, and the God and Goddess within are said to have
been saved by a miracle from *Aurungebe* and his army, to whom
these things are always attributed. At this temple an annual fair
is held in the beginning of November.

the Goor Ghat, or classic knot, and no man who
has not been thus ordained by the high priest, is
permitted to tie it. See *Goor Ghat.* The disciple
receives it respectfully from the high priest in his
right hand, and stands over the victim, with a
shumseea, or holder of hands, by his side. The
traveller is roused on some pretence or other, and
the disciple passes the handkerchief over his neck,
at the signal given by the leader of the gang, and
strangles him with the aid of his shumseea. Having
finished his work, he bows down before his gooroo,
and touches his feet with both hands, and does the
same to all his relations and friends present, in
gratitude for the honour he has attained. He opens
the knot after he has heard or seen the Thibaoo,
or auspice on the right, takes out the rupee and
gives it, with all the other silver he has, to his
gooroo, as a nuzur; and the gooroo adding what
money he has at the time, purchases a rupee and
a quarter's worth of goor for the Tuponee, and
lays out the rest in sweetmeats. The Tuponee
sacrifice is now performed under the neem, the
mango, or the byr, if they are available, and if not,
under any other tree except the babul, the sirsa
(mamosa series) and the reonja. The new disciple
now takes his seat among the Bhurtotes around the
carpet, and receives his share of the consecrated
sugar, and the sweetmeats are distributed to all
the members of the gang of whatever grade. On
his return home after the expedition he gives a
feast to his gooroo and his family; and if he has
the means, to all his relations; and he presents his
gooroo with an entire new suit of clothes for himself and one for his wife, and others for his relations, if he can afford it. The gooroo after a
certain interval, returns the compliment to him and

his family, and the relation between them is ever after respected as the most sacred that can be formed. A Thug will often rather betray his father than the gooroo by whom he has been knighted.

The Bhurtote is not permitted to bathe on the day he has strangled any one: formerly no member of the gang was permitted to bathe on the day that a murder was committed, but now the stranglers alone are forbidden to do so.

Buhup, Buhupna, Buhapjana—To go, or escape; as a traveller from the snares of the Thugs, or Thugs from pursuit.

Bara Muttee—The call of the lizard. At whatever time and place they hear the call of the lizard, they consider it a very good omen. The fall of a lizard, upon a Thug is considered a very bad omen; and if it falls upon any garment, that garment must be given away in charity. If it falls upon the ground it threatens nothing.

Baroonee—An old and venerable Thug woman, who is much respected by the fraternity.

I have heard of only one woman who has gone herself on Thug expeditions, and that is the wife of Bukhtawur Jemadar, of the Sooseea class of Thugs. She and her husband are still at large in the Jypore territory. She has often assisted her husband in strangling; and on one occasion strangled a man who had overpowered and stunned her husband. Mothers, I know, have often made their sons go on Thuggee when they would not otherwise have gone, and wives on some occasions their husbands; and I have heard of one woman in the Duckun who kept herself a small gang of Thugs; but Bukhtawur's wife is the only woman that has, as far as I can learn, gone on Thuggee herself.

Baroo—A Thug of respectability either from the celebrity of his Thug ancestors, or from his own character as a Thug.

Barana, Barawnee kurna—To disperse on the approach of danger or separate into small parties to avoid suspicion.

Birar—The fighting of cats or their screams when fighting. Also the Duckun Thugs' term for Manj.

Agaseebirar—Thunder : a term also peculiar to Duckun Thugs. Agasee signifies turban among both Duckun and Hindoostanee Thugs.

Bhurahur—A pitcher full of water. Bhurehur one empty.

If on leaving their homes on an expedition they meet a woman with a pitcher full of water on her head, it promises a safe return and prosperous journey; if empty, the reverse. The pitcher full promises still more if the female be with child.

Bhurka—Rupees. Peculiar to the Duckunees.

Bhurehur—An empty pitcher, and a bad omen when met on the road.

Bharakee—A gun.

Bhara—Dead bodies of the victims. Term peculiar to the Duckun Thugs. Hindoostanee Thugs call them Ghurtha.

Bora—A Thug; in contradistinction to Beetoo, any person not a Thug. This term is peculiar to the Jumaldehee, Lodaha, Moteea and Bungoo Thugs in Behar and Bengal.

Borkee—A knife.

Borkeeana, or *Borkee Marna*, or *Borkeeas dalza*—To stab with a knife.

Boreeahut or *Bore*—Loud talking, bellowing, uproar.

Borkee—The small deer. If a single small deer

crosses their road from right to left, it threatens evil. If from left to right, it promises good; but its promises and threats are not considered important. A herd of small deer at all times and under all circumstances promise a meeting with other Thugs, and is considered good. The Duckun Thugs consider the crossing of the single deer either from left to right or right to left a bad omen.

Borcha—New clothes; term peculiar to Duckun Thugs. Also a bundle or load of new clothes. Hindoostance Thugs call it scep.

Burauk—The omen of the wolf or wolves crossing their road. If from left to right it threatens great evil. If from right to left it is a good omen. If its call be heard during the day, the gang must immediately quit the country in which they hear it. If between midnight and day light, it is bad; if between evening and midnight indifferent; between midday and sunset it is not so bad as between sunrise and midday. They call it the weeping (Chimmama) of the wolf, and consider the sound mournful. The single wolf portends more than a pair; and the Burauk is, whether for good or for bad, one of their most important omens.

Bursote—One of the seven original clans of Thugs who were all Musulmans.

Burg—Any thing seen upon a man unbecoming his condition, and therefore likely to lead to suspicion.

Burgeela—An accomplice: one who knows the secrets of the Thugs and keeps them.

Burka—A leader or chief of Thugs, or one thoroughly instructed in the art; distinguished from Kuboola, a tyro. Also any man of rank.

The Thugs consider a Burka as capable of forming a gang of Thugs out of the rude materials

around him in any part of India ; and a Thug who
has arrived at this degree of proficiency in the art,
ought not therefore to be left at large. A Kuboola,
or tyro, they think, could do nothing if left to
himself, and he might therefore be left at large
without much danger to society, if he had no leader
to join.

Buroee—An omen from the jackal's call. See
Bhalee.

Buhra—Four travellers, or victims in the hands
of Thugs.

Bees—A low call of the small owl repeated three
or four times: called also Chireya. It always
threatens evil.

Bhusmee—Fine earth or sand, particularly applicable to what is found in digging the graves for
the victims: same as Rewaroo. Flour is also
called by them Bhusmee.

Bhys—One of the seven original clans of Thugs.

Bisul purna—To be awkwardly handled in
strangling: to have the roomal round the face or
head instead of the neck. *Soosul purna*—to have
it round the neck.

Bisnee—A Thug, pick-pocket, thief, or any one
that lives by the plunder of others.

Bisendhee—Fetters. Also a Thulee or metal
utensil of any kind.

Bisul—A person, intended to be killed, who has
clothes round his neck and head, or other impediment to strangling. Also a man on whom the
roomal falls untowardly, either on his head or face,
or is otherwise untowardly handled in strangling.
Also a Thug who has blood upon his clothes, or
other signs of murder that may lead to suspicion.
In all these and other senses, Sosul is opposed to
Bisul. Any Thug in whose hands victims have

been often Bisul, is excluded from the office of strangler, on the ground of presumed unfitness for the duty.

Bous—A large gang of Thugs, above twenty-five; same as Kharoo.

Beeta or *Bheeta*—A hundred.

Beetoo—Any person not a Thug, in contradistinction to Aulae a Thug.

Bhitree—A pair of travellers or victims.

Botoel—A body of travellers too large for the Thugs to manage: see *Tonkul.*

Bote hona—To become inveigled; fall into the snares of the Thugs; in contradistinction to Chuk Jana or Iterjana.

Char—A Bhurtote or strangler. Term peculiar to the Bungoes, Jumaldehees, Lodahas and Moteeas.

Chareeae—Bhurtotee, the office or duty of strangler.

Cheeha—A coward, timid Thug, one who shows sympathy or fear.

Chibiana—To be released from confinement; distinguished from Jhur jana, to escape or break prison.

Chandanee-kee-dhap—A dog seen dunging by moonlight; a very bad omen, which makes the gang suspend all operations for three days if possible, and make sacrifices.

Choukana—To examine or reconnoitre secretly.

Chaukna or *Chouklena*—To see, inspect, examine.

Chookadena—Same as Thibaedena. To cause to sit down and look up; as travellers before strangling them. They direct their attention to the sky or some other object above them.

Chuk—Suspicion.

Chukbele—A place chosen for the murder too near to danger.

Chuk ho juna—To become aware of the designs of Thugs and on one's guard ; as travellers whom they are trying to inveigle.

Chukura—A small gold coin. This term is confined to Duckun Thugs.

Chulub—The interval between the time when the sun sets and about gunfire at night. Evening, Chulub men Ladhna, To kill in the evening.

Chuttoo-Dhuneea—Same as Oorut Kawuree.

Chamoo Jana—To be seized or arrested.

Chamlena—To seize or arrest.

Chimmama—The call of the wolf; considered a bad omen at all times, but particularly during the day. The gang must immediately halt, or go back, and quit that part of the country as soon as possible.

Chimmota—A boy.

Chimmotee—A girl.

Chummun—A Brahmin.

Chummoseea—A holder of hands. Term used by Duckun Thugs for shumseea.

Chummoseeae—The office or duty of Chumoseea.

Chumeeae—The office or work of the Chumeea, viz. seizing the victim.

Chumeea—The person who seizes, or assists the Chamosee in seizing and keeping down the victim. There may be ten Chumeeas, but there can be only one Chumosee.

Chanda—Cloth.

Chandoo—An experienced and expert Thug.

Chingoreea—One of the sects or Bharnts of the Thug clans.

Chinha—A boy.

Chingurce—A clan of Moltanee Thugs, sometimes called Naicks, of the Musulman faith. They proceed on their expeditions in the characters of Brinjaras, with cows and bullocks laden with merchandize, which they expose for sale at their encampments, and thereby inveigle their victims. They use the rope of their bullocks instead of the roomal in strangling. They are an ancient tribe of Thugs, and take their wives and children on their expeditions. They destroy, it is said, their female children; and if they at any time preserve them, they never allow them to marry out of their tribe.

There are, it is said, more than a hundred families of these Moltanees in the neighbourhood of Hingolee. They do not associate with other Thugs, but they use nearly the same technical language, and practise the same trade of murder. They have however a different ostensible employment in the hire of their bullocks, sale of wood and grain, &c. &c.

Chingana—A boy. Term peculiar to Duckun Thugs.

Choundh,na—To bind up in bundles booty or the dead bodies of victims.

Choundh Lena—To tie on the turban. **Agasee** Choundh lena.

Choundhee-Churana—To tie the arms behind.

Chowun—A woman. Term peculiar to Duckun Thugs.

Choundhee—Turband.

Cheeng—A sword. Term confined to **Berar** Thugs.

Chungar—A thief of any kind.

Cheek—A gold Mohur.

Cheyhur—Jungle or forest.

Chirreya—A chirping of the small owlet, which Thugs consider a bad omen, whether made while the bird is sitting or flying; it is said to be a melancholy and low sound, seldom repeated. See *Puttoree*. Judae, Jemadar, who was considered to be one of the best augurers of his day, lived at Murnae, a celebrated Thug village, and it is said that, returning one morning from a walk in the fields, he told his friend that he had heard the the Chirreya in a manner that indicated some great calamity at hand. That night or the night after Mr. Halhed is said to have attacked the village and Lieutenant Monsel was killed. It was I believe in November, 1812.

Chireeapotee—One of the sects of Thugs, said to be from the Bhys clan.

Chira—The call of the Roopareel, or Muhoka (Caculus Custaneous,) or the bird itself. Some Thugs call it also the Bhinjhoda.

Chirchera—The call of the lizard. See *Bara Muttee*.

Chireyta—A Pundit, or any Marhata.

Chourukna—To inform or give information against any one.

Churagee—A Byragee; term peculiar to Duckun Thugs.

Churtec-Pholkee—The time between sunrise and mid-day: see *Pholkee*.

Cheesa—Any good or blessing from Heaven, but particularly a rich traveller.

Checota—Rupees.

Cheyt—Same as Cheek. A traveller who has discovered the designs of the Thugs. Cheyt ho Jana—Cheek ho Jana—To become aware of their designs and on one's guard.

Chutaw—A share of the booty.

Chutae—The same.

Chutae Lena—To divide.

Deo—Used for the same purpose as Bajeed khan.

Deo Sing—The same.

Daee—The road; term peculiar to Duckun Thugs.

Duheea—The call or cry of the hare. They will perish in the jungles, they say, after hearing it, if they do not make sacrifices, and the hare or some other animal of the forest will drink water out of their skulls; if they kill any one whom they have with them at the time, they will find no booty on him, or what they find will tend to their ruin. See *Roopuneea*.

Duhee Phorkana—To gargle and squirt from the mouth sour milk. The means by which the evil threatened by the Kalee kee Manj, is averted in the morning.

Dada Dheera—A very ancient and canonized Thug of the Bhursote class whom they invoke in drinking spirits at certain religious ceremonies. They do not mention him with Jora Naek in the Ghoor offering, or Tuponee; but they make votive offerings of ardent spirits to Dada Dheera. They promise an offering of spirits, and if they succeed in their prayers, they drink the spirits, if their caste permits; if not, they throw it on the ground with the expression of their thanks in prescribed phrases. Dada Dheera's tomb is visited as a holy shrine by Thugs at Kumona in Koel, where he was buried.

Dudh—A man who is not a Thug. See *Beetoo*.

Dhagal—Papers.

Dhaga kurana or dena—To satisfy a suspecting chief or public functionary of the innocence of Thugs suspected.

Dhaga le ana—To search out and report what they require to learn from travellers.

Dhaga—An eliciting of the intentions of travellers; or negociation with native chiefs, or any men in authority for protection, or for release when arrested.

Dhagsa—Hilly or jungly country. Term peculiar to Duckun Thugs.

Dogga—A hookha of any kind; also an old man.

Dhokur—A dog; also a man who seizes Thugs.

Dhonkee—A police man or guard. Same as Ronkee.

Dhilha—A pice.

Dhoulanee—One of the sects of Thugs.

Dholin—An old woman; term peculiar to Duckun Thugs.

Dhulal—Spirit vender; term peculiar to Duckun Thugs.

Dul—Weight.

Duldar—Weighty.

Duller—The head.

Dullar Khan—Same as Surbulund Khan.

Deomun—Used for the same purpose as Bajeed Khan.

Dhamonee-kee-manj—The fighting of cats, during the day, which is a very bad omen. The threatened evil must be averted by a sacrifice.

Dhamree—Metal utensils, peculiar to Duckun Thugs.

Dheema—The belly.

Dheema—Goats or sheep, sense peculiar to Duckun Thugs.

Dant,hee—The noise of jackals fighting; a very bad omen, which involves the necessity of leaving the part of the country in which the gang hears it.

Dhaundhoee—Any man employed in the pursuit of Thugs.

Dunda—Term used by Duckun Thugs for Kanta, or braying of an ass.

Dhons-Jana—To fly or escape.

Dhonsna—The same.

Dhonsana—To come to seize or arrest Thugs. Peculiar to the Duckun Thugs in this sense.

Dhunteroo—The ass. The Thugs think the omen of the ass the most important of all whether it threatens evil or promises good. "Sou puk, heroo ek Dunteroo." The ass is equal to a hundred birds, is a maxim in augury. The omen of the ass is also superior to that of all quadrupeds! If they hear it bray on the left on opening an expedition (Pilhaoo), and it is soon after repeated on the right (Thibaoo), they believe that nothing on earth can prevent their success during that expedition, though it should last for years.

Dhuneea—Breaking wind ; peditum. See *Oorut Kawree.*

Dhungee—Lotah or brass pot.

Dhnoonsa—Dry tobacco.

Doona—Stocks for confining Thugs or other prisoners.

Doonr—The loud screams of a victim for help. See *Senth.*

Doonrkurna, or *Doonree Lakarna*—To scream loudly for help.

Doonreeana—The same.

Dapnee—A dagger. Term peculiar to Duckun Thugs.

Dhap—A dog seen in the act of dunging.

Dhara—Vessels of metal..

Dheree—A Surae or village.

Dhurae—The share of the booty assigned to the leaders before the general division. It is generally the tenth article if there are ten or more of the

same kind ; or one ana in the rupee upon the value,
if there are not. After this deduction and the payment of a small extra allowance to the stranglers,
grave choosers and diggers, and other officers,
they all divide the booty in equal shares, as described under the head of Kowree.

The Motheea Thugs about Patna and Chapra,
give their leaders, as Dhurae, a handful of rupees
out of the booty, and divide with them the rest in
equal shares ; and from this they are said to derive
their name. Their Jemadars are bound in honour
to sacrifice themselves for the good of their followers, whenever required to do so, and have the
character of being more staunch than those of
other classes of Thugs.

Dheerna—The belly. A term peculiar to the
Duckun Thugs.

Dhurdalna—To strangle.

Dhurohur—Strangling.

Dhurohurkurna—To strangle.

Dhurdho—A river.

Dautun—A police guard ; any person found unexpectedly in the neighbourhood of the Bele, or
place chosen for the murder, whether residing
there, or there merely by accident.

Dutoon—The call of the hare ; if on the right, it
is a very bad omen ; all travellers with them must
be let off.

Ekareea—A single or short call of a jackal in
which he seems to have met with a sudden check.
This is considered a very bad omen by Thugs all
over India.

25th May, 1835, I had ordered a party of Spa-
hees, with some approvers, to proceed this morning
towards Gwalior in search of some Thugs who
have lately found an asylum there. About 9 o'clock

last night one of the native officers came to tell me
that they could not move till afternoon to-day as
they had heard a bad omen.   I have just been to
the jail and discovered that this bad omen was the
Ekareea, heard about 8 o'clock last night. · Nun-
hooa, one of the approvers, declared that on leaving Saugor about three months ago for Indore he
heard the Ekareea; and not attending to it, he got
the wound, which he received from a sword in
arresting a noted Thug, Bhyroo, the son of Himmut, between Indore and Baroda.   These men
never go out to arrest their associates or to take
up the bodies of wounded travellers without taking
the auspices, though they rarely tell us of it.

Ekburda.—A Teylee or oil vender.   They never
either kill or employ oil venders, and if they meet
one on leaving home the first day they must return.
No man of this cast has yet been admitted as a
member of their fraternity, as far as I can learn.
The Thugs attribute their arrest in the Mhow cantonment, and all their consequent suffering after
the Dhar affair, to their having murdered a Teylee, though they knew not his cast at the time.

Ektawhona—To assemble together; rendezvous.

Eloo—Any single person not a Thug.

Endh—A woman.

Eentab—Term used by the Duckun Thugs for
Eetuk.   The term signifies contamination from the
following circumstances; 1st, the birth of a child
in a Thug family; 2nd, the first courses of a Thug's
daughter; 3d, a marriage in a Thug's family; 4th,
a death in a Thug's family of any person that has
quitted the mother's breast; 5th, a mare foaling;
6th, circumcision; 7th, a buffaloe or cow giving
calf or dying; 8th, a goat or ewe giving young;

9th, a cat or dog giving young or dying; 10th, menses after the first time. All these involve the necessity of sacrifice.

Eetuk—Contamination from a wife or daughter being under her courses. No man can enter on an expedition while they are in that state, or for a certain number of days after; and if the leader's wife or daughter should be in that state none of his party can go; also contamination from any of the above circumstances. See *Eentab.*

Entha—Rupees or money of any kind. See *Anchta.*

Etrbarkhanee—A sect of Thugs derived from the Bursote clan.

Gobba—The round grave. This is made circular, and a small pillar of hard ground left in the centre. This they think prevents the dogs, jackals and other animals of the jungle from digging up the bodies, and at the same time the ground from cracking and emitting that effluvia that often leads to their discovery in the Kurwa, or oblong grave. The Thugs about Delhi, and the Motheeas of Patna, Chupra, and Guya, and many other classes of Thugs, use the Gobba. The bodies are closely packed round the pillar of round earth.

Godaekurna—*God, dulna*—to perform the God-ae.

Geeda—Contaminated; viz. a Thug by the occurrence of the Eentab. Also à man of the lowest cast; Duckun term.

Ghonghee Phenka, Marna or Dalna—To cast lots with cowries for the booty.

Gugura—A class of Thugs so called.

Gajna—To eat.

Gook,hee—The person who is carrying the bones of his relations to the holy river; a term peculiar to the Duckun Thugs. The Hindoostan Thugs have no peculiar term for such a person, though they can never murder him.

Gael—Treasure.

Ghenae—Fetters. Term peculiar to the Jumaldehee and Lodaha Thugs.

Ghoeela: Pice—term peculiar to the Jumaldeha Thugs of Oude.

Gollee—Coral. Term peculiar to Duckun Thugs.

Gahum—Food.

Geem—Same as Karh, search after Thugs. It also means theft according to the Koolecas.

Goma—Omen of the Bhojunga (Shrike) seen flying from right to left, or from left to right. Both promise good. Its call is not regarded by Thugs.

Gano—A clan of Thugs so called.

Ganoo—The man who feigns the sickness. See *Gan karná*. These terms are peculiar to the Jumaldehee, Lodaha, and Mootea Thugs.

Gheyns—Noise and confusion, uproar.

Gona—The hand: also five according to the Duckun Thugs.

Gonee—A shoe.

Goneeait—A man who has lost his hand, or nose. To murder such a man they consider very unlucky, and therefore rarely venture to do it.

Gunga ram—A word of caution signifying that danger is near.

Gan kurna—To feign sickness in order to bring the travellers into a situation and condition favourable for strangling them. The Ganoo falls down and pretends to be taken suddenly and violently ill; some of his friends raise and support him; others bring water; some feel his pulse, and at last one pretends that a charm will restore him. All are requested to sit down, the pot of water being

in the centre; all are desired to take off their belts,
if they have any, and uncover their necks, and
lastly to look up and count a certain number of
stars if they are to be seen, and in this state the
roomal is thrown over their necks and they are
strangled.

Gunooa—Any fraud or trick of Thugs.

Gorha—Bread.

Gorhonee—Bread.

Gorhna—To strangle.

Goor Ghaunt—The knot of the gooroo or priest
who teaches the use of the roomal in strangling.
The Thug who has learnt from this man scienti-
fically, as a mark of his college education, leaves
the end of the roomal concealed within the knot,
or Ghaunt. The Bhurtote or strangler who has not
been so instructed, leaves the end out, as more secure
for his less skilful hand. The man who has had
his collegiate education is called the Ghoor ponch.

Gurkha—The neck. *Gurkha men dena*—To
strangle.

Gurtha—The dead body of a victim.

Gar—A share of spoil.

Garbung—A share of spoil.

Gharna—To strangle; term peculiar to the
Sooseea and some other few classes of Thugs.

Gharnakhna—The same.

Goraree—The call of the Sarus. See *Jubhur.*

Gorgureea—A low gurgling sound made by the
large owl, which they say resembles the bubbling
of a huka, or goorgooree, whence its name; and
that it always threatens evil. If the Thugs hear it
on first setting out, they must suspend their journey
for some days. If they hear it after the expedition
has been opened, on the left, they must advance far
and fast, as danger pursues in the rear. If on the

right, they must halt as danger lies in front. See *Korra.* Duckun Thugs pronounce it Gulguleea.

Gota—Stones, particularly stones from graves.

Gote hona—Term used by Duckun Thugs for Bote hona, to fall into their snares, become inveigled.

Gote purajana—To come to the aid of the strangler: Duckun Thugs.

Gote—A large city. Term peculiar in this sense to Duckun Thugs.

Guthonie—A knot in a turban, or any other piece of cloth in which money or jewels may be concealed.

Hukka bhur lao—" Fill your pipe," technically one of the signals or Jhirnees for the stranglers to do their work : peculiar to the Koelea Thugs.

Hilla—The rank or grade held by three men in every expedition : 1st. The man who chooses the place for murdering people and burying the bodies. 2. The man who carries the Kusee, or consecrated pick-axe. 3d. The man who brings the goor or coarse sugar, for the Taponee, sacrifice. All these officers are supposed to require peculiar skill and peculiar piety. The man who brings the goor, must be a man of great ability to persuade the people of villages that so large a quantity of goor, as he is required to purchase, is for innocent and ordinary purposes. Three of the most skilful Thugs are selected for these offices on opening every expedition, and they get an allowance out of the booty acquired, over and above their common and equal share with the rest. If the gang has not prospered, two of the three are changed ; the man who carries the pick-axe and the man who brings the goor. They name other two with certain ceremonies, and walk to a certain tree or other mark chosen at a distance on the road. If they hear or see the auspice on the left, the deity is understood to confirm the choice. This is the Pilhaoo. If not, they must name other two men, and so on, till they find the deity approve.

Hingra—A shopkeeper. Term confined to the Duckun Thugs.

Handeewuls—One of the sects of Thugs. They are Musulmans, and reside in Telingana. The Duckun Thugs divide themselves into five districts; those of Berar, Telingana, Duckun or Sholapore, Arcot, Kurnatuk. The term Handeewul they consider as applicable to those of Telingana only; and to them only as a nickname. It is a term of reproach given by the Agureea Thugs to the Telinganas, who are extremely indignant when they hear it. Sahib Khan, a Thug leader from Telingana, and a very respectable and pious man in the opinion of his fraternity, told me when I was revising this vocabulary, that if I intended to send it to government, he hoped I would not designate the Thugs of his district by this odious term. It would imply that they had been in the habit of eating food dressed in old and dirty earthen pots, whereas there were really no men in the world more scrupulous than they were in this and all matters relating to their caste.

Hurwa—A Brahmun; term peculiar to Duckun Thugs.

Huttar—One of the seven clans of Thugs.

Jhawur—Among Berar Thugs signifies a Mahommudan; among those of Berar and Bengal it signifies a Kawur, or the pair of jars in which the the Kawrutties carry Ganges water.

Jokkur—A dog. If the Thug sees a dog shake his head, they give up the design they have formed whatever it may be. If they see the dog dung on the right or left on the first day of opening the expedition, it is a bad omen, and they return and postpone their journey three days. If after having opened the expedition and advanced a day's journey, the dog is seen to dung on the left, they move on fast, as there is danger behind; if on the right, they must rest or move slowly as there is danger in advance. If they see the dog dung by moonlight, they call it the Chandnee kee dhah, or moonlight dhah, and consider it a very bad omen. They must suspend operations for three days. If when preparing to set out from any stage, they see a dog dung, they call it the Mekh kee dhah, or dhah of the tent pins; and the pins are not to be taken up; that is, they are not to move that day. If they see the dog dung in the evening, they call it the Gawdhoor kee dhah, and consider it good and promising a good booty within seven days.

Jheealoo—Same as Jywalas.

Jhuller—The belly.

Julkagura—The call of the large hill crow, while sitting on a tree, with a lake (tank,) or river in sight. This is a very favourable omen, and promises an immediate and great booty. If it calls from the back of a living buffaloe, pig, or from the skeleton of any kind of animal, it is a bad omen. If from rocks on plain grounds indifferent. Some classes of Thugs consider its call from the back of the cow good, others consider it bad.

Julhar—The call of the Sarus. It is considered a very important omen. It must be heard first on the left, on opening an expedition, and if repeated on the right, it is very good. If on setting out from any stage they hear it on the right, it is bad, unless preceded by the call on the left. If on reaching any stage, they hear it on the right, it is good, and if repeated on the left, they expect a great booty in jewels or money. If the Julhar is heard on the left after they reach any stage, it is a bad omen, threatens disputes and arrests. The same rules are applicable to almost all omens.

Jywaloo—A person left for dead but found afterwards to have life in him.

Jheema—The belly; term peculiar to Moltanee Thugs.

Jhummanta—One not a Thug to whom the Thugs are known, and is to be avoided by them.

Jumaldehee—A class of Thugs that are settled in Oude and some other parts east of the Ganges. They are considered very clever and expert, and more staunch to their oath of secrecy than most other classes. They are Agureeas, or emigrants from Delhi through Agra, and supposed to be descendants from a man named Jumalud Deen. They do not commonly allow their females to know their trade, nor permit their sons to join in their expeditions, till they have attained the age of puberty. They assign a full share of the booty to every member of the gang who has been left at home to take care of their families.

Jumaldehee—It is stated that in the time of Munsoor Alee Khan, the Jumaldehees, to the amount of some hundred families, came from Delhi, and established themselves in the purguna of Bhyswara, in the village of Tillohee, under the protection of the Rajah, one of the ancestors of the present Rajah Shunker Sing, to whom they used to give a portion of their booty in the most valuable and rare articles, as horses, jewels, &c. &c. The protection he gave them was reported to Court, and he was obliged to expel all the Thug families who dispersed in different directions. Some established themselves in other parts of Oude. Some went to Goruckpore, Durbhunga, Tirhoot. Those who went to the last two districts, were from that time called Lodahas, while the others all retained the title of Jumaldehees. They are all of the same clan, and use the same Ramasee or slang dialect.

In the time of Asufod doola, some five or six families of the Goruckpore Thugs returned to Oude, and established themselves at Nadhee in Jugdespore, under the protection of Baboo Balwunt Khan, the grandfather of the present chief Allah Buksh Khan. From five or six families they increased to forty or fifty, under his protection and support, when they became so notorious that his sovereign obliged him to expel them; and they dispersed themselves and settled in Kotedeh and Bhurtolee and Bhowulmowe in the Deorhee of Hindoo Sing, and Rudolee, Dureeabad, and the town of Dureeabad itself, in Dutekaporwa Tindolee in Huleeapore, Balahurdoee, Nusseerabad and Tholehreg. The greater part of the *operators* of this class in Oude have now been secured.

Indermun—A woman.

Iter Juna—Term used by Duckun Thugs for Chukjana—to become aware or suspicious of the designs of the Thugs. In contradistinction to Gote hona or Chuk hona.

Jangura—A Rajpoot. Term peculiar to Duckun Thugs.

Jungjore Raja—Term among the Duckun Thugs for the responding of two large owls in their loud full call, called by them the Raja or Mahee; and by Hindoostan Thugs, the Thakur; this is a bad omen, and all travellers whom the gang may then have with them must be suffered to escape. Any ventriloquist, who could imitate this and some other calls mentioned in this vocabulary, might travel from Lahore to Cape Comorin, without danger from Thugs.

Jheer Dalna—To strangle. A term peculiar to the Sooseeas and some other classes of Thugs to the west.

Jeerna—The same as Jheernakhna.

Jhauwur—Term among Berar Thugs for a Musulman.

Jhirnee—The signal for strangling; this is commonly given either by the leader of the gang, or the Belha, who has chosen the place for the murder.

Jhirnee dena—To give the signal for strangling.

Jhowar Khan—Call of spies and scouts to say that danger is near, and the gang must conceal themselves.

Jhowar dena—To conceal things from stranglers.

Jhowar lena—To conceal or hide oneself, or any thing one has.

Jhora Naek—A celebrated leader of the Multan Thugs, and of the clan of Hurtal; his name is mentioned with reverence in their sacrifices—See *Tupuna*. He was a Musulman, and he and his servant Koduk Bunwaree, are said to have killed a man who had in jewels and other articles, property to the value of one hundred and sixty thousand rupees laden upon a mule. They brought home the booty, assembled all the members of their fraternity within reach, and honestly divided the whole as if all had been present. Jora Naek, his wife and his slave, were all canonized in consequence.

Jhurawun ho, or *ho Jao*—Run, fly.

Jhurjana—To run, or fly from pursuit.

Jhurwa—The word made use of by spies and scouts to tell the gang that danger is at hand and they must fly.

Jhurwa Khan, Jhurwa Sing—The same.

Jhurowa—The fugitive Thug, or Thug flying from danger.

Jhoosa—Small or feeble man (either **Thug or** other person,) or small village.

Jeetna, Jeetjana, Jeetae purjana—To take the auspices. When the Thugs are prepared to undertake an expedition, they seat the most learned pundit they can get upon a blanket, with their leader and four of the Thugs, the most respectable in their vocation from birth and character. The rest of the gang sit around outside the blanket. They place before the pundit as an offering a brass plate (Thalee) with some rice, wheat, and two copper coins upon it. The leader asks the pundit, respectfully, what day will be proper to open the expedition, and he after due search and ceremony, pronounces the day, the hour, and the direction. They on the day appointed fill a Lotah (brass jug) with water, which the leader holds suspended by the mouth in his right hand down by his side. In a clean white handkerchief they tie up five knots of turmerick, two copper coins, one silver coin and the pick-axe, and this the leader holds upon his breast in his left hand. He now turns to the direction indicated by the priest, and moves on slowly followed by his gang to a field or garden outside the village. On reaching the spot thought best adapted for the purpose, he stands with his face still in the direction indicated, his left hand on his breast, and his right down by his side with the lotah; and with his eyes lifted to heaven, and his mind abstracted from all earthly things, he says,

"Great Goddess! universal mother! if this our
" meditated expedition is fitting in thy sight, vouch-
" safe us help, and the signs of thy approbation!"
All the Thugs present repeat this prayer, after the
leader, and join in the praises and worship of the
goddess. If within half an hour they hear or see
the Pilhaeo (or auspice on the left,) it signifies that
the deity has taken them by the left hand to lead
them on. If the Thibaoo (or omen on the right)
follows, it signifies that the deity has vouchsafed
to take them by the right hand also. The leader
then puts the lotah on the ground, and sits down
with his face in the same direction. He keeps the
silver and copper pice and turmerick during the
whole expedition, and gives them as an offering to
some poor Brahmun on his return; but if the expedition has been very prosperous he keeps them to
use again in opening others.

The leader remains seated in that spot seven
hours, while his followers bring him food, and
make all necessary preparations for their journey.
When all is ready, they advance a few paces in
the precise direction indicated, but afterwards they
may turn to the right or left as impediments or
incentives present themselves. On arriving at the
first stage, they must hear or see the Thibaoo first,
and the omen is improved by the Pilhaoo afterwards. Having had the auspices favourable thus
far, they proceed next morning to the nearest
water, and there eat the goor and the dal which
the leader takes with him. Any bad omen after
this can be averted by the usual sacrifices, offerings and observance, but any bad omen before it
involves the necessity of returning and opening the
expedition anew. If the lotah should drop from
the Jemadar's hand, he must, they think, die within

that or the following year inevitably. If they hear any one weeping for the dead on leaving the village, it threatens great evil. If they meet the corpse of any one belonging to the village, it is a very bad omen. Or if they meet an oil vender, a carpenter, or potter, a dancing master, a blind or lame man, a fukeer with a brown waist band, or a jogee with long traced hair, all threaten evil.

If after eating the goor and dal, they get the Thibaoo, it assures them a rich booty within a month and a half. It is good also to see a fair in any village but their own on the road. A corpse from any village but their own is a good omen: so also is it good to see a party of friends weeping round a woman taking leave of her parental roof to go to that of her husband.

They must not open an expedition in Sawan, (July,) Koar, (September,) nor in Poos, (December,) nor on a Wednesday nor a Thursday.

Kubita—Term for Bhurtote or strangler among the Jumaldehees and Lodahas.

Kubitae—The office or duty of the Kubita.

Khobba—Beef, mutton, or any other flesh meat. Peculiar to Duckun Thugs.

Khub,ha—A village or hamlet, same as Khugha.

Kuboola—A menial servant of Thugs; or a low raw man on Thuggee. A tyro, as distinguished from Burka, a Thug of distinction.

Kuchunee—One of the seven clans of Thugs.

Khuchooa—A pick-pocket.

Kucha—Unburied, or imperfectly buried: referring to a dead body. Also a Thug who discloses what he knows regarding his associates.

Khodda—An old man.

Khodeylee or *Khoreylee*—An eight ana piece.

Khydura—Barkundauzes, chuprasies, nujeebs,

or any armed police men ; distinguished from Run-
gooas, or sipahees or soldiers.

Koduck-bunwaree—The celebrated follower of
Joora Naek. See *Tuponee*. He was a Lodhee
by cast.

Kode—Dressed rice. Term peculiar to Duckun
Thugs.

Kud,hooa—The head. A term peculiar to the
Koeleea and some other classes of Thugs.

Khugha—Same as Khubha, village or hamlet.

Kugura—The croaking of a large mountain
crow. Contrary to the ordinary rules of augury,
the Pilhaoo, in this omen, is the croaking on the
right ; and the Thibaoo the croaking on the left.
If he croaks from a tree either on the right or the
left, it promises good ; and if water be in sight, it
is better. See *Jul-kugura*, or the water croak. If
heard from a tree while the gang are in camp, it
promises a rich traveller on that spot, and the gang
waits for him. If he croaks while on the back of
a pig, or buffalo, or from any dead body, or skeleton, the omen is bad. If from the back of a cow,
some Thugs think it a good, others a bad omen.

Koojaoo—A Thug informer ; one who denounces
Thugs or extorts money from them.

Kuj—A traveller, or any man not a Thug ; same
as Betoo.

Kujjee—A woman of any kind not of a Thug
family.

Kojeytee—Fetters. Term confined to the Duckun
Thugs.

Khokhee kurna—To hawk up the phlegm from
the throat. See *Thokkee*. A signal to prepare for
action, strangling, marching, or doing any thing
they have in hand.

Khokureea—A Bangureea Thug, applied to them

by other Thugs as a term of reproach, as Harn-
deewal is to the Telingana Thugs.

Kokatee—Duckun Thug's term for the Korra,
or low clinking sound of the large owl, which
always threatens evil to be averted by sacrifices.

Kalunderee—Sweetmeats.

Kalee—Night.

Kaul—A village. Term peculiar to Duckun
Thugs.

Kaulkee—Liquor.

Kalee kee manj.—The fighting of cats heard at
night after the first watch, which is an evil omen.

Khal Khoseea—A barber.

Khullee—A Thug who conceals himself on his
return home from the dread of his creditors.

Khuleeta—A village. Term peculiar to Koeleea
Thugs.

Kulloo—A thief.

Kullooee—Theft.

Kamp—A bribe for the release or ransom of
Thugs.

Khal—Is the term used by the Duckun Thugs
for Kamp, a bribe.

Khom—A door.

Khomusna—To rush in upon travellers when there
is no time for the ordinary ceremonies of murder.

Komil—Something unbecoming one's condition
and cast, and likely therefore to lead to suspicion.

Kanta—The omen of the braying of the ass. It
is an omen of great importance, and must be heard
first on the left on opening an expedition, or on
setting out from any other stage. If on reaching
any stage, or while haulting at any stage, it is heard
on the left, they must leave the place and go on:
for such situations it is good on the right. If the
ass approaches the gang, braying from the front, it

is a very bad omen, and is called Mathaphore, the head breaker.

Kanthun—A knife.

Kanthana or *Kanth dalna*—To cut up the body of a murdered person in order to prevent its swelling and forming cracks in the soil that covers it. Also to kill with a knife, a person whom they have not time to strangle, on the approach of danger, or stab a strangled person in order to prevent the possibility of his recovery.

Kanee Isd—The name of the wife of Joora Naek—See *Tuponee*.

Khonsana—To return or Khounsana.

Khonchkhana—Same as Tupjana. Term peculiar to Duckun Thugs.

Kondoo—The belly. Term peculiar to the Kooleea Thugs.

Khanjoo—A cut purse. Peculiar to Duckun Thugs.

Kondul kurna or *Dalna*—To pound in the earth upon the bodies when they are securely buried. Term confined to Duckun Thugs.

Konjul—The call of the Saurus. Term peculiar to the Jumaldehee, Lodaha, and Mootea Thugs of Behar and Bengal. Same as Julhar.

Kotuk—A novice or tyro in Thuggee. Term peculiar to the Jumaldehee, Lodaha, and Mootea Thugs of Bengal and Behar.

Kuneelee—Earings, gold.

Kapsee—Corn or grain, or any agricultural produce in the ground, before harvest.

Karthee kurna—Inveigling travellers, or secretly consulting about their murder.

Karthee must kurna—To speak or consult in a low voice or whisper.

Karh—Search or inquiry after Thugs.

Karhkurna—To search after, or molest **Thugs.**

Karhoo—One who searches after, betrays, or molests them.

Khurtae—Any bad omen. Duckun **Thugs.**

Kawree—Breaking wind. See *Oorut kawree.*

Kartheana—Same as *Karthee kurna.*

Kharoo—A gang of Thugs.

Kharoo phootna—To break up or disperse the gang.

Kharkuneea—The passing of a hare across the road in front of the gang; a bad omen either from right to left, or left to right.

Khorae—Pice, copper coinage.

Khour—An army. Peculiar to the Dooab, Oude and Behar Thugs.

Khorchee—A barber.

Khora—Unlucky.

Khoruk—A horse, so called by Duckun **Thugs.**

Khorkanee—A mare, ditto, ditto.

Kurba—Secure or perfect burial, as distinguished from Angjhap, imperfect burial.

Kurbakurree—Term used by Duckun **Thugs** for Lugha, Sexton, when the bodies **are securely** buried.

Kurbakurna—To dig graves when the **bodies** are to be securely buried; all three terms **chiefly** confined to Duckun Thugs.

Khurkha—Same as Kanta, an ass.

Khureyree—(See *Putouree*) Term peculiar to the Jemaldehees, Dooab and Behar Thugs, for the small owl.

Khureynja—A nalah or ravine. Term peculiar to the Jemaldehee Thugs.

Khuruk—Noise made by the pick-axe in digging the grave.

Korra—A low clicking sound made by the large owl. It always threatens evil like the Gorgureca. The Duckun Thugs call this Kokatee.

Kourga—Silver. Term confined to Duckun Thugs.

Korhureeas—The Thugs who resided in the district of Korhur, between Etawa and Cawnpore, after their expulsion from Delhie.

Kouree Phenkna, *Marna* or *Dalna*—To cast lots for the booty. After defraying all extra expenses to leaders and officers, they commonly divide the booty into three equal shares and the gang into three equal parties. A cowree is then given to each party, who, after marking it, puts it into the hand of a man, who, without knowing to which party the cowrees respectively belong, puts one on each of the three piles, and each party takes the pile on which its cowree has been placed, and subdivides it among the individuals.

Kurwa—The grave, made square or oblong, for the bodies of the persons murdered. See *Gobba*.

Kursaul—The large male antelope. If a single antelope or a pair only are seen crossing the road from left to the right, it is a good omen; viz. the Thibaoo. If from right to the left, very bad, viz. the Pilhaoo.

Khurtul—Term used by Duckun Thugs, for Kotar, any bad omen.

Khosman—Term for a Musulman.

Khosur—The month among the Behar Thugs called Khomur Khosir.

Khous—Return, in contradistinction to Pusur, advance.

Kiswara—A well.

Kussee—The consecrated pick-axe. At first Thugs were allowed by Davey, according to their creed, to leave on the ground the bodies of the persons murdered, but were prohibited from looking back to see how she disposed of them. A slave on one occasion looked back, and saw her occupied in throwing them into the air, without any clothes on her body. She was naturally very angry and bid them in future to bury the bodies themselves; but to use in making the graves pick-axes duly consecrated. On ascertaining from the priest or elder of the gang a lucky day for the purpose, the leader of the gang goes to the blacksmith's, and having closed the door that no other person may enter, gets him to make the axe in his presence, without touching any other work till it is completed.

On a day fixed, either Friday, Monday, Tuesday, or Wednesday, they give it the dhoop or incense offering. The place chosen must be either inside a house or tent, so that the shadow of no living thing may fall on and contaminate the axe. The Thug most skilled in the ceremonies, sits down with his face to the west, and receives the pick-axe on a brass dish. A pit is dug in the ground, and the pick-axe is washed with water which falls into this pit. It is afterwards washed with a mixture of sugar and water. Then with dehee or sour milk, and lastly with ardent spirits; all falling successively from the pick-axe into the pit. It is then marked from the head to the point with seven spots of red lead, and placed on the brass dish, containing an entire cocoanut, some cloves, pawn leaves, gogul gum (amyris a gollacha) inderjon, some seed of the sesamum, white sandal wood, and sugar. In a small brass cup close by, is some ghee. They now kindle a fire from some dried cow dung, and some wood of the mango or byr

tree, and throw in upon it the above-named articles, except the cocoanut; and when the flame
rises, they pass the pick-axe seven times through
it, the officiating priest holding it in both hands.
He now strips the cocoanut of its outer coat, and
placing it on the ground, holds the pick-axe by the
point in his right hand, and says, " Shall I strike ?"
All around reply yes. He then says " all hail
" mighty Davey, great mother of all !" and striking
the cocoanut with the but end of the pick-axe,
breaks it in pieces, on which all exclaim " All
" hail Davey and prosper the Thugs !" They throw
all the shell and some of the kernel into the fire, tie
up the pick-axe in a clean piece of white cloth,
and placing it on the ground to the west, all face
in that direction and worship it. This done they
all partake of the kernel of the cocoanut, and collect all the fragments and put them into the pit,
that they may never after be contaminated by the
touch of any one's foot. If after this ceremony
the Thibaoo, or auspice on the right is seen or
heard, the sacrifice has been approved. If the Pil-
baoo, on the left, it is not; and if the cocoanut is
not severed at one blow, the deity is considered to
have disapproved, and another day is appointed for
the ceremony to be performed over again. Hence-
forward the pick-axe is called the Kassee, or
Mahee, instead of Kodalee. The Jemadar keeps
it with great care, and before every expedition the
ceremony must be repeated.

It is given to the shrewdest, cleanest and most
sober and careful man of the party, who carries it
in his waist belt. While in camp he buries it in a
secure place, with its point in the direction they
intend to go; and they believe that if another
direction is better its point will be found changed.

They say that formerly they used to throw it into a well, and that it would come up of itself when summoned with due ceremonies; but since they began to do what was forbidden, and neglected what was enjoined, it has lost that virtue. They say that it has it still among some classes of Thugs in the Duckun who have adhered more rigidly to their rites and usages. No foot must touch the earth under which it lies buried; nor may the pick-axe be touched by any man in an unclean state, or by any unclean animal or thing. The burnt offering is repeated on certain holydays, and whenever they have been long without a victim. After every grave made with it, it must be bathed with certain ceremonies.

The oath by the Kassee is, in their esteem, far more sacred that of the Ganges water or the Koran, and I have known men who have been in prison twenty years, entertain the firmest conviction that perjury on the Kassee, when the oath has been administered with due ceremony, must inevitably cause the death of the person within six days, or involve him in some great calamity. I have talked with hundreds who have told all their secrets, and I never yet met a Thug that did not, up to the last moment of his existence, believe the same. They never under any circumstances lose their confidence in the Kassee; and if it fail them they attribute it to accidental neglect of the prescribed ceremonies. In prison, when administering an oath to each other in cases of dispute among themselves, I have known them to frame the image of the Kassee out of a piece of cloth, and consecrate it for the purpose. The deponent puts his hand on it while he deposes, or holds it in both hands, and after having sworn he drinks water in

which the Kassee has been washed, or he goes
before the image of Davey with the Kassee in his
hands and swears.

If the Kassee at any time falls from the hands of
the man who carries it, it is a dreadful omen, and
portends that he will either be that year killed, or
that the gang will suffer some grievous misfortune.
The gang must deprive him of his office, return
home, or change the road, and consecrate the
Kassee anew; and no other party will ever encamp
or associate with one whose Kassee has so fallen,
lest they should be involved in the calamity.
Many are the curious stories they relate to illustrate all this.

Kathur—One of the sects of Thugs. They are
supposed to derive their name from a man, who
attended the feasts of the seven classes at Delhie
with a wooden dish or trencher, called Kathur,
took to their trade, and left it as an inheritance
to his descendants.

Kautgurree—The office of a scout or spy.

Kautgur—A scout or spy.

Kotar—A bad omen. Duckun Thugs.

Kotuck—A novice or tyro in Thuggee.

Keyta—Ardent spirits.

Khotana—To set out with travellers before daylight in the morning.

Khotub—The interval between midnight and
daybreak or sunrise.

Khotub men Ladkna—To murder in that interval.

Khoturna—To encamp or lodge. Term peculiar to some classes of Thugs.

Khutana, or Khutae, or Khutae dena—To inform
against the gang in consequence of a quarrel; or
to become their enemies.

Khuteeae.—The doing so, or Khutheae.

Khutowa—A Thug who informs against his associates.

Koot--Theft committed by Thugs among themselves out of the booty. Duckun Thugs call it Bhons.

Koot kur lena—To steal from the booty acquired.

Kootha—The Thug who so steals.

Kottar—Any bad omen ; same as Ardhul.

Kuthowa—The man who cuts up the bodies of the victims before they are buried. This they do to prevent their emitting a smell, and being thereby discovered by jackals, and dug up and exposed. If they leave the bodies entire, the ground that covers them cracks as they decay, and the stench rises to the surface.

Kuthae--The office of doing so.

Kutheeana—Same as Kat,hna.

Kutoree—Same as Bele—place for the murder. Kutoree signifies a brass cup, and when, in the heaping of their victims, they apprehend that the term Bele might excite suspicions, they say, " Jao, " kutoree manj lao ;" literally, " go and clean the " cup ;" technically, go and choose the place for the murder.

Kutoree Manjna—To choose a place for the murder.

Kutkola—A carpenter.

Kote—Ducken term for the feast or sacrifice to Davey, peculiar to Thugs, but common to all classes of them. Having collected goats, rice, ghee, spices, and spirits, they assemble on a Tuesday or Friday, in a room chosen for the purpose, the doors and windows of which must be so closed that nothing can be seen from without. The floor must be cleaned, and plastered with cow dung;

and in the centre, a square is drawn of a cubit each
side, with the kokoo, or mixture of tumerick and
lime. Upon this square is spread a white sheet,
and upon this sheet, the rice when boiled is placed.
Upon the rice is placed the half of a cocoanut,
filled with ghee, in which is inserted two wicks,
lying across each other, and lighted each at both
ends, so as to give four lights. If a cocoanut cannot be found, a vessel of dough of the same form
will answer. This kind of lamp is occasionally
made by all kinds of people, and is called Chou
mukh. Upon the white sheet is now placed the
consecrated pick-axe and the knife of the gang;
and all the spirits brought for the feast. From
among all the goats purchased for the occasion,
two are now selected, black, and perfect in all
their parts. They are bathed, and washed, and
made to face to the west, and if they shake themselves lustily to throw off the moisture from their
bodies, they are immediately sacrificed as having
been accepted by Davey, or if one does so, both
are sacrificed. If neither of them does this, it is a
sign that she has rejected both; and the party eats
the rice and drinks the spirits, but postpones the
sacrifice to another day, considering the feast as
in the light of a simple meal. This they do if any
other bad omen is observed on that day, considering the goddess to be displeased with something.
While the Eentak obtains among the gang, this
offering cannot take place.

The goats are sacrificed after the Mahomedan
form, having their throats cut while grace is said
over them, if the party be Mahomedans; but if
they are Hindoos, the goats have their heads struck
off as at Hindoo sacrifices. If the two goats are
accepted and sacrificed, all the other goats pur-

chased for the feast are killed and eaten: if not
they are kept for a better day. A pit is dug in the
floor into which is thrown the skins, bones, and
offal of all kinds; for nothing brought in for this
sacred feast must be seen by any living thing but
a Thug eligible to partake of it; and they believe
that if any man not a Thug see the lamps, or any
part of the preparations, or any fire falls on the
white sheet and burns any part of it, or any animal
touches the bones or offal, the leader of the gang
must die within the year, and all the members be
involved in some great calamity.

If they are on an expedition they must take the
same precautions, and conceal themselves and their
ceremonies by means of curtains, if they have not
walls. After feasting, they must all wash their
hands and faces over the pit, and then fill it up
securely. The expenses of this feast are defrayed
commonly by subscription, when it is called the
Punchaetee Kote, and is given whenever they
choose; but most commonly in the Hooly or
Dusera festivals, during which they may, if they
choose, have it on any other day as well as Tues-
days and Fridays. Sometimes the feast is given
by the leader or any individual member of a gang.
No Thug is eligible to partake of this feast in any
part of India till he has attained the rank of
strangler, unless his family have been Thugs for at
least two generations. The above is considered
the complete ceremony, and in the Duckun every
part is strictly attended to. In Hindoostan some
minor points, as the form of the lamp and the
drawing the square, are omitted. They have no
peculiar term for the feast; the term they use
Kurhae kurna or Kurahee dena, being common to
all people for a feast.

Lodh—A bullock among the Thugs of Hindoostan. Among the Duckun Thugs it signifies blood.

Lodaha from Lodh, a bullock—A class of Musulman Thugs, either descended from or grafted upon the Jumaldehee stock of Oude Thugs. These Thugs reside in Chupra, Goruckpore, Ghazeepore, Pooruneea, Dinajpoor, Rungpore, and other parts of Behar and Bengal, but now the principal seat of them is said to be in the Turae, north-east from Dhurbunga, where they occupy several villages on the frontier between the Nepaul territory and our own. The most noted of this class at present are Jhoulee Khan the black, and Jhoulee Khan the fair, who are, I believe, cousins. They are said to have got their name from loading bullocks, though it does not appear that they trade in that way now. Lodha or Lodhee, without the vowel after the ohais, a cast of Hindoos common all over India, and of this cast the greater part of the gangs of Thugs between the Ganges and Jumna were composed.

The Lodahas may be estimated at about three hundred, I believe.

Lubba—A bullock.

Lickha—A Musulman. Term peculiar to Duckun Thugs.

Luchmun or Lutchmun Sing—Term made use of by scouts to indicate the approach of danger. See *Bajeed*.

Luchee Ram—The same.

Ladhna—To strangle; common to all classes of Thugs.

Ladhka—Goor or coarse sugar.

Lode—Bullock among the Hindostan Thugs; but among the Duckunees it signifies blood.

Ludohur—Killing. Ludohur kurna, to murder.

Lugha—A grave digger.

Lughae—The office of grave digger.

Lughouta—Dead bodies of victims.

Lokaree—A gun.

Lokharna—To scream loudly when being murdered. See *Doonr.*

Lukeer—Fakeer, a religious mendicant.

Lewalee—A blanket. Term peculiar to Duckun Thugs.

Lol—The throat. Term confined to Duckun Thugs.

Lamkun—Term used by the Duckun Thugs for the Kurkuneea, or crossing (from the right or from the left) of a hare on the road before them.

Lumbheree—A sword.

Lumpocha—Term among the Berar Thugs for a snake. If a snake crosses the road before or behind the gang, it is a bad omen, and they dare not go on unless they can kill it. If they see it in any situation, it involves a sacrifice unless they kill it.

Lumbhereeana—To kill with a sword.

Lendkeea—A washerman, peculiar to Duckun Thugs.

Lond,hlena—To plunder.

Londh,hhona—To be plundered.

Lapna—To kill goats or other animals for food. Term peculiar to the Duckun Thugs.

Leepra or *Leep*—Cloth in pieces, not made into garments.

Leepurna—To strangle. Peculiar to the western Thugs of Ojeyn.

Lopna or *Lop Ruhna*—To lie hid or asleep.

Lopee, or *Lopee Khan*, or *Lopee Singh*—A term made use of by scouts to intimate that danger approaches.

Lopee Kurna—To conceal.

Lopee Hona—To be concealed.

Luppooa—Thief.

Lohurburheya—A pair of jackals crossing the the road in front of the gang from the right or from the left, indicating prison and chains; from Lohar, a blacksmith, and Burhey, a carpenter, a very bad omen; a single jackal passing from right to left, is a good omen; from left to right, bad, but of little moment.

Lurheea—A shop-keeper.

Lutkuneea—A very small purse, worn only by Thugs and thieves, and therefore a distinctive mark.

Luhtar—A dagger.

Moeh—A bullock, among the Duckun Thugs.

Muchhooa—A Bhutteeara, or keeper of a surae for the accommodation of travellers. The greater part of these people are in the interest of the Thugs, often permitting them to perpetrate murders in their suraes, and giving them useful information regarding travellers and pursuers.

Mudoreea—Name given to the Maunj or fighting of cats, by the Koeleeas and some other Thugs.

Mekhkee Dhap—See *Jokkur* or *Dhap*.

Mukkaur—A Rajpoot of whatever calling.

Mykureea—A barber. Term peculiar to Duckun Thugs.

Maulee—The man who bears home money for the subsistence of their families from Thugs engaged in distant expeditions. Peculiar to the Korhareca and Lodhee Thugs.

Mawil—A horse.

Mawilee—A mare.

Maulee—Parole of rendezvous among the Duckun Thugs; the same as Phool among the Hindoostanees.

Maulee dena—To give the parole of rendezvous.

Mohil—A chief. Peculiar to the Duckun Thugs.

Mahee—The sacred pick-axe, called also Kussee. The Duckun Thugs always use the term Mahee, never Kussee, for the pick-axe. The Duckun Thugs give this term to the Thakur, or full call of the large owl also. See *Thakur.*

Mooltaneas—A class of Thugs, all Musulmans, who are said to have emigrated direct from Delhi, and not through Agra, and therefore not among the Agureeas. They are said to call themselves Naiks, and to travel and trade as Brinjaras. They kill the greater part of their female children, and never allow what survive to marry out of their own class. They travel with their families, and strangle travellers with the cords with which they are accustomed to drive their bullocks, and not like other Thugs, with the handkerchief. They are among the ancient Thugs, and are considered strict in their observances, and staunch to their oath of secrecy.

Mamoo—One who knows Thugs, and takes advantage of his knowledge to betray, or to extort money from them.

Maun—The place for the grave. A term peculiar to Duckun Thugs. (See *Belee.*) Maunkurree, the man who selects the place for murder.

Maunj—The omen of the cats heard fighting. If heard during the first watch of the night it promises good; if during the night at any time after the first watch, it is called " Kalee kee Maunj," and threatens evil. If heard in the day time, it is called the "Dhamonee kee Maunj," and threatens very great evil. If the cats fall down from a height while fighting, it threatens still worse.

Maunghee—Treasure. A term peculiar to some classes of Thugs.—Gael is the more common term.

Minukeea—A Gosaen.

Minuk—A Gosaen or Byragee; Hindoo religious mendicant.

Munkhela—A man.

Munjwar—A jackal. To prevent their digging up the dead bodies, Thugs throw over the grave either very thorny bushes or ispaghole, the seeds of the flea wort, to which they say jackals and dogs have a strong antipathy. They say that with the ispaghole there is no danger from any animal, but the bear and hyena.

Mourheea—A gold mohur.

Morna—To go slowly; peculiar to Duckun Thugs.

Mirgmaul—A herd of deer. This at all times and under all circumstances is favourable, as promising a meeting with more Thugs.

Morka—The extra share given to distinguished or principal Thug leaders, who command each a party of not less than twenty Thugs. If, including the jemadar, the party consists of twenty, they divide the booty into twenty-one shares, the leader takes one as his morka, and he has another share with the rest. If there are five such leaders and parties, they have five separate shares. This is after the deduction of the dhurae or leader's share, in which jemadars, great and small, share alike.

Margee—A cheyla or disciple; term peculiar to Duckun Thugs; a mere tyro before he becomes initiated. Hindostan Thugs call them kyboolas or betoos.

Mururee—A party of Thugs assembled in council.

Mururee ka Dhuneea—A peditum, heard from one of the Thugs, while they are assembled in council. It is considered a dreadful omen, and involves the necessity of great sacrifices.

Must Katee Kurna, or *Katee must Kurna*—To speak softly in whispers.

Matungee—A lizard. Peculiar to Duckun Thugs.

Motheea—A class of Thugs that reside chiefly about Rangpore, Dinapore, Purnea, and derive their name, it is said, from their usage of giving their leaders a handful (Motheea) out of every booty consisting of rupees or other money, as their share over and above what they receive in the general division.

They have the same dialect as the other Thugs, and assume like them the disguises best suited to times and circumstances; but, like the Thugs of Behar and Bengal generally, they have their Beles or places of murder, and Thapas or resting place, chiefly on the banks of large rivers or running streams, into which they can throw the bodies of their victims. They are almost all of the meaner caste or Tantooas.

Mat,haphore—(Literally head breaker.) The approach of the ass braying from the front upon the gang. It indicates that the gang will have their heads broken, if they rest at the place they had intended to halt at: they must go to some other.

Mahasutee—Call of the single jackal which people call the Faoo. Term among Duckun Thugs for what the Hindostan Thugs call the Bhalee or Barohee. Bhaloo is said to be a term used for this call among all people in the Duckun, Thugs or not Thugs. It is always a bad omen among Duckun Thugs. Among Hindostan Thugs it is subject to the ordinary rules.

Now—The weeping of a woman. Term peculiar to Duckun Thugs.

Nudh—A village.

Naga kur dena—To exclude from association with Thugs. Term peculiar to Duckun Thugs; and among them peculiar to exclusion for the murder of a Sweeper, Chumar, Teylee, Dhobee, Sonar, Dancing Girl, Bhart, Nanukpuntee, Jattadaree, Bunjara, Hatheewan (elephant driver.) For the murder of any one of these classes, knowing him to be such, the Thug is turned out of-caste, and never admitted back to their society.

Naga Lugna—The occurrence of this crime, the most dreadful of all crimes in the estimation of a Duckun Thug.

Nughoo—A body of soldiers.

Nukhna—An affix signifying Kurna, to do, in general use it is said with the Punjab, Multan and Kanthur Thugs.

Nakee or *Nukaree*—Sneezing. This is a bad omen on setting out on an expedition, or on leaving any stage: and requires expiatory sacrifices. If they have travellers with them when they hear this omen, they must let them all escape, as they dare not put them to death; all Hindoos have the same dread of this omen on setting out on an expedition; and so have the Mahommedans in spite of their creed.

Nemee or *Nemee Khan*—A call to signify speak or walk slowly and softly.

Neeamut—A traveller in the hands of Thugs; same as Bunj.

Neera—Water.

Nareal—The head. Term confined to the Duckun Thugs.

Narta—Any soldier or police man. Term peculiar to Duckun Thugs.

Nowureea—A tyro or new Thug while on his

first expedition. The Thugs of the Jumaldehee and Lodaha clans always make the Nawureea kick the body of the first person they murder on the expedition five times on the back, thinking that it will bring them good luck. The Moteeas do the same.

Nureehur—Unsafe or disturbed, in contradiction to Bajeed or safe and undisturbed, i. e. the scene appointed for murder.

Nissar—Free from danger; any place where the Thugs intend to murder, divide property, or lodge, in contradistinction to Tikkur, dangerous— *Kaul Nissar*, a safe village. *Kaul Tikkur*, unsafe village.

Nizam Oddeen Ouleea—A saint of the Sonnee sect of Mahommuduns, said to have been a Thug of great note at some period of his life, and his tomb near Delhi is to this day visited as a place of pilgrimage by Thugs, who make votive offerings to it. He is said to have been of the Bursote class, born in the month of Suffer Hidgeree, (March, A. D. 1236,) died Rubee Olowul, 725, (October, A. D. 1325.) His tomb is visited by Mahommudun pilgrims from all parts as a place of great sanctity, from containing the remains of so holy a man; but the Thugs, both Hindoo and Mahommudun, visit it as containing the remains of the most celebrated Thug of his day. He was of the Sonnee sect, and those of the Sheeah sect find no difficulty in believing that he was a Thug; but those of his own sect will never credit it. There are, perhaps, no sufficient grounds to pronounce him one of the fraternity; but there are perhaps some to suspect that he was so at some period of his life. The Thugs say he gave it up early in life, but kept others employed in it till late, and derived an

income from it ; and the " Dustul Ghyb," or supernatural purse, with which he was supposed to be
endowed, gives a colour to this. His lavish expenditure, so much beyond his ostensible means, gave
rise to the belief that he was supplied from above
with money.

Ogalna—To set out. A term peculiar to Duckun
Thugs.

Oogur Jana—To escape, fly from danger. Same
as Jhurjana.

Oogaul—Old clothes, term peculiar to Duckun
Thugs.

Oguera—A servant of a Thug or other man of
rank ; term confined to the Duckun Thugs.

Oondana—To eat ; term peculiar to Duckun
Thugs.

Oorut putoree—The chattering of the small owl
when flying. See *Putoree*.

Oorutkawree—The " crepitus ventris" heard from
a Thug when on the road. They either change
the road or avert the omen by a sacrifice. They
collect and burn a pile of cow-dung, and each
member of the gang throws one of the burning
embers at the offending party who runs the gaunt-
let among them. If any Thug is heard to break
wind while they are at their phur, or resting place,
dividing the booty, it is called " Phur ka Dhuneea,"
and considered a very bad omen. They remove
the offender from among them, and kindle a fire
upon the place where he sat, and quench it with
water, saying : " As the signs of the water disap-
" pear, so may the threatened evil pass away." Five
blows of a shoe inflicted upon the head of the
offending person mitigates the evil to be apprehended, but cannot avert it altogether. If any one
break wind between the point they set out from,

9*

and the first resting place, it is considered an extremely bad omen.

Ooharna—To strangle.

Oorwala—A stone; also a Shumseea, or holder of hands. Term peculiar to Duckun Thugs.

Paoo—An acquaintance and accomplice of Thugs.

Puchbheya—One of the sects of **Thugs**; it is derived from the Bursote clan.

Pucka kurna—To bury in a deep **and secure** grave.

Puck heyla—Paper in general: written upon or not.

Peeada byth lana—Same as poolakurna.

Pykee—Treasure in money.

Pehloo or *Pulloo*—The handkerchief with **which** they strangle people: the roomal.

Pholkee—The time from sunrise till sunset. From sunrise till midday, *Churtee Pholkee.* From midday till sunset is the *Oturtee Pholkee;* a bad omen during the first is much worse than the same during the Churtee Pholkee.

Palwee—A ring for the finger, nose, or ear; term confined to the Ducken Thugs.

Phool—Parole or engagement to meet again at a certain place when suddenly dispersed.

Phooldena—To appoint the place of meeting; "Agra kee Phool deea. He appointed Agra as the place of rendezvous."

Phoola—The person who takes home money for the subsistence of the families of Thugs.

Pilhaoo—The appearance or voice of the animals from which omens are taken, on the left. The reverse of the Thibaoo. If the Pilhao promises good according to their rules of augury, it is always the better from being followed by the Thibaoo soon after. If it threatens evil, that evil is mitigated by the Thibaoo.

Different casts and clans of Thugs have in some few instances different rules for interpreting these sounds and appearances, and what is considered to threaten evil by some, is thought to promise good by others; but on such occasions they all follow the rules of the leader who opens the expedition, or leads the greatest number of Thugs associated together in any expedition.

The Pilhaoo, or omen on the left, must be observed first on opening an expedition, and it must be followed by the Thibaoo immediately after, or the expedition cannot be entered upon. It signifies that the Deity has taken the gang by the left arm, to lead them on; but she must give them the Thibaoo, to signify that she has taken them by the right arm also, or the party appointed to take the auspices returns home, and the gangs wait till the omens are unexceptionable.

The Pilhaoo perceived on leaving any stage during the expedition, or preparing to leave it, promises good. The Thibaoo threatens evil, and the gang halts. On reaching any stage, the Pilhaoo threatens evil, and they must move on without resting. The Thibaoo promises good, and they rest securely.

There are some few exceptions to the general rule, that for the Pilhaoo, the omen must be on the left. Some animals must be heard or seen on the right to constitute the Pilhaoo, and vice versa, but these are very few indeed.

Pola—The sign made at a cross road to guide the members of the gang who are behind, in the direction the others have taken. They draw their feet along the dust in the direction they have taken;

and if their friends are to follow quickly, they leave the dust piled up at the end of the line where the foot stops, or make a hole in it with the heel. If the road affords no dust, they leave two stones piled one on the other in the line they have taken, and strew a few leaves of trees along the road. If their friends are to make haste, they leave a long line of leaves. They have other signs for the same purposes.

Polakurna—To make the signs.

Puloee—A ring.

Pulloo or *Pehloo dena*—To instal as a strangler, or invest with the roomal.

Panderphulee—Pearls; term peculiar to Duckun Thugs.

Phankdena—To throw away any victim or other thing as worthless or unsuitable, as one or more of a party to be murdered, when they have more than they can manage, or he, she or they are not suited for their purpose.

Phangola—Pearls. Among Duckun Thugs a cock.

Phangolee—Small gold coins. Among Duckun Thugs a hen.

Phankura—The call of the hare by night or day when the Thugs have travellers with them. It is a bad omen and the travellers must not be killed.

Phank—Any useless thing not worth the keeping, but particularly a traveller without property.

Pungoo—A river Thug of Bengal, who carries on his murders on board his boat, which he calls a Kuntee.

Puneeara—Pearl.

Parnakhna—To strangle. Term peculiar, it is said, to the Thugs of Ojeyn and the west.

Phoorkana—A horse.

Phoorkanee—A mare.

Phur—Any place where they murder their victims or divide their booty.

Phurka Dhuneea—A " crepitus ventris," heard from any one while they are sitting down and dividing their booty: a very bad omen. See *Oorut Kawree.*

Phur jharna—To clean the place of murder. After a murder has taken place at night, some members of the gang are left behind to remove any signs that may be seen when day appears.

Phurjhurowa—The man who is left behind for that purpose.

Phuruck dena—To wave any cloth to warn associates of danger.

Purta purna—To be recognised, viz. any article taken from a murdered person.

Phosurna—To fly or escape. Term peculiar to Duckun Thugs.

Pusur—The direction or scene appointed for an expedition. Khous, the time of return.

Phutakee—A gun.

Phutkee—A shield.

Potura—A horse.

Poturee—A mare.

Pooturaet—A man on horseback.

Pooturaet-Bhurtote—The man who strangles him.

Poolaraetee—The strangling a man so pulled off his horse.

Potnee (Dhotee)—A waist band. Term peculiar to Koeleea Thugs, or Thugs of and from the district of Koel.

Putlee ho jana—To disperse or divide into small parties when it is dangerous to remain assembled.

Putunee—A sneeze.

Puthoree or *Kosut*—The loud and continued chirping or calling of the small owl. If made by the bird while sitting, it promises good. If while flying, it threatens evil. The chatter or call when sitting is interpreted according to the rules of the Thibaoo or Pilaoo.

Puteear—The call of the partridge. If heard while the Thugs are travelling, the call on the left promises good, and on the right threatens slight evil. If they are halting at the time, the call on the right is good, that on the left bad.

Putoree—The small owl.

Qulundera—One of the sects of Moltanee Thugs, who travel with bears and monkeys.

Rooh—An affix to the number of persons killed in any affair; a single person killed in an Eeloo, when two persons are killed, the affair is a Bhitree, three Singhore, four Behra, five Puchrooh, six Chehrooh, and so on.

Raba—Any trick of Thugs.

Richee—Behind. Peculiar to a few classes, and obsolete.

Rugon—An omen good or bad.

Rugnoutee—Taking the auspices.

Even the most sensible approvers who have been with me for many years, as well Musulmans as Hindoos, believe that their good or ill success always depended upon the skill with which the omens were discovered and interpreted, and the strictness with which they were observed and obeyed. One of the old Sindouse stock told me yesterday (May 30th, 1835) in presence of twelve others from Hydrabad, Behar, the Dooab, Oude, Rajpootana, and Bundelcund, assembled for the purpose of revising this vocabulary, that had they not attended to these omens they could never have

thrived as they did, and that in ordinary cases of
murder a man seldom escaped after one of them,
while they and their families had for ten generations thrived, though they had murdered hundreds
of people. " This," said he, " could never have
been the case, had we not attended to omens, and
had not omens been intended for us. There were
always signs around us to guide us to rich booty
and warn us of danger, had we been always wise
enough to discern them and religious enough to
attend to them." Every Thug present concurred
with him from his soul.

Raja—Term among Duckun Thugs for Mahee
or Thakur: the loud full call of the large owl.
Jungjore Raja: Two large owls responding to
each other; at all times and in all situations a bad
omen.

Raookar—Sahookar, a banker.

Roukee—A police choukedar or guard—Rou-
keea, a police-man.

Rukut Beej[1] Dana—The Thugs have a tradition
that a demon by name Rukut Beej Dana infested
the world and devoured mankind as often as they
were born or created; and to enable the world to
be peopled Kalee Davey determined to put him to
death. This demon they say was so tall that the
deepest ocean never reached above his waist; and
he could, consequently, walk over the world at his
ease. Kalee Davey attacked him, and cut him
down; but from every drop of his blood another

---

[1] Rukut, blood, and Beej, seed. All Hindoos believe in this
demon having been destroyed by the consort of Mahadeo in the
form of Kalee, but those who are not Thugs suppose that when
she found every drop of blood, as it reached the ground producing
another demon to wage war with her, she licked them all off with
her enormous tongue as she cut off their heads.

demon arose, and as she cut them down, from
every drop of their blood another demon sprung
up, and the numbers increased at this geometrical
rate, while she became fatigued with the labour.
On this she formed two men from the sweat
brushed off from one of her arms; and giving them
each a handkerchief, told them to put all these
demons to death, without allowing one drop of
their blood to fall upon the ground.

After their labour was over, they offered to
return to the goddess the handkerchiefs with which
they had done their work, but she desired them to
keep them as the instruments of a trade by which
their posterity were to earn their subsistence and to
strangle men with these roomals, as they had
strangled the demons, and live by the plunder they
acquired; and having been the means of enabling
the world to get provided with men by the destruction of the demons, their posterity would be entitled
to take a few for their own use. The roomal they
call the " Goputban," and the goddess told them
that they should leave the bodies of their victims
on the ground and she would take care that they
should be removed, provided they would never
look behind them to see in what manner, and that
if they observed this and all the other rules she
prescribed for them, no power on earth should
punish them for what they did.

These creations from the sweat of Bhowanee's
arm are not supposed to have themselves used the
roomals, but to have bequeathed them with all their
privileges to their children, who did not avail themselves of them for several generations.

Raul—Duckun term for Rareyn, the clamorous
call of many jackals. Among the Duckun Thugs

this is always a good omen, whether by day or night, right or left.

Rumasee—The peculiar dialect of the Thugs.

Rumujna—To recognize or detect.

Rungwa—A Seepahee, so called from his red coat.

Rungeela—Coral.

Ruhna—A temporary grave.

Rahna kur dena—To bury bodies in a temporary grave.

Rooaran—Any call of the jackal. Term peculiar to Jumaldehee, Lodaha and Moteea Thugs of Oude, Behar, &c.

Roopareyl—The Sawa Mamoola, or water wagtail. Its omen is interpreted according the ordinary rules of the Thibaoo and Pilhaoo.

Roopauneea—The call of the hare at night on the left hand—a good omen.

Rareyn—The general clamour of a pack of jackals. Heard at night it is good on the left, and of little or no importance on the right, except on the day of opening the expedition. Heard then on the right, it threatens evil, and the expedition cannot be opened. Heard at any time in the day, from half an hour after sunrise to half an hour before sunset, it is a very bad omen.

Rewaroo—Fine earth or sand from a grave, same as Bhusma.

Ratee bolee Teetura, Din ko bolee seear, Tuj chulee wa deysra, nuheen puree achanuk Dhar—If the partridge call at night, or the jackal during the day, quit that country, or you will be seized.

Seeu—Gold.

Shah Mahommud—Same as Lucheeram. Term used to signify that danger is near.

Sodh—Money or any property concealed, or search made for it.

Sodhna or *Sodhlena*—To endeavour to ascertain the extent of a traveller's property.

Sofedee—Silver.

Sheikh Jee—Same as Shah Mahommud.

Sikka*—The roomal, or handkerchief with which they strangle.

Sewalee—A fox. Term peculiar to Duckun Thugs.

Sambhur—Treasure.

Shumseea—The person who holds the hands and feet of the person while the Bhurtote strangles him.

Shumseeae—The office of the Shumseeas.

Santh—A sword.

Sancha—The grave.

Singore or *Sankhole*—A party of three travellers.

Sireepotee—A sect of Thugs derived from the Bhys clan.

Siskar—A washerman. Term peculiar to Jumaldehee, Lodaha, and Moteca Thugs.

Soon—A Thug by birth who has not yet attained the rank of a strangler.

Sainee—Term used by Duckun Thugs for Jhirnee, the signal for murder.

Sonoka—The first murder committed after opening the expedition. The person murdered must not be of the female sex, or a Brahman, a Kaet, religious mendicant, oilman, potter, carpenter, blacksmith, goldsmith, elephant-driver, any person having a domestic animal with him, no one having gold conspicuous upon his person, no man carrying

---

* Siva and his consort Parbuttee or Kalee are often represented with the Pasha in one hand, which is a rope or roomal carried for the purpose of binding and strangling offenders.

the bones of his parents to the holy river, nor musician, nor dancing master.

Soonaree—A kite. Term peculiar to Duckun Thugs.

Seyp—Any sleight or trick of a Thug made to deceive travellers, same as Gunooa; also the exterior or appearance, when respectable, of a Thug or traveller.

Soopureea—A class of Thugs that reside about Sooper in Scindhea's territories. They adopted the trade, after some of the original emigrants from Delhie through Agra had married into their families. They are called also Bungureeas and Kokureeas.

Sirwa—A shopkeeper. Term peculiar to a few classes of Thugs in Behar and Bengal.

Siharna—To count.

Sirma—The head.

Saur—Any man that escapes from the hands of the Thugs, when they attempt to strangle him.

Surbalund Khan—The name pronounced by the leader to direct the stranglers to be ready at their post to fall upon the victims, when the final signal or Jhirnee is given. It is also used to signify that some one approaches, or overhears, and that the Thugs must be on their guard. Dulur, Dulur Khan and Surmust Khan are used for the same purpose.

Surdhuneea—A Dhotee or waist-band.

Sosalladhna—To strangle a Sosal.

Sosal Kurna—To wash or bathe; also to bind up the booty when Bisul or scattered for the purpose of dividing it; also to prepare a victim for being strangled, by persuading him to uncover his head or neck.

Soosul—A person whose neck and head are uncovered and therefore convenient for being strangled; one who is strangled without any untoward circumstance of screams, blows, struggles, &c. &c.; also a Thug after he has cleansed himself from stains of blood, or any signs of murder. In all these senses, and in every other in which the term is technically used, it is opposed to Bisul.

Sooseeas—A class of Thugs of the Dhanuk, or lowest Hindoo caste, who call themselves Naeks, and Thories, and reside about Jypore, Kishengur, Onhecara, Boondee, Joudpore, Khasnode, Shahpore, Rutlam, Jhubooa, Mundisore, Tonk, and other parts of Malwa, and Rajpootana. They have been increasing in numbers for many generations, though they are not considered very ancient; and from their low caste are looked down upon by all the other classes of Thugs, who never eat with them, though often associated with them in their expeditions. They often dress themselves as merchants, and pretend to travel through the country on business in parties, in which their leaders figure as merchants of rank, and the rest as his followers and friends of different grades. The head man is often in a hackery or a palanquin, and the rest appear very assiduous and respectful in their attentions to him. Sometimes they are found as sipahees in search of service; at others as treasure bearers, or in whatever disguise seems best for the occasion and country in which they operate, most commonly Guzerat and Rajpootana or Kandesh. They strangle and bury like the other Thugs, and with but few exceptions use the same dialect.

Sath-zut—The seven original clans of Thugs who were all Mahomedans, and from them all others are supposed to be derived. They are Bhyns, Bursoth, Kachunee, Huttar, Ganoo, Tundil, Buhleem. The Thugs say that the Sath-zut, or seven

clans, were all that were at Delhie as Thugs; and
that they derived their descent from sevēn brothers.
This however is not probable. Musulman Thugs
all over India are very proud to trace their descent
from one or other of these great stocks, and he who
can do so is generally treated as a man of superior
birth.

Satha—The first seven days of an expedition,
during which the families of those engaged in one
expedition admit no visits from the families of
Thugs who are absent on another expedition, lest
the travellers destined for the one should go over
to the other gang; neither must they eat any thing
that has belonged to the familes of such other
Thugs. The Thugs engaged in the expedition do
not till the seventh day dress any food in ghee, nor
nor eat any animal food but fish; nor shave, nor
allow their clothes to be washed by a dhoby, nor
indulge in any sexual intercourse, nor give in
charity, not even part of their food to a dog, cat or
jackal. They must not bathe nor eat any sugar,
except what the leader brought with him on setting
out. Formerly they never ate any salt or turmerick, but now they do. On the seventh day they
have a good meal of which greens of some kind or
other must be a component part. During the
whole time the expedition lasts, if within one year,
they take no milk, nor do they clean their teeth
with a brush (miswak.)

If the Sonrka, or first murder, takes place within
the seven days, or Satha, they consider themselves
relieved by it from all these restraints. Formerly
they never used to murder as the Sonrka (or first
victim) any Brahman, or Syad, or any very poor
man, nor any man with gold upon him, nor any
man who had a quadruped with him, nor a dhobee,

10*

nor a sweeper, nor a teylee (oil vender), nor a bhaut (bard), nor a kaet (a writer), nor a blind man, nor maimed persons, nor a leper, nor a dancing woman, nor a pilgrim or devotee. Some classes and individuals neglect these rules and the misfortunes which have fallen upon Thugs lately are attributed principally to this cause.

Setna—To snore when sleeping, or when being strangled.

Seet,h—The slight chirp of the small owl three or four times only repeated. This is a very bad omen while the bird is sitting, and still worse when flying.

Santa—A bracelet; confined to the Duckun Thugs.

Siharna—To count.

Sitkala—Gold coins. Term peculiar to Duckun Thugs.

Situk—Gold. Term peculiar to Duckun Thugs.

Sotha—The person employed to inveigle travellers; always the most eloquent and persuasive man they can find.

Sothae—The office of inveigler.

Sootlee—Twenty rupees.

Suthote—Same as Bhurtote; a strangler.

Suthna—A Musulman.

Sutheea dalna—To kill with a sword.

Sutheeana—The same.

Syt—Term used by the Berar Thugs, for phool or parole of rendezvous. Other Thugs of the south call it maulee.

Taw—A gang or party of either travellers or Thugs.

Taw must Chowkaw—Keep out of sight, conceal the gang from view.

Tubae dalna—To kill. Tobae jana, to be killed.

Thibana or *Thibae dena*—To cause travellers

to sit down on some pretence or other, that stranglers may conveniently do their work of murder.

Thibaoo—The auspice or omen on the right hand. In opening an expedition the omen must be seen or heard first on the left, Pilhaoo; and be soon followed by one on the right. They will not open their expedition if the omen is first observed on the right, nor when observed on the left, unless followed on the right.

Thibna—To sit down or rest, as a traveller.

Tubae dalna—To strangle. A term peculiar to some classes of Thugs.

Tubae Nakhna—The same.

Tighunee—The eye.

Tighunee kurna—To search.

Togree—The turban. Term confined chiefly to Berar and some other Duckun Thugs.

Taujna—To eat.

Thakur—The loud full call of the large owl, said to be like the word "ghoo ghoo." This they interpret according to the ordinary rules of the Thibaoo and Pilaooo. See also *Gorgoreea* and *Kurra*. Duckun Thugs call it Mahee or Raja Teekula.

Teekula—Any suspicious thing taken from a murdered person, which it is dangerous for a Thug to carry.

Teekula purna—To be recognized, as any thing taken from a murdered person and found upon a Thug. Peculiar to Duckun Thugs; same as Purta purna among other Thugs.

Thokee kurna—To spit. When the leader of the gang for the time being, wishes every man to be at his post ready to perform the office assigned to him, he gives the Khokhee, which is hawking aloud or casting up the phlegm preparatory to spitting. When they are all ready, he **gives the** Jhirnee, or signal to set to, if all is clear. If **he** sees cause to suspend operations, he **gives the** Thokee, that is, spits out the phlegm; **when all** retire again. Commonly it is the signal for **the** stranglers to take post near their respective **victim,** but sometimes it is used on other occasions.

Tikhur—Dangerous to Thugs, either **a place or** person.

Tookna—To die.

Took jana—To die.

Tukrar—Search made by villagers or **others** after Thugs or their proceedings.

Tail—A company or individual who has **escaped** by being left behind out of a party of **travellers** murdered. Same as Adhoreea.

Teel—A person found watching or **dodging** the Thugs.

Thola—A Thana or police guard; term **peculiar** to the Koeleea and Dooab Thugs.

Tilha—A spy or scout.

Tilhae—The office of scout.

Tooluk ruhna—To sleep, or Toolukna.

Thumonee—Bribery. *Thumonee dena*, **To bribe.**

Tombako kha lo, or *pee lo*—Eat or smoke **your** tobacco, technically " strangle;" one of **the signals** for murder.

Tome—Any thing particularly good or **valuable** in the spoil; a thing which the gang thinks **worthy** of being preserved for the head man of their vil-lage, or any great patron as a present.

Townaree—Pretence, or trick to beguile **travel-**lers.

Tankee dena—To rouse travellers from **their** sleep.

Thenga—A sword; term peculiar to the Telingana or Duckun Thugs.

Tinnooa—A boy.

Tinna—The same.

Tonga--An Anghurka or vest. A term peculiar to the Thugs of the Dooab.

Tonkal—A party of travellers larger than the Thugs can manage to destroy.

Tona—A Thug's trick, pretext or deceit.

Tongur—Any Marhatta man. Term peculiar to the Duckun Thugs.

Tundul—One of the seven original clans of Thugs. They and the Bahleems went direct from Delhie, after their expulsion, to Multan and the Duckun, and did not rest at Agra. None of these clans are to be found in the Dooab or Bundlecund.

Tupounee—A sacrifice of goor to Bhowanee. This sacrifice is offered at the first convenient place after every murder. One rupee and four annas worth of goor, or coarse sugar, is purchased and put upon a blanket or sheet spread upon the cleanest place they can select. Near the pile of sugar and on the blanket they place the consecrated pickaxe, and a piece of silver, as a "Roop Darsun," or silver offering. The most esteemed leader of the gang who is supposed to be most in favour with the goddess, and best acquainted with the modes of propitiating her, is placed on the blanket, with his face to the west. As many noted stranglers as it can conveniently contain, sit on each side of this leader, with their faces in the same direction. They must be, including the leader, an even number. The rest of the gang sit outside the blanket. The leader now makes a hole in the ground, and having put into it a little of the goor, he lifts his clasped hands and eyes towards heaven,

and with his mind fixed upon the goddess, he says,
" Great Goddess! as you vouchsafed one lack and
" sixty-two thousand rupees to Joora Naig, and
" Koduk Bunwaree in their need, so we pray thee,
" fulfil our desires." In this prayer all the Thugs
fervently join; repeating the words after the
leader. He then sprinkles some water over the
pit and pick-axe; and places a little goor upon the
extended hands of every Thug seated upon the
blanket with him. One of the gang now gives the
Jhirnee, or signal for strangling, in the same manner as if they were going to commit murder, and
the Thugs upon the carpet eat their goor in solemn
silence. Not a word is spoken till they have eaten
the whole, and drunk some water. The pile of
goor is now distributed, as consecrated food to the
whole of the gang entitled from their rank to partake of it. They eat it all with silent reverence,
so that no part may fall to the ground, and if any
fall, it is put into the pit that it may not be soiled
by the foot of any one. The silver is then given
back to the person who lent it for the purpose.

No one but a man who has strangled with his
own hands, and is at the same time a free man, is
suffered to partake of the goor thus consecrated.
For those who have not yet strangled a victim, or
are not freemen, sugar is set apart from the pile
before consecration, and they eat it at the same
time as the others on the signal given. If any thing
improper or indecorous in language, manner, or
conduct, takes place during this ceremony, they
consider it an evident sign of the displeasure of the
deity, and despair of further success during the
expedition.

If any particle of the consecrated goor should
be left on the ground, and eaten by a dog or any

other animal, they would, they believe, suffer under
the displeasure of the deity for years. If any other
human being should taste the goor, they are persuaded that he would immediately take to the trade
of Thuggee, and never be able to leave it off, whatever may have been his rank or condition in life.
If they have any young disciple about whose
advancement they are very solicitous, they try to
get for him a little of the consecrated goor, assured
that he would advance rapidly in his profession
after eating it. See *Joora Naig,* and *Koduk Bunwaree.*

Tippana—To watch, observe.

Tuparna—To search or scrutinize, or arrest.

Thapteea—A potter. Peculiar to Duckun
Thugs.

Taup—Bread. Term peculiar to Duckun Thugs.

Teep—A fire kindled among Thugs for evil purposes; *teep kurnd* to murder, divide booty, bury,
or cover up the grave. They use this term whenever they require to mention fire before those who
are likely to hear, but ought not to understand them
commonly.

Thap—The place of encampment where the
Thugs spend the night, commonly outside a village.

Thapa—The same.

Thapa—A river among the Behar and Bengal
Thugs, from its banks being their general resting
place.

Topka—Cloth of any kind.

Tupponee kurna—Performing the ceremony of
Tupance.

Tup jana—To quit the road on which they are
moving and take another direction.

Tuppul, or *Tuppowal,* or *Tupole*—The by-path or
Pugdundee, into which Thugs lead the travellers

from the high road in order to murder them without danger.

Tareea—A gold mohur.

Tawree—Bread.

Tirkeea—A goldsmith. Peculiar to Duckun Thugs.

Tharee—The Sooseea Thugs are called Thories by other classes of Thugs.

Tirheea—A bag or knapsack.

Tarndee—A gold mohur.

Tormee—Thug, thief, or robber of any kind.

Tortunkur—A searching after, seizing, or molesting Thugs.

Tas—The neel kunt, or blue jay. If they see it to the right, or crossing from the left to right, it promises good. If to the left, or crossing from the right to left, it promises no good, but threatens no evil. Its cry they consider as nothing. **Tas**, as the name of the jay, is not peculiar to Thugs.

Wahurna—To strangle.

Walgee—Duckun term for Burauk, the crossing of a wolf or wolves on the road before the gang. Whether they cross from right to left, or left to right, it is considered a very bad omen among Duckun Thugs, and they dare not advance.

W. H. SLEEMAN,
General Superintendent.

OFFICIAL PAPERS

RELATING TO

TRIALS OF THUGS

BY THE

BRITISH AUTHORITIES IN INDIA.

CORRESPONDENCE BETWEEN CAPTAIN SLEEMAN AND MR. STOCKWELL.

Saugor, 7th February, 1833.

DEAR SIR,

I have now before me several private and public letters written by you so long back as 1816 on the subject of Thugs, and as you may be pleased to learn something of the subsequent history of the leading characters whom you then mentioned as being at large and at their "dreadful trade," I take the liberty to enclose a few genealogical tables of the families of some of the approvers now under my charge. Should you not have preserved copies of these letters I shall have much pleasure in forwarding them to you, for I have often referred to them with interest and advantage.

I hope you will pardon the liberty I take in saying that it is to me, and must be to every one who knows any thing of the subject, and feels anxious for the success of an attempt so interesting to humanity, a source of sincere gratification to find you again so unexpectedly placed in a situation where your abilities and former experience are likely to be of such important advantage. Indeed I may very honestly say, and without any wish to be complimentary to a gentleman whom I have never had an opportunity of seeing, that I consider your appointment to the Dooab *providental;* and to complete our success all that is wanting seems to me to be your appointment as a special commissioner to try all the Thugs arrested in the different districts of the Dooab and kingdom of Oude; and health and strength to enable you to get through the Herculean labour. This tribute I pray you to accept from one who has known you only through your repute as a public officer, and who may perhaps never have an opportunity of becoming personally acquainted with you.

My part in the work I consider as an episode in my life. It is a duty to which I have devoted willingly and zealously all the little ability that God has given me, but it is one to which none of us would be led from taste or inclination. It is one requiring the finest abilities, but one to which fine abilities would not from choice be directed. If the protection of life and property be the first duty of government, never did any object more imperatively call for the application of all its energies than this; and I trust no considerations will induce it to relax, or its public officers to withhold their cordial co-operation in the work.

Believe me, dear Sir, your's very faithfully,
(Signed) W. H. SLEEMAN.
G. Stockwell, Esq.

Note.—Mr. Stockwell had for some years been Commissioner in Orissa, and his return to the Dooab was to me quite unexpected.

Cawnpore, 24th October, 1893.

My dear Sir,

An experiment is about to be made of what can be done with Thug cases in our courts of law, for Mr. Wilson's Shawl case will come before me immediately, and we shall see what effect is produced by the result of this trial. I have done what is in me to have the preliminary proceedings indisputably correct—1st, by obviating cavil at my holding a trial while the sessions judge is on the spot, which has been done by obtaining the opinion of the Nizamut in favour of my so doing; 2ndly, by avoiding a chance that a commitment by Mr. Wilson is not deemed quite legal. He has no letter making him a joint magistrate, nor has he been gazetted as such, while the letter from government to the Nizamut only speaks of the districts in which he ought *to be* made joint, not that he *has been* so made. This we overcome by getting the magistrate to join in the commitment without however touching the case, and thus I think we start fair.

Of Wilson I will not pretend to give you any accounts. You are aware of his activity and zeal and doubtless he keeps you acquainted with his movements and their results. He may too tell you, though he might not tell me and has not, if any thing is done by me or my subordinates which frustrates his endeavours. And if so you will possibly let me know what does thwart him, for certes he has my anxious wishes for the success of the most important police measure that has been adopted in my time. May your health so rally and your strength be so renovated that you may remain to superintend that measure to its triumphant conclusion. I can hardly say more of it than that I have heard persons equally unknown to you and to me, but who have travelled through your districts call down blessings on your head for the security to the lives and property of travellers which had been brought about by your exertions and penetration. This is the sort of praise which must come home to a man's breast, and as I said, the persons knew neither you nor me personally, so it is genuine. I hope you got lists of Thugs sent to you under two separate covers from Futtehghur and Cawnpore.

Believe me very truly yours,
(Signed)   G. STOCKWELL.

To Captain Sleeman, &c. &c.

Cawnpore, 5th November, 1833.

My dear Sir,

Wilson's commitment came before me at the close of last month. It took me two days to make extracts from his proceedings, and five more to take the trial. Of a jury of nine who were called, only six attended, of whom one deserted on the third, another on the fourth day of trial, leaving four by whom the verdict was delivered. Their judgment was more free from bias than that of an English jury, because there were no advocates to lead, nor was there any summing up by me, whence my leaning might have been discovered. At first the business seemed to go against their grain, and to be beyond their belief; but, as point after point was developed, and each fresh head of evidence fitted into that which had gone before, conviction entered their minds. After retiring for an hour into a separate room they returned a verdict of guilty: they brought in three men guilty of the actual murder and the same three with three others guilty of removing the bodies, stabbing, and throwing them into a well; and a seventh guilty of being with them though not at the murder. The nine accused of receiving, sharing and passing the stolen property were also convicted. Of these last I have acquitted and released two. The rest must await the orders of Nizamut by whom I suppose some will be hanged. But the trial will not yet be submitted, as it came out before me that two of the Jemadars, Rumdeen and Bhugga, had been for three years in the Furruckabad jail on a charge of Thuggee, whence they were released but two months before they set out on this expedition. The papers have been sent for from that Zillah. Should you desire a more detailed account, I will send over my notes of the evidence, though notes are rarely useful to any but him by whom they are made, and with them a copy of my address, which will be brief, to the Nizamut when laying my proceedings before them.

As I am about to quit the Dooab, it will be beyond my power to lend that aid to Wilson's operations which I trust they have received in my character of moderator between him and our magistrates. But I hope the foundation which has been laid by his own good sense and conciliatory manner towards functionaries and people, and the footing on which I have put him with them, will preserve to him all necessary influence. And that it may be rendered efficient, I have to-day in a demi-official to Mr. Macsween, advised that Wilson should be joint magistrate in the districts within this and the Alahabad division. Any particular trials can still be referred to me, if it be so wished, at Moradabad; and in respect to hearing them, there is no objection or reluctance on my part. I cannot however but think that an arrangement is required for trying the Jumaldahee Thugs whose depredations are committed in Oude. The venue cannot be changed to our courts, and Saugor appears to me too distant. Would not the government instruct the resident to hold those trials?*

Believe me, my dear Sir, very truly and faithfully yours.

(Signed)   G. STOCKWELL.
To Captain Sleeman, &c. &c.

* This has since been done.

English proceedings of the Thug trials held at Gazepoor and Benares in 1833-34.

To Welby Jackson, Esquire,

Register to the Nizamut Adawlut for the Western Provinces at Allahabad.

Court of Sessions of Zellah Ghazeepoor trial, No. 5. of the Calendar for Sessions of August, 1833.
1. Shewsahao Loll, Gomastah of Persotum Doss Shah, Prosecutors.
—2. Musst. Phooleeah,—3. Jhannoe,
Versus
1. Peer Bukhs Khan,—2. Kurrum Bukhs Khan,—3. Bechook Noorbaff,—4. Khoda Bukhs Khan,—5. Sheikh Durvoish,—6. Peeroo Khan,—Sheikh Bucktour,—and—8. Sheikh Ammoe.
Charge.
1st Count.
Thuggee, attended with murder of Purdil Khan, and Buddhaie, labourer.
2d Count.
Murder of Purdil Khan, and Buddhaie, labourer.
1st April, 1833.

Sir,

I herewith transmit, to be laid before the Nizamut Adawlut, the proceedings upon the trial noted in the margin, held at the station of Gazeepoor on the 24th, 26th, 27th, 29th and 30th days of August, 1833, A. D.

2. There are three prosecutors—Shewsahae Lall deposes that he is a Gomastah of Persotum Doss Shah, a Mahajun of the city of Benares, by whose directions he, the prosecutor, purchased a quantity of Kinkaubs and other costly clothes of Benares manufacture, in value about 450 rupees, placed them in a wooden box, sent the box to the Benares custom-house, where he took out a Rowannah, and had the box properly secured with rope and moom-jamah, the fastenings being secured by wax, bearing the custom-house seal, entertained Purdil Khan as Peon in charge, and Buddaie Cooley to carry the box; and upon the 28th March, 1833, corresponding to the 22nd Chait, 1240 Fy., sent off the said Purdil Khan and Buddaie, with directions to deliver the box to the house of Gourdeal Ram and Bunarsee Ram, Muhajuns, residing in the town of Chuprah, Zillah of Sarun.

He further declares, that the distance between Benares and Chuprah is travelled in six days, but that eighteen days elapsed without his receiving any tidings that the goods had reached Chuprah, or of those to whom he had entrusted them; when upon the nineteenth day, a letter reached him by the Dak from Sungumlall and Bullakeedoss Muhajuns of the town of Ghazeepoor, acquainting him with the apprehension of a gang of robbers having in their possession considerable property of a nature similar to that which he, the prosecutor, had entrusted to Purdil Khan.

That he then repaired to Ghazeepoor, taking with him the Beejuck of the property, and having made known the occasion of his coming to the magistrate, the property in Court was compared with the Beejuck and found to correspond, and that after inspection he was enabled to swear to the whole property as being that which by his directions Purdil Khan and Buddhaie took from Benares to carry to Chuprah.

Musst. Phooleah,—The wife of Purdil Khan corroborated the circumstance of her husband having been engaged for the trip by Ghous Khan, a Jemadar in the employ of Shewsahae Lall last named, and to her husband having sent her a message on the day he set out, saying he should return in six days. That he never has returned, and she now hears he has been murdered; she recognises a sword and a dagger in Court as having been her husband's weapons.

The third prosecutor, Jhannoo,—A Chowdry of Coolies at Benares, corroborates the dispatch of a box by Shewsahae Lall in charge of Purdil Khan, and his having furnished Buddhaie Cooley in virtue of his office, to carry the box. He appears as a prosecutor in consequence of his being Buddhaie's uncle.

Evidence for the prosecution. 3d. The facts stated by the prosecutors, that is the purchase of the property, the taking out a Rowannah at the Benares custom-house, the entertaining of Purdil Khan and Buddhaie, and the dispatch of the box in their charge, and the identity of the property with that in the Court, is firmly established by the following evidence:

Ramlowtun Raie,—Who was employed by Shewsahae Lall to purchase the goods.

Baboo Noorbaff,—Who himself manufactured the greater part of the goods, sold them to Shewsahae Lall, and who was present at the purchase of those articles not made by himself.

Suhaie,—A tailor in the employ of Shewsahae Lall, who sewed the cloth packing cases, who sewed on the fringes to a number of articles, who assisted in packing the goods, and who afterward saw the box, with the custom-house seals and moomjamah attached to it.

Ghous Khan,—Jemadar of Shewsahae Lall, who engaged Purdil Khan and Buddhaie Cooley, and assisted in packing the box.

4th.—I now proceed to the evidence which is adduced to prove that this property of the prosecutor Shewsahae Lall was found upon the prisoners.

Sheikh Oudan, a Burkundaz in the Thannah of Bansdee,—Deposes that, on the 2d April, 1833, he was travelling along the road upon business connected with the police, in an easterly direction, when just as he was about to enter the village of "Meiree Tal," he met seven men coming from Meiree Tal. That he at once recognised Kurreem Bukhs, Peeroo Khan and Kurrum Ali, having chanced to see them once before, when they were under trial for a former offence; that he spoke to them slightly, and then, passing them, entered the village. That suspecting their purpose, he got together some of the Zemindars and Goraits of Meiree Tal, and gave immediate pursuit; that coming in sight of them about a mile from the village he found they had divided into two parties and taken different roads, one party consisting of Peeroo Khan, No. 6, Sheikh Durveish, No. 5, and Khodah Bukhs Khan, No. 4, having taken a road due west, and the other party of four persons, Peer Bukhs, No. 1, Kurreem Bukhs, No. 2, Beechook No. 3, and Kurrum Ali having gone by a road in a N. W. direction; that seeing this, he sent At- chumbit Sing and Lalsa Goraite after the first party; and himself accompanied by Shewdeal Sing, Keener Sing, Pran and Gunga, pursued the second party, and that he was thus enabled to appre- hend the whole of these seven persons, upon four of whom Peer Bukhs, (No. 1,) Kurreem Bukhs, (No. 2,) Bechee, (No. 3,) and Durveish, (No. 5,) he found bundles of property.

That he then proceeded with the whole party in the direction of his Thannah, and had reached a Pokerce in Bandsdee, when the prisoners entreated for their release, offering him fifty rupees cash, for which one of their party was to be sent, and a piece of Kinkab; that he declined their offers, and lodged them safely at the Thannah, where the property found on them was duly examined, &c.

The whole of the above testimony, from the moment that Sheikh Oudan entered Meiree Tal and gave the alarm, till he delivered the prisoners into the custody of the Thannadar, is corroborated by the following evidence:

Shewdeal Sing, Reener Sing, Atchumbit Sing, Lalsa Goraite, Pran Goraite,—resident Zemindars and Gooraits of the village of Meiree Tal, added to which the prisoners* when examined by the Thannadar, and in their subsequent depositions, admitted having the property in their possession, though they attempted to account for that circum- stance in a way which will be noticed in the defence.

* The four prisoners on whom it was found.

5th.—Having thus traced the property with which Purdil Khan and Buddhaie set out from Benares to carry to Chuprah, into the possession of the prisoners, I now proceed to the evidence, tending to show how far Purdil Khan would appear to have reached on his way.

It is to be observed that Purdil Khan having charge of goods liable to pay duties, and for which he held a Rowannah of the Benares custom-house, was obliged to present himself and show his Rowannah at all the custom-house Chowkees on the road. We have accordingly the evidence of the following persons to the point in question:

Kurramut Ali,—Stationed at the custom-house Chowkee Goomtee Mohamah at Patna, to whom Purdil Khan showed the box and Rowannah, and who took a copy of the Rowannah on the 28th March.

Lalljeelall,—Stationed at the Chowkee Bulleah, 31 coss east of Patna on the road to Chuprah, who took a copy of the Rowannah which was presented to him by Purdil Khan; he forgets the date, but from other sources it appears to have been the 31st March.

Bussunt Sing,—Stationed at Chowkee Bursund, 2 coss east of Chowkee Balleah on the Chuprah road, who minutely details the person and dress of Purdil Khan, the Cooley, the box with red Moomjamah and seals, his questioning Purdil Khan, who described himself as travelling from Benares to Chuprah, and to whom he assigned a lodging in the house of Shewchurn Candoo for that night (31st.)

Shewchurn Candoo,—In whose house at Bursund, Purdil Khan slept.

Sunker Gorait,—Of Bursund, who described the

person, dress, &c. &c. in a similar manner to Bussunt Sing.

Kurrum Ali,—An accomplice to whom, under the provisions of Section III. Regulation X, 1824, a pardon was tendered by the magistrate,—

Who describes how he and the other eight prisoners were out on the road in question, in quest of some victims on whom to exercise their profession (Thuggee) ; that they remained the night of the 30th March under a tree, south of the village of Balleah above-mentioned, the night of the 31st March opposite to and a little south of Bursund, and that on the 1st April, when about 2½ coss from Bursund, they fell in with Purdil Khan and the Cooley carrying the box, with whom some of them joined company and accompanied them to Murlee Chupra, 6 coss distant from Bursund; that there they all passed the night under a tree at a little distance from the village, and that so early as 3 A. M. on the morning of the 2d April, they all set out and had proceeded but a short distance, when Purdil Khan and Buddhaie were deprived of their lives in the usual way by strangulation; their bodies deposited in a ditch between two gardens near the spot ; the box opened and property packed in bundles, and their apprehension at noon the same day near Meiree Tal by Sheikh Oudan Burkundaz.

Connecting this evidence with that to the seizure of the prisoners at Meiree Tal about noon on this very second of April, a distance of 8 coss west of Murlee Chuprah, we have undoubted proof that Purdil Khan and Buddhaie Cooley appeared at Bulleah and Bursund Chowkies, and slept at the latter place on the 31st March, and that the prisoners were apprehended at Meiree Tal proceeding westward and 8 coss from Murlee Chupra by a cross road in an opposite direction on this 2d April, that consequently Purdil Khan and Buddhaie could not possibly have reached more than one stage beyond Chowkee Bursund when deprived of the property.

6th. The evidence to the following points has thus been detailed :

1. The purchase and despatch of the property in charge of Purdil Khan and Buddhaie en route to Chupra on the 25th March.

2. The identity of the said property with that in the Court.

3. The seizure of the prisoners on the 2d April, having this property in their possession.

4. Evidences showing that Purdil Khan could not have reached beyond a day's journey east of Bursund, where he slept on the 31st March.

The fate of Purdil Khan and Buddhaie, and the circumstances attending the robbery are detailed in the evidence of Kurreem Ali alone, from whose deposition a brief abstract of a part only has been made. It is now however necessary to give it more in detail, as several connecting proofs have been elicited in consequence of the disclosures made by him. But first it is necessary to mention that at the Thannah, and in the first instance before the magistrate, he made a defence similar to that of the other prisoners, and that it was not until the 6th of May, being one month and four days subsequent to his apprehension, that he gave his evidence upon oath before the magistrate.

He declares that in the month of Phagoon, the eight prisoners assembled at the house of Khader Bukhs (4), in the village of Tupnee, and set out along the road to Mirzapore in the hope of falling in with some booty. That he, Kurreem Ali, had

promised to meet them for the same purpose in the
month of Chait, and agreeably to his promise, he
in the month of Chait went to the village of Tupnee,
and through Musst. Choheeah, a female slave of
Khader Bukhs, inquired where he was to meet the
gang. That Musst. Azeema, the wife of Khader
Bukhs, was ill, and he did not see her, but that
she sent him word by Choheeah* that he would
meet the gang at the village of Bulleah : that he
set out for Bulleah, and upon the same day, the
30th March, reached Bulleah, where he found the
prisoners, and was informed by them that they had
been unsuccessful; that they remained that night
under a tree south of Bulleah; that the next day
they removed to the vicinity of Bursund, where
they passed the night of the 31st; that in the morning of the 1st April they proceeded eastward, and
six men had gone ahead, while three of the party,
Khader Bukhs (4), Durveesh (5), Peroo Khan (6),
sat down by the road side to eat ; that after a while
these three persons appeared, having Purdil Khan
and the Cooley in company; that in the act of
passing their companions who were smoking by
the road side, one of the three, Durveesh (5), falling
behind joined them, and told them to come on to
Murlee Chupra about dusk in the evening. That
they joined company at Murlee Chupra, and took
up their lodging under a tree near the village, being
the usual resting place for travellers; that at 3
A. M. of the 2d April, Ammee awoke Purdil Khan,
and proposed to proceed, but Purdil Khan, saying
it was too early, declined; that shortly after however the whole party proceeded, and while their
companions scattered themselves to a little distance

* This is corroborated by the evidence of Musst. Chohceah.

with a view to prevent the approach of strangers
Khader Bukhs (No. 4), Durveesh (No. 5), Buktour
(No. 7), and Ammee (No. 8), who continued near
to Purdil Khan and Buddhaie, having seated them
to ease themselves, took advantage of the opportunity and strangled them; that Ammee (No. 8),
threw the phausee, and Durveesh (No. 5), pulled
out the legs of Purdil Khan, while Khader Bukhs
(4), threw the phausee round Buddhaie's neck, and
Buktour (7), held his legs; that the same persons
then removed each their own victims and placed
the bodies in a ditch between two Baggechas; that
Kurreem Bukhs (2), took up the box, and Khader
Bukhs the dagger and sword, belonging to Purdil
Khan, and they all of them then proceeded westward, in the direction of Peeroo Khan's house by
a cross road; that when they had reached a distance of about one coss, they by Ammee's desire
went into a field, and broke open the box, where
they divided the contents into four bundles, one a
piece being given to Durveesh (5), Kurreem Bukhs
(2), Buctour (7), and Ammee (8); that after having
buried the pieces of the box and the strings and
red moomjamah in the field, they again set out,
and when near to Meiree Tal, Buktour (7), and
Ammee (8), proposed to get home by a shorter
route, and giving their bundles to Peer Bukhs and
Beechook, separated from them when just entering
Meiree Tal. That the gang then went up to the
Tukkeah of Allee Bukhs Shah Faqueer, with whom
Peeroo Khan (No. 6), deposited the sword belonging to the deceased; that going onward, they met
Sheikh Oudan Burkundaz outside Meiree Tal, who
suspecting them, and knowing some of them to be
bad characters, got a party of Zemindars and
Goraits from Meiree Tal, and apprehended them;

that they offered large bribes to Sheikh Oudan, but
he would not listen to them, and lodged them at
the Thannah; he also declared that the dagger
had been taken from Khader Bukhs by Sheikh
Oudan.

The evidence of Kureem Ali presented several
peculiar circumstances, each susceptible of independent proof, and upon the truth of which the
credit due to that evidence would mainly depend,
such as the finding of the sword, the dagger, the
pieces of box and appendages, and the bodies in
the places indicated by Kureem Ali.

The magistrate at once observed the importance
of investigating these points, and lost no time in
deputing the Darogah of the jail, an active and
intelligent officer, to make these investigations,
accompanied by Kureem Ali. The result of this
inquiry substantiating more or less the above
points I shall now detail from the evidence examined before this Court.

Sword.

Allee Buksh Shah, Faqueer,—Describes the
sword being deposited with him by Peeroo
Khan (6), on the day when the prisoners were
seized. He also identifies the said Peeroo Khan
and swears to the recognition of prisoners, Nos. 1,
2, 3 and 4, as well as Kureem Ali, saying they
were standing near his Tukkeah when Peeroo
Khan begged him to keep the sword.

Dullum Koeree,—Inhabitant of Meiree Tal,
deposes to the same facts as Ali Bukh Shah, but
even in a more particular way, recognising all the
prisoners, save 7 and 8, describing what bundles
he saw with each, his evidence in this respect

tallying with that at the Thannah respecting the search of the prisoners.

The sword was found in the Chupper of the Tukkeeah.

The Dagger.

Was found by search in the presence of witnesses, in the petarah of Sheikh Oudan Burkundaz, who accounts for the circumstance by stating, that when he apprehended the prisoners, he espied the dagger in the kummer of Khader Bukhs (4), and fearing lest that prisoner in dispute should attempt to do him an injury, he took it from him, and having put it away in his petarah, and being instantly sent upon other police duties, he had never thought again of the dagger till it was found in his petarah.

The dagger is a shabby article, and worth scarcely one rupee; some of the witnesses who assisted to seize the prisoners also depose to seeing the dagger in the kummer of Khader Bukhs.

Pieces of Box—Rope with Seals—Red Moomjamah.

Nerkoo Chumar, Ruhum Alli Noorbaff,—Who reside in the adjoining village, depose to being called upon to attend the Darogah; that upon reaching the spot, a person whom they identify as Kurreem Ali, took them all to a field and by his directions they began to dig the ground, when after a little they found the rope with the seals and red moomjamah; that again he took them to another field where a little below the surface they found some pieces of a box; that the first field was Beharie's, and the second field belonged to Reghar; that both fields adjoin each other, with the road running between them.

12*

The bodies.

Kurreem Ali, it appears, pointed out the exact spot corresponding with his evidence where the bodies had been deposited, but they were not found there.   Upon this point—

Bhoabul Raie, Hurrie Raie, Moheet Raie, Sewchurn Geer, Omrao Noorbaff and Barosa Koiree,—Who reside in the surrounding villages, depose to having heard that two bodies of murdered travellers were lying between the gardens of Thakoorduth Missir and Gunnaishduth Missir, for some days about the time in question, but they either know not or are averse to disclose the manner in which they were removed.   The latter seems the most probable.

By a Roobekaree of the magistrate under date the 27th July, 1833, it would appear that after a full inquiry he considered this point to be established and punished by imprisonment and fine, those who had abetted the concealment of the bodies, instead of reporting the circumstance to the police.

The defence.—The prisoners deny the charge in toto, and account for having the stolen property in their possession in the following manner—that upon the day on which they were seized, it chanced that they were passing Meiree Tal, some upon one errand, and some upon another, but without connection with each other, and that upon their reaching the well at Meiree Tal, Sheikh Oudan Burkundaz laid hold of them apparently as beggars or coolies, and ordered them to assist in carrying some bundles, lying by the side of the well, to the Thannah; that they objected to this coercive measure without effect, and ultimately were forced to obey, and that when they reached the Thannah they were denounced as Thugs, and saddled with the property as proof of their guilt.

The prisoners have not attempted to prove this story, but they called witnesses principally to establish their good conduct.

Their evidence, however, far from establishing their claim to good character, represent them as men who have no ostensible livelihood, and in corroboration of the character assigned to them, mention their frequent absence from their homes for unknown purposes.

Such is the evidence brought by the prisoners Nos. 2, 3, 7 and 8; Khader Bukhs No. 4, and Peeroo Khan No. 6 are own brothers. The former brought two witnesses, one of whom denies all knowledge of him, and the other hears he is a bad character, having been apprehended twice or thrice before. The latter brought two witnesses to prove he was a servant in an indigo factory near to Meiree Tal, and had incurred the enmity of the inhabitants in the discharge of his duty as a peadah; one of these witnesses has been 10 years, the other 6 years a servant of the factory. They positively swear that the prisoner (No. 6,) never has been a servant of the factory during the above period.

The Futwah,—Of the Law Officer is to the following effect; that from the corroboration of the several circumstances in the evidence given by Kurreem Ali, such as the finding of the pieces of the box and the cords bearing the seals of the custom-house at Benares, in spots pointed out by that witness, as well as the finding of the sword in the possession of Allee Bukhs Faqueer, with whom Peeroo Khan had placed it, and the dagger with Sheikh Oudan, both of which latter circumstances had been previously narrated by the said witnesses; also, from the prisoners having been apprehended together with the property, as well as from the story told by the prisoners, "that Sheikh Oudan Burkundaz put the property on them by force," being quite unworthy of credit, and as it would appear that the prisoners offered large bribes to the said Sheikh Oudan to induce him to release them; also from the evidence that the prisoners are bad characters, have been before apprehended and obtain a livelihood by highway robberies, &c.; from all these circumstances, there is strong presumptive proof that the prisoners did, in concert with each other, murder Purdil Khan and Buddhaie, and rob and plunder the property in their charge now in court; and further, that from the evidence of Kurreem Ali, the declaration of Beechook, and evidence of Lalsa Gorait, the prisoners Buktour (No. 7,) and Ammee (No. 8,) are proved to have been aiders or abettors in the said murder and robbery; that the prisoners are liable to akoobut either by lengthened imprisonment or by sentence of death against the whole or a portion of the prisoners.

Judge's opinion,—After a perusal of the evidence for the prosecution, which is so arranged as to show the gradual progress of the investigation and its tendency to substantiate the charge, I feel no difficulty in arriving at the conclusion that the prisoners are all of them professed Thugs, and that the prisoners, No. 1, 2, 3, 4, 5 and 6, did actually murder Purdil Khan and Buddhaie Cooley, by strangulation in the manner usually made use of by Thugs; plundered and carried off the property with which the murdered persons were entrusted, and within a few hours after, and not twelve miles from the spot, were apprehended, having the plundered property, and a weapon of the murdered Purdil Khan in their possession while hurrying in a straight line from the spot where the murders were perpetrated to the house of Peeroo Khan (No. 6,) which is situated about a mile beyond Meiree Tal.

Respecting the guilt of the prisoners, I do not see any reasonable doubt to be urged in their favour; the evidence of an accomplice whose very act of deserting and denouncing his companions is one of treachery dictated by the desire of self-preservation, is ever viewed with suspicion; but in the present case, the evidence of Kurreem Ali would scarcely be necessary to substantiate their guilt, for there would still remain a mass of proof sufficient to convict the prisoners.

To be circumspect however, and not attach any further credence to that evidence than so far as its truth is established beyond dispute by subsequent investigation, we may add to the proofs already obtained when Kurreem Ali made his disclosure,— 1st, the finding of the pieces of the box, the cords having the custom-house seals, and the moomjamah cover; 2d, the finding of the sword with the Faqueer at Meiree Tal; 3d, the finding of the dagger with Sheikh Oudan, both of which weapons belonged to Purdil Khan; and 4th, the result of an investigation, which shows that the two bodies were lying for some days on the spot pointed out by Kurreem Ali. All these are facts elicited from the evidence of Kurreem Ali, which, while they tend greatly to strengthen the proofs against the prisoners in question, undoubtedly show, if well considered, that the evidence of Kurreem Ali may be depended on as truth, an opinion to which the evidence of the prosecution, corroborating the details of that evidence in other respects lends additional weight.

Had Kurreem Ali made the disclosure immediately after the arrival of the prisoners at Ghazeepoor, there is little doubt that the bodies would have been found, as indicated ; but as there was a lapse of one month and six days between the perpetration of the murders and the arrival of the Darogah with Kurreem Ali on the spot, there could be little hope that the bodies would be left undisturbed so long in such a frequented place. There appears little doubt that the Zemindars, having omitted to report the circumstance to the police from a dread of the inconveniences of a visit from the police, particularly at a season when every one was busy cutting their crops, removed the bodies, and afterwards when the Darogah did arrive, used every means in their power, though without success, to prevent their own neglect being made known. For fuller details on this head, I beg to refer the Court to the Roobekaree of the magistrate, dated the 8th May, 1833, and 27th July, 1833.

After a full consideration of the case, I am therefore constrained to give my opinion that the prisoners Nos. 1, 2, 3, 4, 5 and 6 are guilty of the heinous crime laid to their charge, and with reference to the prevalence of Thuggee in the Chuprah, Goruckpoor and *Ghazeepoor districts, to neither of which do the prisoners seem to be strangers, to the many proofs exhibited in this case that the prisoners have no honest means of living, but subsist by spoliation and destruction of their fellow crea-

* A list of cases ascertained by that police of this district between the year 1826 and the present year : 1 of Thuggee with murder, 2 of highway robberies, is annexed.

tures, to the impunity which in ninety-nine cases in a hundred attends the perpetration of this insidious and most cruel mode of robbery and murder, which calls for exemplary punishment, and an example such as shall strike terror into the minds of those who pursue a similar course, I recommend that the prisoners 1 to 6 be sentenced to death, and suffer the full penalty of their crimes.

With reference to the two remaining prisoners Sheikh Buktour (7), and Ammee (8), their case requires a separate consideration.

In their cases, two of the most important of the proofs against the prisoners 1 to 6 are wanting, for neither were these two prisoners apprehended on the 2nd April, the day of the murders, nor was there any part of the property found in their possession.

I shall therefore carefully note down the proofs that have been adduced against them and then give my opinion. It has already been shown that Sheikh Oudan Burkundaz, with the assistance of the Zemindars and Gorait of Meiree Tal, succeeded in apprehending the whole of the gang of seven men. Not one escaped. The first intimation therefore by which these two prisoners were implicated was Kurreem Ali's evidence upon the 8th May, prior to which their names had not been even mentioned. To begin therefore with his evidence, it has already been recorded that—

Kurreem Ali,—Includes Buktour and Ammee as having accompanied the gang up to Mirzapoor, and as having continued with them till after the perpetration of this offence, in which he gives both of them a prominent character, the one (Buktour) as having pulled Buddhaie's legs, while Khadar Bukhs threw the phansee round his neck, and

Ammee as having cast the phansee round the neck of Purdil Khan, while Durveish held his legs. We are now to inquire how far Kurreem Ali's evidence, so far as it relates to these two prisoners, has been substantiated by other testimony.

1. Before the magistrate—

Musst. Choheeah,—A female slave belonging to Khadar Bukhs (4), corroborated Kurreem Ali's evidence as to the departure of the gang from Khadar Bukh's house in Phagoon, and mentioned these two prisoners by name as having accompanied them.

In this Court, when the evidence of this witness was examined, there appeared the usual intimation that she had been tampered with, a circumstance not to be wondered at, when her dependence on one of the prisoners is considered.

The existence of such an influence manifested itself not in a total denial of her former evidence, but in such omissions as rendered it nugatory; however, no sooner was she reminded of her former testimony, than she readily admitted its truth, and gave up her previous intention to screen the prisoner.

Lalsa Gorait, 2,—Who assisted in apprehending the prisoners 1 to 6 at Meiree Tal, declared that while occupied in securing the prisoners, he observed two persons standing at a short distance, who then went away. He subsequently identified Buktour and Ammee as the persons in question.

His evidence, however, is inadmissible, for when examined before the magistrate upon the 9th April, he did not mention the circumstance, although he was questioned whether there were any others with the seven men then apprehended; in short, he did not mention it till after Kurreem Ali's evidence had been taken, and Buktour and Ammee' had been seized.

Beechook 3, Prisoner (3.)—When first examined touching the property found in his possession, declared it had been given to him by two persons; subsequently when Buktour and Ammee were brought to the magistrate's Court, he was re-examined, and then declared that the property had been given to him by these two prisoners Buktour and Ammee.

In this deposition of Beechook is a corroboration of Kurreem Ali's evidence, who had previously deposed " that near Meiree Tal where Buktour and Ammee were about to leave their companions and get home by a shorter road, this Buktour gave his bundle to Beechook."

Towukul Gorait of Mouzah Peprah.
  Chintamun ditto of ditto.
  Beechook Raie Rajpoot of ditto.
  Purdan Koiree, Nonid Koiree of ditto,
    and
	Witnesses for the Prosecution and evidence of Buktour's village,	Corroborate Kurreem Ali's evidence with reference to Buktour (No. 7,) having been absent from his village from the month of Phagoon.

Chumroo Gour of ditto. Roopun Rae Rajpoot of ditto.	Witnesses called by Buktour,	

5. In like manner Mundil and Pirthee Raie, whom Ammee called to exculpate himself, both declare that Ammee was absent from his home, on what errand they know not, from the month of Phagoon.

6. All the witnesses called by these two prisoners, as well as some of the witnesses to the prosecution, denounce them as men of bad character, without ostensible means of livelihood, absenting themselves from their homes, and generally con-

sidered from their having been before apprehended by the police, to be dangerous.

I have thus enumerated the proofs exhibited against Buktour and Ammee. My opinion is as follows:

Judge's opinion.—The degree of proof against these two prisoners for reasons already stated, is in its nature less conclusive than that against the prisoners, Nos. 1 to 6.

I have already stated the strong grounds which exist for inducing me to attach credit to the whole testimony of Kurreem Ali, for after a careful investigation not a single circumstance narrated by him has been invalidated, while upon many essential points, it has been singularly corroborated.

In the case of these two prisoners, their absence from their homes from a period coincident with that stated by Kurreem Ali as that in which the gang set out, their notoriously bad character, their former apprehensions, and general conduct in life, corresponding with what would be the conduct and habits of men engaged in Thuggee, is established, their own witnesses whom they brought to the defence, assisting powerfully to produce this impression.

I would further observe, that if Kurreem Ali had, causelessly and to gratify some former enmity, included them in his evidence, they would not have failed to plead such in extenuation and exculpation.

Taking the evidence of Kurreem Ali, Musst. Chooheeah and the witnesses for the defence, I consider it established that Buktour and Ammee did accompany the other prisoners in their going forth to commit robbery on this occasion, that there is strong presumption that they aided and abetted in the perpetration of the offence charged, and that there is full proof that both the prisoners are bad characters and robbers by profession.

I recommend that the prisoners Buktour and Ammee be imprisoned for life with labours and irons.

Recommends the zealous conduct of the Magistrate to the favourable notice of the Court.—I cannot conclude this address, until I have noticed to the Court, the unwearied assiduity, patience, and activity displayed by Mr. E. P. Smith, the magistrate, in conducting the voluminous investigation requisite to the success of the indictment in this important case, which I consider the more exemplary in this officer, since in his double eaparity of collector and magistrate, he has such a multiplicity of business to encounter.

Rewards to the Sherishtadar, Darogah and Sheikh Oudan.—To the Sheristadar of the Criminal Court, and to the Darogah of the jail, whom the magistrate particularly recommends for a suitable reward, which he deems their activity and able services to have merited, I have awarded each the sum of fifty rupees, with a Purwannah expressive of the sense entertained of their conduct.

To sheikh Oudan, whose presence of mind and tact in apprehending the whole gang, and integrity in having resisted the large offers made to him by the prisoners is alike conspicuous, I have ordered one hundred rupees to be paid, recommending him, if properly qualified, to the favourable notice of the magistrate for promotion.

I have, &c.

(Signed)   C. W. SMITH,
Officiating Sessions Judge.

Zillah Ghazeepoor, the 17th Sept. 1833.

To Edward Peploe Smith, Esq.
Magistrate of Zillah Ghazeepoor.

Sir,

I herewith transmit for your information and guidance copy of the proceedings of the Court of Nizamut Adawlut under date the 28th September, 1833, held on the trial of Peer Bukhs Khan and others charged with Thuggee, attended with the murder of Purdil Khan and Buddhaie, together with a copy of the futwa of their law officer on the said trial, and request you will call the prisoners before you and make them acquainted with the sentence passed upon them.

2d. The usual warrant is herewith forwarded, together with a copy of the letter from the register to the Nizamut Adawlut, forwarding the above proceedings.

I have, &c.

(Signed)   C. W. SMITH,
Officiating Sessions Judge.

Zillah Ghazeepoor, the 4th October, 1833.

To the Sessions Judge of Zillah Ghazeepoor.

Nizamut Adawlut Western Provinces.
Present—
W. Ewer, Esq. Offg. Judge, and A. J. Colvin, Esq. Judge.

Sir,

I am directed by the Court of Nizamut Adawlut for the Western Provinces, to acknowledge the receipt of a letter from you dated the 17th instant, with the proceedings held on the trial of Peer

Bukhs Khan and others charged with Thuggee and murder, and to transmit to you the accompanying extract from the proceedings of the Court of this date, for your information and guidance, together with the copy of the futwa of their law officer on the said trial.

2d. The Court desire that you will issue your warrant to the magistrate of Zillah Ghazeepoor to carry the sentences passed upon the prisoners into execution, instructing him at the same time to call the prisoners before him and to make them acquainted with the sentences passed upon them.

3d. You will direct the magistrate to order his police officers to be careful that the bodies of Peer Bukhs Khan (1), Kurreem Bukhs Khan (2), Beechook Noorbaff (3), Khoda Bukhs Khan (4), Sheikh Durveish (5), and Peeroo (6), be not removed by their friends or by any other persons.

4th. You are requested to direct the magistrate of Zillah Ghazeepoor to deliver to Sheikh Oodan Burkundaz an additional reward of 200 rupees, and one of 10 rupees each to the Chokedars of Meiree Tal, who assisted in the apprehension of the prisoners, viz. Lal Sah, Pran and Gunga.

5th. The Court observe that you have omitted to mention the age of the prisoners in the heading of the case, as well as to unite with wax and the seal of the Court, the ends of the string on which the papers are filed; you are requested to attend strictly on these points, to the rules laid down in the Circular Order of 16th July, 1830.

6th. The Court have much pleasure in remarking the judicious manner in which this trial has been conducted by you, and have taken measures for bringing it to the notice of the government; they have at the same time, called the attention of the government to the activity and assiduity evinced by Mr. E. P. Smith in the investigation previous to trial, which appears to the Court highly creditable to that officer.

7th. The original proceedings of the magistrate are returned under a separate cover.

I have, &c.

(Signed)   WELBY JACKSON, *Register.*

Allahabad, the 28th Sept. 1833.

———

Allahabad, 28th Sept. 1833.

N. A. W. P.

At a Court of Nizamut Adawulut for the Western Provinces held at Allahabad,

Present:

W. Ewer, Esq. *Offg. Judge,*

and

A. J. Colvin, Esq. *Judge.*

Read the following letter from the Sessions Judge of Ghazeepoor, the proceedings held on the trial of Peer Bukhs Khan (1), son of Rustum Khan, Kurreem Bukhs Khan (2), son of Nurkoo, Beechook Noorbaff (3), son of Ahayd Noorbaff, Khoda Bukhs (4), son of Dowlut Khan, Sheikh Durveish (5), son of Sheikh Sawdoola, Peeroo Khan (6), son of Dowlut Khan, Sheikh Buktour (7), son of Sheikh Koodrutoollah, and Sheikh Ammee (8), son of Sheikh Dussy, charged in the first count with Thuggee, attended with the murder of Purdil Khan and Buddhaie, and in the second count with the murder of Purdil Khan and Buddhaie, and the futwa of the law officer of this Court thereon.

Zillah Ghazeepoor—No. 5, of the Calendar for the Sessions of August, 1833.

Nos. 90 to 92.

The Court having duly considered the proceedings held on the trial of Peer Bukhs Khan (1) Kurreem Bukhs Khan (2), Beechook Noorbaff (3), Khoda Bukhs Khan (4), Sheikh Durveish (5), Peeroo Khan (6), Sheikh Buktour (7), and Sheikh Ammee (8), charged in the 1st count with Thuggee, attended with the murder of Purdil Khan and Buddhaie and in the 2d count with the murder of Khan and Buddhaie, and the Futwa of the law officer on the said trial pass the following sentence:

The futwa of the law officer of the Nizamut Adawlut convicts the prisoners Peerbux Khan (1), Kurreem Bukhs Khan (2), Beechook Noorbaff (3), Khoda Bukhs Khan (4), Sheikh Durveish (5), Peeroo Khan (6), Sheikh Buktour (7), and Sheikh Ammee (8), on strong presumption of the crime laid to their charge, and declares them liable to discretionary punishment by Akoobut-i-shudeed, extending to death by Seeasut.

The Court convict the prisoners Peer Bukhs Khan (1), Kurreem Buksh Khan (2), Beechook Noorbaff (3), Khoda Bukhs Khan (4), Sheikh Durveish (5) and Peeroo Khan (6), of the crime charged against them, and Sheikh Buktour (7) and Sheikh Ammee (8), of aiding and abetting them, and seeing no circumstances in favour of the prisoners Peer Bukhs Khan (1), Kurreem Bukhs Khan (2), Beechook Noorbaff (3), Khoda Bukhs Khan (4), Sheikh Durveish (5), and Peeroo Khan (6), to render them proper objects of mercy, sentence the said Peer Bukhs Khan (1), son of Rustum Khan, Kurreem Bukhs Khan (2), son of Nurkoo, Beechook Noor-

baff (3), son of Ahoyd Noorbaff, Khoda Bukhs
Khan (4), son of Dowlut Khan, Sheikh Durveish (5), son of Sheikh Sawdoola, and Peeroo
Khan (6), son of Dowlut Khan, to suffer death by
being hanged by the neck until they are dead, and
order that their bodies be afterwards exposed upon
gibbets at the spot where the murder was committed, or as near to it as circumstances may admit;
and Sheikh Buktour, son of Koodruttoollah, and
Sheikh Ammee, son of Sheikh Dussy, to imprisonment, with labour for life, in the jail at Allypoor.,

Ordered, that the original proceedings of the
magistrate be returned through the Sessions Judge.

(Signed) W. Ewer, *Officiating Judge.*
(Signed) A. J. Colvin, *Judge.*
(True Extract,)
(Signed) Welby Jackson, *Register.*
(True Copies,)
(Signed) C. W. Smith,
Officiating Sessions Judge.

———

Office of the Session Judge of Zillah Ghazeepoor,
Trial No. 5 of the Sessions for the month of
August, 1833, and case No. 5 of the Magistrate's
Calendar for the month of August, 1833.

To E. Peploe Smith, Esquire,
Magistrate of Zillah Ghazeepoor.

Whereas, at a Jail Delivery of Zillah Ghazeepoor
for the August Session of 1833, holden at Ghazeepoor on the 24th, 26th, 27th, 29th and 30th days
of the month of August in the year 1833, Peer
Bukhs Khan, (No. 1), Kurreem Bukhs Khan, (No.
2), Bechook Noorbaf, (3), Khoda Bukhs Khan, (4),

Sheikh Durveish, (5), Peeroo Khan, (6), having been convicted of Thuggee attended with the murder of Purdil Khan and Buddhaie, and sentenced by the Court of Nizamut Adawlut Western Provinces, to suffer death by being hanged by the neck until they are dead, after which their bodies to be exposed upon a gibbet, as near to the spot where the offence was committed as circumstances may admit; it is hereby ordered that execution of the said sentence be made and done upon the said Peer Buhks Khan, (1), son of Rustum Khan, Kurreem Bukhs Khan, son of Nerkoo, (2), Bechook Noorbaf, son of Ohayd Noorbaf, (3), Khoda Bukhs Khan, son of Dowlut Khan, (4), Sheikh Durveish, son of Sheikh Sawdoola, (5), and Peeroo Khan, son of Dowlut Khan, (6), on or before the tenth day of the month of October, 1833, A. D. and that you do return this warrant to me with an endorsement attested by your official seal and signature, certifying the manner in which the sentence has been executed, as commanded by the regulations enacted by the Governor General in Council and now in force. Herein fail not.

Given under my hand and seal of office, this fourth day of October, in the year 1833.
Judge's seal.   (Signed)   C. W. SMITH,
Officiating Session Judge.

I hereby certify, that the sentence of death passed on Peer Bukhs Khan, (1), son of Rustum Khan, Kurreem Bukhs Khan, (2), son of Nerkoo, Bechook Noorbaf, (3), son of Oheyd, Khoda Bukhs Khan, (4), son of Dowlut Khan, Sheikh Durveish, (5), son of Sheikh Sawdoola, and Peeroo Khan, (6), son of Dowlut Khan, by the Nizamut Adawlut, has been duly executed, and that the said persons were accordingly hung by the neck till they were dead, at the town of Ghazeepore, on Thursday the 10th of October, 1833. I further certify, that the bodies of the said persons were afterwards conveyed to the place where the crime of which they were convicted, was committed, and there suspended on a gibbet.

Given under my hand and the official seal of this Court, this 16th October, 1833.

(Signed)　　E. P. Smith,
　　　　　　　　　　　Magistrate.

Magistrate's Seal.

———

Court of the Sessions Judge of Ghazeepore for the month of August, 1833, case No. 5 of the Magistrate's Calendar for the August Sessions of 1833.

To E. P. Smith, Esquire,
　　　Magistrate of Zillah Ghazeepore.

Sheikh Buktour and Sheikh Ammee, to be imprisoned with labour for life in the jail at Allipore.

Whereas at a Jail Delivery of Ghazeepore for the Zillaz Ghazeepore, holden at Ghazeepore on the 24th, 26th, 27th, 29th and 30th days of the month of August, in the year 1833, Sheikh Bucktour, son of Koodruthollah, (7), and Sheikh Ammee son of Sheikh Dussy, (8), having been convicted of aiding and abetting in a case of Thuggee, attended with the murder of Purdil Khan and Buddhaie, and sentenced by the Judges of the Nizamut Adawlut Western Provinces, to imprisonment with labour for life in the Jail at Allipore, it is hereby ordered that execution of the said sentence be made and done upon the said Sheikh Buktour, son of Koodruthollah, and Sheikh Ammee, son of

Sheikh Dussy, without delay, as commanded by the regulations, and that you do return this warrant when completely executed, with an endorsement attested by your official seal and signature, certifying the manner in which the sentence has been carried into execution. Herein fail not.

Given under my hand and the seal of this Court, this fourth day of October, in the year 1833.

(Signed) C. W. SMITH,
Officiating Session Judge.

Judge's Seal.

Sentence explained to the prisoners herein named (Sheikh Bucktour and Sheikh Ammee), this 7th day of October, 1833.

(Signed) E. P. SMITH.
Magistrate.

To E. P. Smith, Esquire.
Magistrate of Zillah Gazepore.

N. A. W. P.
Present—
C. T. Sealy, M. H. Turnbull, W. Ewer, *Offg.* A. J. Colvin, Esquires, Judges.

Sir,

I am directed by the Court to transmit for your information the accompanying copy of a letter under date the 14th instant, received from the Secretary to Government Judicial Department.

I am, &c.

(Signed) WELBY JACKSON,
Register.

Allahabad, the 25th Oct. 1833.

(No. 1998.)
To W. B. Jackson, Esq.
Register of the Nizamut Adawlut in the Western Provinces of
Allahabad.

Judicial Department.

Sir,—I am directed to acknowledge the receipt of a letter from you dated the twenty-eighth ultimo, with its enclosures, and to request that you intimate to Mr. E. P. Smith and Mr. C. W. Smith, that the Right Honourable the Governor General in Council has noticed with approbation the creditable and judicious manner in which they conducted the proceedings in their respective departments connected with the trial of Peer Buksh and others for Thuggee.

I am, &c.

(Signed)   C. MACSWEEN,
Secy. to Government.

Council Chamber, the 14th Oct. 1833.

True Copy.

(Signed)   WELBY JACKSON, Esq.
Register.

———

To W. Jackson, Esq.
Register to the Nizamut Adawlut, Allahabad.

Court of Sessions Judge Zillah Benare Trials, Nos. 2, 3 and 4, of the Calendar for the January Session of 1834.

Government

versus

Shamsherah, son of a father unknown, aged 25 years.—Bukus, son of Meer Ali or Bonolla, aged 32 years.—Oozurah, son of Jeetoo, aged 30 years.—Neher Ali, son of Gholam Ali, aged 40 years.—Asmut, son of Behoo, aged 30 years.

Charge.

For being privy to and concerned in the murder by strangulation (Thuggy) of traveller, name unknown.

2d Charge.
Ditto of two travellers, names unknown.
3d Charge.
Ditto, of three travellers, names unknown.
Futwah Jageer.

Sir,

I transmit herewith to be laid before the Nizamut Adawlut, the proceedings in three trials noted in the margin, held at the station of Benares from the 18th to the 21st of February, 1834.

The following is an abstract of the case:—

The prisoners are Thugs and were concerned in three expeditions during the month of Jeit 1240 fuslee, corresponding to part of June and July, 1833, in which six persons were murdered.

The Thannadar of Juggut Gunge with the Foujdaree Nazir, and the spies Goplah and Bhuggoo went to Raja-ka-Tullao described as a halting place of the prisoners and others, who were proved to have purchased various articles of food from the grocers' shops, and to have slept there. Towards morning they took their departure accompanied by a Musulman traveller, and, leaving the high road at Sarai Mohun to the right, followed a path-way for about a mile, where having found a convenient place they strangled the traveller and threw his body into a well. The Thannadar and his party proceeded to the well which was pointed out, and on examining the Goraits of the neighbouring village, it appeared that there had been a body taken out in the month of Jeit, which had been concealed by the Zemindar's orders all day in some sugar canes, and at night thrown into the Sambhar Nullah: some bones were found in the Nullah; which were declared to

be human, and supposed to be those of the murdered traveller.

The second Thuggy expedition occurred in the
jurisdiction of the Kilia-Khonah Thannah. The
shopkeepers there sold spice, &c. to some of the
Thugs who passed the night at the Dhurm Salah
of Bukt-Pooree at Kupuldhara. There were about
five and twenty Thugs and two Musulmen tra-.
vellers with them, with three bullocks. They all
left before day-break and having proceeded about
a mile towards the Ganges, the two travellers were
strangled and their bodies thrown into the river.

The third Thuggy excursion took place in
Huroah Thannah's jurisdiction. Three persons
were strangled and the bodies thrown into Hur Dho-
bey's well, in searching which three skulls, several
human bones, and a pair of shoes, the latter evidently a sepoy's were discovered.

As the atrocious crime of " Phansegare or
Thuggy" is fortunately very uncommon in this
district, and no instance has occurred during the
periods I have been resident at Benares, I shall
submit for the Court's consideration the evidence
of two of the witnesses, and likewise the confession of the prisoner Shumsherah, which last was
given before the magistrate, and affords perhaps a
clearer insight into their proceedings.

The first witness to the fact in each of these
cases is Bhuggoo; his evidence, however, is so
contradictory, and agrees so badly with the deposition given before the magistrate, that I prefer
sending the examination of the second witness
Kadir Khan, a Patan, son of Jumum Khan, inhabitant of Moujah Punnah, Perganah Moneah, Zillah
Patna, aged forty-three years, formerly a culti-

vator, but for the last twenty-one years a Thug by profession.

In the month of Augun, 1840, fuslee, Shumsherah, Oozerah, Moradun, Bukus, Asmut, Mehar Ali and myself, went on a Thuggee expedition to the westward, and reached the "Oude" territory. At "Chand Pertaubpoor" we met Chuta, Thug, in company with a traveller who was afterwards strangled, and eleven rupees with two or four cloths found on him. We journeyed on to Alahabad, and thence eastward. Near "Burount" we met Goplah Beekah, and nine other Thugs, and they accompanied us to Mirza Morad's Serai. There we found Mohur Singh, a Jemedar of Thugs, with ten others whose names I do not remember. We all went on together and rested at night near the temple at Rajah-ka-Tullao. On the road we met a traveller whom Mohur Singh entered into conversation with, and persuaded to join our party. At the last quarter of the night we renewed our march and quitting the high road near Serai, Mohur followed a pathway for about half a cose, and strangled the traveller. Seven rupees, with two or four clothes were taken, and Goury and Mehar Ali threw the corpse into a well.

After walking some distance in the direction of Benares we overtook two Musulmen travellers with three bullocks. They went in with us to our halting place the Dhurm Salah, at Kupuldharah. Towards day break we departed, and about a mile off near the banks of the Ganges, Mohur Singh and Goury strangled the travellers. We found on them five rupees, a sword and two or three pieces of cloths. Mohur Singh took all and drove the bullocks on before us. Our people threw the bodies into the river. After taking some refreshment we proceeded to "Sydpoor." There "Salaroo," a Burkundaz, recognized Mohur Singh, who in consequence gave him five rupees. The three bullocks were sent by Mohur Singh to his home. From "Sydpoor" we went to Kytee, and the next day to Rajghaut. Very early the following morning we proceeded towards the west. It was then the month of Jeit, and the period of the *Ghazymeean* festival. When we reached a tank we found two Sepoys and a bearer sitting there. We drank *toddy* with them and all went on together. Mohur Singh asked them where they came from and whither they were going. They replied from the east towards the west. Mohur Singh said I am also going towards the west. In the evening we halted at the "Hurooah Bazar." When one quarter of the night only remained, we continued our journey and went two miles on the Punch Cossy road, where there is a pucka well with two mangoe trees near it. There "Moma" and "Imaum Bux" strangled the travellers, I standing by. Thirty rupees, ten pieces of cloths and two brass pots were found on them. There was also a horse and a mare. We were then twenty-five persons. Some of us threw the bodies into the well. My share was a doputta and a rupee eight anas. The other Thugs had their proportion. I took the mare and Mohur Singh the horse. From thence my companions and myself separated from the gang and went home. The other Thugs likewise travelled in the direction of their homes. After being at home for some days the *Tomandar* and Foujdaree Nazir of the city of Patna apprehended me. I was never taken up before, during the twenty-one years I have practiced "Thuggy." I have been in many excursions in Oude and to the eastward, but excepting the three expeditions above alluded to, I have never done any thing in the Benares division. I have spent all my share of the plunder. The mare was taken from my house to the Patna Adawlut. There are only eight men connected with me in this business. Their names are Moradhun, Bukus of Siveree, Shumserah, Oozerah, Imambux of Khutary, Asmut, and Hunoman, a Brahmin of Jurrowah. Of these eight Moradhun and myself are Sirdars. Mohur Singh has twenty-five men and is a Sirdar. All the men were in these expeditions, but I cannot remember their names. We do not go armed; perhaps two may be armed. We strangle our victims generally, and never use a weapon excepting in case of necessity. No wounds were inflicted on any of the victims of this district. Those who strangle receive an additional rupee.

Third witness Goplah, son of Dyar of the *Lode* caste, inhabitant of Muteepurwa, Zillah Cawnpore, aged twenty-six years. A year ago, I had left home alone on a Thuggy expedition towards the east. When I reached Bhaugur Mow, in the Oude country, I met Kisseree Singh with twenty-five Thugs, and Bekram and Muhadut Jemadars with Mukdoom Bux and others. After travelling fifteen coss we fell in with three travellers, whom Bekram, Mukdoom and Chudu strangled and took their property. The bodies were thrown into a well. I had my share. Going by Meean Gunge and Hussun Gunge to Noel Gunge, we strangled five travellers. On arriving on Burount near Choby Bazar, Moradhun, Kadir and Mohur Singh, Jemadars of Thugs, joined us with twenty-five men. Bekram and the other Oude Thugs returned thence.

On the road from Mirza Mourad to Rajah-ka-Tullao we met a Musulman who went with us to the latter place where we rested at the Buneah's house near the temple, and after taking some food passed the night there. When the night was nearly over, we resumed our march towards Benares, and leaving the high road in a northern direction, struck into a path-way for a mile until we came on a plain at some distance from a village. Mohur Singh strangled the traveller, and I and another threw the body into a well; we found on him seven rupees, a sword, two or four brass pots, and four or five cloths. In the division my share was a turban. The cloths and pots were divided amongst us, and the rupees soon spent. We then came to Benares, and passed a day at the Serai Aurungabad. We crossed the Sepoy lines and entered the Orderly Bazar, where we met two travellers and three bullocks. We inquired whence they came and where they were going. They said from Hansy to Goruckpore. Mohur Singh said "I am on my way to Goruckpore; come with us." We proceeded to Kupuldara and put up at the Dhurm Salah, for the evening. At the sixth hour of the night we renewed our journey. When we reached the Ganges, east from Kupuldara, some of us seized the hands, and others the feet of the travellers, whom Chutu and Imaum Bux strangled. We then threw them into the river. Five rupees, a lotah, a sword, and a pair of *pyjamahs* were taken. Mohur Singh took the three bullocks. We travelled afterwards to Sydpore, Kytee and Rajghaut, putting up at the Luckah Serai. The next day we went towards Sheopore, and stopping at Shunkur Talao we drank some toddy. We saw two Sepoys and a bearer sitting there, whom Mohur Singh asked where they were going and whence they came. Their reply was from Cuttack and their destination Lucknow. We all went on to Sheopore and from that place to Huroah, where we rested at a Buneah's shop. In the latter part of the night we continued our march, and after walking a mile on the Punch Cossy road, Beeka, Bheegoo and Moraudun threw the travellers down, when Imaum Bux, Mohur Singh, and Goury strangled them. The others remained on the watch. Twenty-five rupees, a gold mohur, fifteen pieces of cloths, and twenty brass pots were gained. Six men and a Jemadar threw the bodies into a well. In the division of the plunder a lotah, a merzai, and a rupee were my share. The witness mentioned that all the prisoners were Thugs and concerned in the three expeditions that took place in the Benares division, with the exception of Asmut.

The prisoner Shumsherah is an inhabitant of Purneah, Pergunnah Moneah, Zillah Patna, twenty-five years of age, of the weaver caste. Moradun supported and protected him whilst a child, and whenever he went on a Thuggy excursion the prisoner accompanied him. The deposition before the magistrate is as follows:—In the month of Aghun, 1240 Fusly, Moradun, Kader Khan, Bukus, Oozerah, Meher Ali, Asmut, Imaum Bux, and myself proceeded on a Thuggy expedition. We strangled several persons in Oude, remaining there until the month of Maug, and then went to Allahabad, from whence we travelled in an eastern direction, until we came to Burount. We found Goplah and Beeka there and further on the road Mohur Singh with four other Thugs. We met a traveller as we proceeded. Mohur Singh, and his

party went on with him. We rested in the evening at Hunoman Chokey. When the night was
nearly spent, we went on and Huna strangled the
traveller. Seventeen rupees, some cloths, and
brass pots were found on him, and the body was
thrown into a well. I being the adopted pupil of
Moradhun, he took my share. He gave me food
only, and I was his follower. Proceeding on our
march we met a Musulman travelling. Imaum
Bux attached himself to him. We halted for the
night at Rajah-ka-Tulloa, and towards morning
recommenced our journey. Leaving the high
road at Serai Mohun to the right, we followed a
small pathway. After walking a mile, we came
near a garden where Imaum Bux strangled the
traveller. Ten rupees, a sword, two dhotees, a
lotah, and some old cloths were the plunder. Two
or three men took the corpse and threw it into a
well. Near Benares we met two travellers with
three bullocks. Moradun, Kadir Khan, Goplah
and Beeka joined them, and in the evening we made
Kupuldhara our resting place, stopping at the
Dhurm Sala. When one quarter of the night only
remained, the march was resumed, and near the
banks of the Ganges, about a mile off, Beeka and
Unna strangled the travellers. I don't remember
what plunder was obtained. Meher Ali, Moradhun, Kader Khan, and Beeka threw the corpses
into the river. We then went to Sydpore. A
Burkundaz, Salaroo, recognized Mohur Singh, who
in consequence gave him four rupees, and Moradhun sent the three bullocks by Bukus to his house.
We afterwards returned to the village of Bettree,
and going by Chundwuk, arrived at Rajghaut.
Remaining there all night, we marched very early
the next morning in a western direction. After

leaving the city we met two Sepoys and a bearer. Beeka entered into conversation with them, and they came on in our company. We halted at Huroah Bazar. Towards daybreak we resumed our route, and going about two miles on the Punch Cossy road, where there is a pucka well, with two mangoe trees, Mohur Singh, Ramsuhoy and Selwunt Rai, strangled the three travellers. They gained thirty-two rupees, some cloths and brass pots. The bodies were thrown into the well. The travellers had a horse and a mare with them. Kadir took the first and Goplah the latter. We afterwards went to Burogong, where we divided the plunder and separated going to our respective homes. I have never strangled any one, but have aided in throwing bodies into wells. Eight annas is a very good remuneration for murdering a man. We often strangle a victim who is suspected of having two pice. We are unrestrained by any fears in pursuing our vocation. We do not sell our plunder, but when there is· a large quantity send it to our homes.

Bukus once accompanied Moradhun and others on a Thuggy expedition in Oude, and was with them two years, but has never practised in the Benares district and is unjustly accused.

Oozerah declares that he is innocent. He once found himself with Moradhun, &c., in Oude, but ran away the moment he could, when he discovered his companions were Thugs.

Meher Ali served Moradhun as a grass-cutter for five or six months. He acknowledged before the magistrate at Patna to having been his servant for the above number of years, and to having accompanied him in his Thuggy expeditions.

Asmut was formerly called Dubery, alias Neea-

mut Ali, at present /   le attributes his name
being mentioned to   dispute he had with
the two brothers Ka   1an and Moradhun, with
whom he is connect   rriage, and of course
asserts his innocence: lepositions of Nanuk,
Ramphul, Rujoo Si   1, .   kgur, Purshad, Jug-
gernat, Thakooree,   o. sseredyeal, Uchalall
and Matadyel, point out   nalting places of the
Thugs in these expediti , and the wells, &c.
where the bones and o   r remains of the murdered persons were discov   1.

The Law Officer has gi   n his futwahs "Ta-
zeer" in each case. As I cannot consider myself
vested with discretionary power to punish the
heinous offences which the risoners have committed, I have the honour to submit all the papers
connected with these cases for the Sudder Nizamut's consideration and orders.

I have, &c.
(Signed)   R. J. TAYLER,
                        Session Judge.

Office of Session Judge,
City of Benares, the 21st Feb. 1834.

———

Allahabad, the 3d April, 1834.

N. A. W. P.
At a Court of Nizamut Adawlut for the Western
Province held at Allahabad—
                Present—
Seal.   W. EWER, Esq., *Judge,*
                and
A. J. COLVIN, Esq., Judge.

Read the following letter from the Sessions

Judge of City Benares in reply to the Court's order of the 13th ultimo, resubmitting proceedings held on the trial of Shumsherah (1), son of a father unknown, Bukus (2) son of Meer Ali or Bonolla, Oozerah (3), son of Seetoo, Mehar Ali (4), son of Gholam Ali, and Asmut (5), son of Beechoo, charged, firstly, with being privy to and concerned in the murder by strangulation (Thuggy) of a traveller, name unknown; secondly, with ditto of two travellers, names unknown, and thirdly, with ditto of three, names unknown, and the futwah of the law officer of this Court thereon.

Nos. 7 to 14.
City Benares Trials, Nos. 2, 3, and 4 of Calendar for January Sessions, 1834.

The Court having duly considered the proceedings held on the trial of Shumsherah (1), Bukus (2), Oozerah (3), Mehar Ali (4), and Asmut (5), charged as above, and the futwah of their Law Officer on the said trial, pass the following sentence :—

The futwah of the Law Officer of the Nizamut Adawlut convicts the prisoners Shumsherah (1), Bukus (2), Oozerah (3), and Mehar Ali (4), of being accomplices in the crime charged against them, and declares them liable to punishment by Akoobut extending to death, by Seasut with reference to the prisoner Shumsherah. It acquits the prisoner Asmut, and declares him entitled to his release.

The Court convict the prisoners Shumsherah (1), Bukus (2), Oozerah (3), and Mehar Ali (4) of the charges preferred against them, and under all the circumstances of the case, sentences the said Shum-sherah (1), the son of a father unknown, Bukus (2), son of Meer Ali or Bonolla, Oozerah (3), son of Seetoo, and Mehar Ali (4), son of Gholam Ali, to be imprisoned in transportion with labour for life. The Court acquit the prisoner Asmut (5), son of Beechoo, of the crime laid to his charge, and direct that he be immediately released.

Ordered, that the original proceedings of the magistrate be returned through the Sessions judge.

(Signed)   W. Ewer, *Judge.*

(Signed)   A. J. Colvin, *Judge.*

(True extracts,)

(Signed)   Welby Jackson, *Register.*

(True Copies.)

D. B. Morrieson, *Magistrate.*

Copy of a letter from Mr. C. Fraser to Mr. Wilder, on the commitment of a gang of Thugs.

To F. Wilder, Esquire,

      Agent Governor General.

Sir,

The whole of these prisoners were sent to me by Captain Wardlow for examination, together with five others whom I immediately released, as they appeared innocent of all connection with them.

On their first examination, they all denied the charges brought forward against them, but subsequently nearly the whole of them confessed a variety of murders which they had committed of travellers, who had joined them on their route, and entered into particulars of their crime almost too horrible to record.

The following statement is founded on those confessions, which being supported partially by other evidences, may, 1 consider, be taken as a correct detail of their proceedings.

Baz Khan, Shewa, Kurreem, Khoda Buksh, son of Lall Khan, Gunesh, alias Dhonkul, Khoda Buksh, alias Ghoorun, Nungoo, alias Hormut Khan, Kesur Khan, alias Khezzur Khan, Assulut Khan, son of Khyreat Khan, Hoshun, Boodhoo alias Hurry Sing, Zubur Khan, Dhurm Khan, son of Noor Khan, Zoolfeekar Khan, alias Budul Khan, alias Budloo, Durroo, alias Munsookh, Islama Khan, (absconded,) Peer Buksh (absconded,) and Husnoo (absconded) :—

Entered the Baitool district together,. and near Neempanee, which lies on the direct road from Hussingabad to Baitool, falling in with two persons, a Sikh and Choomar at different places, Shewa and Kurreem, with others of the gang, seized, robbed, murdered and buried them.

These two murders are proved independent of their confessions, by the discovery of the remains of the deceased, which were disinterred under the superintendance of Kurreem, and also some articles found on the prisoners.

The manner in which the prisoners are in the habit of waylaying travellers, and the secrecy observed by them, makes it almost impossible to find out the persons of those who fall a prey to their villainous practices, and therefore nothing has been ascertained, that could enable me to discover who these two individuals were or whence they came.

The gang proceeded from Baitool to the Dekhan and they confess the following murders perpetrated by them when there; pointing out the property received by each as his share of the spoils, collected on these occasions, viz.

Five persons beyond Lukhunwara; five persons between a village called Borlgaon and Omrowtee; one person at Moostuzzurpoor, and one person near it. Of these crimes there is no proof, but what can be collected from their confessions; but since their confessions have been corroborated by evidence on the other murders committed by them, there is unfortunately but little reason for hoping that their statements of the destruction of so many individuals are false, and unfounded on fact.

At Omrowtee or near it, they were joined by Phoolell Khan, Sheikh Shuhadut, alias Assulut, Jhao Khan, Dhurm Khan, son of Bukhtawur Khan, Sheikh Islama, Kalo Khan, alias Kunnoo, and probably by others whom they have not mentioned who were on their way home from the Dekhan where they had indulged themselves in murdering their fellow beings, and whence they were returning to feast on the property which they had thus acquired by their crimes.

They had fallen in on the road with Chintaman Jemadar and six other persons, who were proceeding to Hindostan on leave of absence, from the cantonment of Ingholee, and who had unsuspiciously associated with them for greater safety.

On arriving at a deserted spot near the village of Haingaun, on this side of Omrowtee, the prisoners taking advantage of the solitude of the place and the darkness of the night, seized their fellow-travellers, and one with another the whole seven were murdered, and would have been buried, but for the appearance of some strangers at a distance.

The murder of the seven persons is sworn to by Adhore Singh Jemadar, and Herpersaud Havildar, who went to the spot, and subsequently hearing of the apprehension of the prisoners attended on me, deposed to the circumstances they were acquainted with, and recognized a portion of the property found on the prisoners as belonging to the deceased, which, however, is but a trifling part of what the prisoners acknowledge was taken from them.

From Haingaon they came towards Seonee Chuprah by Nagpoor, and on this side of Nagpoor the remaining prisoners associated themselves with them; viz. Surroop Singh, Dhurm Khan, son of Bushorant Khan, Goolab, his son, Assulut Khan son of Man Khan, Islam Khan, soon of Peer Khan, Akbur Khan, and Bahadoor, and others who have not been apprehended.

On passing from Sookhtowa to Chonree in the Seonee district, five travellers whom they had met, and one of whom was a woman, were disposed of by them in their usual method, and the property taken from them, divided amongst them.

The bodies of these five persons were dug up by Bahadoor Khan, whom I sent for the purpose to Captain Wardlow, and therefore there can be no doubt on this occasion, that the murder was committed, and their own confession clearly brings it home to the party who had by this time collected.

After this murder, they came to Chuprah, where they were all seized, together with Khoshal, alias Laljou, who is not implicated in these successive offences, but who nevertheless is an old Thug, and has been educated and bred up in a family of Thugs.

The two other persons, Munnoo and Mahadeo, are committed with the rest, but on a separate charge of keeping up a criminal intercourse with the Thugs, which is fully proved by the statement of Mahadeo, by the present received by them, and also by the confession of more than one of the other prisoners.

It probably would have been more correct had I sent the whole of the prisoners back to Captain Wardlow, as they were guilty of no offence within my jurisdiction; but on the whole from the agent being present at Jubulpore, I determined on committing them at once, leaving their subsequent disposal for him to determine; a Persian statement is attached to the Roobukaree of the property found on the prisoners, and of the murders acknowledged to have been committed by them previously in different parts of the country, with a descriptive roll of some of their gang, who escaped when they were apprehended, and likewise of several individuals named by them, who are now at large, and who subsist like them, on property procured by murder.

In conclusion I may observe, that the discovery of their crimes is chiefly to be attributed to the confessions of Shewa, one of the prisoners; and that although I have given him no distinct promise, still I have told him that I would mention the circumstance, in the belief, that it would be the means of alleviating the punishment he might otherwise be sentenced to.

(Signed)   C. Fraser,
P. A. A. G. G.

(True copy,)
Signed)   R. Low,
P. A. A. G. G.

Extract of a Letter to F. Wilder, Esquire, Agent to the Governor General, from the Chief Secretary to Government.

The Vice President in Council having duly considered the above report, adverting to all the circumstances of the case, and not seeing any thing to render the prisoners Kurreem Khan and Nungoo fit objects of mercy, confirms the judgment of the agent to the governor general, whereby the said prisoners Kurreem Khan, (1) alias Kuramut Khan, son of Khezzur Khan Pathan, and Nungoo, (2) alias Hormut Khan, son of Maun Khan, are convicted of murder and robbery, and are declared liable to suffer death, and directs that they be hung by the neck until they are dead, and that their bodies be afterwards exposed upon a gibbet in chains, at such place as the acting agent to the Governor General may determine.

The Vice-President in Council also confirms the judgment of the agent to the governor general, by which the prisoners—

3 Baz Khan, alias Bhuga, son of Nuthee Khan.
5 Khoda Buksh, son of Lall Khan.
6 Gunesh, alias Dhokul, son of Kunhey Tewaree.
7 Khodabuksh, alias Ghoorun, son of Sheikh Ruhmud.
8 Kesur Khan, alias Kheszzur Khan, son of Peer Khan.
9 Assulut Khan, son of Hormut Khan, alias Khyreat Khan.
10 Hoshun Dyer, son of Kulloo Dyer.
11 Muduree, son of Kulloo.
12 Boodhoo, alias Hurry Sing, son of Mukhun.

15*

13 Zubur Khan, son of Lal Khan.

14 Dhurm Khan, son of Bussarut Khan.

15 Zoolfeckar Khan, alias Budul Khan, son of Bheekum.

16 Durroo, alias Munsookh, son of Persaud.

17 Phoolell Khan, son of Iktiar Khan.

18 Sheikh Shuhadut, alias Assalut, son of Sheikh Bukshoo.

19 Jhao Khan, alias Mudaree, son of Darab Khan.

21 Shiekh Islama, son of Sheikh Sooltanoo.

22 Kaloo Khan, alias Kunnoo, son of Iktiar Khan.

23 Surroop Singh, son of Sookeh Lall.

24 Dhurm Khan, alias Izzut Khan, son of Noor Khan.

25 Assalut Khan, son of Man Khan.

26 Islam Khan, son of Peer Khan.

27 Bahadoor Khan, son of Imam Khan, and

29 Akbur Khan, alias Hukooa, son of Peer Khan, are convicted of being accomplices in murder and robbery, and sentenced to imprisonment and transportation for life.

With regard to the prisoner Shewa, the Vice President in Council observes, that the discovery of the crimes of this gang is represented by Mr. Fraser to be chiefly attributable to his confession, and that although he, Mr. Fraser, gave no distinct promise to the prisoner, he told him that the circumstance would be mentioned, in the belief that it would be the means of alleviating the punishment to which he might otherwise be sentenced.

Adverting to this circumstance, and to the want of sufficient evidence to convict the prisoners Dhurm Khan, (20), son of Bukhtawur Khan, and Khoshal, (28), alias Laljoo, son of Sooklall, of any active participation in the criminal acts of the gang, the Vice President in Council resolves that the sentence to which the said prisoners Shewa, (4), Dhurmo Khan, (20), and Khoshal, are severally liable by the judgment of the agent to the governor general, be remitted: but with reference to the fact of their being the associates of Thugs, and to their having been apprehended in their company, directs that they be kept in confinement till they find substantial security for their future good conduct and appearance when required.

The Vice President in Council observes that the prisoners Goolab Khan (30), Munnoo and Mahadeo, have been sentenced to specific periods·of imprisonment by the agent to the governor general.

Ordered that a copy of the foregoing resolution, together with a copy of Mr. Robertson's report and the whole of the proceedings in the case, be transmitted to the acting agent to the governor general in Saugor and Nurbudda Territories for his information and guidance, with orders to carry the sentence of death passed on the prisoners Kurreem Khan and Nungoo (2) into execution, by causing them to be hanged by the neck till they · are dead, at such time and places as he may deem proper; and with directions to send the prisoners Baz Khan (3), Khoda Buksh (5), Gunesh (6), Khoda Buksh (1), Kesur Khan (8), Assdut Khan (9), Hoshun Dyer (10), Muduree (11), Boodhoo (12), Zubur Khan (13), Dhurm Khan (14), Zoolfeekar Khan (15), Durroo (16), Phoolell Khan (17), Sheikh Shuhadut (18), Jhao Khan (19), Sheikh Islama (21), Kalo Khan (22), Surroop Singh (23), Dhurm Chan (24), Assalut Khan (25), Islam Khan (26), Badadoor Khan (27), and Akbur Khan (29), in custody at a proper season, with the requisite warrants to the magistrate of the suburbs of Calcutta, who will be instructed to carry the sentence of transportation passed upon them into effect.

(True Extract)

(Signed)   F. C. SMITH,

Agent Governor General.

9th November, 1826.

W. H. SLEEMAN.

BURWAHA GHAT AFFAIR.

Deposition of Moklal, Jonooa and others, taken at Saugor before Captain W. H. Sleeman.

In the month of Kartick, about six years ago, I, Bukhut Jemadar, and Thukoree, at large, Dhokul Meraea Pande, (hung at Saugor) and Moklal approver, left our homes at Poorah in Jhansee, on an expedition to the Duckun, and after taking the auspices outside the village, we proceeded via Jhansee, Bhilsa, and Rehlee. Leaving Bhopaul on the right, we crossed the Nurbudda at Cheepanere, and encamped outside of the village, under a Bur tree on the bank of the river where we found a gang of fifty Thugs under the following leaders:

Roshun Jemadar hung at Saugor, with ten followers.

Khuleel ditto hung at ditto, with ten ditto.

Ghureeba Dhadee hung at ditto, with seven ditto.

Zolfukar Jemadar hung at ditto, with seven ditto.

Golab Khan, alias Puhara, hung at ditto, with three ditto.

Sheikh Madaree hung at Joura.

Moollooa Aheer . . ⎫
and ⎬ Died in the Saugor jail;
Kehree Lodhee, . . ⎭

Nunha Musulman, ... ⎫
Manoola, ... ⎪
Bhowanee, son of Rostum, ⎪
Mahomed Buksh, ... ⎬ Approvers;
Pawn Mahomed, ... ⎪
Sheikh Chotee, ... ⎪
Daood, and . . . . ⎪
Pawn Khan, ... ⎭

also encamped, and we joined them. They had reached this place from their homes without committing any murder. The next morning we all fifty-six set out on the road to the Duckun, and arrived at Hurda where we passed that night. Thence we proceeded by Singeea Deo Boregow and Asseer to Borhanpore, and encamped outside of the town in a grove where there was a Muth (Gosaens lodging). We halted there the next day, and about noon a gang of fifty-six other Thugs, under the following leaders, came up from their homes and joined our gang:

Purshaud Lodhee hung at Saugor, with ten followers.

Purusram Jemadar, ... ⎫
Sirawun, brother of ditto, . . ⎬ at large, with fifteen ditto.
* Munohur Partuk, Jemadar, ⎭

* Munohur lately cut his throat near Jhansee, when he found the guard from Jhansee coming up with him upon the open plain, and died on the spot.

Khooman Brahman, bro- } (at large), number
ther of ditto, and . . . . } of followers not
} remembered.

Mahraj Patuck who drowned himself in the lake at Dhamanee, on his way to Saugor, under an escort 1832.

We all amounted to one hundred and twelve persons.

From this place we set out on the road to the Duckhun; on reaching the bank of the Taptee river we sat down, and while we were talking and smoking, two Musulman travellers came up on their way from Bhopaul to Aurungabad. Roshun Jemadar acted as Sothae and won their confidence. They sat down with us and smoked the hookah, and Roshun gave them some food to eat as he was himself eating. After resting here sometime we went on with the travellers and reached Tankolee, a village six cose south from Borhanpore, and encamped on the bank of the river on the north side of the village. After we had taken our dinner, about two ghurries after sunset, we sent some people of our gang to converse with the travellers, and while they were engaged in talking they were both seized and strangled upon their beds by Khoda Buksh Musulman and Bukhut Brahman, both at large, assisted by others as Shumsheeas, who were sitting near them. We got from them one hundred and fifty rupees in cash, two matchlocks, one tattoo and some other articles. In the division we got one rupee each.

After this affair the next morning we proceeded on the road to the Duckhun and reached Edulabad, about ten cose south from Borhanpore, and encamped outside of the town at a Fukeer's Tukeea under some trees. The same day eight Rokureeas,

of whom six were armed with matchlocks, and
two camel drivers, came up with Tippoo Sahee
rupees (Spanish dollars) from Dunraj Seth's house
at Bombay, on their way to Indore, and lodged in
a shop in the Bazar. We sent Khoda Buksh (at
large) and Molloo Jemadar as Tilhaes (spies) to
watch them. They went and put up in one of the
shops near them. The next morning the Rokureeas set out and both our spies followed them.
We conjectured that they would probably encamp
at Tankolee that day, and as we had already committed a murder there we did not think it advisable
to follow them to that place. We accordingly
went on to Caund Devee. The Rokureeas did not
however go to Tankolee, but to Borhanpore—on
the following morning :—

Khuleel, ... ⎫
Mahraj Patuk, ... ⎬ Jemadars,
Purusram, ... ⎪
Zalim and Bukhut, . . ⎭

with fifty select Thugs from the gang, set out for
Borhanpore, thinking that the Rokureeas would
arrive there from Tankolee. The remainder of
the gang returned from this place to Deoleea, in
the Bhopal district, having appointed to rejoin them
there after perpetrating the murder of the above
Rokureeas. About one watch before sunset our
party arrived at Borhanpore and encamped outside
of the town towards the north. Here both of the
spies brought information that the Rokureeas had
put up in the Bazar. On this we sent Molloo and
Ghureeba Jemadars to make inquiries, and on
reaching the Bazar they found three other camels
lodging there, but not the Rokureeas we were in
search of. They returned and reported, and we
sent off Khuleel and Monohur Jemadars, and

Mudara Thugs to trace them, offering to give them one hundred rupees reward over and above their share of the booty. They were to proceed to Asseer and thence on to Boregow, where we would wait for them. These three men arrived at Asseer about midnight, but could not discover the Roku-reeas, although they were at the time lodged in the Bazar. The next morning we reached Asseer without finding any trace of the Rokureeas, and sent Ashraff (at large) and Monga (died in Saugor jail) to the Bazar to purchase some flour, &c. and went on to a nullah about one half cose distant from Asseer. Soon after we had sat down at this nullah, these two men returned and told us that they had seen the Rokureeas settling the duties at the custom-house. On learning this we were much gratified and leaving Moonga and Ashruff, as Tilhaees to watch their movement, we went on to Boregow; a little after our arrival there the spies brought information that the treasure bearers would not pass that way, having gone to Punch-puhar. On hearing this we immediately set out for Punchpuhar but could not find the Rokureeas. We passed the night there, and in the morning we sent six other active Thugs in different directions. to trace them. Two to Asseer, two to Boregow, and two to Sherpore, on the Indore road, while the main body halted at Punchpuhar. About a watch before sunset the two men from the Sher-pore came back and told us that the Rokereeas had lodged in the Bazar at Sherpore the preceding night, and had set out on the road to Indore that morning, and intended to put up at a village about eight cose from Sherpore, name not remembered. They got this information from the people at Sher-pore and it was correct. Here the four other men rejoined us also. On learning this, although we were all much tired, we immediately set out for that village, leaving Sherpore on the right; we arrived there at midnight and encamped outside of the village under a large Peepul tree. The next morning when the Rokureeas set out from this village we followed, and about a cose from the village we were detained by the Chokeedars of the custom chokee, and during our detention the Rokureeas went on out of our sight; we paid the Chokeedars one rupee four annas and went on; during this interval the treasure bearers had, we found, crossed the Nerbudda at Burwahaghat and gone on to the Bazar of Burwaha, a village the other side of the river, and put up in a shop. We followed and crossed the Nerbudda at the same ghat and encamped outside of the same village under a bur tree near the small reservoir. The next morning the Darogah of the custom chokee detained the treasure bearers to settle duties on their treasure, and we were detained also by the same authority, but we did not intend to pay them till the treasure bearers had settled, with the view of following them.

The treasure bearers had great altercation with the people of the chokee who demanded a high rate of duty from them, when Maharaj Patuck went to the Tarogah and admonished him, and asked why he did not let the treasurer bearers go, as, in the event of any accident happening to their treasure if they moved at a late hour, he would be responsible for it; on this the Darogah became alarmed and took from them whatever they had intended to pay. It was now late and the treasure bearers would not move that night. We advanced to a garden about two cose on the side of the road, where we cooked and ate our dinner and passed the night. The next morning, while we were preparing to move, we saw the camels and the treasure bearers coming on, and we immediately set out and went on to a nullah in an extensive bamboo jungle, where there was an uninhabited village. Here we all sat down, after cutting some large bamboo sticks, thinking this a suitable place for murder. While we were smoking, a man on horseback who had been the companion of the Rokureeas ever since the preceding night, came up and sat down with us to smoke. Soon after the Rokureeas arrived and sat down to rest. We surrounded them from every side, and seized and strangled the six matchlock men, then the horseman, and lastly we pulled down the surwans from the camels with the bamboo sticks we had cut there, and strangled them. We buried the bodies of the whole in the nullah and instantly made Ghureeba mount on the sowar's horse, and took the treasure camels by a bye road through the jungle, leaving the high road to Indore on the left. Going on about two cose from the place where we had committed the murder, we sat down and took the loads off the camels, put them on our tattoos, and turned the camels loose in the jungles. Here we left the Indore road altogether, and took another in a direction to the east. In three days we reached Sundulpore and encamped on the bank of a tank. Here we cut the treasure khoorjees with tulwars and knives, and took out the treasure, in which we found 15,000 Tippoo Sahee rupees (Spanish dollars), silver bullion 100 rupees weight, and a small brass box stamped. When we broke open this box, we found in it four diamond rings set with jewels, eight pearls, and one pair of gold kurras or bangles. The whole of these articles amounted to 1000 Tippoo Sahees rupees in value. From this booty Zalim took out a handful of money as an offering to Davee, which we intended to give to priests of Bindachul; but not finding an opportunity for doing so it was left with Zalim. Afterwards we divided the booty and got about 150 rupees each, Tippoo Sahee rupees (Spanish dollars). The pearls and jewels were divided according to their value which had been then estimated. The shares of those who left our gang for the Bhopaul district as before described were given to their friends and relations. Hurry Sing (at large, adopted by Khoman, died in Jubulpore jail), took the horse for 10 rupees. We passed that night at Sundulpore, and afterwards returned to our homes by regular stages. A few days after our return home, the part of our gang whom we had left behind at Dooleea returned, having heard that the treasure had been robbed at Burwaha ghat.

(True Translation)
(Signed)   W. H. SLEEMAN,
                                P. A. A. G. G.

To G. Wellesley, Esq.
            Resident, Indore.
SIR,
        I have the honor to forward the deposition of Moklal and others on the subject of the murder of the escort with the treasure of Dhunraj Seth, and to request that you will have the goodness to endeavour to procure the depositions of the men who burnt or buried the bodies. They were, I understand, discovered by the people of the place soon after the affair. Any information regarding the camels left on the ground would also be imper-

tant. The guard at the Burwaha ghat belonged, I understand, to His Highness the Holcar.

I have, &c. &c.

(Signed)   W. H. SLEEMAN,

P. A. A. G. G.

Saugor,

P. A. A. G. G. Office,

The 10*th Oct.* 1831.

(True Copy,)

(Signed)   W. H. SLEEMAN,

P. A. A. G. G.

Deposition of Narooha Kumusdar, of the Purguna, of Burwaha, taken on the 5th November 1831, before Captain Sandys, Assistant to the Resident at Indore, and in charge of the Nunar district.

In the year Sumbut 1884, on the 29th January 1829, A. D., three camels loaded with treasure belonging to Dhunraj Seth of Omrowtee, came to the town of Burwaha, rested the 30th and 31st, paid the duties demandable at the Custom-house, and marched again on the 31st January towards Indore, by the village of Naen, which was then unoccupied and waste. On the bank of the Nullah, near that village, the men escorting the treasure were all killed, and the treasure taken off by robbers, and on the 3d of February, 1829 Khosala Balar, of the village of Omureea, came to the guard in the evening, and reported it. It was then late, and the horsemen of the guard had gone to escort treasure to Mundlesur, and I deferred going out till the next morning, when I, with Runa Ragonauth Sing, Zemindar of the Purguna, and Chutter Duffadar, and three foot soldiers of the guard, went towards Naen, the place where the murders had been committed. On the road we met Golbeea, a Pardhee of the village of Nadeea, who told us that the three camels were left in the jungle, one with his legs tied and the other two free. On coming to the Nala, at about a hundred paces distant from the road to the west, on the dry bed, we found three bodies. They were under the branches of a Golur tree, covered with leaves, dry sand and stones. We took them out and found all their throats cut, apparently with swords. On one of the bodies was a black coat, and by that coat he was recognized to be Meer Futah Alee, a Merchant of Borhanpore. He often passed by Burwaha on business, and became known to the Peeadahs of the guard. We then went to Omureea and asked Humtah, the Putel of that place, where the bodies were that he had reported, and he took us to a part of the Nala in which some water remained, with Girdhur Mukatee and Nana Putwaree, and about fifty paces west from the place where we discovered the first three bodies, we saw two more bodies lying on the ground on the edge of the water. Their throats had been cut in the same manner as those of the other two, and they had been mangled by animals. From this place we returned to the first three bodies, and searching further found two more about ten or twelve paces from them covered with sand, leaves, and stones, and lying one over the other. We took them up and found their throats cut in the same manner as those of the others. There was no other wound discoverable on any of the seven bodies. We now went in search of the camels, and about a quarter of a cose from the bodies to the east, we found one camel lying down with his legs tied. We took him

16*

up and came on to the village of Nadeea where we found the two other camels browsing in a field, and sent all three without ropes or saddles to Burwaha, and I collected the Baloes from Nadae Rampoora, and Agarwara, and Omureea to bury the bodies, and returned to Burwaha, and at the Custom-house chokee ascertained from the books of Gunpot Raw, the Agent on the part of the farmer of the customs, that on the 30th of January, 1829, Dhunraj Seth's three camels had paid duty, and that on the same day, a Bhowanee Persaud, and others his companions, bearing arms, and residents of Bundelcund, thirty persons, with six ponies, had been entered as paying Rahadaree duties, and on the same day, Meer Tullah Alee, the merchant, had passed on his way to Indore. After learning these particulars, I sent off in pursuit of the robbers.

Davey Sing, Peeada of the guard, deposed on the same day to the same effect. So also did Gobind Apa, Peeada of the same guard, and Chutter, Dufadar of the same guard. Also Rana Rugonath Sing, Zemindar of the Parguna of Burwaha. The men employed to bury them, depose to their having buried the seven bodies by order of the Kumasdar.

Deposition of Bijan Naek Nahil, of Omureea, in Burwaha, 3d November, 1831.

In the year Sumbut 1884, three camels laden with treasure from Dhunraj Seth, were robbed at the Nalah of the village of Naen, and seven men who escorted it, murdered. Narabad, Kumasdar of the Purguna, called me and ordered me to search for the murderers. I took three other Nahils from Omureea, and two Danuks from Nadeea, and Bheela Raw, a Peeada of the guard of Burwaha,

with me, to pursue the track (*many*) at the place
where the bodies lay. We could find no trace, but
after a good deal of search we found the *many* on
the road to Key, about a cose from the village of
Naen east, near the deserted village of Khoree,
and from that place we followed it through the
villages of Gidwara, Jugutpoorah, Ramgolah,
Chorurnudee, Khamkee, Khargee, Baroul, and
Kutkote, Holkar's territories. From this place
Bhula Raw returned home to Burwaha, and we
took Zemeendars, one Dhanuk and one Bilae, to
follow on the *many* or trace. We found it through
Ranjhunna, Gowarbar, Gureegoor, Chundere Gurh,
Sankola, Byroogow, Kop Gowra, Beetora, up to
the Bowlee of the village of Portula, in the Purguna of Neemunpore, Mukoar, in the territories of
Bunnear, which Bowlee is situated about two hundred paces from the village. From that Bowlee
no trace could be found. We told the Putel of that
village, Dew Chund Kolee, and two other people
to carry on the trace, and if they could not, they
must answer to their government for the murders,
and having told them this we returned. On our
way we saw the people of Kutkote cutting wood,
and asked about the people who had passed of late.
They said they had seen on the Nuddee, under
Kutkote, twenty-five or thirty men from Bundelcund
Awud, with five or seven ponies, and asked them
whence they came. They said they were from
Malwa, and were going to Pootula, but had lost
their road. We returned and reported all to the
Kumasdar of Burwaha.

Deposition of Tejula Bular, of the village of Nadeea, Purgunna of Burwaha, 1st November, 1831.

In the Sumbut year 1884, on a Nalah, in the village of Naem, in the Purgunna of Burhawa, three camels laden with treasure, belonging to Dhunraj Seth, were robbed, and the men who escorted them murdered. I had been taken as a *begar* with a Kafila of government servants, who were going with a Palkee and other things from Borhanpore, as far as village of Omureea, and was on my return, and warming myself at a fire left burning on the ground which a party of Brinjaras had just quitted near the village of Naen, when I saw a number of carrion birds, such as vultures and others descend from the sky and collect on the bank of the nalah; on seeing this I went to the village of Rampora in the above Purgunna, and told Omrow Bhugwan and other Bulaes, that some animals must be lying dead in the nalah of Naean, as carrion birds were there collected, and they all accompanied me to the nalah to see, and we found two human bodies lying in the nalah close to the edge of the water. On seeing them, my companions returned to Rampora and I came home. On my way I met Heera Rajpoot, of the village of Agurwara, feeding his cattle in the grounds of Naen, and I told him that I had seen the bodies of two murdered travellers in the bed of the nalah, and at his request I went again and pointed them out from a distance.

Deposition of Heera Rajpoot, of Agurwara, 1st November, 1831.

I was grazing my cattle on the boundaries of Naen when Tejula Bular of Naneea, came towards me from the nalah, and said some people had murdered two travellers and thrown their bodies into the nalah, and at my request he went and pointed them out to me. At that time Nana Putwaree, of Naddera, was on his way from Burwaha to Omureea, and meeting him I mentioned the circumstance. He went on towards Omureea, and I returned to my cattle.

Nana Putwaree deposes, 1st November, 1831.

That on hearing the circumstances from Heera Rajpoot he went to Omureea and told Girdhur Muktee and Himota Patel, and went with them and Bichun Nahil and Shamila Bilae, to see the bodies. After seeing the two we returned, and I requested Shamila Bular to go and report to the guard at Burwaha, but he sent his brother Khosala to do so. Khosala deposes that he was sent to report the circumstance to the guard at Burwaha, and reached the place towards evening, and reported accordingly.

Urzee of Dhun Raj Seth, 5th November 1830, forwarded through Captain Robinson of Ellichpore.

About thirty-three months ago, 45,000 rupees of my property, on three camels and one pony, with nine men on their way from Bombay to Indore, were taken by twenty-nine Thugs, four cose from Alvee Bureyra and twenty from Indore. The men were all killed and the pony taken with the property, but the camels were let go: Behareelal and Gomanee Ram, my Gomashtas, went with Dolla Hurcara of Holkar's, in search of the Thugs, found them in Jhansee, and gave information to the Governor General's Agent at Humeerpore, who

got them seized and put in irons. They confessed
that the property had been taken and divided into
a hundred and one shares, and the agent sent them
all to the resident at Indore, and the resident sent
them back to the Agent at Humeerpore, who made
them over to the Jhansee Rajah's Wukeel, with
orders to recover and make good the property.

Some time before this, gold to the value of
twenty-two thousand rupees, in charge of four
Hurcaras, and another batch of gold to the value
of eleven thousand rupees, on their way from Poona
to Jeypore, were taken by Thugs, and the people
murdered. The robbery was traced to these same
Thugs, some of whom were in the Gwalior, and
some in the Dutteea territories; many were taken
and made over to Kishen Persaud, Holkar's
Wukeel, and put into his Highness's Fort of Alumpore. I have recovered fourteen or fifteen thousand
rupees out of the whole; but my agents have in
thirty-three months spent in the search fifteen or
sixteen thousand.

The officer in charge of the Jubulpore district,
has seized seven of the Thugs, and sent them to
the Resident at Indore, and their case is not yet
decided. All these Thugs reside in Jhansee and
Jubulpore, and they should be made to give up my
property. My Gomashta at Humeerpore wanted
a Hurcara and a letter, but the agent of the Governor General would not furnish them, out of regard
for the Jhansee chief, though the Residents of Nagpoor and Gwalior and other places have written to
him in my behalf.

Urzee of Nanik Ram, Gomashta of Dhunraj Seth, forwarded through Mr. Graem, the Resident at Nagpore, 2d September, 1831.

About three years and four months ago, three camels and a pony were laden with twelve thousand five hundred Reals of silver, value forty thousand rupees, and under the escort of seven matchlockmen, were on their way from Bombay to Indore. On the road about six cose from Indore twenty-nine Thugs killed all the escort and took the pony but left the camels. Beharcelal and Gomanee Ram, my Gomashtas at Indore, heard of the robbery and informed the Court of Holkar, who sent Dolla Hurcara with them to search for the Thugs. They found them at Jhansee and informed the agent at Humeerpoor, who got them secured, and when they had confessed the crime he sent them off to the Resident at Indore with the Jhansee Rajah's Hurcara. Twelve hundred rupees and three of the Reals were found upon them, and made over to the Gomashtas, and the Resident, having proved the theft, sent them back to the Governor General's Agent at Humeerpore, who made them over to the Jhansee Rajah's Wukeel, with orders to request his master to make good the property.

Some time before this, silver and gold to the value of thirty-three thousand rupees were on their way in charge of Hurcaras from Poona to Jypore, and the men were all killed by Thugs and the property taken. This was made known to the Agent at Humeerpore, who discovered that the Thugs were from Gwalior. They were seised and sent to the Resident at Gwalior, who ascertained the truth and recovered gold to the value of four thousand rupees, and put it in deposit at Gwalior, and afterwards made it over to my Gomashta. Four Thugs had been seized by the gentleman at Jubulpose, with fourteen hundred rupees of gold upon them, and on my representation through the then Resident of Nagpore, Mr. Wilder, they were forwarded to Indore. The gold was there made over to my Gomashta and the Thugs sent to Humeerpore, where the Agent made them over to the Jhansee Rajah, with orders that he should satisfy me and get my Razeenameh, as he must have received a share of the booty.

The Wukeel sent them all to Jhansee but remained himself at Humeerpore; and the Rajah detained my Gomashtas a month, and then told them to go to Humeerpore, and he would send them the thieves. They went accordingly to the Agent at Humeerpore, who promised to recover the property for them, but it is not yet forthcoming. The Gomashtas are reduced to despair, and have expended thousands of rupees. The Saugor gentleman is now in charge, and three hundred and twenty Reals have been found upon the Thugs, and as Behareelal and Hursahee my Gomashtas, are now at Saugor, I pray a letter to his address, to request he will cause the Jhansee Rajah to make good my losses.

W. H. SLEEMAN.

DHOOLEEA MALAGOW AFFAIR.

To G. WELLESLEY, Esquire.
Resident at Indore.

SIR,

I have the honour to forward the deposition of

Feringcea, one of the gang engaged in the affair commonly called Dhooleea Malagow, and request you will do me the favour to have the depositions of some of the people of Jokur, who are said to have seen the bodies of the murdered people, taken by the local authorities and forwarded to me, that they may be filed as part of the evidence against the members of the gang now in this jail. I must pray you to excuse the trouble which my ignorance of the local jurisdiction occasions.

I must also request you to do me the favour to ascertain whether the money was sent as stated by Kishenchund from Poona for the house of Maun Sing at Indore.

I have, &c. &c.

(Signed),   W. H. SLEEMAN,
P. A. A. G. G.

Saugor P. A. A. G. G. Office, }
    29th June, 1831.   }

DEPOSITIONS TAKEN BEFORE THE BOMBAY AUTHORITIES AND FORWARDED TO CAPTAIN SLEEMAN BY MR. WEL-LESLEY.

Bheeka and Luchmun, 25th March, 1828.

We went from Jhorya to Arohee on the 22nd of Cheyt last, on a Sunday, and on our way home at a ruined Bowlee near Jhorka, we smelt something like dead bodies, and coming home told the public officers, who went to ascertain what it was.

Deposition of Sukharam, Luchmun, Mohun Ram and other Bankers of Poona, 22d July, 1831, A. D.

Our Seth master at Poona sent three men on

the 2d of Mag,* (January) from Poona to Indore, with gold to the value of eleven thousand rupees, and as they did not reach their destination, he sent us to seek them. We searched from village to village as far as Joorka, and one cose from it in advance on the road to Dhooleea, on the right hand, in a ploughed field, we found the bodies of the three murdered men, and reported to the Sahib.

Deposition of Oda Putel taken at Malagow, 22d July, 1831.

The Mamlutdar at Malagow asked whether I had gone upon Dusrut Bheel's report to search for bodies. I said that on the 7th March, on Saturday, Dusrut Bheel of Jhorka, came to me and said that in the Gya Pokar field were dead bodies. Papa Bheel told me the same thing. I told the —, and he, I, and Raghoo Putel and Meerab, Kulkarnee, and four others went, and I saw in a hollow place bodies with stones over them: animals had devoured part of the flesh: we uncovered and took out bones and two or three skulls. About ten cubits from this pit, we found bones of two or three other people, but the skeletons were not entire. The hair on the head was about a cubit long, and part being cut off showed they were men. We reported to the Court at Malagow.

Deposition of Dusrut Putel, 22d July, 1831.

Papa Bheel of Dharureea, on Thursday came to

---

* These were the three men murdered at Dhorecots, and not those whose bodies were found. These were the bodies of the seven persons murdered the year before, three were buried in the field, and the rest buried under stones in the Bowlee.

Manjee Naek while we were together, and said he had seen dead bodies in the field of Gya Pakur, the day before while hunting. I sent Gurha Bheel with him. He saw them and returned. I next day, with Dusrut Shikdar and Oda Putel, and three or four others, went and saw bodies under stones in a ditch. There was little flesh upon the bones. At another place twenty cubits distant were the bones of two or three people, but the skeletons were not entire and we could not see the wounds. We came to Malagow Kutcheree and reported.

Krishna Putel, 22d July, 1831.

On the 22d of Cheyt, Saturday, Bhika Bheel, on returning from Aumee to Jhorka, smelt a bad smell, and came to Shikdar and reported. I and Oda Putel were sitting with him. He said there was a bad smell in the Bowlee and it should be searched. We went and were joined by Shukaram and Luchmum from Poona, who had just come from Dholeea in search of three men who had been sent with money from Poona to Indore. Having arrived at the Bowlee we smelt the stink, and looking down saw the body of a man under stones. He had on a white Ungarka, with blood about the collar of it. We threw it in again after looking at it. There was long hair on the head. We concluded he had been murdered by Thugs. We returned home and reported. Next day further search made, but no more were found in the Bowlee. Some time before five or six bodies had been dug up about five hundred paces from the Bowlee on the Purola road, but Shukaram thought the one in the Bowlee must have belonged to his three, as the others had been buried too long.

DHOREE AFFAIR.

To W. S. Boyde, Esquire,
Magistrate, Candeish.

Sir,

I have the honour to forward the translation of
the deposition of Dulela, one of a gang of Thugs,
who are said to have perpetrated some murders in
your neighbourhood, and as several of the members
of that gang are now in the Saugor jail, and about
to be brought to trial for that and other crimes, I
must request you to do me the favour to send me
copies of any proceedings held in that case at
Dholeea.

(Signed)   W. H. SLEEMAN.

15th August, 1831.

To. W. S. Boyde, Esquire,
Magistrate, Dholeea.

Sir,

Permit me to request, that you will have the
goodness to furnish me as soon as possible with
any information you may be able to procure regarding the case mentioned in my letter to your address
of the 15th August last.

(Signed)   W. H. SLEEMAN.

25th October, 1831.

Dhoreea Affair, No. 46.

(Copy.)

To Captain W. H. Sleeman,
Princl. Assistt. Saugor.

Sir,

I have the honor to forward all the information my records afforded on the subject of your dispatch of the 25th ultimo.

(Signed)   W. BOYDE,
Magistrate.

Candeish, Dholeea, 18th Nov. 1831.

No. 25.

To Captain H. W. Hodges,
Acting Collector in Candeish.

Sir,

In reply to your favour of the 13th instant, I lose no time in forwarding the enclosed petition this day received by me from the agents or owners of the property therein mentioned, and have only to add that four persons by name Rutteeram, Premrauj, Tillukchund, and Sidpersaud, on behalf of the above mentioned parties, this day proceed to appear before you at Dholeea. A Muckadum of Cossids by name Juggajee Rajpoot accompanies them.

(Signed)   J D. DEVETRE,
Senior Magistrate of Police.

Bombay Police Office,
The 21st February, 1829.

17*

To the Worshipful J. D. Devetre, Esquire,

     Senior Magistrate of Police, &c. &c. &c.

Most respectfully sheweth,

That your petitioners on the 28th of January had dispatched some goods, valued altogether at about rupees 72,322, belonging to them, directed to Joypore, by the persons named Jootadass, Rajpoot, Jullajee Cooly Raoe Putel, Busta Putel, Busta Calooka, Beta Ravajee Putel, Jewraj Cooly, and Jeetajce Rajpoot, through the recommendation of the following Muccadums, viz. Pudmajee, Jasajee and Askurrun.

Intelligence has been received by your petitioners, that the men above named have been plundered on the road and killed by the highway men, except one, whilst on their way to Joypore. It was understood that some of the thieves are apprehended by the Honourable Company's Officer in charge of authority at that place, and also it is given to understand to your petitioners that some of the goods have been found there. In noticing to you the above circumstances your Worship ordered the petitioners to give a list of the goods and marks on the bundles so plundered, that your petitioners may perhaps obtain some relief.

Pursuant to your Worship's order the petitioners beg to annex a detailed list of the goods and marks of the bundles as above specified.

And your petitioners as in duty bound shall ever pray.

     Jonuvmul Bahadoor Mull.
     Mohun Ram Girdhurlall.
     Arjoondas Soorujmull.
     Tarachand Seetaram.

Bombay, 21st Feby. 1831.

Goods belonging to Jonuvmul, marked in Guze-
ratee, Nos. 1, 2, 3 and 4.

4 bundles of pearls, value Rs.	16,842

Marked in Gozeratee letters.

1 bundle of Europe piece goods, 1 piece,	5

Marked with wax seal in Gozeratee.

	16,847

The detail of the above is as follows:

Bundle No. 1, valued Rs.	8,400
Ditto " 2, "	3,550
Ditto " 3, "	4,300
Ditto " 4, "	592

On every of this bundle Gozeratee, No. 151½.

Total,	16,842

Goods belonging to Mohuman Girdurlal—

4 bundles of pearls, 2 of which marked in Gozeratee, numbers 1 and 2, Rs.	10,500

The detail of it as follows:

Bundles No. 1, containing pearls, value Rs.		2,150
Ditto No. 2, ditto, ditto,	4,175	
Ditto ditto diamonds,	35	
Ditto ditto Pana Manic,	40	
		4,250
1 bundle without number, containing powder of pearls,	550	
1 bundle ditto ditto, contg. pearls,	3,100	
		3,650

Seal of wax in Gozeratee on every bundle
Mohomernom Sree Kishundass,

Total Rupees,	11,810

Goods belonging to Arjoondass Soorujmul—

1 bundle of pearls, marked with different numbers, Rs.	11,750

Marked with wax seal in Gozeratee, Husband Bo-
hies, name 3 and 4, mark 15½.

1 bundle of gold and silver, marked with
Surendass Hursook's name, value Rs.   60
<small>Nos. 1, 2 and 3, marked 33½, with Bhijachund Sunkur-
dass Mooltan Chund's name,</small>

                         11,810

Goods belonging to Tarachund Seetaram—
11 bundles of pearls, value Rs.   30,340
1 box of ditto ditto,   5,400
<small>Marked with wax, seal in Gozerat, with Jeyram Mun-
ja's name, No. 15½,</small>

            Total Rupees, 35,740

            (True Copy.)
      (Signed)   J. STEVEN, A. M.,
                  Judicial Department.

To CHARLES NORRIS, Esquire,
          Secretary to Government, Bombay.

An account of murder and robbery as required
by the Secretary's letter of the 6th instant transmitted.—Sir, I have the honour to acknowledge
the receipt of your letter of the 6th instant, in reply
to mine of the 20th ultimo, and conformably to the
instructions contained in the fourth paragraph of
it, beg to transmit the following account of the
murder and robbery which took place in the Dholeebaree pass, of the Sathpoora Hills, on the 6th
February last.

Description of the persons robbed, and amount
of the property in charge.—2d. The persons robbed and murdered were six men, who together
with a seventh, had been entrusted with twenty-
seven packages of pearls, a small package of cloth,

and a few rupees, by four mercantile houses at Bombay, on whose account they were to have been conveyed to Jeypore. At Malegaon and Parolah, the persons entrusted with these commodities, the value of which is stated by the Gomashtas of the several houses to be rupees 72,322, took under their charge some gold mohurs, and Venetian ducats, and it is not improbable that from this circumstance it became known to the gang by whom they were plundered, that they had such valuable property under their charge.

Intimation of the robbery first received.—3d. The first intimation of the robbery was conveyed to the Mamlutdar of Chofrah, on the day after it was committed, by Dusrut, the Bheel Naig, of the Dholeebaree pass, who stated by letter that, at about eight o'clock in the morning of the preceding day, seven Beemawallas, of the designation of the persons robbed, had passed by Dholeebaree, and represented in reply to his inquiries on the subject that they were come from Bombay, and were going to Indore, and had no property of value in their possession. He added that they were followed shortly after by twenty-two men, with five tattoos, who had among them two swords and a dagger, and who stated that they had been in the service of the British government, from which they had received their discharge and were proceeding to Cawnpore.

Intimation of the robbery, by what means communicated to Dusrut Naig.—4th. The circumstance of the robbery became known to Dusrut Naig in consequence of one of the Beemawallas having proceeded in advance of his companions as far as Gudurghaut, about four cose from Dholeebaree, where he waited for his companions during that day   d afterwards, finding he was not foll   b   , returned to Dholee-baree.

By what means t   o   ence of the robbery was first discovered.—   n his way to Dholee-baree this person was   med by a traveller whom he met on the r   at he had seen the body of a murdered man   nalah near the road, and proceeding hi   e spot where it was reported to have been seen, ne recognised it to be the body of one of his co   anions. From that spot he proceeded to Dholee aree, and obtaining some of Dusrut Naig's   o   to accompany him returned to the nalah whe   e bodies of his other five companions were a   nd, on one of them concealed in his clothes a bag of pearls was found, and on another a rupee and   half.

Conduct of Dusrut Naig nd his followers in tracing the thieves.—6th.   usrut Naig shortly afterwards joined his followers at the nalah where the bodies had been fo   , and traced the footsteps of men and horses as lar   a deserted village, on the way to a deserted   t of country, between two ranges of the i   Hills called the Pall Tuppa. From   ce ne states some footsteps were traced in   d c   of a village called Chinahpanee, in the Ar   w d Purguna, but the footsteps of the horses   greater part of the gang were traced to a village named Dhegaum, in the Yawull Purgunah,   b   by this time late in the evening no further t   es could be discovered, and the Naig came to i   Yawull.

Measure taken at Y   obtain intelligence of the robbers.—7th.   u   iol wing morning every Sowar whose services   vailable for the pur-pose, and several of the n   lute   H rcarahs, mounted on tattoos, were sent out in quest of intelligence of the robbers.

Proceedings of two Sowars and Hurcarahs from Yawull.—8th. Three Sowars and one of the Hurcarahs having obtained intelligence on the road that some persons answering to the description of the robbers given by Dusrut Naig, had been seen at a village called Nahnee, in the Yawull Pergunnah, proceeded to that village, and one of the horsemen being in advance of the others entered the village by himself, and standing near a Buneeah's shop, met a man who on inquiry described himself to be a Sepoy of the 4th Regiment; upon being asked if he had any companions with him he said he had two, who were preparing their food at a well near the village. Afterwards the person addressed accompanied him to the gate of the village, near which he pointed out two persons who he stated to be his companions. These two persons on being called to, stopped in the first instance, but after accompanying the horsemen a little distance ran off. The horseman gave the man whom he had first accosted in charge to a Sebundy, and went in pursuit of the others, who he says ran towards a place called Martunachee Warra, and he observed that they were preceded by five other persons, all of whom were running away. The Sowar came up with five of the party who stood on their defence against him, one of them drawing a sword for the purpose, and in the end, by the assistance of other persons the whole five were apprehended. The Sowar stated that the other two were apprehended also at Fyzpoor, to which place he followed them, but there is not yet sufficient evidence that two persons who were apprehended there are the same he had seen at Nahnee.

Statement of the prisoners taken at Nahnee.—9th. The prisoners, six in number, who were taken at this place (Nahnee) all describe themselves to be persons without employment or connexions in the country, and most of them state that they have recently come from Hindoostan. They all agree that they come to Nahnee together, but give different accounts of the time and place of their first meeting each other, some of them saying it was Dholia, others at Maligaum, and others between these two places, and notwithstanding they acknowledge they had been travelling together for some days past, they generally professed an ignorance of each other's name.

Mode in which part of the plunder was discovered.—10th. A short time after they were apprehended, a Chowdry of the village of Nahvee observed a sword and some other things without any person near them in the place called Martunchawarra. He communicated the circumstance to another Chowdry of the village, who taking a dirk with him brought the things found there to a Shaikhdar, who was in the village, and upon examining one of the things found, it was discovered to contain among other things two sealed bags which proved to be two of the bags of pearls of which the murdered Bimbeewallas were robbed.

Nature of the evidence against the prisoners taken at Nahvee.—11th. I cannot obtain any clear and certain evidence that the persons apprehended had been seen in the place where the stolen property was found, but all the circumstances under which they were apprehended point them out as the persons in whose possession it had been, and their guilt is further established by the important circumstance of two of them being recognised by one of the followers of Dusrut Naig, as two of the party that passed Dhooleabaree immediately after the Bimbeewallas, by which party there can be no doubt the murder and robbery were committed.

Proceedings of a party of Sowars from Borhanpore.—12th. The party of Sowars whose operations have been described, proceeded from Yawull, and another party of five proceeded from Russoelpoor in the Rewair Purgunnah, and went to Borhanpore in quest of the robbers; they there learnt that some strangers with tattoos had just arrived, and alighted in a garden near the city. They proceeded to the spot and found three men together, two of whom were in the act of unloading their tattoos, and the third was standing near them with a sword under his arm. Other two were observed at some little distance from them, who when they found the Sowars questioning the three men ran off and made their escape. The three men were secured by the Sowars. The sword of the man described to have been standing unemployed, was on examination found to be stained with blood from the point to the hilt. Suspended to the neck of the same man was a tobacco pouch containing some rupees, gold mohurs, and Venetians—the latter the exact number that had been in charge of the Bimbeewallas. On examining the baggage that had been taken from the tattoos, four of the bags of pearls that had been plundered were discovered.

Nature of the evidence against the prisoners apprehended in a garden at Borhanpore.—13th. The evidence against these three persons appears to be quite conclusive. They themselves, however, deny their guilt, assert that all the Sowars have sworn to is false, and that they know nothing about things pretended to have been found with them. There is not the slightest reason to doubt the truth of the Sowars' statements, which are perfectly clear and consistent, and in confirmation of them, one of the three persons is recognised to have been with the party of twenty-two persons who followed the Bimbeewallas at Dhooleebaree.

Circumstance under which four prisoners were apprehended.—14th. On the same day and about the same time that the three persons were apprehended as abovementioned, other four were stopped by some persons employed in the collection of the Zukat near Borhanpore, and detained until some of the party that had been in quest of the robbers arrived. The four persons are stated to have been going towards the garden where the other three were apprehended. They had with them two swords and two tattoos. Both the swords were stained with blood, and one of them considerably so. The loads on the tattoos were not examined on the spot, but taken to a place where the Sowars were, and there examined. Nothing of value was found with the baggage of these persons, but two brass vessels were found with it, which are recognized by the Bimbeewalla that escaped to have belonged to one of his murdered companions. Of the two tattoos taken with these prisoners, one of them was seen at Dholeebaree by a follower of Dusrut Naig, in possession of the party of two and twenty men that followed the Bimbeewallas and is recognized by him. Two of the prisoners are said to have been seated on the tattoos when the party was stopped by the Zakat collectors, but unfortunately these last cannot point out which of the prisoners were so seated, nor can I ascertain on satisfactory evidence from which of them the swords were taken. One man only can swear to one of the swords being taken from one of the prisoners in particular.

Statement of the prisoners.—15th. Three of the prisoners acknowledge that the four had been travelling in company together before they were apprehended, but give discordant accounts as to the time and place of their first meeting. One of the prisoners denies that he had previously been in company with the other three before he was apprehended, and alleges that they were merely following him on the road unconnected with him. One of the swords is stated by the prisoners to have been in the possession of one of his companions, but that companion denies that he had any sword in his possession. The other sword none of the prisoners will acknowledge. One of the tattoos, but not the one which was recognized at Dholeebaree, is acknowledged by one of the prisoners to have been in his possession, but the other tattoos none of them will acknowledge.

Remarks on the evidence.—16th. Such is the evidence against the prisoners who have been apprehended on suspicion of having been engaged in this atrocious robbery and murder. I regret with regard to some of them it is not so perfect as could be desired, although it appears to me that there is sufficient to warrant the committal of thirteen of them and to leave little doubt of their guilt. I have in vain endeavoured by every proper means to induce some of them against whom the evidence is least perfect to turn king's evidence, and merit pardon by a full confession and disclosure of all the circumstances connected with the robbery.

17th. Considering the hazard to which so large

a property was exposed by the manner of its conveyance through a wild and deserted country, and
that the recovery of a considerable part of it, I
believe about one-third of the whole in value, has
been effected quite independently of the exertions
of the owners of it, it may perhaps appear to the
Honourable the Governor in Council, but just, that
whatever may be now given in the shape of rewards to those by whose exertions it has been
recovered, should be paid to government by the
owners of the property after the trial of the prisoners has taken place, and it may be a question
whether the owners of the property should not
also be required further to reward the Sowars and
others by whose means their property has been
recovered by the payment of a salvage, in addition
to the rewards which they may be deemed entitled
to under my proclamation.

(Signed)   H. W. HODGES,
Acting Magistrate.

Bhurgaon, 24th March, 1829.

(True Copy.)
(Signed)   W. BOYDE,
Magistrate.

To W. Boyde, Esquire,
Magistrate, Candiesh at Dhooleea.

Sir,

I have to express my thanks for the documents
you have done me the favour to forward with your
letter of the 18th instant, but in order to complete
the case I shall feel much obliged if you will have
the goodness to procure for me any reply that
government may have sent to Captain Hodges's

address to the Secretary to government of the 24th March, 1829, and let me know what ultimately became of the men therein mentioned as under his custody.

Several of the gang who then escaped have been seized by me, and I hope to secure the greater part of those still at large, but it is too late to expect to recover much of the property taken off by them. Should you not have a copy of Mr. Secretary Norris's reply, may I beg the favour of your making application for one in order to save delay, as the men are to be put upon their trial, if possible, next month.

   (Signed) W. H. SLEEMAN,
        Principal Assistant.
Saugor, P. A. Office, 8th November, 1831.

———

     (Copy.)
To Captain W. H. Sleeman,
   Princl. Assistt. A. G. G., Saugor.
Sir,

  I have the pleasure to acknowledge the receipt of your letter of the 30th ultimo, and to enclose a copy of the reply from this government required by you to Major Hodges's letter of the 24th March, 1829.

  2. I also enclose a memorandum of the manner in which the Thugs you allude to were disposed of.

  3. With best wishes for the success of your able exertions in protecting the country from the atrocious acts of these detestable miscreants.

   (Signed) W. S. BOYD, *Magistrate.*
Candeish, Magistrate's Office,)
 Dhoolea, 13th Dec. 1831.)

MEMORANDUM.

No.	Names of Convicts.	Sentence.
1	Sheikh Emam, Ud. Sheikh Buscon,	Was sentenced to be hung, but he committed suicide, on the 2d August, 1829.
2	Munsaram, Ud. Kalooram,	Transported beyond seas on the 2d September, 1829.
3	Madaree, Ud. Rajaram,	
4	Oody Sing, Ud. Punchum,	
5	Peerbux,	
6	Qasim Khan, Ud. Noor Khan,	
7	Hossein Khan, Ud. Peer Khan,	
8	Sheikh Rynoo, Ud. Sheikh Loothan,	Hanged at Raware on the 11th September, 1829.
9	Manick, Ud. Buhader,	Released, now in Saugor.
10	Gunesh, Ud. Mungul, at large,	Acquitted on the 29th June, 1829.
11	Massook, Ud. Mudoo Sing, in Saugor,	
12	Bhowanee Ud. Munsook, at large,	
13	Sheikh Kalloo Ud. Sheikh Munnoo,	Imprisoned for natural life—died on the 22d December, 1829.

(Signed) W. S. BOYDE,
Magistrate.

No. 545 of 1829.

No. 46.

Judicial Department.

To Captain H. W. Hodges,
Acting Collector and Magistrate in Candeish.

Sir,

I am directed to acknowledge the receipt of your letter of the 24th ultimo, and to convey to you the sanction of the Honourable the Governor in Council for the distribution of a reward of rupees six hundred and fifty, among the persons through whose exertions certain delinquents, supposed to have been concerned in a robbery and murder, were secured, and for the offer of a reward of rupees fifty, for the apprehension of every other person engaged in the said robbery.

(Signed)   C. NORRIS,
Secretary to Government.

Bombay Castle, 3d April, 1829.

(True copy)

(Signed) W. S. Boyds, Collector.

(No. 102.)
SHIKARPORE AFFAIR.

To Colonel Briggs,
Resident, Nagpore.

Sir,

I have the honour to request that you will do me the favour to let me know whether Mr. Jenkins, while he was resident at Nagpore, paid a visit to Bundelcund about the year 1816 or not.

(Signed)   W. H. SLEEMAN,
Princl. Assistt.

Saugor, 25th April, 1833.

To Captain Warde,
Assistant Resident, Nagpore.

Sir,

Will you do me the favour to ascertain for me the names of any officer who passed up through Nagpore and Jubulpore in the early part of 1816. Some people following in their train were murdered between Jubulpore and Bandah, and some of those who were present at the murder say that they had very large establishments, and that they think one of them was a near relation of the Resident of Nagpore, Mr. Jenkins. They add, that the servant of the gentleman talked of their having been on some expedition against the French.

At that time we had not taken possession of Jubulpore, and no information could be expected from reference to that place.

(Signed)   W. H. SLEEMAN,
Princl. Assistt.

Saugor, 23rd May, 1833.

To Captain Warde,

Assistant Resident, Nagpore.

Sir,

I have the honour to request that you will do me the favour to ascertain whether Ram Buksh Tumbolee ever recognized and recovered the property of his relations from Budelcund, as he is stated in Mr. Jenkins's letter of the 6th September 1816 to have claimed them, but no documents relating to it can be procured from the Agent's Office. Some of the perpetrators of that murder are now under trial, and the Court is very anxious to ascertain this point, which it considers of great importance; and I shall feel much obliged if you can afford me the necessary information.

(Signed)   W. H. Sleeman,

Princl. Assistt.

Saugor, 27th February, 1833.

————

To Captain W. H. Sleeman,

Princl. Assistt. Agent Gr. Gl. Saugor.

Sir,

In reply to your letter of the 27th ultimo, I have the honour to inform you that there does not appear to be any record in the Residency Office in the case of Ram Buksh Tumbolee of a subsequent date to Mr. Jenkins's letter alluded to by you. Ram Buksh is dead, and by what I have been able to ascertain from persons recollecting the circumstance, it appears that he went to Bundelcund with the hope of recovering a child and his property, but returned unsuccessful.

(Signed)   W. Warde,

Offg. Assistt.

Nagpore Residency, 13th March, 1834.

Shikarpore Affair.

Murder of 27 Persons.

Deposition of Sheikh Inaent, 11th April, 1833.

About fifteen years ago, in the year when **Mr.
Jenkins,** the Resident, went from Nagpore to Banda,
I was with a gang of one hundred and twenty-five
Thugs, under Nathea, Noor Khan, Bhudae, Gholab
Khan, Hyput Jemadars, at Sehora, in the District
of Jubulpore. We heard of Mr. Jenkins's approach
from Jubulpore and waited a day for his party,
and when they came to Sehora we joined them,
and made acquaintance with the travellers. Some
pretended to be on their way home from service,
others to belong to the Resident's camp. They
went on to Cowreea, and we continued with them,
and went on the second day with them to Belhree,
where we inveigled to join us, twenty-seven of the
party, including five women and two boys about
three years of age each. We persuaded them that
they suffered much loss and inconvenience by
travelling with so large a camp, that food was
much dearer, and often not to be got for money,
that the water was always scarce and muddy,
and that we should escape all this by leaving the
camp, and taking the road by Powae. To all this
they agreed and assented, and the next morning
we left the camp which was going by way of Lohar-
gong and took the road through Powae. We
reached Shikarpore in Punna, which is three cose
on this side of Powae, and encamped in the grove,
and in the afternoon we sent on Kurhaea and
Mutholee, to select a place for the murder of this
party. They chose a place on the bank of a river,

between Powae and Shikarpore, where the jungle
is thick and extensive, and about midnight we set
out with this party. As soon as we reached the
appointed place, we recommended them to sit down
and rest themselves, as a good deal of the night
still remained; about half of them sat down and
the other half remained standing, and the signal
being given, twenty-five of the party were strangled.

Jowahir took one boy, and the other boy was
taken by Kehree. The bodies were thrown into a
dry pit in the Nalah, and some stones and branches
of trees thrown in upon them to conceal them.
The boy, whom Jowahir had taken, on seeing the
bodies thrown into the pit, cried loudly, and Jowahir dashed him against a stone and killed him.
We concealed the bodies of all but that of the boy,
which we forgot to throw in upon the rest, and it
lay by the stone exposed. We went on to Powae,
and purchased five rupees worth of goor, which
we took on with us to a village whose name I
forget. In the morning a bearer going to the river
to fish, saw the body of the boy, and gave information to Burjore Sing, the Thakoor of Powae;
and he went to the place with his people, opened
the pit, and took out the bodies, and proceeded in
seach of the murderers. He searched all day and
the following night in vain, and the next day he
came up with us at a river, where we were washing our hands and faces, after having left the small
village where we had eaten our goor. He had
before him two matchlock men, and suspecting his
design we formed into a close body and proceeded
on our road. They ran upon us, but we kept
waiting with our matchlocks ready, and pointed
towards them, but they had some horsemen with
them, and they charged in upon our body, and

they wounded Hyput with a spear in the breast, and Bhugwan on the face with a sword ; and finding it vain to attempt resisting any longer, we dispersed and fled. They each seized his man, and after possessing themselves of what property they found upon them let them all go, except Hossein Khan, alias Kunheya, Roshun, Khoosalee and Kureema, whom they sent to Bandah, where they were kept in confinement four years and then released.

The boy's name who was saved was Gunesh, and he was taken by Kehree Patuk, who brought him up as a Thug, and he died about three years ago. (Signed) W. H. SLEEMAN.

To Captain Sleeman,
Princl. A. A. G. G., Saugor.

Sir,

I am directed to acknowledge the receipt of your letter under date the 25th ultimo, and to acquaint you in reply that Mr. Jenkins, while he was Resident at Nagpore, paid a visit to Bundelkund, either before or subsequently to the year 1816.

(Signed) W. WARDE,
Nagpore Residency, 3d May, 1833. Offg. Assistt.

To Captain Sleeman,
Pl. A. A. G. G., Saugor.

Sir,

I have the honour to acknowledge the receipt of your letter of the 23d ultimo, and in reply beg to acquaint you that particular inquiries have been made regarding the information required by you, but I have not been able to procure any trace of officers passing up through Nagpore and Jubulpore in the early part of 1816. In December of that year or January following, Captain Jenkins, of the Bengal Artillery, came by that route. He accompanied the force under the command of Colonel Adams as far as Bellary, where he was met by an escort from this, but there was no report of any of his followers having been murdered.

(Signed) W. WARDE,

Offg. Assistant.

Nagpore Residency the 14th June, 1833.

No. 102.

My Dear Sir,

On examining the records of this Residency I find allusion made to the murders regarding which you require information.

Captain Close must, I conceive, have been the officer whose name you were desirous of ascertaining. I have not been able to find the four depositions referred to. They probably were never transmitted. I have sent copies of these documents officially, supposing you may wish to record them.

(Signed) W. WARDE,

Offg. Assistant.

Nagpore, 23d July, 1833.

To Captain Sleeman,

P. A. A. G. G., Saugor.

Sir,

In continuation of my letter to your address under date the 14th June last, I am now directed to transmit to you the enclosed copies of correspondence which took place between Mr. Jenkins and Mr. Wauchope in the early part of 1816, on the subject referred to in your letter of the 23d May last, and which it is hoped will be found correct and satisfactory.

(Signed)   W. WARDE,
Offg. Assistant.

Nagpore Residency, the 23d July, 1833.

To R. Jenkins, Esquire,
Resident at Nagpore.

Sir,

I beg leave to transmit to you the enclosed copy of my proceedings of the 13th instant, containing a statement of a most heinous robbery, with murder, which was committed on a party of travellers in the Rajah of Punna's territory, in the month of March last, accompanied by a list of articles taken from the robbers.

2. The party of travellers who appear to have proceeded from Jubulpore, consisted of eighteen men, seven women and two children, every one of whom seem to have been murdered by the gang of robbers, which appears to have been very numerous. My object in addressing you on the occasion is, that in the event of your being able to discover the relations of the unfortunate sufferers, you might have the goodness to direct them to depute an authorized person to receive the recovered property.

(Signed)   J. WAUCHOPE,
Suptt. of Poll. Affairs.

Foujdaree Adawlut,)
Zillah Bundelcund, }
The 22d June, 1816.)

To J. Wauchope, Esquire,
     Suptt. of Poll. Affairs, Bundelcund.

Sir,

I have the honour to receive your letter of the 22d of June, enclosing a copy of your proceedings, containing a statement of a robbery committed on a party of travellers in the Rajah of Punna's territory in March last, and a list of articles recovered, and requesting that in the event of my being able to discover the relations of the sufferers, I would direct them to depute an authorized person to receive the recovered property.

The bearer Ram Buksh Tumbolee has presented himself to claim a part of the property as belonging to his family, who he believes were amongst the unfortunate sufferers. Enclosed is a copy of the list of articles which he has given in, as having been in the possession of his family, and one of his verbal statements on the subject, taken down in my cutchery.

    (Signed)   R. Jenkins, *Resident.*
Nagpore Residency, 6th September, 1816.

    (True Copies.)

    (Signed)   W. Warde,
                  Offg. Assistant.

Roobukaree, 27th March, 1816—14th Cheyt Sumbut 1873, by the Magistrate of Banda.

As it is understood from the superintendent of these territories that twenty-five persons on their way from Jubulpore, have been strangled by murderers who were from the west and have taken the road to Huttah, and it is probable that they are from Gohud and Gwalior, purwanas are to be

addressed to all the Thanahs to use all their efforts
to arrest them.

Roobukaree of the Superintendent Mr. Wauchope,
13th April, 1816.

On the 7th March a Purwana was addressed to
Burjore Sing to require the arrested robbers by
whose gang the twenty-seven persons had been
murdered at the Pass of Shikarpore. This day
Bukshee Chitura, the Punna Wukeel, has presented
a Hindee letter from him in reply with a list of
property, and stated that the four* arrested men
are present—*Husun Khan, Imambuksh, Shumsera,*
and *Bahader.* These men have been examined
and they declare that they were not concerned in
the murders, and state that they were innocent
travellers. The Wukeel states that the men who
took them have not come with them; but are with
their masters at Powae; that among the things
taken from them was a phansee, or noose, and one
of the Row's Sipahees took it to draw water from
a well; that Buhader, one of the four taken, had
confessed that they murdered the people in the
Nalah; but Shumshera, who calls himself also
Kuramut, forbad him, and said he would get hung
if he confessed, and he remained silent; although
they deny the crime, still it is clear that they are
men of bad character, and the suspicion is very
strong against them, and they are to be sent to the
magistrate with the list of things taken with them.

---

* Husun Khan alias Hunna, dead.
 Imambuksh alias Khosal, hung at Dholeea Malagow.
 Shumshera alias Roshun, hung at Jubulpore, 1832.
 Buhadur, somewhere in Hyderabad, in service 1st battalion.
 Moghobee in Hingolee Aurungabad.

and Burjore Sing is to be thanked for his meritorious conduct and to be requested to send the other evidence required.

(True Translation.)

(Signed)   W. H. SLEEMAN,

P. A. A. G. G. Saugor.

Roobukaree, 27th March, 1816, by Mr. Wauchope.

This day Bukshee Chitara, the Wukeel of the Punna Rajah, came and presented an Urzee, stating that twenty-five persons had been murdered on their way from Jubulpore, by fifty robbers, near the Pass of Shikarpore, in the Punna Rajah's territory, and that six or seven of them had been wounded, and four taken by the people of Row Burjore Sing, a relation of the Rajah's. The Wukeel stated that Omrow Zumeendar of Bumhoree was present, and would be able to give further information, and his deposition has accordingly been taken, and as it may lead to the discovery of their associates, the four robbers arrested are to be demanded from the Rajah, who will also be desired to take care of the property for the heirs of the murdered people. The Rajah is at the same time to be thanked for his exertions on this occasion, and as these robbers may pass through these territories, the following chiefs are to be written to, and conjoin to aid in their arrest.

Gwalior, Bijawur, Tehree, Jhansee, Duttees, Kour, Sonee Sa and Kour Purtab Sing.

19*

Urzee of Bukshee Chitara, Wukeel of the Punna Rajah.

Row Burjore Sing, a Jemadar of my master, in the Purgunna of Powae, writes to me that near Shikarpore, about five cose south of Powae, near the Pass, in the middle of Phagun, twenty-five travellers, on their way from Jubulpore, a district of the Nagpore government, were murdered by fifty robbers, and their property taken off. That after the murder the robbers came to Powae, and purchased food at the Bunceas' shops, but without sitting down went on. The Bunceas asked who they were, from whence and whither going, and they said they were from the Duckun on their way to Banda, saying this they went on; that contrary to their professed design they took the road to the west, and rested at the village of Chowmooka, in my master's territory, and left the place again at midnight for Tighurra, in the Jytpore territory. As soon as Row Burjore Sing heard these circumstances he sent on twenty-five of his soldiers after them, and they came up within the boundary of Tighurra, and unable to prevail upon them to surrender, they wounded six or seven of them, and took four out of the number into custody. They secured seven ponies, and brought them with other things, to Burjore Sing. Unable to stand against the sipahees the robbers sought shelter in Tighurra, and the villagers came to their support and escorted them to Simareea in Jytpore, and the holder of that village entertained them one day, and the next dismissed them, but took kfrom them all their property, first understanding that it amounted to ten or twelve thousand rupees. Burjore Sing wrote to the Simareea man and desired him to keep them in custody but he would not.

Deposition of Omrow, Zumeendar of Bumhoree, 27th March, 1816.

I heard that twenty-seven persons, male and female, had been killed on their way from Jubulpore to Chutterpore, by fifty or sixty decoits, and all their property taken off—that they had gone after the murders to Powae and thence to Tighurra in Jytpore, and that Row Burjore Sing had sent after them twenty-five of his followers, who seized four and two more that had been wounded, and brought them with seven ponies to Powae to the Row who still has them. An action took place between the Rowe's people and robbers at Tighurra, but the people of that place came to the aid of the robbers, and as night came on they effected their purpose and escorted them to Simareea. Burjore Sing's people sent a message to the Thanadar of Simareea by the Zumeendar of Pourneea, to say that the Tighurra people had sent the robbers to him, and he must secure them. The robbers remained there all night, till noon the next day, and then took the road to Deoree in Huttah. I heard that all the property they had with them was taken by the Zumeendar of Simareea in Jytpore. I hear that the four taken confess they are from Gwalior and that the robbers had with them twenty-five matchlocks, and the rest had bows and arrows, and were all dressed differently, and talked like people from the west.

Urzee of Koonjbehareelal Akbur Nuvees at Punna.

I have received your Purwanas of the 27th March, stating that you had enclosed two Purwanas, one to Burjore Sing and the other to the Aumil of Simareea in Jytpore, and directing me to forward them immediately. I have done so by two Hurcarahs.

———

Copy.
To Captain W. H. Sleeman,
Princl. Assistt. Saugor.
Sir,

With reference to your letter of the 5th instant, I have the honour to transmit an extract from Major Close's letter dated December 3d, 1815.

(Signed) R. CAVENDISH, *Resident.*
Gwalior Residency, 13th August, 1833.

———

Extract from a Letter from Major Close to the Secretary to Government, dated Poona, December 3d, 1815.

" I had yesterday the honour to receive your
" letter dated 10th of November, notifying my
" appointment to succeed Mr. Stacy as Resident
" at the Court of Dowlut Row Scindia. I shall
" proceed to that chief in obedience to the Gover-
" nor General's commands, with the least practi-
" cable delay, and shall adopt the route of Aurun-
" gabad, Nagpore, and Bundelcund, as being the
" most open and the least liable to impediment."

(A true Extract)
(Signed) R. CAVENDISH, *Resident.*

SURGOOJA AFFAIR.

To Major Smith,
Commanding at Ellichpore.

Sir,

I have the honour to forward the deposition of Dorgha, regarding the murder of some people, on their way from Ellichpore to the Dooab, about the year 1809 or 1810, and shall feel obliged if you will do me the favour to ascertain whether any such people disappeared about that time.

(Signed)　　W. H Sleeman,
Principal Assistant.

Saugor P. A. A. G. G. Office,
14th February, 1834.

Deposition of Dorgha, 13th February, 1834.

In 1810 or 1809 we were 200 Thugs at a village near Suhajie in Nagpore, when we met 40 persons, some from Ellichpore, and some from Gwalior, and Jhalna, and Aurungabad. We came on with them seven stages, and in a jungle between Chóree and Sutrumju, we killed them all, and buried their bodies under stones in the bed of the river; one was a Subadar, a Brahmin, belonging to the regiment of Sulabut Khan and Behlal Khan, Newabs; one was a Brahmin Tewaree, with two daughters, he was going home to get married. They were murdered with their mother and father. There was another Tewaree Brahmin, with an old woman, his wife, and a young daughter. The old woman was killed, but the daughter was preserved and married to Hunce Rao, nephew of Kasal, Subadar of Thugs; she had two or three children by him, but they are dead; all three were residents of the purdesee Mahulla, in Ellichpore, and they were going to the provinces on the Ganges.

(True Translation,)
(Signed)   W. H. SLEEMAN,
P. Asst. Agent Governor General.

————

To Captain Sleeman,
Princl. Assist. Agent Governor General, Saugor.

Sir,

With reference to your letter of the 14th ultimo. and deposition of Dorgha annexed, I have the honour to forward to you the undermentioned papers containing all the information I have been able to obtain relating to the affair detailed therein, and which I trust, considering the long period which has elapsed, will be found satisfactory.

No. 1. Copy of a letter from Nawab Namdar Khan to Major Smith, commanding at Ellichpore.

No. 2. Statement of Bapajie Pundit in the service of Major Smith, commanding at Ellichpore.

No. 3. The depositions of Gobind Sing Subadar, Maun Sing Subadar, and Subsookh Jemadar, pensioners, residing in the cantonment at Ellichpore.

The occurrence to which they refer must have happened in November or December 1809, because it is stated in the accompanying papers that the persons supposed to have suffered quitted this in the cold season previous to the march of Colonel Close's force to Seronge, which took place in December or January 1809-10, to which I can speak myself, having been present with that force. If however you should wish to ascertain the precise date (for I speak from recollection only) it can be ascertained by reference to the public records of the Residency at Nagpore.

(Signed)   H. SMITH, *Major*,
                    Commanding Ellichpore Division.

Ellichpore, 10th March, 1834.

———

Copy of a Letter from Newab Namdar Khan to Major Smith, Commanding at Ellichpore, 1st *March,* 1834.

I have received your letter with a Roobukaree from Saugor regarding the murder of some people from Ellichpore of the Purdessee quarter of the town. Twenty-five years have elapsed since that event, and the people of that quarter have dispersed, and no information can be got regarding them, but should I get any it will be forwarded to you.

Deposition of Gobind Sing Subadar, Maun Sing Subadar, Subsookh Jemadar, Pensioners, residing in the Ellichpore Cantonments, before Major Smith, Commanding.

8th March, 1834.

Colonel Close marched with the Division of Newab Sulabut Khan of Ellichpore towards Seronge, and before that time in the cold season twenty-one persons, purdessees (foreigners), residing in Bundelpoora in Ellichpore, set out for Hindostan, with all their families in order to celebrate the marriage of their children. We afterwards heard that they had all been murdered in the Nagpore territories, but from that time we have received no further accounts of the matter. We heard that one girl who was saved on the occasion was still living at Nagpore, but Subsookh Jemadar in 1831 went to Hindoostan with his family, and on his return he said he could not discover what had become of this girl though he had made inquiries about her.

NAMES OF MURDERED PERSONS.

1 Gunga Tewaree of Dhondkhera, servant of Buhloll Khan Bahadur, deceased.
3 His wife and daughter about nine years of age.
4 Bodhee Sing Subadar of Bhyswarra, servant of Newab Subahdar Khan deceased.
5 Needhan Sing, his father-in-law.
6 His mother-in-law.
7 His sister-in-law.
8 Alpee, his nephew.
9 The wife of Alpee's brother.
10 His niece.
11 Makun, his brother-in-law.
12 Wife of Makun.
13 Makun's brother.
14 Sunthoo Tewaree Havildar of Bhyswarra.
15 Byjnauth Sookul Havildar of ditto, servant of Sulubut Khan.
16 Gomaun Tewarry, of Sukraen.
17 Achuroo, his brother.
18 Wife of Gomaun.
19 His son's wife.
20 Dewan Choube Sing.

21 His brother.
22 Bawun, an old woman of Bhyswarra.
(True Translation)
(Signed)   W. H. Sleeman.
P. A. A. G. G.

Statement of Bapoojie Pundit in the service of Major Smith, Commanding at Ellichpore 4th March, 1834.

About twenty-five years ago, fifty persons, Rajpoots, with all their arms and necessaries, left in company with Rumakunt, a Brahmin, about twenty-five years of age, and his mother set out for   on Teeruth; and we afterwards heard that they had been robbed on the Hatee Nalah.   At that time the roads were much infested by robbers, and we never could learn any thing more about any of them, nor did the Brahmin and his mother ever return.
(True Translation,)
(Signed)   W. H. Sleeman,
P. A. A. G. G.

Deposition of Bukteen Brahmin, 14th April, 1834, about thirty years of age.

My mother and father resided in some town in the Duckun, but their names I do not recollect, as I was only three or four years of age, when my uncle and mother took me with them on a journey towards the Ganges. On the road my mother and uncle were killed by Thugs, with many other travellers. Kasal Sing Putuck Jemadar preserved my life and took me with him to Pahlun in Gwalior, where he brought me up, and when I became of age he married me to his son, Hunce Rao, who is now dead. As long as he lived, I lived with him, but he has been dead several years, and I have since lived with his mother and earned my subsistence by my labour. Your Sipahees found me out and have brought me into Saugor. I had two sons by Hunce Rao. The first died when fifteen months old; the other is eight or nine years of age, and is named Buksh; he is in Khyrawa in Jhansee, with his grand-mother. I was the only person out of the party saved. There is now no Thug left in the family of Hunce Rao, who can provide for me. If you will maintain me I shall be glad to remain here, but I have never heard whether my parents have any surviving relations or not. I was in advance of the party when they were killed. The other two girls who were killed were not related to me, but our parents resided at the same place, and we used to call each other sisters. I had no other relation killed but my uncle and mother.

(A true Translation,)

(Signed) W. H. SLEEMAN,

P. Assist. Agent Governor General.

CHUTTERKOTE AFFAIR.

To Captain Robinson,
Paymaster Ellichpore.

Sir,

I have the honour to forward the deposition of a noted Thug leader regarding the murder of a party of travellers, among whom is said to have been an officer by name of Gholab Khan, who had been Killadar of Gawilgur, under the Nagpore government, and as you are in the vicinity shall feel obliged if you will endeavour to ascertain whether such an officer ever commanded that garrison.

(Signed)   W. H. SLEEMAN,
P. A. A. G. G.

2d August, 1833.

Extract of a letter from Captain Robinson to Captain Sleeman, dated Ellichpore, 20th August, 1833.

"Since the receipt of your letter of the 9th I have endeavoured to get information on the subject of the horrid murder, and though the information I have got in some respects differs from the Thug statement, I fear the leading facts are all too true. The person, who gives the Persian statement, which I send you, was a Jemadar of 300 men, in 1817—18, when I was sent up by General Doveton to take possession of Gawilgur. His family had been servants in the fort for three generations. His name is Gopie. The family are originally from Tilin-ganah. He himself is in charge of the villages immediately under the fort at present, and I have no doubt as to the truth of his statement, so far as his memory serves him, for he cannot write, and there are no documents to be found ; for even at the time I first went into the fort I inquired for the archives, but all I got was some old Sadre accounts, which only went back a few years, and were consequently of no use. I don't know what became of them. Gopie, in order to show that there is no Killadar of the name of Gholab Khan, has mentioned the names of the Killadars in succession for a number of years, though I am sorry to say he could not give the periods of each reign; but he seems to be quite certain as to the fact that Gureeb Sing sent his brother to Hindoostan and a sum of money for recruits, and that there was no more heard of them after they left Jubulpore. The exact number of people in his suit he cannot tell, but to the best of his recollection about 100 people left the fort with him, though some of them may have only been going to Nagpore, and the number mentioned by the Thugs may have been that which really accompanied Gureeb Sing's brother. Is it not terrible to think what horrid deeds were almost every where perpetrated with impunity in former times? In making the above inquiry I was informed of a still more frightful murder which took place close under Gawilgur, a very few years before, of five hundred recruits, that had come from some place for Gawilgur, and were pitched in tents for some reason or other below the fort. Some how or other a quantity of treasure for the fort, for the night halted in this camp, and shortly after about one thousand, of apparently discharged

sipahees, came up, said they were from Hindoostan, and wanted service and encamped at night in
the same place, but in morning there were none to
be found of the latter.   The rest were all laying
strangled, and the treasure gone.   People were
sent all over the country but none of the Thugs
were caught.   The person who has told me the
above says he came to this place, or rather *Arkote
Arkote* about one year afterwards, and though his
story may not be correct in all its points there was
no doubt a very great number murdered on the
occasion.   I expect to get a better account of it
from another person expected here.   If I get such
as may be worth sending, you shall have it.
      (Signed)   W. H. Sleeman,
                          Princl. A. A. G. G.

Saugor, 29th August, 1833.

No. 100.

Statement of
    sent by Captain Robinson of Ellichpore.

The fort Gawilgur was first held by Shahjie,
under the Pewsha's government, and after his death
by Makatmun Tija Raw.   He made it over to
Madhajie Ghosla, Rajah of Nagpore, who appointed
Pygoojie Ghosla to the command.   He held it five
years, after which he was replaced by Jam Sing,
who died and was succeeded by Surnaum Sing,
who held it sixty years, when in 1813, Murhatta,
it was taken by the English, who made it over
again to the Nagpore government, who appointed
to the command of it Gumbheer Sing, the son of
Surnam Sing, who appointed as his substitute his

uncle Ghureeb Sing, who sent ....
Dhyan Sing, to Hindoostan; he ....
nearly a hundred followers and ....
value of twenty thousand rupees, and ....
Adhartal, in the district of Jubulpore, ...
all his party were plundered. What became of
Dhyan Sing we could never learn, ...
twenty-four years ago. No Ghoohib ....
commanded the fort of Gawilgur, but a ......
Sing commanded the fort of Peeruala, where he
died.

(Signed)   W. H. SLEEMAN,
                   Prin. ....

Saugor, 30th August, 1832.

No. 100.

*Deposition of Mahasook, the 16th April, ... con-
firmed by Dorgha alias Dulole and ....*

About twenty years ago I was with a gang of
three hundred and fifty Thugs under Ghasee Subahadar, Noor Khan, and other leaders ....
Some of us were at Gopaulpore and some ....
at Adhartal, and some in the Bazar. We were
there three days, and on the third day ....
Khan, the Killadar of Gawilgur, in Nagpore, ...
Kadher Khan and a party of sixty persons, including seven women and a boy, came up ....
encamped on the bank of the Gopaulpore ....
a grove of mangoe trees. Ghasee Khan Subahadar
went to them as our *Sotkae*, and told them that he
was a Subadar in the service of Rughoojee, the
Rajah of Nagpore, and on his way home on leave

with a number of the men of his regiment. Gholab
Khan said he had been the Killadar of Gawilgur,
and having been deprived of the command of that
fortress was now on his way home. Ghasee said
he and his friend should be glad to travel in his
company, and finding the Killadar pleased with
his proposal, he returned to us. The Killadar
remained the next day and we remained also, and
the following day went to Punnagurh, and thence
to Sehora; from this place we quitted the high road
through Belchree and took that through Rewa, and
encamped at a village, whose name I forget; we
sent on people to choose a place for the murder,
but no suitable one could be found, and we went
on in this manner for eight days, searching every
day in vain for a convenient place for the murder.
On the eighth day we reached a village called,
from a large Bur tree, the Burwala village, five
cose from Birsingpore, and encamped under trees,
and sent on men to search for a Bele. At a place
two and a half cose distant between this village
and Chitterkote, they found a place suited to our
purpose on the bank of a Nalah, and about a watch
before daylight we set out with the party of travellers; and contrived as we went along to put a
Bhurtote (strangler) and a Shumseea (holder of
hands) by every traveller's side; on reaching the
spot chosen, Ghasee Subadar gave the signal, and
the travellers were seized by the men placed by
their sides for the purpose and strangled. Their
bodies were buried in the sand in the bed of the
Nalah, and we got from them nineteen thousand
rupees in money and seven or eight thousand
rupees worth of other property, which we took on
to Chitterkote. From thence we sent back men to
bury the bodies deeper, and they found one body

exposed which they buried, but the rest had been all washed down by the flood arising from some heavy rain that fell; alarmed at this we all dispersed and returned to our homes.

The boy was preserved by Mungul and Laljoo, brothers and Brahmins of Sindouse. He was a Brahmin and transported in 1834 for murder.

We passed through Rewa and Simereea and Chandeeah also, and another town, a few cose from Bundoogur.

(A true translation.)
    (Signed)   W. H. SLEEMAN.

END OF VOLUME II.

2)

LaVergne, TN USA
04 April 2010
178127LV00003B/48/P